Praise for *Learning Agile*

Another amazing book by the team of Andrew and Jennifer. Their writing style is engaging, their mastery of all things agile is paramount, and their content is not only comprehensive, it's wonderfully actionable.

—*Grady Booch*
IBM Fellow

The biggest obstacle to overcome in building a high-performance agile team is not learning how, but learning why. Helping teams discover the why is the key to unlock their potential for greater commitment and more creative collaboration. With a focus on values and principles Andrew and Jennifer have provided an outstanding tool to help you and your team discover the why. I can't wait to share it.

—*Todd Webb*
Technical Product Leader at a global e-commerce company

While I was already sold on agile, what I learned from Learning Agile will help my efforts to sell agile across my organization. This book provides more than "just" an engaging way to gain a deep understanding of agile's principles and practices. The easily relatable stories will help make agile compelling to members across your team, so you can begin reaping its rewards.

—*Mark Denovich*
Senior Business Consultant and Head of US development, Centriq Group

An excellent guide for any team member looking to deepen their understanding of agile. Stellman and Greene cover agile values and practices with an extremely clear and engaging writing style. The humor, examples, and clever metaphors offer a refreshing delivery. But where the book really shines is how it pinpoints frequent problems with agile teams, and offers practical advice on how to move forward to achieve deeper results.

—*Matthew Dundas*
CTO, Katori

As an engineer, I always thought the problems that Agile practices help to solve are a direct hit for the industry. As it turns out, becoming Agile is hard; it's more than just the practices. A piecemeal approach to Agile gives, as the the authors call it, "better-than-not-doing-it" results. If you are just getting started, or Agile is only "better-than-not-doing-it", Andrew and Jennifer have a lot of practical advice on how to read between the lines of the Agile Manifesto and really become Agile.

—*James W Grenning*
Founder of Wingman Software (*http://www.wingman-sw.com*) and co-author of the Agile Manifesto

Andrew Stellman and Jennifer Greene have done an impressive job putting together a comprehensive, practical resource that is easily accessible for anyone who is trying to 'get' Agile. They cover a lot of ground in Learning Agile, and have taken great care to go beyond simply detailing the behaviors most should expect of Agile teams. In exploring different elements of Agile, the authors present not just the standard practices and desired results, but also common misconceptions, and the positive and negative results they may bring. The authors also explore how specific practices and behaviors might impact individuals in different roles. This book is a great resource for new and experienced Agile practitioners alike.

—*Dave Prior PMP CST PMI-ACP*
Agile Consultant and Trainer

If you want to learn about any of the specific approaches to agile, you need to read the specific relevant books. That means you know what you want to do in advance. Not very agile of you, is it? What Andrew and Jenny have done is create an approachable, relatable, understandable compendium of what agile is. You don't have to decide in advance what your agile approach is. You can read about all of them, and then decide. On your way, you can learn the system of agile and how it works.

—*Johanna Rothman*
Author and Consultant, *www.jrothman.com*

The culture of a software development team often has a greater impact than their expertise or tools do on the success of their project. Stellman and Greene's advice on how to transform an assortment of fragmented individual perspectives into a collaborative unit with shared values and practices should help any software manager regardless of the organization's official methodology. Their comparison of Scrum, XP, Lean, and Kanban techniques analyze the many ways in which Agile principles can be applied. The entertaining case studies illustrate the human dilemmas—and the rewards—of learning to become Agile.

—*Patricia Ensworth*
President, Harborlight Management Services LLC

Learning Agile

Andrew Stellman and Jennifer Greene

Beijing · Boston · Farnham · Sebastopol · Tokyo

Learning Agile

by Andrew Stellman and Jennifer Greene

Published by O'Reilly Media, Inc., 1005 Gravenstein Highway North, Sebastopol, CA 95472.

O'Reilly books may be purchased for educational, business, or sales promotional use. Online editions are also available for most titles (*http://safaribooksonline.com*). For more information, contact our corporate/institutional sales department: 800-998-9938 or *corporate@oreilly.com* .

Editor: Mary Treseler	**Indexer:** Judy McConville
Production Editor: Nicole Shelby	**Interior Designer:** David Futato
Copyeditor: Jasmine Kwityn	**Cover Designer:** Ellie Volckhausen
Proofreader: Rachel Monaghan	**Illustrators:** Andrew Stellman and Jennifer Greene

November 2014:   First Edition

Revision History for the First Edition
2014-11-03:   First Release
2016-02-05:   Second Release

See *http://oreilly.com/catalog/errata.csp?isbn=9781449331924* for release details.

978-1-449-33192-4

[LSI]

For Nisha and Lisa,
who have been very patient with us

Table of Contents

Foreword

It seems that people always need something to debate. Was Van Halen better with David Lee Roth or Sammy Hagar? Pepsi or Coke? Lennon or McCartney? Cats or dogs? One such debate in the early days of agile was principles versus practices. Early agilists agreed on a set of principles enshrined in the Agile Manifesto, and many practices were shared across multiple agile approaches. However, there was fierce debate about whether a team should start by understanding the principles of agile software development or whether they should begin by performing the practices even before developing a deep understanding of why.

Proponents of starting with practices took a wax-on/wax-off view of the world. If a team were to act agile, they would be agile. By going through the motions of being agile—pair programming, automating tests and builds, using iterations, working closely with a key stakeholder, and so on—a team would gradually develop an understanding of the principles of agile.

Proponents of starting with principles, on the other hand, contended that practices without principles were hollow. Going through the motions without understanding why did not lead to agility. Agility was (and still is) a focus on continuous improvement. The argument went that a team could not improve continuously if they didn't understand why they were doing the things they were doing.

In *Learning Agile*, Andrew Stellman and Jennifer Greene do the best job I've encountered of stressing the principles of agile without de-emphasizing its practices. They point out that following practices without knowing why is likely to lead only to what they call a "better-than-not-doing-it" level of success. That is, implementing practices alone is helpful, but it falls far short of the true promise of what becoming agile can truly deliver.

I first met Andrew and Jennifer six years ago when they interviewed me for their *Beautiful Teams* book. Although that book does not include *agile* in its title, in many ways the book was about agile. A team that has embraced the principles of agile, mastered the practices it needs, and discarded practices it found unnecessary is truly a beautiful team. In *Learning Agile*, Andrew and Jennifer focus their discussion on agile by concentrating on today's three most common agile methods—Scrum, Extreme Programming, and Kanban. You'll see how their shared principles have led to different practices within each approach. For example, if you've wondered why Scrum requires end-of-sprint retrospectives but Extreme Programming does not, you'll find the answer here.

In joining Andrew and Jennifer through their exploration of Scrum, Extreme Programming, Lean, and Kanban, you'll read lots of stories. This makes sense—after all, a common practice for many agile teams is telling user stories to describe what a system's users want. You'll meet teams struggling to build the right functionality, taking too long to deliver last year's requirements, mistaking agile for just another form of command-and-control management, being whipsawed by change rather than embracing it, and more. More importantly, you'll read how those teams overcame those problems and how you can, too.

Learning Agile puts an end, once and for all, to the question of which should come first, practices or principles. Its engaging stories and discussions illustrate the simple truth that in agile there can be no separation between principles and practices. In these pages, you'll gain a deeper understanding of how to get started (or get back on track) on your journey to becoming a genuinely beautiful team.

Mike Cohn

Author, *Succeeding with Agile*

Boulder, Colorado

Preface

Acknowledgments

We wrote this book to help you learn agile—but we didn't do it alone. First and foremost, we want to thank our fantastic editor, Mary Treseler. She championed this project from the day we first discussed it with her in an Indian restaurant in downtown Manhattan all the way through to the finished book that you're reading today. She's been an important part of everything we've done with O'Reilly, and we couldn't have done this without her.

We'd also like to thank other friends at O'Reilly, without whom this would not be possible: Mike Hendrickson, Laurie Petrycki, Tim O'Reilly, Ally MacDonald, Andy Oram, Nicole Shelby, and especially Marsee Henon, Sara Peyton, Kathryn Barrett, and all of the fantastic press and PR folks in Sebastopol.

We want to thank Mike Cohn for his wonderful foreword, as well as the really good advice he's given us over the years. We also want to thank him for his great books, because we learned a lot from them! We'd also like to thank David Anderson for giving us some really excellent feedback on Chapters 8 and 9. We want to thank Grady Booch, Scott Ambler, James Grenning, Scott Berkun, Steve McConnell, Karl Wiegers, Johanna Rothman, Patricia Ensworth, Tommy Tarka, Keoki Andrus, Neil Siegel, Karl Fogel, and Auke Jilderda for giving us some really good material and input over the years, especially in *Beautiful Teams*—and especially Barry Boehm, not only for contributing a really fantastic story to that book, but more importantly for laying the intellectual groundwork that much of agile is built on. And we want to thank Kent Beck, Alistair Cockburn, Ken Schwaber, Jeff Sutherland, Ron Jeffries, Tom Poppendieck, Mary Poppendieck, Lyssa Adkins, and Jim Highsmith for their groundbreaking work in agile. We literally would not have been able to write this book without them.

We also want to thank all of our technical reviewers for their excellent feedback and thorough review: Faisal Jawdat, Adam Reeve, Anjanette Randolph, Samuel Weiler, Dave Prior, Randy DeFauw, Todd Webb, Michael DeWitt, and Paul Ellarby.

And finally, we'd like to thank the hundreds of software team members who have been kind enough to talk to us about their problems, solutions, stories, and experiences over the years.

Andrew would like to thank Lisa Kellner. He'd also like to thank everyone in the Computer Science department at Carnegie Mellon who helped him learn some really important ideas, especially Bob Harper, Mark Stehlik, and Randy Bryant. He'd like to thank Tony Visconti, who's been a true mentor and a friend over the years. He'd like to thank his friends Sara Landeau, Greg Gassman, Juline Koken, Kristeen Young, and Casey Dunmore—thinking back, it's kind of amazing how much he's learned about teamwork from these great musicians. He'd also like to thank some really fantastic teammates he's had over his career, including Dan Faltyn, Ned Robinson, Debra Herschmann, Mary Gensheimer, Lana Sze, Warren Pearson, Bill DiPierre, Jonathan Weinberg, and Irene O'Brien. And last but not least, he'd like to thank the two best software teams he's ever worked with, especially Mark Denovich, Eric Renkey, and Chris Winters from Optiron, and Mike Hickin, Nick Lai, Sunanda Bera, and Rituraj Deb Nath from Bank of America.

Jenny would like to thank Nisha Sondhe. She'd also like to thank Christopher Wenger, Brian Romeo, LaToya Jordan, Mazz Swift, Rekha Malhotra, Courtney Nelson, Anjanette Randolph, Shona McCarthy, Ethan Hill, Yeidy Rodriguez, Kyle Mosier, Achinta McDaniel, Jaikaran Sawhny, and Kit Cole for all of their support, laughter, and shenanigans. She'd like to thank her family for their patience and encouragement during the nearly three years this book was under construction. She'd like to thank Tanya and Dilan Desai for their support and help. Finally, she'd like to thank the many colleagues she's learned from over the years. There are too many people who deserve thanks to list them all, but here are a few: Joe Madia, Paul Oakes, Jonathan Weinberg, Bianka Buschbeck, Thor List, Oleg Fishel, Brian Duperrouzel, Dave Murdock, Flora Chen, Danny Wunder, David San Filippo, and Rasko Ristic.

Safari® Books Online

 Safari Books Online is an on-demand digital library that delivers expert content in both book and video form from the world's leading authors in technology and business.

Technology professionals, software developers, web designers, and business and creative professionals use Safari Books Online as their primary resource for research, problem solving, learning, and certification training.

Safari Books Online offers a range of product mixes and pricing programs for organizations, government agencies, and individuals. Subscribers have access to thousands of books, training videos, and prepublication manuscripts in one fully searchable database from publishers like O'Reilly Media, Prentice Hall Professional, Addison-

Wesley Professional, Microsoft Press, Sams, Que, Peachpit Press, Focal Press, Cisco Press, John Wiley & Sons, Syngress, Morgan Kaufmann, IBM Redbooks, Packt, Adobe Press, FT Press, Apress, Manning, New Riders, McGraw-Hill, Jones & Bartlett, Course Technology, and dozens more. For more information about Safari Books Online, please visit us online.

How to Contact Us

Please address comments and questions concerning this book to the publisher:

O'Reilly Media, Inc.
1005 Gravenstein Highway North
Sebastopol, CA 95472
800-998-9938 (in the United States or Canada)
707-829-0515 (international or local)
707-829-0104 (fax)

We have a web page for this book, where we list errata, examples, and any additional information. You can access this page at *http://bit.ly/learning-agile*.

To comment or ask technical questions about this book, send email to *bookquestions@oreilly.com*.

For more information about our books, courses, conferences, and news, see our website at *http://www.oreilly.com*.

Find us on Facebook: *http://facebook.com/oreilly*

Follow us on Twitter: *http://twitter.com/oreillymedia*

Watch us on YouTube: *http://www.youtube.com/oreillymedia*

CHAPTER 1

Learning Agile

The most important attitude that can be formed is that of desire to go on learning.
—John Dewey, *Experience and Education*

It's an exciting time to be agile! For the first time, our industry has found a real, sustainable way to solve problems that generations of software development teams have been struggling with. Here are just a few of the solutions that agile promises:

- Agile projects come in on time, which is great for teams that have struggled with projects delivered very late and far over budget.
- Agile projects deliver high-quality software, which is a big change for teams that have been bogged down by buggy, inefficient software.
- Code built by agile teams is well constructed and highly maintainable, which should be a relief to teams accustomed to maintaining convoluted and tangled spaghetti code.
- Agile teams make their users happy, which is a huge change from software that fails to deliver value to the users.
- Best of all, developers on an effective agile team find themselves working normal hours, and are able to spend their nights and weekends with their friends and families—possibly for the first time in their careers.

Agile is popular because many teams that have "gone agile" report great results: they build better software, work together better, satisfy their users, and do it all while having a much more relaxed and enjoyable working environment. Some agile teams seem to have finally made headway in fixing problems that have vexed software teams for decades. So how do great teams use agile to build better software? More specifically, how can *you* use agile to get results like this?

In this book, you will learn about the two most popular agile methodologies, Scrum and Extreme Programming (XP). You'll also learn about Lean and Kanban, and how they help you understand the way you build software today and help you evolve to a better state tomorrow. You'll learn that while these four agile schools of thought focus on different areas of software development, they all have one important thing in common: they focus on **changing your team's mindset**.

It's that mindset shift that takes a team from superficially adding a few token agile practices to one that has genuinely improved the way it builds software. The goal of this book is to help you learn both sides of agile: the practices that make up the day-to-day work, and the values and principles that help you and your team fundamentally change the way that you think about building software.

What Is Agile?

Agile is a **set of methods and methodologies** that help your team to think more effectively, work more efficiently, and make better decisions.

These methods and methodologies address all of the areas of traditional software engineering, including project management, software design and architecture, and process improvement. Each of those methods and methodologies consists of **practices** that are streamlined and optimized to make them as easy as possible to adopt.

Agile is *also* a **mindset**, because the right mindset can make a big difference in how effectively a team uses the practices. This mindset helps people on a team share information with one another, so that they can make important project decisions together —instead of having a manager who makes all of those decisions alone. An agile mindset is about opening up planning, design, and process improvement to the entire team. An agile team uses practices in a way where everyone shares the same information, and each person on the team has a say in how the practices are applied.

The reality of agile for many teams that have not had as much success is quite different from its promise, and the key to that difference is often the mindset the team brings to each project. The majority of companies that build software have experimented with agile, and while many of them have found success, some teams have gotten less-than-stellar results. They've achieved some improvement in how they run their projects—enough to make the effort to adopt agile worth it—but they haven't seen the substantial changes that they feel agile promised them. This is what that mindset shift is all about; "going agile" means helping the team find an effective mindset.

But what does "mindset shift" really mean? If you're on a software team, then what you do every day is plan, design, build, and ship software. What does "mindset" have to do with that? As it turns out, the practices you use to do your everyday work depend a lot on the attitude that you and your teammates have toward them.

Here's an example. One of the most common agile practices that teams adopt is called the **daily standup**, a meeting during which team members talk about what they're working on and their challenges. The meeting is kept short by making everyone stand for the duration. Many teams have had a lot of success adding a daily standup to their projects.

So imagine that a project manager is just learning about agile, and wants to add the daily standup to his project. To his surprise, not everyone on his team is as excited about this new practice as he is. One of his developers is angry that he's even suggesting that they add a new meeting, and seems to feel insulted by the idea of attending a meeting every day where he's asked prying questions about his day-to-day work.

Figure 1-1. A project manager who wants to have the team start holding a daily standup is surprised that not everyone is immediately on board with it.

So what's going on here? Is the developer being irrational? Is the project manager being too demanding? Why is this simple, well-accepted practice causing a conflict?

Both the project manager and the developer have different—and valid—points of view. One of this project manager's biggest challenges is that he puts a lot of effort into planning the project, but when the team runs into problems building the software they deviate from the plan. He has to work very hard to stay on top of everyone on the team, so that he can make adjustments to the plan and help them deal with their problems.

The developer, on the other hand, feels like he's interrupted several times a day for meetings, which makes it very hard for him to get his work done. He already knows what he needs to do to get his own code built, and he doesn't need another person nagging him about plans and changes. He just wants to be left alone to code, and the last thing he wants is yet another meeting.

Figure 1-2. Both people seem to have a valid reason for their attitude toward the daily standup meeting. What effect will this have on the project?

Now imagine that the project manager is able to get everyone—even this reluctant developer—to start attending a daily standup meeting. What will that meeting look like? The project manager will be thinking mainly about how people are deviating from his plan, so he'll concentrate on getting status from each person. The developer, on the other hand, wants the meeting to end as quickly as possible, so he'll tune out everyone else while he's waiting to give his update, then say as little as possible when it's his turn, and hope that the whole thing ends quickly.

Let's be clear: this is how many daily standups are run, and while it's not optimal, a daily standup that's run this way *will still produce results*. The project manager will find out about problems with his plan, and the developer will benefit in the long run because those problems that *do* affect him can be taken care of sooner rather than later—and the whole practice generally saves the team more time and effort than it costs. That makes it worth doing.

But what would happen *if the developer and the project manager had a different mindset*? What if each person on the team approached the daily standup with an entirely different attitude?

For example, what would happen if the project manager felt like everyone on the team worked together to plan the project? Then the project manager would genuinely listen to each team member, not just to find out how they've deviated from *his* plan, but to understand how the plan *that everyone on the team worked together to create* might need to change. Instead of dictating a plan, handing it to the team, and measuring how well the team is following it, he's now working with the team to figure out the best way to approach the project—and the daily standup becomes a way to work together to make sure everyone is doing the most effective thing possible at any given time. As the facts of the project change each day, the team uses the daily standup to work together to make the most effective decisions they can. And because the team meets every day, changes that they discover in the meeting can be put into effect immediately so they don't waste a lot of time and effort going down the wrong path.

And what if the developer felt like this meeting wasn't just about giving status, but about understanding how the project is going, and coming together every day to find ways that everyone can work better? Then the daily standup *becomes important to him*. A good developer almost always has opinions not just about his own code, but about the whole direction of the project. The daily standup becomes his way to make sure that the project is run in a sensible, efficient way—and he knows that in the long run that will make his job of coding more rewarding, because the rest of the project is being run well. And he knows that when he brings up a problem with the plan during the meeting, everyone will listen, and the project will run better because of it.

Figure 1-3. When every person on the team feels like they have an equal hand in planning and running the project, the daily standup becomes more valuable—and much more effective.

In other words, if people on the team are in the mindset that the daily standup is simply a status meeting that must be endured, it's still worth doing, but it's only slightly more effective than a traditional status meeting. But if everyone on the team shares the mindset that the daily standup is their way of making sure that everyone is on track, they're all working toward the same goal, and they all have a say in how the project is run, it becomes much more effective—and also more satisfying. The developer has the attitude that this meeting helps him and his team in the long run. The project manager has the attitude that when each person on the team can contribute to the plan, the project gets better results. And when everyone shares these attitudes, the daily standup helps them all work faster, communicate more directly, and get things done more easily.

This is just one small example of how the mindset and attitude of the team have a big effect on how well they'll adopt agile practices. An important goal of this book is to help you understand how your own team's mindset affects your projects and your own agile adoption. By exploring Scrum, XP, Lean, and Kanban, you will learn both sides of the agile coin—principles and practices—and how they come together to help you build better software.

Who Should Read This Book

Do any of these scenarios describe you and your team?

You tried an agile practice, but it didn't really work out. Maybe you implemented daily standup meetings, and now your team meets every day—but you still get blindsided by problems and miss deadlines. Or you started writing user stories and reviewing them with your team and stakeholders, but your developers still find themselves dealing with just as many last-minute changes to add extra features that continue to pop up. Or maybe your team tried to go agile wholesale by adopting a methodology like Scrum or XP, but it seems somehow "empty"—like everyone is going through the "required" motions, but your projects are only marginally improving.

Or maybe you haven't tried agile yet, but you recognize that your team is facing serious challenges, and you don't know where to start. You're hoping that agile will help you with those demanding users who constantly change their minds. Each change your users make requires more work for your team, and leads to "duct tape and paperclips" spaghetti code solutions that make the software increasingly fragile and unmaintainable. It could be that your projects are simply controlled chaos; the primary way software is delivered is through long hours and personal heroics, and you think that agile may offer your team a way out.

What if you're an executive who's worried that teams working on important projects will fail to deliver? Maybe you've heard about agile, but you don't really know what it means. Can you simply tell your team to adopt agile? Or will you need to change your own mindset along with the team?

If any of those situations is familiar to you, and you want to improve how your team works, this book will help.

We explain the agile methodologies: why they're designed the way they are, what problems they address, and the values, principles, and ideas that they embody. By giving you the "why" in addition to the "how," we'll help you to recognize the principles that apply to the particular development problems specific to your team, company, and projects. And we'll show you how to use that information to guide your choice of methodologies and practices.

There's one other sort of person we wrote this book for: the **agile coach**. Teams and companies are increasingly relying on agile coaches to guide them in adopting agile methodologies and practices, and to get each team member into the right mindset. If you're an agile coach, we will give you tools to help you better communicate these ideas to your team, and to overcome some of the challenges that you face every day when helping a team become more agile.

Our Goals for This Book

What we want for you:

- We want you to understand the ideas that drive effective agile teams, and the values and principles that bring them together.

- We want you to understand the most popular agile schools of thought—Scrum, XP, Lean, and Kanban—and how they can all be agile, even though they're very different from each other.

- We want to teach you specific agile practices that you can apply to your projects today—but we also want to give you the framework of values and principles that you'll need to implement them effectively.

- We want to help you understand your own team and company better, so that you can choose an agile approach that matches your mindset (or comes as close as possible)—but also help you and your team start to learn a new way of thinking that will help you become a more effective agile team.

How do all the different agile methodologies and practices give you better software? Why do they give your team the ability to handle change better? Why are these things agile? Does it really matter that you're using, say, index cards for planning, or that you're standing up during meetings? These questions are difficult and often confusing for people just starting their path to agility. By the end of this book, you'll be able to answer them for yourself.

If you look at many of the blogs and articles out there discussing agile software development, one of the first things you'll read is that "Agile is good, and waterfall is bad." Why is agile "good," and waterfall "bad"? Why are they in conflict with each other? Is it possible to work on a team that follows a waterfall process and still be agile? By the end of this book, you'll able to answer those questions, too.

Getting Agile into Your Brain by Any Means Necessary

This book is called *Learning Agile* because we *really* want you to learn agile. We've spent the last 20+ years working with real teams building real software for real users day in and day out. We've also spent the last 10+ years writing books about building software (including two very successful books in the O'Reilly *Head First* series about managing projects and learning to code). This experience has helped us find many different ways to get complex and technical ideas into your brain without boring you to death.

We've done our best to take this material and make it as interesting and engaging as possible...but we need your help to do it. Here are the tools and techniques you'll find throughout this book to help make these ideas stick in your head:

Narratives

Denoted by the ▣ icon. Think about the last technical book that you read. Can you remember all the major topics it covered, and in what order? Probably not. Now think about the last movie you saw. Can you remember the major plot points, and the order in which they happened? Almost certainly. That's because your brain is wired to remember things that cause you to have an emotional reaction. In this book, we use that to our advantage. We'll use narratives—with people, dialog, and conflict—to show you what it looks like when real people encounter agile. These people will run into problems.

What we need from you: Try to imagine yourself in their situation, because that will give you an emotional connection to these ideas, and make it easier for you to remember and understand them. Keep an open mind about these narratives, especially if you're the sort of learner who doesn't like to read fiction. There's real learning in each narrative, and they're part of the core material in this book.

Illustrations

Different people learn in different ways. Some people are more visual learners, and ideas will "click" much more easily for them when they see a picture. We want to give you as many tools as possible to learn, so we included many illustrations throughout this book. In some cases, we rely heavily on visual metaphor, like using geometric shapes to represent different features, or gears to represent complex software.

What we need from you: If you're not a visual learner, some of the illustrations may seem superfluous at first, and you may find yourself thinking that a specific illustration doesn't make sense. This is a good learning opportunity for you, and if this happens then you should take a minute and try to figure out what someone who *is* a visual learner might get from the illustration. That will help you gain a deeper understanding of the concept.

Redundancy

Most technical books introduce an idea, describe it completely, and then move on to the next one. That's an effective way to get as much information into a book as possible, but that's not how our brains work. Sometimes you need to see the same concept more than once before you get that "aha!" moment. This is why we will sometimes come back to the same concept several times within a chapter, or in different chapters. **This redundancy is intentional**—we do it to help you get to that "aha!" moment.

What we need from you: When you run across a concept for the second or third time, you might be tempted to think, "Didn't they already cover this?" Yes, we did, and it's really good that you noticed it! There are other readers who didn't notice it, the same way you probably won't notice every time we use redundancy. It's all done to help you learn.

Simplification (at first!)

Sometimes it's easier to understand a complex subject by first just scratching the surface, and letting that sink in. We do that many times in this book, introducing a simplified (but still technically correct!) version of a concept, and elaborating on it later. This works on two levels. If it's an idea that you already understand in depth, then you'll recognize the simplification and react to it emotionally—and that keeps you engaged. On the other hand, if you aren't aware of the concept, it helps give you a gentler introduction to prepare you for the more in-depth description later on.

What we need from you: If you feel like something is oversimplified, don't just dismiss it, and definitely don't assume that we missed a major idea or that we glossed over or forgot an important point. Chances are, you'll find the point that you're looking for later on in the book. If it helps, think of a simplified introduction of a difficult concept as a sort of "Hello, World!" program for your brain—it gives readers who aren't familiar with the concept a feeling of encouragement so that they know they're on the right track, and it sets the stage for a deeper understanding later.

Conversational/casual tone

We keep a casual tone throughout this book in order to keep the material as engaging as possible. We use humor and occasional cultural references, and will sometimes speak directly to you or refer to ourselves using pronouns like "us" and "you." There's actually science behind this—cognitive research[1] that shows that your brain remembers more when you feel like you're in a conversation.

What we need from you: While most people have no problem with a casual tone, some people really dislike it. For example, some readers bristle every time they see a contraction. For others, a casual tone makes them feel like the book isn't authoritative enough. We understand that. Believe it or not, you'll actually get used to it faster than you might think.

Key Points

Denoted by the icon. Throughout each chapter we'll summarize key points that were covered recently. This helps you make sure that you "got" everything, and that you didn't miss an important concept. It also gives your brain a quick break from learning.

---

1 If you're interested in learning more about how conversational tone helps you learn, have a look at *E-Learning and the Science of Instruction* by Ruth C. Clark and Richard E. Mayer (Wiley, 2011).

What we need from you: Don't just skip over the Key Points sections. Take a minute and look through them. Do you remember each of those points? If not, don't be afraid to flip back a few pages and refresh your memory.

Frequently Asked Questions

Denoted by the ⓘ icon. We spend most of our time actually working on software teams building real software for real users, but we've also spent years giving talks and presentations about agile, and talking to many, many people. And over all of that discussion, there are some questions that people kept asking over and over again.

What we need from you: Read the Frequently Asked Questions at the end of each chapter. Was this a question that you had? If so, do you like the answer? You may not always like the answer, but try to find the truth in it. If it wasn't a question that you had, try to figure out why someone might ask it—that can help you see the material from a different perspective (and you'll learn in Chapter 2 why that is important for a team).

What You Can Do Today

Denoted by the ☑ icon. The most effective way to learn something is to do it! At the end of each chapter, we include a short section that gives you a few things that you can do today, right now, either alone or with your team.

What we need from you: Obviously, the best thing that you can do is actually try those things! But the reality is that not every team or company is open to this— and one of the most important things you'll learn throughout the book is that trying to put a practice in place on a team with an incompatible mindset can end badly. So before you try these things, think about how your team will respond. That can be as effective a learning tool as actually doing it.

Where You Can Learn More

Denoted by the ⬚ icon. Isaac Newton once said, "If I have seen further it is by standing on the shoulders of giants." We're lucky to be writing this at a time when there have been so many groundbreaking books written about agile software development. After each chapter, we'll give you a few places where you can learn more about what we just taught.

What we need from you: Keep learning! This book is a thorough overview of Scrum, XP, Lean, and Kanban, but we can't cover every detail of each of these ideas. We didn't come up with most of the ideas in this book; luckily, you can learn from the people who did.

Coaching Tips

Denoted by the 📋 icon. An agile coach is someone who helps teams learn agile. This book is written for someone who is learning agile, but it can also be used as a guide to help an experienced agile coach introduce these ideas to her team. If you're an agile coach, look for the coaching tips at the end of each chapter. They'll help you take the ideas and the approach that we use and adapt them to your own team.

What we need from you: Even if you're not a coach, you should still read the coaching tips. That's because one effective way to learn is to put yourself in the shoes of someone who is teaching others. If you're learning these concepts for the first time, imagine how you might use these coaching tips to help your team learn more about agile.

How This Book Is Structured

This book is structured to help you understand agile by teaching the values and principles of an effective software team, the schools of thought that embody those values, and the practices that make them up.

The next two chapters will help you understand the values and principles that will help you to adopt an agile mindset. They will give you the tools to figure out if your team and your company are ready to adopt agile, which parts of agile will resonate with your team, and which might be more difficult to implement:

- Chapter 2, *Understanding Agile Values*, describes the core agile values. We will show you an example of a team struggling with a software project, and help you recognize that a main source of the struggle is a "fractured perspective." We'll explain the agile values, and use a metaphor to help you see how those values bring the team's perspective together.

- Chapter 3, *The Agile Principles*, describes the principles that agile teams use to make decisions about how to run their projects. We'll show you the purpose and idea behind each of the principles, illustrating them with a practical example from a software project.

The following six chapters will teach you about the most popular agile schools of thought: Scrum, XP, Lean, and Kanban. You'll learn their basic application in a way that you can put in place on your team today:

- Chapter 4, *Scrum and Self-Organizing Teams*, uses Scrum, a popular agile methodology, to teach you how self-organizing teams work. We'll give you advice for adopting Scrum on your own projects, and tools to help your team learn to self-organize.

- Chapter 5, *Scrum Planning and Collective Commitment*, shows you specific practices that Scrum teams use to plan their projects, and how those practices help your team commit as a whole to delivering valuable software. We'll show you how real-life adoption of Scrum depends on how well the Scrum values match the culture of your team and your company, and what to do if they don't.

- Chapter 6, *XP and Embracing Change*, teaches you about the primary practices of Extreme Programming, and the XP values and principles. You'll learn how they help get each team member into the right mindset to build better code: instead of hating change, every person on the team learns to embrace it.

- Chapter 7, *XP, Simplicity, and Incremental Design*, teaches you about the final three primary practices of XP, and how they help you avoid serious code and design problems. You'll learn how all of the XP practices form an ecosystem that leads to better, more maintainable, flexible, and changeable code.

- Chapter 8, *Lean, Eliminating Waste, and Seeing the Whole*, teaches you about Lean, and the values that help you get into the lean thinking mindset. And we show you how the Lean thinking tools can help your team identify waste and eliminate it, and see the whole system that you use to build software.

- Chapter 9, *Kanban, Flow, and Constantly Improving*, teaches you about Kanban, its principles and how they relate to Lean, and its practices. You'll learn how its emphasis on flow and queuing theory can help your team put lean thinking into practice. And you'll learn about how Kanban can help your team to create a culture of continuous improvement.

The world of agile includes more than mindsets, methodologies, and schools of thought. Companies are increasingly relying on agile coaches to help their teams adopt agile. This is why we included the final chapter in the book:

- Chapter 10, *The Agile Coach*, teaches you about agile coaching: how teams learn, how an agile coach can help a team change their mindset so that they can more easily adopt an agile methodology, and how that coach can help you and your team become more agile.

Figure 1-4.
Live graphic recording of Andrew Stellman's talk at the STRETCH 2013 conference in Budapest, Hungary. The talk was based on the material in this chapter.

Graphic recording: Kata Máthé and Márti Frigyik
www.remarker.eu

CHAPTER 2

Understanding Agile Values

We do not act rightly because we have virtue or excellence, but we rather have those because we have acted rightly. We are what we repeatedly do. Excellence, then, is not an act but a habit.

—Aristotle, *Nichomachean Ethics*

Agile, as a movement, is different from any approach to software development that came before it, because it started with ideas, values, and principles that embody a mindset. It's through the lens of these ideas that you can begin to become more agile as a practitioner, and more valuable as a member of your project team.

The agile movement is revolutionizing the world of software development. Teams that adopt agile have consistently reported improvements—sometimes huge leaps—in their ability to build great software. Teams that successfully adopt agile build better, higher quality software products, and they do it faster than before.

Our industry is at a turning point with agile. Agile has gone from being the underdog to becoming an institution. For the first few years of agile, people adopting it struggled to convince their companies and teammates that it worked, and that it was worth doing. Now, there is little question that agile development is a highly effective way to build software. In fact, in 2008, an important survey[1] found that more than half of all software teams surveyed were using agile methodologies, practices, or principles—and agile has only grown since then. And agile teams are increasingly going beyond the problem of how to be agile themselves, and are starting to figure out how to spread agile development throughout their companies.

But it wasn't always like this. Traditionally, companies have used a **waterfall process** when running their software projects, in which the team defines the requirements up

---

1 The Forrester 2008 Global Agile Company Online Survey

front, plans the project in its entirety, designs the software, and then builds the code and tests the product. Plenty of software—great software, but also lousy software—has been built this way over the years. But as the decades went on, different teams in different companies kept running into the same kinds of problems...and some people started to suspect that a major source of project failure might be the waterfall process itself.

The story of agile started when a small group of innovative people got together to try to find a different way of thinking about these problems. The first thing they did was come up with a set of four core values that are common to successful teams and their projects, which they called the *Manifesto for Agile Software Development*:

- Individuals and interactions over processes and tools
- Working software over comprehensive documentation
- Customer collaboration over contract negotiation
- Responding to change over following a plan

In this chapter, you'll learn about these values—where they came from, what they mean, and how they apply to your project. You'll follow a waterfall-weary team through their first attempt at implementing agile before they really understand how those values apply to them. As you read their story, see if you can spot how a better understanding of these values could have helped them avoid their problems.

Narrative: a team working on a streaming audio jukebox project

Dan – lead developer and architect

Bruce – team lead

Joanna – newly hired project manager

Tom – product owner

A Team Lead, Architect, and Project Manager Walk into a Bar...

Dan is a lead developer and architect at a company that makes coin-op games and kiosks. He's worked on projects ranging from arcade pinball machines to ATMs. For the last few years, he's been working with a team lead, Bruce. They bonded on a release of the company's biggest product, a Vegas slot machine called the "Slot-o-matic Weekend Warrior."

Joanna was hired a few months ago as a project manager to head up a project building software for a new line of streaming audio jukeboxes, which the company wants to introduce and sell to bars and restaurants. She was a real prize—they poached her from a competitor that already has a successful jukebox on the market. She's been getting along really well with Dan and Bruce, and she's excited about getting started on a new project with them.

Dan and Bruce are much less excited about the new project than Joanna. They all went out for drinks after work one day, and Bruce and Dan started explaining why the team came up with their own name for the slot machine project: the "Slog-o-matic Weekend Killer."

She wasn't happy to learn that in this company, failing projects are the rule, not the exception. The last three projects were declared a success by the company's managers, but they only got out the door because Dan and Bruce worked incredibly long hours. Worse, they held their noses and took shortcuts in the code that are causing support nightmares today—like when they hastily patched up a prototype for one feature and pushed it out into production, and it later turned out to have serious performance problems because pieces of it were never built to scale up.

As they talked, Joanna recognized the pattern, and knew what was causing the problem: the company follows a particularly ineffective *waterfall process*. A team following a waterfall process tries to write down as early as possible a complete description of the software that will be built. Once all of the users, managers, and executives agree on exactly what the software must do (the *requirements*), they can hand a document that contains those requirements (the *specification*) to a development team, and that team will go off and build exactly what's written. Then a testing team comes in afterward, and verifies that the software matches the document. Many agile practitioners refer to this as "big requirements up front" (sometimes abbreviated BRUF).

But Joanna also knew from her own projects over the years that theory often differed from practice, and that while some teams have a very effective waterfall process, many of them struggle with it. She was starting to think that this team might be one of those that struggled.

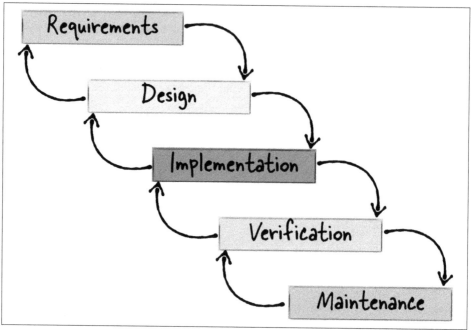

Figure 2-1. The waterfall model.

As they talked, Bruce and Dan confirmed a few things that reinforced her opinion. Just as Joanna suspected, there were a lot of specifications sitting in large binders and gathering dust on shelves all across the company. Somehow, everyone expected a group of users, managers, and executives to create a perfect requirements specification. In real life, the spec had a nasty habit of changing so that it would be inaccurate by the time the team got their hands on it, and would progress to being disastrously wrong by the time the team finished building the software. Bruce, Dan, and a lot of other people at the company knew that it was unreasonable to expect the perfect spec, but they still ran their projects as if it were possible.

As the evening went on, Bruce got more comfortable (and tipsy), and he brought up another problem that had been nagging him: that many teams he'd been on at their company had a lot of trouble actually building their software. Even if the users got the requirements right (which rarely happened), and even when the team understood those written requirements perfectly after reading them (which had yet to happen to this day), they often used inferior tools and had a lot of trouble with software design and architecture. This led to Bruce's teams repeatedly building software that had a lot of bugs, and was often an unmaintainable mess.

Both of these problems led to many failed projects, especially because they considered any project where they had to work many 90-hour weeks and deliver buggy code to be a failure. Joanna explained that the biggest cause of those failures was the *inability of the waterfall process the company followed to handle change.* In a perfect world, the waterfall process would work just fine, because at the start of the project everyone would know exactly what they'd need at the end. That way, they could write it all down in a neat spec and hand it off to the team to build. But real-life projects never seemed to work out that way.

Dan and Bruce were now officially drunk, and deep into a marathon gripe session with Joanna. Dan told her that on almost every project that they'd worked on, the customers decided partway through that they needed the team to build something different than what they'd originally planned on. Then everyone had to go back to the beginning of the waterfall. According to the strict waterfall process the team was following, they were supposed to write entirely new specifications, come up with a different design, and build a whole new plan. But in reality, this almost never happened, and it was rare that they had time to throw out all of the code that had been written so far. Instead, they usually ended up hacking together a solution out of the existing code. This rework led to bugs, because taking software that was designed for one purpose and hastily modifying it to do something else often results in messy, tangled code—especially when the team is under pressure. Adapting it to the new use would have taken up precious project time, so they ended up with poor workarounds and brittle code.

What Dan, Bruce, and Joanna were starting to realize by the end of the night was that their project's problems were caused by *overly rigid documentation*, *poor communication*, and *bugs*, which led to projects that could not keep up with normal project changes.

At the end of the evening, the bartender called taxis for all three of them. Just before they left, Dan said he was relieved to get a lot of that off of his chest. Joanna was happy to have a better picture of the project that she was joining...but a lot less optimistic. Will she be able to find a way, she wondered, to fix some of these problems?

No Silver Bullet

Today we know that there's no single "best" way to build software. But while that's not a controversial statement now, for much of the last century many people in the industry would have loudly disagreed. There was a general feeling among many practitioners that they could discover a single, highly prescriptive "silver bullet" method that would solve project problems for everyone, everywhere. Many people felt that developers could build software just by following a set of instructions, like following a recipe or assembling a product on an assembly line.

(Ironically, one of the most quoted papers in software engineering is Fred Brooks's 1986 essay, "No Silver Bullet," in which he shows conclusively why this is an impossible goal. That has yet to stop people from trying to find one!)

There were many proposed silver bullet solutions to these kinds of problems. They typically came in one of two forms: a **methodology** that claimed to give teams a fool-proof way of building software, or a technology that programmers could use to prevent or eliminate bugs. The idea was that if a company decided on a methodology and a technology, then all the team had to do was to follow the company orthodoxy, and great software would start pouring out.

Dan and Bruce know firsthand that this doesn't work, because they lived through years of managers in their company throwing methodologies and technologies at their projects without any real, lasting improvement. The company's attempts at finding a silver bullet software process were usually enormously disappointing for everyone involved—and especially for Bruce and Dan, because they were asked to follow an ever-changing series of processes that they hadn't asked for.

Joanna was also no stranger to this from her own career. At her last job, she was routinely handed a rigid set of requirements, and ordered to come up with a plan to build them out into software. Teams were then given her plan, and ordered to follow it to the letter. Teams that "planned the work, and worked the plan" were doomed to build software that was often outdated and not useful to their users even on the day that it was deployed.

One thing that gave Joanna pause was that some teams she worked on actually did manage to get great software out the door by following a waterfall (or waterfall-like) process that was heavy on up-front documentation. She'd managed some of her best projects at a company that built software for medical devices using waterfall practices.

Waterfall really can work. In fact, if you actually know what you need up front, then writing it down first is a pretty efficient way to build software. Joanna's medical device software projects were rare examples where the requirements were actually right from the beginning, and needed very few changes during the project.

But it takes more than just stable requirements to run a successful waterfall project, which is why they run into so many problems. Teams that build great software using a waterfall process typically have a few common characteristics:

- Good *communication*, because the teams that were successful in a company that mandated waterfall were the ones that consistently talked to their users, managers, and executives throughout the project.

- Good *practices*, especially ones like code reviews and automated testing, which are aimed at finding bugs as early as possible in the process. They usually called this "defect prevention," and it required teams to actively think about how those bugs got into the code in the first place.

- Drawers full of documentation that have rarely been opened, because the people on the team understand that the act of writing down the plan—and the questions that get asked during that planning—is more important than mindlessly sticking to it afterward.

There's one other piece of the puzzle. Dan started his career after the 1990s revolution in software development tools and technology, so he's only ever worked on teams that used object-oriented development to build better software designs. Version control systems, automated testing, better integrated development environments (IDEs) that include features to automate coding practices like refactoring and class design, and other revolutionary tools all help Dan keep control of the code. Bruce has been working on projects longer than Dan, and he watched developers on his teams increasingly adopt software tools over the years to automate routine and repetitive tasks. Bruce and Dan know from their own projects that the most successful ones made effective use of these practices, tools, and ideas. That left more time for them to talk to their users and teammates, and to think about the problems they had to solve instead of fighting with the code.

And as it turns out, when waterfall projects are run effectively, it's because their teams take to heart *many of the same values, principles, and practices that agile projects follow*. Projects that are run using some agile techniques and practices—but that don't really follow the agile values and principles—often end up running into the same kinds of problems that plague waterfall projects.

Unfortunately for Bruce, Dan, and Joanna, they're about to learn this the hard way.

 Key Points

- A **waterfall process** requires a team to write down a complete description of the software at the beginning of the project, and then build exactly what they wrote.
- The waterfall process made it difficult to respond to change because of the focus on documentation rather than collaboration.
- There is *no silver bullet* process or practice that makes projects run perfectly.
- Teams that make waterfall work do it by *adopting effective software practices and principles*, especially ones that improve communication.

Agile to the Rescue! (Right?)

You probably know what a waterfall process feels like, even if you're just learning the term "waterfall" for the first time.[2] Joanna, Bruce, and Dan do, too. Before jumping into planning the jukebox project, they talked about how waterfall processes had caused problems for their teams in the past.

On their last project, Bruce and Dan worked with Tom, a customer account manager at the company, who spent a lot of time on the road helping customers at arcades, casinos, bars, and restaurants install and use their products. The three of them spent the first few weeks of the project building up a specification for the new slot machine. Tom was only in the office half the time, which gave Bruce and Dan time to start designing the software and planning the architecture. Once all three of them had agreed on the requirements, they called a big meeting with the CEO and senior managers of the company to review the requirements, make necessary changes, and get approval to start building.

At that point, Tom went back out on the road, leaving the work up to Bruce and Dan. They broke the project down into tasks, dividing them up among the team, and had everyone start building the software. When the team was almost done building the software, Tom gathered a group of business users, project managers, and executives into a big conference room to do a demo of the nearly complete Slot-o-matic Weekend Warrior software.

It didn't go nearly as smoothly as they'd expected.

At the demo, they had an awkward conversation where the CEO asked, "The software looks great, but wasn't it supposed have a video poker mode?" That was an unfortunate discovery. Apparently, the CEO was under the impression that they were working on software that could be deployed to either the slot machine hardware or the video poker hardware. There had been a lot of discussion of this between the senior managers, the board, and the owners of their two biggest customers. Too bad nobody had bothered to tell the team.

The worst part about it was that if Dan had known about this earlier in the project, it wouldn't have been difficult to change direction. But now, they had to rip out enormous amounts of code they'd already written, and replace it with code retrofitted from the video poker project. They spent weeks troubleshooting weird bugs that were caused by integration problems. Dan spent many late nights complaining to Bruce that this was 100% predictable, and that this almost always happens when code built

---

2 If you're a project manager and you've prepared for the PMP exam, you've learned all about a waterfall process. To be fair, that's because a PMP certification spans many different methodologies across many industries, not just software. When you build a skyscraper or a bridge, it's generally a good idea to have a complete set of blueprints up front, even if they do change along the way.

for one job is hastily repurposed to do something else. Now he's going to be stuck with a tangled mess of spaghetti code. It's going to be difficult to maintain this codebase, and the team is frustrated because it clearly didn't have to be this way.

And this wasn't just a problem for Dan and Bruce. The project manager for that project was so unhappy that he left the company. He had trusted the team's estimates and status, which were completely destroyed by the video poker change. The team had no idea that they would have to deal with the unexpected hardware change, but that didn't make the project manager's life any easier. Even though the facts on the ground had changed, the deadline was set in stone. By the time the project ended, the plan was out of date and basically useless, but the project manager was being held accountable for it anyway. After being raked over the coals by the senior managers in the company, all he could say in his defense is that his team didn't give good numbers to start with. Pretty soon, he left the company for another job—and Joanna was hired shortly after that.

Tom may have been the most frustrated of the group, because he was the one who had to face the customers when they ran into problems. Their biggest customer for this product was the Little Rock, a casino in Las Vegas that wanted to customize all of their slot machines with themes to match their reproductions of cities in Arkansas. The customer had requested this new feature so they could change games between shifts without having to move kiosks around. Their engineers kept running into bugs left in the software by Bruce's team, which meant that Tom and Dan had to spend weeks on the phone with the engineers coming up with patches and workarounds. The Little Rock didn't cancel any contracts, but their next big order was with a competitor, and it wasn't a secret that the CEO and managers blamed the Slot-o-matic Weekend Warrior project for the loss of business.

In the end, everyone knew that the project went wrong. And each person had a pretty good idea of how it was somebody else's fault. But nobody seemed to have any idea how to fix these types of recurring problems. And the software that they'd delivered was still a mess.

Adding Agile Makes a Difference

Bruce, Dan, and Joanna took Tom out to lunch the next time he was in town. After spending time commiserating about their past project problems, Joanna suggested that it was time to go agile.

Like many teams beginning their move to agile, they started with a discussion about what the word "agile" really meant to each of them. To Bruce, it just referred to the world of agile development: the specific books, practices, training courses, blogs, and people who practice agile. To Joanna, agile specifically meant "the ability for a project to handle changes," and it was mainly a set of practices focused on that goal. Dan thought agile meant not writing any documentation, and just jumping straight into code. And Tom had no idea what they were talking about, but he was happy that they were talking about giving him lots of demos along the way, so he could avoid what happened last time.

Members of a team that has started to "go agile" typically start educating themselves on agile techniques, practices, and ideas, and this team was no exception. Dan joined the Agile Alliance (*http://www.agilealliance.org*) and started connecting with other agile practitioners. Bruce and Joanna started reading blogs and books about agile development and project management. Both of them saw great ideas, and took it upon themselves to use what they learned to start anticipating and fixing their project's problems. Each of them discovered different things, and immediately started adding them into the mix.

Dan had already written automated unit tests for his previous projects, but a lot of the developers on the jukebox project had never written any. He started working with the developers to do unit testing and **test-driven development**. He created an **automated build script**, and set up a **build server** that would check out the code, build the software, and then run the tests once an hour. And it worked! They immediately saw an improvement in their code. Every day a developer found a bug that they never would have caught without the automated tests, and it was clear that they were avoiding weeks of debugging and tracking down nasty problems in the field. Not only were they creating fewer bugs, they also felt like the code they were building was easier to change.

(It's OK if you don't recognize all of these practices—like test-driven development— right now. You'll learn all about them throughout this book, and we'll put these new practices in **boldface** to make it easy for you to spot them.)

Joanna attended **Scrum** training, and now the team has taken to calling her the Scrum Master (although she learned in her training that there's a big difference between a Scrum Master and a project manager, and she isn't 100% sure that the role that she's playing on the project really deserves to be called Scrum Master). She helps the team break the project down into **iterations**, tracking their progress on a **task board** and using project **velocity** and **burndown charts**—line charts that track the amount of work left on the project on a daily basis, "burning" down to zero when the work is done—to keep everyone up to date. This is the first time the team has actually been interested in what their project manager is doing, and it makes an improvement in how the work progresses.

Tom also wanted to get in on the agile improvement. Dan, Bruce, and Joanna started calling him the **product owner**, and Tom began to write **user stories** for the team so they could have a better idea of what the software needed to do. He worked with them to build **release plans** based on the stories, and now he felt like he had direct control over what the team would build.

Best of all, Bruce started holding **daily standup meetings** with Joanna, Dan, and all of the programmers, and Tom started attending them as well. It was a little awkward at first, but by the time the project was rolling, everyone was very comfortable giving each other real feedback and honest assessments of how the project was going. Bruce convinced the team to start holding **retrospectives** together at the end of each iteration, and he was pleased to see the team genuinely trying to carry out the improvements that they talked about during the retrospectives.

"Better-Than-Not-Doing-It" Results

It all worked. The team improved, and the project got better...up to a point.

By "going agile," everyone on the team got better at their jobs. Dan and the developers started to develop better habits and write better code. Joanna had a better handle on where the project was at any time. Tom communicated with the team much more, and that gave him better control over the software that they built, which meant he could do a better job of delivering what the users needed. Bruce could concentrate on improving his team's skills and communication.

But have they *really* become an agile team?

They adopted a lot of great practices. Many of those practices were better versions of what they had previously been doing, and all of them made each person more productive at their job. And that was definitely an improvement.

But while the team was happier, and the jukebox project really was going better than any of their previous projects, they also had some reservations about the new, more agile world they found themselves inhabiting. Dan, for instance, thinks that the team is definitely building better code now than they were before, but he finds himself making some technical sacrifices to meet the schedule.

Joanna is happier with the fact that she has some control over the way the project is run. But breaking the project down into short iterations makes her feel a bit blind. Instead of having a big, top-down schedule that she can use as a roadmap, she now finds herself increasingly depending on the team to tell her what's going on at the daily standups. The daily standups are useful, but they mainly consist of each team member reciting his or her status—which Joanna dutifully writes down and communicates to the stakeholders. It's starting to feel more like she's just a coordinator or organizer than a project manager in control of a project. She only focuses on status now, and that makes it difficult for her to spot obstacles and remove them for the team. The team is better at reacting to change, but that puts Joanna in a somewhat uncomfortable position where that's all she's focusing on: reacting, rather than planning.

Now that Tom's a product owner, he's thrilled with his increased ability to define what the team builds. But he's also torn, because he feels like he's expected to work for the team full time. He has to attend these daily meetings, and constantly respond to emails and questions from developers who ask about details of the software they're building. Sometimes they ask questions that he doesn't know the answer to, and other times he wishes they could just answer those questions themselves. He already has a job, and he doesn't feel like the others are meeting him halfway—he feels like they're pushing all of the responsibility for building a great product back on him, and he doesn't have all of the answers. After all, his "real" job is account manager—those jukeboxes won't sell themselves. How can he stay up to date on his accounts and what his users need if he's spending all of his time answering questions for the programmers?

As for Bruce, he's happy that the team is delivering more often. But when he takes a step back and really looks at what's going on, something seems unsatisfying and incomplete, and he's not sure why. Clearly this is an improvement, considering most of his previous projects felt like they were a hair's breadth from failure. It seems to Bruce like the agile adoption made things better, cut down on the personal heroics, and reduced the number of long nights and weekends of work. But he also feels like going agile brought its own set of problems.

It's not uncommon for team members, and especially team leads, to feel the way Bruce does: a little disappointed after their first attempt at agile adoption. The blogs and books they've read and the training they've attended talked about "astonishing results" and "hyper-productive teams." This team feels like the jukebox project is an improvement on their previous projects, but they definitely don't feel "hyper-productive," and nobody's really been astonished at the results.

There's a general feeling that the project has gone from dysfunctional to functional, and that's very good. They've gotten what we like to call **better-than-not-doing-it results**. But is this really all there is to agile?

A Fractured Perspective

Teams have been running into problems for as long as they've been building software. In fact, back in the 1960s, people openly talked about the idea that software development was fundamentally broken. They used the term *software crisis*, which was coined at the same NATO Software Engineering Conference in 1968 as the term *software engineering* was.[3] The "software crisis" referred to the state of software development in a typical company in the 1970s and 1980s, because serious (and now-familiar) problems were very common and led to failed projects. Over time, our

---

3 Peter Naur and Brian Randell, ed., *Software Engineering: Report on a Conference Sponsored by the NATO Science Committee, Garmisch, Germany, 7th to 11th October 1968* (Brussels: Scientific Affairs Division, NATO, 1969), 231.

industry started to understand a major source of the software crisis. An important milestone was when Winston Royce, an engineer at Lockheed, published a paper in 1970 that described a model of software development that was very popular, yet highly ineffective. By the early 1980s, this method was widely known as the waterfall process; it took another 10 to 20 years before many teams made any real headway past blindly adopting it. Like Bruce, Dan, and Joanna, many teams have discovered that agile practices can help them with the problems of a typical waterfall process—but many have also found that it's not as straightforward as they'd expected.

Developers use software tools every day to build their code, and a developer who's proficient with many tools is always more marketable than his neighbor who doesn't know as many. So when many developers first encounter agile, they immediately see it as a set of tools, techniques, and practices. Almost any developer who has been working with agile for a few months has updated his résumé to include the practices that he's been working with. This first impression of agile is a good thing, because it helps make the agile practices attractive to developers who might otherwise be uninterested in them.

But seeing only the tools, techniques, and practices is just the first step in "going agile," and it has a problematic side effect. Think about things from Dan's perspective. As a developer and architect, he's going to concentrate mainly on things that directly affect development: techniques that help him improve the code by removing or preventing bugs, tools that make builds faster and easier to run, and practices that help improve the way the code is designed, reviewed, and built. A project manager like Joanna, on the other hand, cares deeply about how much work it will take to build the software and the quality of the results. So she'll concentrate on the tools that help her understand and communicate schedules, estimates, and effort. A business user like Tom is generally interested in the value that the software delivers to the business, and will be attracted to any practice that helps the team understand exactly what the users need, so that the software they build is valuable. And team leads like Bruce want to make sure that everyone on the team is moving in the same direction, communicating well, and learning from their experiences. They look for the tools that help with those things.

Take the agile practice of writing **user stories**, for example. A user story is a way to express one very specific need that a user has. It's usually written out as a few sentences, often on an index card, sometimes in a strict structure but other times in a flexible format. One user story from the jukebox project, for example, went like this: "As a bar patron, I want to be able to play the newest hit that was just released today."

Each of the people on the team sees user stories a little differently:

- Joanna, the project manager who's trying to become a Scrum Master, sees a user story as work to be done, neatly packaged up and ready to build. She wrote each of the user stories on index cards and taped them all to a whiteboard to help keep everyone on track.

- Dan, the lead developer and architect, sees a user story as a small piece of functionality, written out in a simple, easy-to-understand way. He can break it down into tasks, create an index card for each of them, and write his name on a task card when he starts working on it. When he's done building it, he moves it to a section of the whiteboard reserved for completed tasks.

- Tom, the product owner, sees a user story as value that will be delivered to the company, because it lets him see a clear connection between what the team is building and what the users will do with the software once it's built. The user stories help him talk to the customers at the accounts he manages so he can figure out what they're looking for in the jukebox software, and he makes sure that each story represents something a user actually needs.

- Bruce, the team lead, sees a user story as a specific goal that the team can organize around. He helps them figure out which stories should be done next, and uses the progress to keep them motivated.

Adding user stories to a team like this will help improve the way they build software, because each of the people in those four roles will see a way that user stories helps him or her personally.

But this can work against the team, too. On Dan's past projects, he had a detailed spec that left little room for flexibility, and now he had the freedom to make broader decisions about what he built. That can be a good thing, but it led to some problems on the project. When Dan wrote the code for the "newest hit" user story, he thought it meant building a feature to let bar patrons play any hit as soon as it was uploaded to their server. But when he demoed that feature to Tom at the end of the iteration, it led to a big argument. Tom had to explain that the newer songs played on the jukebox meant that bar owners had to pay higher royalty fees. He'd worked out details with them to let the patrons play the latest hits often enough to be happy to hear them, but not so often that it ran up excessive costs. Dan was pretty upset about this, because it meant that he had to go back and completely rewrite a large part of the feature, and Tom was angry because it meant that the first release of the software wouldn't include the feature.

Had Dan understood that the user story was valuable to Tom for validating what the users needed, he might have had a discussion with Tom about what the software had to do before he started coding. Conversely, if Tom had taken the time to understand a little more about how Dan was going to build the software based on his limited knowledge of the user story, he might have made sure that conversation happened at the beginning of the iteration. But they didn't have that conversation, and the project ran into the same kind of problems their past waterfall projects ran into: developers making incorrect assumptions, jumping into programming, and having to make changes to the code that could have been avoided, and that leave it more fragile.

When each person thinks only about his role and that one particular way the user story helps him, and doesn't look past it to see how the entire team uses the user story —or any other agile tool, technique, or practice—it can cause exactly the kind of problem that Dan and Tom ran into. We call this a **fractured perspective**, because everyone has a different view of the agile practice.

Let's leave our streaming audio jukebox team to their project—we won't be seeing any more of them in this book. Will they overcome their problems and deliver their software? As you read the rest of this chapter, see if you can spot ideas that might help them.

How a Fractured Perspective Causes Project Problems

When each person on a project team only sees a practice from his or her perspective, the same old problems crop up. In the software crisis years, developers would dive right into the software without taking the time to understand the users' needs. Invariably, they'd find out about some new requirement halfway through the project, and they'd have to rip out a bunch of code and replace it. Many agile practices are aimed at giving teams a better understanding of the customer's needs from the beginning of the project, which helps them avoid a lot of that inefficiency. But when people on a team don't communicate—like when a developer builds code and throws it "over the wall" to a product owner without ever really talking about what the users need—it can lead to problems that need to be corrected, often more than once.

In the meantime, product owners are happy that agile gives them a way of directing the project toward things that users need. This is a big relief to any product owner who felt a lack of control over the project, and who watched helplessly as programming teams built last year's software rather than next year's, because that's the last time the programmers talked to the users. But a product owner will still get frustrated if he writes down user stories only to find that the team didn't build exactly what he had in mind. To the team, it seems like the product owner expects them to read his mind; to the product owner, it feels like the team wants him to work with them full time in order to constantly answer any questions they have.

The same kind of fracture happens with other roles on the project, too. Project managers and team leads are happy that the developers have taken it upon themselves to add structure and concrete goals. They see incremental improvement, but not a fundamental change to the way they work, because real change to the way they operate is thwarted when team members work against each other. A project manager who sees user stories taped to a whiteboard as a direct replacement for a Gantt chart in a Microsoft Project file, and who hasn't shifted her "command and control" attitude toward the project, will frequently react to a change on the project by demanding overtime from the team to stick to the original plan. The team lead may respond defensively, protecting the team from the extra work by pushing back against the tighter schedule, and demanding a more relaxed deadline or a reduction in scope. Both the project manager and team lead may be making good points, but had they seen each other's perspectives from the beginning, they might have been able to avoid the conflict while still arriving at a good result.

In other words, when the team doesn't communicate, the people in each of the project roles can adopt a new tool (user stories), but still hold onto the old attitudes that caused friction and team problems. The new tool is better, so the project runs more smoothly. But to the people on the team, it doesn't really feel like much of a change, because many of the old conflicts still come up. And that's when they start to wonder if this is all there is to agile.

There's evidence that many teams have experienced this kind of problem, where adopting individual practices leads to better-than-not-doing-it results. VersionOne is a company that builds agile software tools, and also contributes to the agile community in many other ways. One of the most important things they do is conduct their annual State of Agile Development survey. From the 2013 results,[4] it's easy to see that many teams have made some improvement by adopting agile:

- 88% of respondents to the VersionOne State of Agile Development Survey 2013 said that their organizations were practicing agile development.
- 92% of the respondents reported year-over-year improvements in all areas measured by the survey, with the leading categories being the ability to manage changing priorities (92%), increased productivity (87%), improved project visibility (86%), improved team morale (86%), and enhanced software quality (82%).

But while teams see agile projects move more quickly and team members are better able to respond to change, when agile projects fail, it's often because of cultural and philosophical differences between waterfall and agile methodologies. Survey respondents cited "lack of experience using agile methods," "company philosophy at odds with agile values," and "external pressure to follow waterfall practices" as the three largest sources of agile project failure.

When teams new to agile run into trouble, it's most often because they haven't really changed from their old, waterfall-like ways. As we saw with the jukebox team, just adding practices isn't enough to break them out of the problems that cause conflict and avoidable changes. Everyone on the jukebox team might describe themselves as having gone agile. But in truth, in many ways they're still a waterfall team; they're just one that's adopted some great agile practices. (Dave West of Forrester Research came

---

4 You can request the latest VersionOne State of Agile report at *stateofagile.versionone.com*.

up with a term for this: "Water-Scrum-Fall."[5]) In other words, they've become the most efficient waterfall team that they can be.

Why Does a Fractured Perspective Lead to Just Better-Than-Not-Doing-It Results?

What people deliver will often vary based on what they're focused on. The more people focus on their own goals, and not on the goals of the team, the less likely it's going to be that what they deliver has real value for the company.

This presents a paradox for a team trying to go agile. Teams that concentrate only on the individual practices do end up seeing improvement, but only in the areas that they're already pretty good at. The reason is that team members can only concentrate on what they know already, because for any one of them to expand past what they already know, they would need to have a good handle on what they don't know yet. Asking a team to improve what they don't know seems like a tall order!

---

5 Dave West, "Water-Scrum-Fall Is the Reality of Agile for Most Organizations Today," *Forrester*, July 26, 2011, *http://bit.ly/water-scrum-fall.*

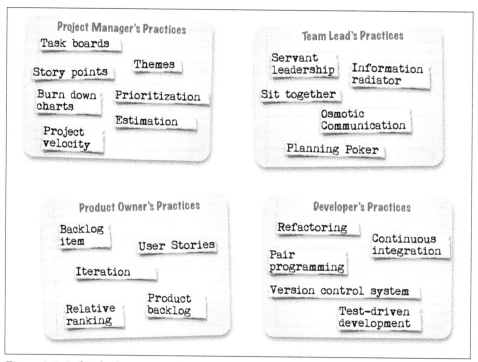

Figure 2-2. Individual team members tend to add agile practices in areas of the project that they're already good at, so the team only improves in those areas—and that's why a fractured perspective leads to better-than-not-doing-it results.

That's why a team that adopts agile practices one at a time will often only get better-than-not-doing-it results. They've applied better practices to the things that they already do, so they'll do those things better. But they haven't touched the areas of the project that they don't already pay attention to, because the practices that affect those areas don't appeal to anyone on the project; therefore, any problems affecting those areas won't be improved. And those areas may be exactly what's keeping the teams from being hyper-productive and delivering those astonishing results.

How does a team get past this problem?

Key Points

- **Better communication** helps a team manage change better.
- **Planning as a team** is more important than over-documenting a plan and mindlessly following it.

- Software projects have been unpredictable and had poor results since the 1960s, and a name given to this situation at the time was the "software crisis."

- Many teams try "going agile" by **adopting great agile practices** that improve on what they already do well today.

- Adopting better practices leads to **better-than-not-doing-it results**, because the teams have not fundamentally changed the way they communicate or work.

- **User stories** are an agile practice in which a team member (often the product owner) describes individual ways that a user will work with the system in one or a few sentences, using language the users can understand.

- Adopting individual practices one at a time is the most common way to adopt agile today, but it is not the most effective path to agile.

The Agile Manifesto Helps Teams See the Purpose Behind Each Practice

The Manifesto for Agile Software development, more commonly known as the Agile Manifesto (*http://www.agilemanifesto.org*), was created in 2001 by a group of 17 like-minded people who came together at the Snowbird Retreat in the mountains outside of Salt Lake City, Utah, to come up with a solution to the software development problems they had all seen throughout their careers. After days of discussion, they agreed on a core set of ideas and principles (and also on the name "agile"). They bundled them into a single document, which started a shift in thinking across the software development world.

The Agile Manifesto contains four simple values. Here's the entire Manifesto:

> We are uncovering better ways of developing software by doing it and helping others do it. Through this work we have come to value:
>
> **Individuals and interactions** over processes and tools
> **Working software** over comprehensive documentation
> **Customer collaboration** over contract negotiation
> **Responding to change** over following a plan

That is, while there is value in the items on the right, we value the items on the left more.

Understanding and effectively working with agile starts with understanding these values.

Individuals and Interactions Over Processes and Tools

People can go wrong when they blindly follow a process. A great tool can sometimes help you do the wrong thing faster. The software world is full of great practices: not all of them are appropriate for every project and every situation. However, it's universally important to understand the people on the team, how they work together, and how each person's work impacts everyone else.

This is an especially useful idea for anyone who needs to improve the way his or her team works. That's why agile teams value individuals and interactions over processes or tools: because it's not enough to have the "correct" process or "best" practice. If the people who need to use a process or tool don't buy into it, it will fall by the wayside—or, even worse, people will follow the letter of the process, even if it leads to incoherent results. Before you're able to implement a process, even if it logically makes a lot of sense or is rationally the right thing to do, you need to sell it to the people who are working with you. If people don't get why you're doing what you're doing, all they'll see is that you're asking for an arbitrary change.

That's why it's always, in every situation, important to recognize that you're working with a group of people. Each of those people has his or her own motivations, ideas, and preferences.

There are many agile practices that support this principle, across lots of different ways of thinking about agile. That's why you'll see practices that support individuals and interactions—like **daily standup meetings** and **retrospectives** (where everyone talks about how the project or iteration went, and what lessons can be learned)—throughout this book. And **user stories**, too—the stories themselves are less important than the fact that they help the team have a conversation about what the story means.

Working Software Over Comprehensive Documentation

There are binders full of complete and comprehensive software documentation sitting unopened on shelves all over the world. There is so much that can be documented in a software project, and it's often difficult during the heat of the project to predict what's going to be useful in the future, and what will gather dust. Because of that, a lot of teams—and especially their managers—will decide on a comprehensive approach, where every little thing must be documented, no matter whether or not there's a potential reader for the document.

Agile teams value working software over comprehensive documentation. But the term "working software" may seem vague—after all, what does the word "working" really mean? To an agile practitioner, working software is software that adds **value** to the organization. It could be software that a company sells to make money, or it could be software that people who work at the company use to do their jobs more efficiently. For a project to add value, it needs to deliver or save more money than it cost to build. Value really does come down to money most of the time, even if that's not something the team talks about directly. And the team should emphasize building and delivering working software that delivers value. Documentation is only a means toward that end.

Valuing working software over comprehensive documentation does *not* mean that you should not document. There are many kinds of documents that are very useful for the team. But it's important to keep in mind that the people writing the documentation are often the same people who are writing the software. Documentation that helps them understand the problem, communicate it with the users, and correct problems before they make it into the software is documentation that saves more time and effort than it costs. It often also happens to be the kind of documentation—like wireframes or sequence diagrams—that programmers don't mind writing.

Concentrating on working software, on the other hand, is a great way to make sure that the team keeps on track. When the team is working on documentation that is clearly headed toward working software, it's making a positive contribution to the project. In fact, the team can often take a novel approach to documentation that allows it to be embedded in the software itself. For example, one such agile practice is **test-driven development**, in which the programmers build automated unit tests *before* they build the software that it tests. These automated tests exist as code that is stored alongside the rest of the code for the software. But it also serves as documentation, because it gives developers a record of what the code is supposed to do, and of the expected behavior for individual elements of the software.

Customer Collaboration Over Contract Negotiation

A lot of people might read "contract negotiation" and assume that this value only applies to consultants and contractors who work within a contract. Actually, this applies to many teams that work within a single company. When programmers, testers, business owners, and project managers all work on different teams, and don't really collaborate toward a single goal of delivering working software, they often treat each other as if they're working on a contract. In many companies, they will explicitly discuss SLAs (service-level agreements) between programming teams, between testers and developers, and between teams and their users.

This may reduce the risk of getting in trouble with the boss (because it makes it easier to point a finger and blame another team for failing to deliver software), but it is highly counterproductive if the goal is to get working software out the door for the users. A developer who is constantly trying to protect himself will be less able to try new ways to collaborate and innovate with the people who need to use the software being built.

One way agile teams put this value in place is to have a product owner who is a real, first-class member of the team. She may not be actively developing code, but she does attend meetings, contribute ideas, and, most importantly, feel ownership for the final product. Product owners will often use user stories as a way to collaborate with the rest of the team.

Responding to Change Over Following a Plan

There's an old project management saying: "plan the work, work the plan." Unfortunately, if you work the wrong plan, you'll build the wrong product. That's why teams need to constantly look for changes, and to make sure that they respond appropriately when there's a change in what the users need, or in how the software needs to be built. If the circumstances change, the project needs a new plan.

It's not uncommon for the person or people who built a plan to resist change, because it takes work to change a plan. For example, there may have been a lot of effort put into breaking the work down into packages, and estimating each one of them. A change could require a project manager to have to redo all of that work, and if he values following a plan over responding to the change, he might dig his heels in. This makes for a smoother project, but, if the change is really needed, it will be much harder to make it later on, after the code is more complete.

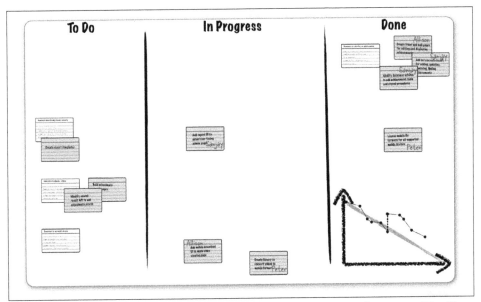

Figure 2-3. Agile teams often use task boards to show tasks and track progress. They'll write tasks or user stories on index cards, and move them across the board as they progress. Many teams also draw charts on their task boards to help them track progress.

A **task board** is a good example of a practice that helps a team make the right decisions about responding to changes. Each element of the work (typically a user story) is written on an index card and attached to a board—like the one that Joanna used for the jukebox project—usually in columns that show the status of each one. A task board can also be managed with a computer program, but many teams find it more effective to physically put it on a wall because standing in front of the board, talking, gesturing, and moving stories is a much richer form of communication than simply talking. The board is set up in a way that anyone can rearrange the order of tasks, and is even encouraged to do so. If changes happen, everyone is encouraged to add index cards to the task board, rather than having to clear each change through a single project manager hub. This helps keep everyone in the loop on changes, so the plan doesn't get stale.

Principles Over Practices

Our better-than-not-doing-it jukebox team got good results because they adopted some great practices, and those practices improved their projects. But because of their fractured perspective, they didn't get the full benefit of working together toward an improved way of building software. There's a mindset of agile that goes beyond practices, and teams who find their way to the ideas behind agile find better ways of collaborating and interacting.

In other words, a team that uses the agile practices to help attain the goal of building working software that customers value through interaction, collaboration, and responding to change *will get more out of their projects* than the team that simply adopts better planning, programming, and documentation practices.

Jim Highsmith does a very good job of summarizing this idea in his book *Agile Project Management: Creating Innovative Projects*:

> Without concrete practices, principles are sterile; but without principles, practices have no life, no character, no heart. Great products arise from great teams—teams who are principled, who have character, who have heart, who have persistence, and who have courage.[6]

So how does a team go beyond simply adopting practices and become "principled," so they can create great products?

 Key Points

- The **Agile Manifesto** contains common values and ideas that lead to effective teams.

- "Individuals and interactions over processes and tools" means the team should focus on the people on the team and how they communicate first, and the tools and practices that they use second.

- "Working software over comprehensive documentation" means that delivering software that does what users need is more important than delivering a specification that describes it.

- Working software means software that delivers *value* to the company.

- "Customer collaboration over contract negotiation" means treating everyone *like they're on the same team.*

- Many effective agile teams treat the **product owner** as a member of the project team to collaborate with, rather than a client or customer to negotiate with.

- "Responding to change over following a plan" means recognizing that plans become inaccurate, and that it's more important to deliver the software than it is to work the plan.

---

6 Jim Highsmith, *Agile Project Management: Creating Innovative Products*, 2nd Edition (Upper Saddle River, NJ: Pearson Education, 2009).

- A **task board** is an agile planning tool in which user stories are attached to a board and categorized into columns based on their status in the current project or iteration.

Understanding the Elephant

Lyssa Adkins, in her book *Coaching Agile Teams*, explains how a metaphor can be a valuable tool to help understand a concept:

> Metaphor is a powerful thing. Professional coaches have known this for a long time. In fact, "metaphor" is a core skill taught in professional coaching courses. ... Coaches ask questions that help clients create their own metaphor, one that is visceral and resonant. Clients use the metaphor to guide them through the events unfolding in their lives.[7]

There's a useful metaphor that can help us get a better handle on what it means to have a fractured perspective, and why that leads teams down a less effective path. It's the story of the blind men and the elephant.

> Six blind men were asked to determine what an elephant looked like by feeling different parts of the elephant's body. The blind man who feels a leg says the elephant is like a pillar; the one who feels the tail says the elephant is like a rope; the one who feels the trunk says the elephant is like a tree branch; the one who feels the ear says the elephant is like a hand fan; the one who feels the belly says the elephant is like a wall; and the one who feels the tusk says the elephant is like a solid pipe.
>
> A king explains to them: "All of you are right. The reason every one of you is telling it differently is because each one of you touched the different part of the elephant. So, actually the elephant has all the features you mentioned."[8]

Teams that get better-than-not-doing-it results from agile are often teams who are already able to get software out the door reasonably well before starting with agile, and were hoping that agile adoption would help them make a good project even better. The problem is that even before the team started adopting agile practices, they were already experiencing problems—not the serious, software crisis problems that caused their projects to fail outright, but problems that caused friction and discomfort on the team. This is what "fractured perspective" really means: the developers think about developer stuff, project managers think about project manager stuff, and they throw the code over the wall to a business user who thinks about business stuff. Everyone is really busy thinking about his or her own project work—so much so that

---

7 Lyssa Adkins, *Coaching Agile Teams: A Companion for ScrumMasters, Agile Coaches, and Project Managers in Transition* (Boston: Addison-Wesley, 2010).

8 From the Wikipedia page (*http://bit.ly/elephant-tale*) of the "Blind Men and the Elephant" story (retrieved June 25, 2014).

they actually use phrases like "throw it over the wall," which explicitly divide the team and kill collaboration. When each person only thinks about his or her own practices, there isn't a lot of communication between people, and they're really functioning as individuals working separately toward compatible goals, not as a team.

That's where the "Blind Men and the Elephant" story comes in. In a fractured agile adoption, each person uses only the practices that impact his or her work, the same way each of the blind men feels only one part of the elephant. Developers concentrate on, say, test-driven development, refactoring, and automated builds. Project managers like task boards, project velocity, and burndown charts. Business users use release planning and user stories to get a better grasp on what the team is doing. Team leads use daily standups and retrospectives to manage and improve the team. Everybody wants something different from the project, and they each see a few practices that do something specific to help them. (Again, we'll cover each of these practices later in the book, so don't worry if you aren't familiar with them yet.)

Now, adopting those practices individually will definitely improve things, because agile practices are really good. The problem is that because everyone—developers, project managers, business users, and team leads—sees the project from a different perspective, they'll concentrate on only those practices that immediately appeal to them. There's a paradoxical effect ("See! I was right all along"), where each person now sees only the part of agile that affects his specific project work, and draws the conclusion that agile is all about getting everyone else to come around to his point of view.

So while the agile "elephant" is made up of many great practices, the whole thing is even greater than the sum of the parts. And if you only see the individual practices—especially if you're only looking at the practices that directly affect your project work—then you'll only see one small piece of agile. The "elephant" of agile is made up of the day-to-day practices, but it's much bigger than just those practices.

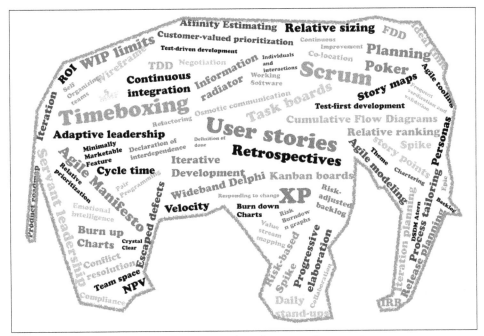

Figure 2-4. The agile "elephant" is greater than the sum of its practices.

A team whose members only see the practices and don't think about the principles will miss out on the important interactions between people. Their perspective stays fractured; the team members stay separate, and don't really function as an effective unit. They'll still get their work done, but they miss out on the great team interactions and collaboration that make agile really powerful.

This is built into agile. Take another look at the very first value in the Agile Manifesto:

> Individuals and interactions over processes and tools

Processes, methodologies, and tools are still important (which is why the Manifesto ends with, "...while there is value in the items on the right, we value the items on the left more"). But even more important than specific practices are the individuals and interactions. It's these values (along with the 12 principles, which you'll learn about in Chapter 3) that show us how the practices work together, and serve as a guide for how teams adopt those practices.

Methodologies Help You Get It All in Place at Once

There's a big gap between understanding the values in the Agile Manifesto (and the principles behind it) and actually changing the way your team builds software. Luckily, there's another important aspect to agile development that specifically helps with this. There are **agile methodologies** that are actually intended to help teams adopt agile and improve their projects.

Agile methodologies are valuable to you because they help you see the practices in context. They are especially useful for teams that are not familiar with all of the agile practices. Each methodology was developed and improved over the years by agile experts focused on all of the different parts of the elephant. Adopting a methodology in full means you'll be following a tried-and-true path that takes you from the beginning to the end of a software project, without the trial and error that can lead to a fractured perspective.

An agile methodology is a collection of practices combined with ideas, advice, and often a body of knowledge and wealth of experience among agile practitioners. An agile methodology will outline different roles and responsibilities for everyone on the project, and will recommend certain practices for each of them at various stages of the project.

The VersionOne State of Agile Development 2013 survey results contain a list of the most popular methodologies, and topping the list are **Scrum**, followed by a hybrid of Scrum and **XP**. Respondents also reported using Lean and Kanban, which are not agile methodologies (as you'll learn about in Chapters 8 and 9), but are still core to agile.

Alistair Cockburn has this description of Scrum in *Agile Software Development: The Cooperative Game*, 2nd Edition:

> Scrum can be summarized (but not executed) very simply:
>
> - The team and the project sponsors create a prioritized list of all the things the team needs to do. This can be a list of tasks or a list of features. This is known as the product backlog.
> - Each month, the team pulls off the top section of the list, which they estimate to be one month's worth of work. They expand it to a detailed task list, called the sprint backlog. The team promises to demo or deliver the results to the sponsors at the end of the month.
> - Each day, the team meets face-to-face for five to ten minutes to update each other on their status and on any roadblocks that are slowing them down. This is called the daily standup meeting.
> - One particular person is designated the Scrum Master. It is this person's assignment to remove, or get someone to remove, whatever roadblocks the team mentions in the standup meeting.[9]

---

9 Alistair Cockburn, *Agile Software Development: The Cooperative Game*, 2nd Edition (Boston: Addison Wesley, 2006).

For many teams beginning their move to agile, this translates to specific practices (which we've highlighted in boldface here, and which we'll explain in detail in Chapter 4):

- The product owner creates and maintains a **product backlog**, a list of requirements for the software.

- The team runs timeboxed month-long **sprints**, where they pull a month's worth of requirements from the product backlog to build, test, and demo. The requirements for the current sprint are called the **sprint backlog**. (Some Scrum teams use sprints that are two or four weeks long.)

- The team meets for a **daily standup meeting** in which everyone talks through the work they did the day before, the work they plan to do today, and any obstacles in their way.

- The **Scrum Master** acts as leader, coach, and shepherd to guide the team through the project.

But adopting Scrum requires more than just adopting those great practices. Every one of those practices could potentially be used in a way that doesn't reflect the values and principles of agile. A daily standup, for example, works very well if the team uses it to collaborate and work together to move the project forward. But it could also be a meeting where a project manager informs the team of their individual assignments and gets status updates from each of them, one at a time. And each developer uses the meeting to tell the project manager, "Here are obstacles blocking my way—you go deal with them." If each person clings to his role—"That's *your* responsibility, not mine!"—he starts to treat each new obstacle as someone else's problem. The meeting turns into a contract-like negotiation, instead of an opportunity for collaboration. A team that falls into this trap may have adopted Scrum-like practices, but they aren't using Scrum.

(You'll learn more about how Scrum works and its practices later on in the book.)

A second methodology is **eXtreme Programming** (or XP). *The Art of Agile Development (http://bit.ly/art-of-agile-development)*, by James Shore and Shane Warden, summarizes XP like this: "Using simultaneous phases, an XP team produces deployable software every week. In each iteration, the team analyzes, designs, codes, tests, and deploys a subset of features." (Many XP teams use iterations that last one week, but others use two-week or month-long iterations. Scrum can also be adapted to use different iteration lengths. You'll learn more about adapting agile methodologies later in the book.) XP prescribes specific development practices aimed at improving collaborating with users, planning, developing, and testing. But XP goes beyond that, using those practices to help the team build simple, flexible software designs that are easy for the team to maintain and extend.

Scrum and XP have many things in common, including the fact that they are both **iterative**. This means that the project is divided up into iterations, in which the team performs all of the activities of a complete project to produce working, deployable software at the end of each iteration. Many XP teams use iterations that last one week, while many Scrum teams use one-month iterations. Putting a limit on how long an iteration lasts is called **timeboxing**, and it helps users to know when they can expect new features to be delivered.

Many teams find adopting methodologies—especially Scrum and XP—to be more effective than simply adopting individual practices. While adopting individual practices allows each team member to select those practices specific to his or her job, adopting an entire methodology encourages the entire team to get together and figure out as a team how to adopt all of the practices for that methodology. To do this, they need to change the way they think about doing their jobs. Methodologies are constructed around the agile values and principles, so this change in attitude is generally toward collaboration and interactions, working software, and responding to change. This transition is often made easier by the books and knowledge already collected by other agile practitioners, and encouraged by existing communities formed around those methodologies.

Lean is not a methodology. Rather, it's a name for a mindset—it has its own set of values, and thinking tools to help you adopt it. Lean is just as important in the agile world as XP and Scrum, and you can learn a lot about what it means to be agile by understanding what's common among all three of them. **Kanban** is an agile method for improving the way that a team builds software. It's built on the values of Lean, and it includes its own practices to help a team improve and evolve.

The practices in XP, and in many ways much of the focus of XP, are different than the practices and the focus of Scrum. Lean and Kanban take yet another approach, with different practices and focus. How is it possible that these different approaches to agile can have entirely different focus and practices, yet all be considered agile? It's because all agile methodologies are based on the same principles, and they all rely on everyone on the team to work together and collectively own every aspect of the project. The values and principles of the Agile Manifesto are what tie all methodologies and methods together.

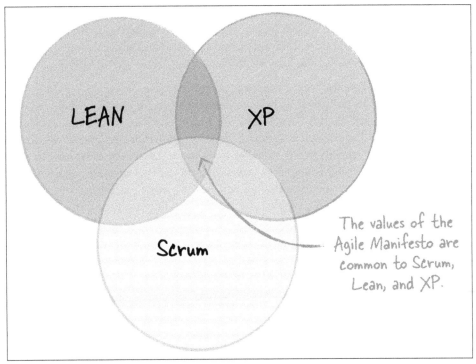

Figure 2-5. Scrum, XP, and Lean all have the agile values at their core, and share some values, ideas, and practices with each other.

Where to Start with a New Methodology

By coming together and working toward the single goal of adopting a methodology, everyone on the team begins talking about each other's practices, ideas, and perspectives. This is the opposite of a fractured perspective. By looking at the methodology as a whole, teams start to understand how the individual practices interact with each other. And that's where Bruce, Dan, Joanna, and Tom want to be—but they don't know quite how to get there.

When the team initially tried out the new practices and ideas, they didn't yet understand how those new practices would relate to the ones they were already familiar with. That understanding will come as the team gains experience with the methodology. This works because an agile methodology is a complete system that includes a set of practices that are known to interact well together, and which teams have used successfully to become more productive. Adopting a complete set of practices will help give the team a foundation for learning about those interactions.

But adopting an entire methodology is more difficult than picking and choosing practices that fit in with the team's current way of working. If a team can adopt the methodology all at once, they stand a much better chance of getting the most out of their agile effort. In part, this is because in addition to the practices that are similar to what each person already does, they also adopt practices and ideas that they may not think they need at first.

As we learned, the jukebox team ran into problems because Bruce, Dan, Joanna, and Tom all approached agile practices independently. To get the greatest benefit of agile in the future, instead of just diving into the practices, they should first sit down together and have a real discussion about what each of those practices will do for them and their project. But this is a challenge, because they don't know how to start that discussion. Like many teams, they face a dilemma: if they already knew what the agile practices would do for their project and how to work together to put them in place, they wouldn't need to have that discussion. But because they don't know that already, the discussion is difficult to have.

There's a solution: the 12 principles that go hand-in-hand with the values of the Agile Manifesto. You'll learn about them in Chapter 3.

Key Points

- A team that only focuses on the individual practices can *lose sight of the larger goal* of better communication and responding to change.

- An **agile methodology** is a collection of practices combined with ideas, advice, and a community of practitioners.

- Agile methodologies like Scrum, XP, and Lean include great practices, but they also emphasize ideas that keep the team focused on those goals.

- Agile coaches often use metaphor as a tool to help their teams learn.

Frequently Asked Questions

When the Agile Manifesto talks about not having comprehensive documentation, does that mean we don't have to write anything down?

This is a really common question about the Agile Manifesto. Take another look at what it says about comprehensive documentation:

> We value ... Working software over comprehensive documentation

This doesn't mean that as agile practitioners we don't value comprehensive documentation. And it certainly doesn't mean that we think you shouldn't write any documentation at all! That's because there's plenty of documentation that's useful without being "comprehensive."

What this means is that putting working software into your users' hands is the best way to communicate how well we, as a team, are progressing. But there's also a place in our projects for writing things down. We'll document our code using code comments (for example, to explain why we made a decision, or why we didn't write the code a different way or use a different algorithm). Later in the book, you'll learn about a specific kind of documentation called a **user story**, which is typically written on an index card and helps you, your team, your users, and your stakeholders work together to figure out exactly what you'll be building. There are many other kinds of documentation, some more comprehensive than others, that agile teams use.

Are you sure? I've definitely heard that agile means not writing anything down or doing any planning, and instead jumping straight into programming. Isn't that more efficient?

One of the most common myths of agile software development is that agile teams don't plan. In fact, agile teams do a much more thorough job of planning than many traditional project teams. But to a developer who's new to agile, it may look like there isn't a lot of planning going on, because the whole team is involved—and nobody is groaning or complaining about it (which, let's be honest, is a programmer's typical reaction when he or she receives an invitation to a planning meeting).

Scrum teams, for example, typically spend a whole eight-hour day planning for a 30-day iteration. Then they have a daily meeting (often timeboxed to 15 minutes) where they review the plan together. For a five-person team, this amounts to 40 person-hours of planning at the beginning of the iteration, and another 40 person-hours of planning spread out across the next 30 days. This is far more planning than many traditional software teams do for 30 days of software development. No wonder Scrum teams do such a good job of meeting their deadlines! However, to the team members, it often doesn't really feel like "boring" planning work. This is because they're engaged in the process, they care about the outcome, and they get a very good sense that the work they're doing to plan the project will make the rest of the iteration go well. (You'll learn more about the mechanics of planning a Scrum project in Chapter 4.)

To a developer looking in from the outside, however, this may actually look a lot like jumping straight into the project without planning. When the team only spends a single day at the beginning of the 30-day iteration planning, it means that on the second day the team can start programming (if that's what makes the most sense to them). So that often looks like they're barely doing any planning, even though it's actually a lot of planning when the effort-hours are added up.

Doesn't that mean that agile is only for very experienced developers who are good at planning?

No, agile is for everyone at every skill level. Planning is a skill, and the only way to get better at it is to practice. Even experienced developers blow their estimates sometimes (in fact, pretty often!). We've run across and read many stories of real-world teams of junior developers who did a great job of becoming agile, and it helped them deliver software that was far beyond what their companies expected of them. However, there's one caveat: junior developers on effective agile teams don't stay junior for very long, and this may be one of the reasons that some people think agile is only for experienced developers.

Can I have the developers on the team go agile, but leave the rest of the team (testers, business analysts, UX designers, project managers, etc.) alone?

Yes, you can. However, it will probably not be very effective. When people talk about putting agile in place for just the developers, what they're really talking about is having those developers adopt some of the practices in a methodology. This will give those developers a boost in their own productivity that makes it worth doing (better-than-not-doing-it results). But because the team has not changed the way they think about their projects, this approach seriously limits the positive impact that agile thinking can have on the team's productivity. This is one way that teams end up in the "Water-Scrum-Fall" scenario that leaves the team members feeling like their agile adoption is somehow empty or incomplete.

If I'm not using Scrum, XP, Lean, or Kanban, does that mean my team isn't agile?

Absolutely not. There are many agile methodologies—we're concentrating on a few here, because we're using them to teach you about the ideas behind agile. But more importantly, one goal of this book is to help you answer the question, "What does 'agile' really mean?" Throughout the rest of this book, you'll learn about the values and practices of different methodologies and methods, and through them you'll learn what it means to be agile—and how such different methodologies and methods can all be agile, even if they don't resemble each other.

Things You Can Do Today

Here are a few things that you can try today on your own or with your team:

- Write down a list of all of the practices that you and your team use when you build software. They may be things like writing a specification, or checking your code into a version control system, or using a Gantt chart to document your project plan, or holding a daily standup meeting.
- Ask someone else on your team to write down her own list of all of the practices that you and your team use. Compare your lists. What practices are on one list but not the other? Have a discussion about that practice. Can you find a difference in perspective between the two of you?

 Where You Can Learn More

Here are resources to help you learn more about the ideas in this chapter:

- You can learn more about the agile values and principles in *Agile Software Development: The Cooperative Game*, 2nd Edition, by Alistair Cockburn (Addison-Wesley, 2006).
- You can learn more about how principles relate to practices in *Agile Project Management: Creating Innovative Projects*, by Jim Highsmith (Addison-Wesley, 2009).
- You can learn more about agile coaching in *Coaching Agile Teams*, by Lyssa Adkins (Addison-Wesley, 2010).

 **Coaching Tips**

Tips for agile coaches helping their team to work the ideas in this chapter:

- When coaching a new team, talk to individual team members separately and try to understand how perspectives differ across the different roles.

- Ask individual team members specifically about the values in the Agile Manifesto: what they think of them, which ones they consider important, or if they think the values apply to them at all.

- Teams often have a sense that they're getting better-than-not-doing-it results, but have trouble putting that feeling into words. Bring up this concept directly, and ask team members to come up with examples of practices that feel "empty," or that take a lot of effort with little payoff.

- Start a conversation about an individual value or principle in the Agile Manifesto—for example, if a team talks about a "contract" that they forge with their users, use that as a starting point for talking about contract negotiation versus customer collaboration. Help them understand where they're making choices.

CHAPTER 3

The Agile Principles

If I had asked people what they wanted, they would have said faster horses.
—Henry Ford[1]

There's no single recipe that results in perfect software every time. Agile teams recognize this. Instead, they have ideas and ground rules that help to guide teams to make the right choices and avoid problems—or deal with those problems when they inevitably happen.

We've already seen the four values in the Agile Manifesto. In addition to those values, there are 12 principles that every agile practitioner should use when working on a software project team. When the 17 original signers of the Agile Manifesto met at Snowbird, Utah, they came up with the four values in the Agile Manifesto quickly. It took them longer to come up with the 12 additional principles that accompany the Manifesto. Manifesto signer Alistair Cockburn recalled:[2]

> The group of 17 quickly agreed on those value choices. Developing the next level of statements proved more than we could settle on in the time left in the meeting. The values included in this section make up the current working set.

> These statements should evolve as we learn people's perceptions of our words and as we come up with more accurate words ourselves. I will be surprised if this particular version isn't out of date shortly after the book is published. For the latest version, check the Agile Alliance (*http://www.agilealliance.org*).

---

1 There's some debate over whether Henry Ford actually said this, but almost everyone agrees that he would have liked it.

2 Alistair Cockburn, *Agile Software Development: The Cooperative Game*, 2nd Edition (Boston: Addison Wesley, 2006).

Alistair was right, and the language on the website for the principles is, in fact, currently slightly different than the language in his book. The language may always be evolving, but the ideas and principles have stayed constant.

In this chapter, you'll learn about the 12 principles of agile software: what they are, why you need them, and how they impact your project. You'll see how these principles apply to a real project by following a practical example. To make it easier to learn, we've gathered these principles into four sections—delivery, communication, execution, and improvement—because they represent consistent themes throughout the principles and agile in general. But even though that's an effective way to learn about them, each principle stands on its own.

The 12 Principles of Agile Software

1. Our highest priority is to satisfy the customer through early and continuous delivery of valuable software.

2. Welcome changing requirements, even late in development. Agile processes harness change for the customer's competitive advantage.

3. Deliver working software frequently, from a couple of weeks to a couple of months, with a preference to the shorter timescale.

4. The most efficient and effective method of conveying information to and within a development team is face-to-face conversation.

5. Businesspeople and developers must work together daily throughout the project.

6. Build projects around motivated individuals. Give them the environment and support they need, and trust them to get the job done.

7. Working software is the primary measure of progress.

8. Agile processes promote sustainable development. The sponsors, developers, and users should be able to maintain a constant pace indefinitely.

9. Continuous attention to technical excellence and good design enhances agility.

10. Simplicity—the art of maximizing the amount of work not done—is essential.

11. The best architectures, requirements, and designs emerge from self-organizing teams.

12. At regular intervals, the team reflects on how to become more effective, then tunes and adjusts its behavior accordingly.[3]

---

3 Source: *agilemanifesto.org/principles.html* (as of June 2014)

The Customer Is Always Right...Right?

Flip back to the beginning of the chapter and reread that quote. What is Henry Ford really saying? He's talking about giving people what they actually need, and not just what they ask for. The customer has a need, and if you're building software to meet that need, then you have to understand it—whether or not he can communicate it to you. How do you work with a customer who can't necessarily tell you at the beginning of a project that he needs a car, and not just faster horses?

That's the motivation behind the 12 principles: getting the team to build software that the user actually needs. The principles depend on the idea that we build projects to deliver *value*. But that word, "value," is a little bit tricky, because everyone sees different value in the software: different people need different things from it.

You might be holding a good example of this idea in your hands. If you're reading this book on a handheld ebook reader, you're using software that was written to display ebooks on that reader. Take a minute and think about all of the different stakeholders (people who need something from the project) for that ebook reader software:

- As a reader, you want the software to make the book easy to read. You care about being able to flip back and forth between pages, highlight sections or take notes, search for text, and keep track of the last page you read.

- As authors, we care very much that the words we write are displayed correctly, that these bullet points are indented so that they're easy for you to read, that it's easy for you to navigate back and forth between the body text and the footnotes, and that you have a good overall experience so you can enjoy and learn from what we write.

- Our editor at O'Reilly cares that it's easy to distribute the book to you, and that, if you like it, you have an easy way to give it a positive review and buy other books from O'Reilly.

- The bookseller or retailer who sold you this book wants to make it very easy for you to browse and buy other books they have for sale, and to download them quickly and easily to your reader.

You can probably think of more stakeholders, and of other things that each of these stakeholders cares about. Every one of these things represents value that's delivered to a stakeholder.

The very first ebook readers on the market didn't do all of these things. It took a long time for the software that runs on those readers to evolve to the point where it is today. And it's almost certain that the software will get better and better as the teams working on it discover new ways to deliver new value.

It's easy to see the value that an ebook reader has delivered, because hindsight is 20/20. It's much harder to see that value at the start of the project. Let's do a quick thought experiment to explore this. Consider this question: how might a hypothetical reader have turned out had it been developed using a waterfall process?

"Do As I Say, Not As I Said"

Imagine you're on a team building the very first handheld ebook reader. The hardware team delivered a prototype device that has a USB port that you can load ebooks into, and a little keyboard that lets you interact with it. It's up to you and your team to build the software that will display ebooks to the user.

Unfortunately, your company has a long history of building software using a particularly ineffective, "big requirements up front" waterfall process. So the first thing that your project manager does is to call a giant meeting with everyone she can find. Your whole team spends the next few weeks in a room with, at various times, the senior managers of your company, a representative from a friendly publisher who wants to publish ebooks that your reader can display, a senior salesperson from an online retailer hoping to sell those books, and any other stakeholder that your project manager can dig up and get to come to a meeting.

After days of intense meetings and heavy debate, your business analysts were able to piece together a large specification with requirements from all of the different stakeholders who were consulted. It was a lot of work, but now you have a spec that everyone thinks is great. There are extensive features for the user that would make it the most advanced handheld reader software available. It includes features to capture marketing statistics for publishers, it provides an entire Internet storefront to make it easy to buy books, and it even has an innovative feature for authors to preview and edit their books as they write them, streamlining the publishing process. This would be truly revolutionary software. After you sit down with the rest of your team to estimate, you've come up with a schedule of 15 months. It seems like a long time, but everyone is excited, and you're confident that you and your team can deliver.

Fast-forward a year and a half. The ebook reader team has worked unbelievably hard, putting in many late nights and weekends, and putting stress on more than a few marriages. It was a huge effort, but the project is done, and you've delivered exactly on plan, practically to the day. (Yes, that seems highly improbable! But for the sake of this thought experiment, try to suspend your disbelief and imagine that it happened, just this once.) Every requirement in the spec has been implemented, tested, and verified as complete. The team is really proud, and every stakeholder who's seen it agrees that they got exactly what they asked for.

So, the product hits the market...and it's a flop. Nobody buys the reader, and none of the stakeholders are happy. So what happened?

It turns out that the software everyone needed a year and a half ago is not the same software that they need today. In the time since the project began, the industry standardized on a new, industry-wide format for ebooks, and because that format wasn't in the spec, it's not supported. None of the Internet retailers want to publish the nonstandard format that the reader uses. And even though the team built that great Internet storefront, it's now far less advanced than the storefronts that the retailers currently use, so it's not attractive to them anymore. And all the work that you and your team put into building the special preview feature for authors isn't nearly as useful as a competitor's support for authors to email MS Word documents straight to their readers and display them.

What a mess! The spec that your team started with had a lot of value to all of the customers, both inside and outside the company. But now the software your team agreed to build a year and a half ago is much less valuable. Some of these changes could have been discovered early on in the project, but many of them would not have been clear from the beginning. The team would have had to change course very quickly at many points during the project in order to take them into account. The "big requirements up front" waterfall approach doesn't give a team much flexibility to respond to these changes.

So how can we find a better way to satisfy stakeholders and customers, but still run a project that delivers software that works?

Delivering the Project

Agile teams recognize that their most important job is to deliver working software to their customers. You already know how they do this from Chapter 2: by working together as a team, collaborating with their customers, and responding to change. But how does that translate to the day-to-day work of a team?

By putting frequent delivery of value first, by looking at each change as a good thing for the project, and by delivering software frequently, the team and the customers can work together to make adjustments along the way. The software that the team builds might not be what they set out to build, but *that's a good thing*—because they end up building the software that the customers need most.

Principle #1: Our Highest Priority Is to Satisfy the Customer Through Early and Continuous Delivery of Valuable Software.

This first principle includes three distinct and important ideas: releasing software early, delivering value continuously, and satisfying the customer. To really understand the core of this principle, you need to know how those three things work together.

Project teams work in the real world, and in the real world things never go perfectly. Even a team that does a brilliant job of gathering and writing down requirements will miss things, because it's impossible to completely and perfectly capture the requirements for any system. That's not to say that teams shouldn't try, and agile methodologies are based on some great practices for communicating and writing down requirements. But the fact is that until customers get their hands on working software, they have a hard time envisioning exactly *how* the software will work.

So if the customer can only give you real, informed feedback after seeing working software, then the best way to get that feedback is through **early delivery**: shipping the first working version of the software to the customer as early as possible. Even if you only deliver a single working feature that the customer can use, that's still a win. It's a win for the team, because the customer can now give informed feedback to help them move the project in the right direction. It's also a win for the customers, because they can do something today that they couldn't do before—with this working software. Because the software works, and because the customers can actually use it to do something they need, the team has delivered real value. It might only be a small amount of value, but it's far better than delivering no value at all—especially if the alternative is an increasingly frustrated user who has to wait a long time before getting his or her hands on software from the team.

The downside to delivering early is that the software that's first delivered to the customers is far from complete. This can be *really* hard for some users and stakeholders to deal with; while some users are used to the idea that they'll see software early, others are much less so. Many people have a hard time when they are handed software that's not perfect. In fact, in a lot of companies (especially larger companies where people have spent years working with software teams), the software team has to literally negotiate the terms under which they'll provide software to their stakeholders. When there's not a great partnership between the team and the people they build software for, if the team delivers incomplete software, the users and stakeholders may judge it very harshly and even panic if a feature they expect to see is missing.

The core agile values have an answer to this: customer collaboration over contract negotiation. A team that's bound to a fixed specification with inflexible bureaucratic barriers to change doesn't have the option to let the software evolve over time. A team working under those conditions has to kick off a whole new change management process, which requires a fresh set of contract negotiations with the customer. On the other hand, a team that truly collaborates with the customers has the option of making all the necessary changes along the way. That's what **continuous delivery** means.

This is why agile methodologies are typically iterative. Agile teams plan the project's iterations by choosing the features and requirements that will deliver the most value. The only way that the team can figure out what features deliver that value is to collaborate with the customer and incorporate the feedback from the previous iteration. This lets the team satisfy the customer in the short run by demonstrating value early, and in the long run by delivering the finished product that delivers as much value as possible.

Principle #2: Welcome Changing Requirements, Even Late In Development. Agile Processes Harness Change for the Customer's Competitive Advantage.

Many successful agile practitioners have a lot of trouble with this principle when they first encounter it. It's easy to talk in abstract terms about welcoming change. But in the heat of a project, when a team runs into a change that will require a lot of work, things can get emotionally charged—especially for a developer who knows that his boss will hold him to the old deadline, no matter how much work the change requires. Getting past this, especially in a culture where people are blamed for delays, can be difficult. But it can also be very rewarding, because welcoming changing requirements is one of the most powerful tools in the agile toolbox.

Why are changes in a project emotionally charged? Understanding that is a key to this principle. Think back to the last time you were working on a project and found out that you needed to change what you were building. How did it feel? Until that moment, you thought the project was going well. You probably made a lot of decisions: how to structure your work, what you were building, and what you promised to deliver to your customers. Now someone outside of the project is telling you that some of that planning and work was wrong—that *you* were wrong.

It's very difficult to accept someone telling you that you've been wrong, especially if you've been doing work for that person. Most software engineers are driven by *pride of workmanship*: we want to deliver products that we can stand behind, and that satisfy our users' needs. A change in a project threatens that, because it's questioning the path that you've taken and the assumptions that you've made.

Very often, someone is telling you to change course after explicitly setting you on that course. If that person told you to build one thing, and you went ahead and built half of it, it's very frustrating for that same person to then come back to you and say, "Actually, now that I think about it, can we build something completely different?" It feels disrespectful of the effort that you put in. Now you have to go back and make changes to things you thought were done. It's hard *not* to get defensive about that! And it gets even worse if you're the one who's held responsible for not reading your customer's mind and, as a result, blowing your deadline.

Almost every professional developer has been through that situation at least once. In light of that, how can we bring ourselves to welcome changing requirements?

The first step toward welcoming changing requirements is to try to see things from the customer's perspective. This is not always easy, but it's enlightening. Do you think that the customer who originally sent you down the wrong path meant to? What do you think went through his head when he realized that he told you months ago to build the wrong software, and now you've wasted months of work because of what he said? Coming to you and requesting the change is, to him, admitting that he made a mistake—a mistake that will cost you a lot of work. That's not easy to do. No wonder customers often wait a long time before coming to the team with a change! It's embarrassing, and they know that they're delivering bad news. Your deadline is going to be blown, but so is his. If he has needs, and if the company is spending money building software to meet those needs, then his needs aren't getting met, and the project isn't delivering value. And it's all his fault, because he told you the wrong thing at the start of the project.

In other words, two people are being asked to do the impossible. You're being asked to read the customer's mind. He's being asked to predict the future. When you look at it like that, it starts to become a lot easier to welcome change. On the other hand, if you want to resist project change and stubbornly stick to the same plan that you wrote at the beginning of the project, it's easy—just make sure to hire only telepathic and clairvoyant team members.

So what does it mean to welcome change? It means:

- Nobody gets in "trouble" when there's a change. We acknowledge—and our bosses acknowledge—that we're human and fallible, and that it's better for the company to allow us to make mistakes and correct them frequently, rather than expect us to do things perfectly the first time.

- We're all in this together. Everyone on the team, including the customers you're collaborating with, owns the requirements and the changes to those requirements. If those requirements are wrong, it's as much your fault as the customer's, so there's no sense in placing blame for a change.

- We don't sit on change until it's too late. Yes, it's embarrassing to have made a mistake. But because we all recognize that, we simply do our best to fix it as early as possible. That way, the damage is limited.

- We stop thinking of changes as mistakes. We did our best with the information we had at the time, and it only became clear that we were wrong because the decisions we made along the way gave us the perspective to recognize the changes that we have to make today.

- We learn from the changes. This is the most effective way for a team to grow and get better at building software together.

Principle #3: Deliver Working Software Frequently, from a Couple of Weeks to a Couple of Months, with a Preference to the Shorter Timescale.

You might be thinking that the idea of welcoming changing requirements is interesting, and could help your projects. But you might also be thinking that it sounds terrible. This is not an uncommon reaction to the idea. Many people who work on software teams—especially traditional project managers—are very uncomfortable with the idea of welcoming changes when they first encounter it. These project managers deal with changes every day, but the agile attitude toward change is very different than what they are used to. Agile practitioners refer to the traditional attitude toward project changes as **command-and-control**.

The term "command-and-control" is borrowed from the military. In our 2010 book, *Beautiful Teams*, we interviewed Northrop Grumman chief engineer Neil Siegel, who gave us a military definition of the term:

> Andrew: I'm not familiar with military systems—what's a command-and-control system?

> Neil: An information system for military commanders. It allows them to communicate with each other, and allows them to maintain situational awareness: where everybody is, what their status is. It's how a commander can understand what's going on. Battlefields used to be small areas—a commander could stand on a hill with a pair of binoculars and could see what was going on. But by about 1900, the battlefields started getting so big that you couldn't stand on the hill like Napoleon did. You had to start using technology to "see" the entire battlefield. And the systems that do that are called "command-and-control systems."

Command-and-control project management is similar to military command-and-control:

- "Command" refers to the way the project manager assigns work to the team. The team may not report directly to her, but she has control over their assignments. She breaks down the work, builds a schedule, and assigns activities to the resources on her team.

- "Control" refers to the way she manages changes. Every project has changes along the way: work takes longer than anticipated, people take sick days or leave the project, hardware is not available or breaks, and all sorts of other unexpected things happen. Project managers constantly monitor for these changes, and then control the project by evaluating each change as it occurs, updating the plans to incorporate the change into the schedule and documentation, giving the team new assignments, and managing their stakeholders' expectations so that nobody is blindsided.

The reason a traditional project manager is uncomfortable with welcoming change when she first encounters it is because she recognizes that those same problems will happen on agile projects too, and the team needs to be able to respond to them. Simply accepting changes and welcoming them seems like a guaranteed way to introduce chaos to the project. If agile teams don't use command-and-control, how do they manage to keep up with all of those changes while still dealing with the normal day-to-day issues that project teams always face?

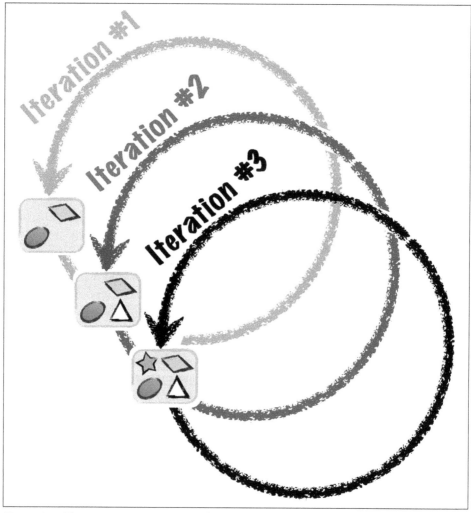

Figure 3-1. The team uses iteration to deliver working software frequently, adding new features with each release.

The key to welcoming changes without introducing chaos lies in delivering working software frequently. The team uses iteration to break the project into regular deadlines. During the iterations, the team delivers working software. At the end of each iteration, the team holds a demo to show the customer what they built, and a retrospective to look back and see what lessons can be learned. Then they start a planning session to figure out what they'll build in the next iteration. The predictable schedule and the constant checkpoints help the team catch those changes early, and give everyone a blame-free environment where they can discuss each change and come up with a strategy to incorporate it into the project.

This is where agile starts to become very attractive to a traditional command-and-control project manager. A command-and-control project manager wants to control the deadline. Timeboxed iterations give the project manager that control. This also solves one of the project manager's biggest challenges: dealing with changes that come in very late in the project. One of the most difficult parts of a traditional project manager's job is monitoring for changes. The daily reviews and iteration retrospectives let the project manager enlist the whole team as eyes and ears to spot those changes much earlier, before they can cause more serious problems with the project.

The project manager's role starts to shift away from command-and-control, where she gave the team a daily battle plan and constantly adjusted to keep them on track. Instead, now she's working with the team to make sure that each person is constantly looking at the big picture and working toward the same goals. It's easier to do that when the team is working on a short iteration that will deliver working software. This gives each person concrete goals, and a much better idea of what everyone is delivering—and a sense that each person is responsible not only for what he built, but also for what the entire team will deliver at the end of the iteration.

Better Project Delivery for the Ebook Reader Project

How can these principles help our troubled ebook reader project? Think back to the problems that the project team faced: their product flopped because it was missing important features that their competitors had (supporting an industry standard format for ebooks, and letting users mail documents to their device), and it had features that were no longer relevant to their market (an Internet storefront).

Let's run the project again, but this time let's have the project manager work with the stakeholders and the team to set one-month sprints. The project turned out very different this time:

- After the third sprint, one of the developers reported that the industry standard for a new format for ebooks had been approved. The team decided to implement a library that supports it in the fourth sprint, and incorporate it into the reader's user interface in the fifth iteration.

- After 10 months of development, they created a working build that can be loaded into prototype machines and given to early beta users. The project manager talked to these users and discovers that they would really like a way to get Microsoft Word documents and newspaper articles onto their readers. The team dedicated part of the next sprint to building email integration into the reader, so users can mail articles to their devices.

- One year into the project, the stakeholders let the team know that the Internet storefront is actually not needed after all, now that the retailers all use the standard ebook format. Luckily, this feature was always low on the backlog and other sprints were dedicated to more important features, so very little work had been done on it.

Because the team had always delivered working software after each sprint, eliminating the features from the backlog meant that they could deliver early! The publishing partner was ready with books, because their senior managers all got early versions of the software and prototype hardware to play with. That kept them involved, and gave them incentive to make sure they had books ready to go as soon as the first version of the product was ready.

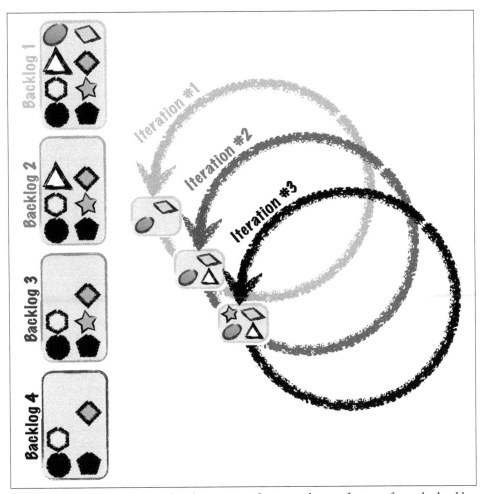

Figure 3-2. At the beginning of each iteration, the team chooses features from the backlog to build.

By using continuous releases, welcoming changes, and delivering working software after each iteration, the ebook reader project was able to deliver a successful product much earlier. Unlike the inefficient waterfall process, which sealed the team off from the customers once the requirements were approved, the agile team stayed engaged with their customers. That let them respond to changes and build a better product.

But things aren't perfect on our ebook reader team—far from it. They're using iterations to deliver working software, but they're getting buried under documentation. Everyone is really happy that they're not stuck building software that won't sell. But every time the team finds a good change they need to make to the project, half the team gets stuck going back to the spec and updating it so that their plans stay up to date and they stay on course. It seems like they're burning as much effort updating documentation as they are writing code.

People on the team have talked about ways to cut down the amount of work it takes to maintain all of these documents. They've had extensive discussions about the "right level of detail" for their documentation. But whenever they try to cut something out, someone always brings up a (valid) point that if they don't write down that particular feature, requirement, design, or test case, then someone might misunderstand it. If it gets implemented incorrectly, they'll get blamed for it. So it seems like every piece of documentation is needed, because otherwise the team will be on the hook for building the wrong software.

Is there any way they can reduce this burden without hurting the project? Is there even such a thing as a "right" level of documentation for a project?

Key Points

- The *12 principles of agile development* that accompany the Agile Manifesto provide agile practitioners with direction and insight into practices and methodologies.

- Agile teams satisfy their customers by *getting feedback early in the project*, and *continuously delivering software* to keep that feedback up to date (Principle #1).

- Agile teams *embrace change* by treating project changes as positive and healthy developments for the project (Principle #2).

- By using timeboxed iterations to *deliver working software frequently*, agile teams constantly adjust the project so that it delivers the most value to the customer (Principle #3).

Communicating and Working Together

Software teams have been struggling with the "how much documentation?" question for as long as they've been developing software. Just like many teams over the years have searched for a "silver bullet" methodology to solve their process, programming, and delivery problems, they've also been looking for a "silver bullet" documentation system or template to magically record everything they need to build the software today and maintain it in the future.

Traditional thinking about software documentation goes something like this: we need a documentation management system so that everyone can put in the information they have, and tie it together with everyone else's information. If we have traceability so that we can fully establish all of the relationships between all of the information, then that will give us near-perfect visibility into what we'll build, how we'll test it, and how it will be deployed and maintained. The idea is that developers can trace every element of the design back to a requirement, and testers can trace every test case back to elements of the design, requirements, and scope. Any time the team needs to change, say, a part of the design, they can see exactly what code, requirements, scope, and test cases will be affected, so they don't have to waste a lot of time doing analysis. Software engineers call this *impact analysis*, and often try to maintain extensive traceability matrices that map all of the elements in the scope, requirements, design, and tests to each other. Then the project manager can use that map to trace code, bug reports, design elements, and requirements back to their sources.

So back to that question that teams have struggled with: how much documentation should they create? The answer, for an agile team, is just enough to build the project. Exactly how much that is depends on the team, how well they communicate, and the problem that they're solving. Think about all of the other kinds of documentation that software teams build: capturing all of the decisions made in every meeting by taking copious meeting notes; creating cross-reference documents that describe every aspect of every data source or store; complex matrices of detailed roles, responsibilities, and rules that each person needs to follow. A case can be made for all sorts of documentation. If it doesn't actually help the team build the software, and if it's not required for some other reason (like for a regulator, investor, senior manager, or other stakeholder), an agile team doesn't build it. But if, for example, a team finds that it *really* helps them to write a functional requirements document, then they can do it and still be agile. It all depends on what works best for the team, and that's one of the freedoms that agile gives you.

All of that work to build the extra documentation beyond what the team needs to build the software—the comprehensive documentation, the traceability matrix, the impact analysis—is done, in large part, to make it possible to fully analyze the impact of any change. While agile has a different (and often much more efficient) approach to managing changes to your project, agile practitioners should recognize that the traditional approach to documentation shares their goal. In a traditional waterfall project, the whole point of comprehensive documentation is to deal with change better.

Ironically, more often than not, comprehensive documentation gets in the way of managing changes. The dream of perfect documentation and traceability is to have a system where the team can automatically generate the impact of any change they need to manage, so that they can pinpoint exactly what needs to be fixed.

For most teams, unfortunately, the reality of managing changes with comprehensive documentation is not nearly so pretty. They have to spend an enormous amount of time at the beginning of the project attempting to predict the future and write it down perfectly. While the project is running, they need to maintain the documents they've written and keep track of any new developments. If there are changes to the original understanding of the product that's being built, they need to go back and make changes to all of the affected documents as well. This can lead to a mess of out-of-date documents over time, and it takes a lot of effort for the team to create and maintain those stale documents.

In fact, because it's not perfect, the comprehensive documentation actually leads to unnecessary changes and wasted effort. Any one piece of documentation is always written from the perspective of a person in a specific role: business analysts write requirements from one perspective, architects build designs from another, and QA engineers create test plans from a third. Then, when they need to tie these all together with traceability matrices, they discover exactly the kinds of inconsistencies that you'd expect these fractured perspectives to introduce. Building the documentation becomes a goal unto itself, and requires an increasing amount of up-front effort. And when a change finally does happen, all of that work that they put into reconciling their perspectives into a single comprehensive set of documentation needs to be redone. This causes the team to spin their wheels rewriting documentation, rebuilding traceability matrices, and resolving conflicts when they should be writing code, testing the software, and deploying the change.

There's got to be a more efficient way to build software.

Principle #4: The Most Efficient and Effective Method of Conveying Information To and Within a Development Team Is Face-To-Face Conversation.

Agile practitioners recognize that documentation is just another form of communication.[4] When I write a document and hand it to you, *the goal is not to write documentation*. The goal is to make sure that the ideas in my head match the ideas in your head as closely as possible. In many cases, documentation is a good tool to accomplish that goal—but it's not the only communication tool that we have.

---

4 To be completely fair, traditional project managers also recognize that documentation is just another form of communication. A typical project manager studies the difference between formal and informal communication, as well as the difference between written and verbal communication. They also study nonverbal cues in communication, and learn that face-to-face communication is the most effective means of getting ideas across. This is actually covered on the PMP exam!

Figure 3-3. When people on the team don't communicate, they may agree on the broad strokes, but end up working toward different goals. Comprehensive documentation can make this worse by making it easy to introduce ambiguity.

Face-to-face communication is almost always a better tool for sharing ideas within a software team than documentation. Everybody knows that talking through a problem in person is the most effective way to understand a new idea. We're all much more likely to retain ideas that were expressed in conversation than if we'd read them on a page or in a Microsoft Word document. That's why agile communication practices focus most on individual people communicating with each other, and reserve documentation for those cases where complex information needs to be recalled in detail later.

Luckily, it's not hard for teams that are used to comprehensive documentation to move to more effective face-to-face communication. That's because most of those teams don't actually try to hit the "ideal" of complete comprehensive documentation and traceability. Software engineers are notoriously practical. When they see how much work is involved in building up that comprehensive documentation, they end up having those face-to-face conversations anyway. In the end, that's the only way they can effectively build software. By recognizing that comprehensive documentation is often inappropriate, they can stop feeling guilty for not accomplishing the impossible—building perfect, comprehensive documentation—because it would not, in fact, be particularly useful for their projects if they did!

Instead, the most efficient way for the team to communicate the important ideas needed for the project is to get everyone thinking the same way. That way, each person can handle every decision as it comes. When a group of people look at the world the same way, and communicate about both positive and negative ideas openly, they end up with a shared perspective. When a change comes along that requires rethinking, the team members don't have to explain as much to each other.

The ultimate goal for team communication is to create a sense of community so that there's a lot of implied knowledge, because it's just not efficient to explain the same thing over and over again. Without that sense of community, people in different roles have to work harder to match each other's perspectives. The closer the team gets to having a sense of community and a shared perspective, the more often each person will independently come to a similar answer when posed the same question. This gives them a much more stable ground for handling changes, because they can get past the conflicts and start working on the code—and won't have to get sidetracked managing documentation.

Principle #5: Businesspeople and Developers Must Work Together Daily Throughout the Project.

Agile teams sometimes forget that the businesspeople they work with have day jobs. This leads to a natural disconnect between software teams and the businesspeople they build software for.

To build software well, teams need to have a lot of face-to-face discussion with businesspeople, because they need to tap into their knowledge of the company's problems that are going to be solved with software. The businesspeople got that knowledge by solving those same problems without software. So for most businesspeople who work with software teams, the software project is typically a small part of their job. For most of them, in an ideal world, the team would have very little contact with them. They'd have a meeting or two, figure out what the software needs to do, and then come back a short time later with perfect, working software.

The teams, on the other hand, want as much contact with the businesspeople as possible. Programmers need to learn about the business problem that needs to be solved. They do this by talking to businesspeople, watching them work, and looking at what they produce. A programmer who needs this information would love to have each businessperson's full-time attention. The longer they have to wait to get their questions answered, the slower their projects progress. But the businesspeople don't want to spend all of their time with the software team, because they have jobs to get back to. So who wins?

Agile teams have a way past this problem that lets both the businesspeople and the developers win together. They start with an understanding that the team is delivering *valuable* software to the company. The finished software is worth money to the company. If that value is more than the cost to build the software, it's worth it for the company to invest in its development. A good project should be valuable enough that the businesspeople can see that it's worth the effort they'll need to put in over the course of the project.

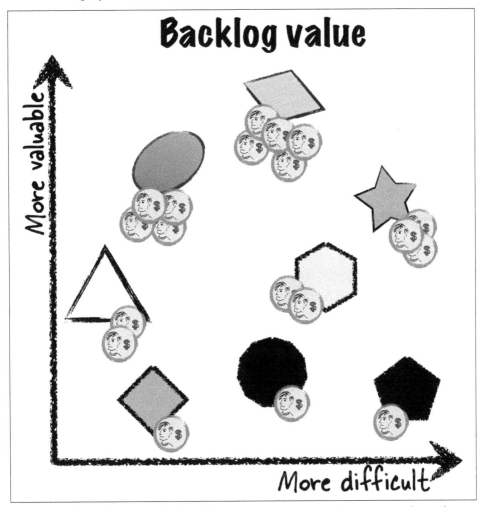

Figure 3-4. Some features in the backlog are more valuable to the company than others. The team has to balance the value (how much a feature is worth) against the cost (how much work it takes to build) when they determine which ones to include in each iteration.

When businesspeople and developers build software as a team, it's most efficient in the long run to work together daily throughout the project. That's because the alternative is to have the businesspeople wait until late in the project to look over the team's work and give feedback, and it's much more expensive to make changes at the end of the project. It takes a lot less of everyone's time if they catch those changes as early as possible. Working daily with the team actually requires less of each business-person's time over the course of the project.

This is why teams that deliver working software frequently should prioritize the most valuable features first—so the businesspeople can get that value delivered early. It's part of the bargain. It's also why good agile teams consider the businesspeople to be an important part of the team, and equal members with the programmers. That's a big distinction between an agile team and a traditional team. The traditional team treats the business user as a customer to be negotiated with; the agile team *collaborates* with the customer (typically the product owner) as someone with an equal say in the way the project is run. (That gets back to the core agile value of customer collaboration over contract negotiation!)

A good product owner can help reduce the amount of time the businesspeople spend with the team. They still need to meet daily, but the product owner can concentrate on understanding the value of the software and the business problem that needs to be solved. That way, the team can use their face-to-face time with the businesspeople to validate information that they've already learned from the product owner.

Principle #6: Build Projects Around Motivated Individuals. Give Them the Environment and Support They Need, and Trust Them to Get the Job Done.

Projects run best when everyone in the company recognizes that the team is building valuable software, and when everyone on the team—including the product owner—understands what makes the software valuable to the company.

On the other hand, projects can break down in an environment where people don't see the value in the software, or where they aren't rewarded for building the software well. It's actually not uncommon for companies to set up performance reviews and compensation systems that discourage people from building software in an effective, agile way, and this can work against the project. Some common "incentives" that work against agile teams include:

- Giving programmers poor performance reviews when code reviews routinely turn up bugs, and rewarding them for "clean" code reviews. (This just leads programmers to stop finding bugs in code reviews.)
- Rewarding testers for the number of bugs that they report. (This encourages nitpicking and poor reporting, and discourages them from partnering with the programmers, because it sets up an antagonistic relationship between them.)

- Basing business analysts' performance reviews on the amount of documentation they produce (rather than the amount of knowledge they've shared with the team).

Ultimately, everyone's performance should be based on what the team delivers, rather than the specific role that they played in it. Now, that's not to say that a programmer who does a poor job or is disruptive shouldn't be called out for it in a review with his boss. People should be reviewed based on their contribution (or lack thereof) toward the whole team's goals. But they should *definitely not* be discouraged from looking beyond the strict confines of a specific role. A good environment for a team will reward a programmer who recognizes a part of the business problem that isn't being addressed and fixes it, or a tester who sees a problem with the code or architecture and raises that with the team. An environment like this gives everyone on the team the support they need, and makes the project more successful.

Comprehensive documentation and traceability matrices are a particularly insidious source of problems with a team's environment and support. Instead of encouraging an environment of trust, they encourage a "cover your ass" (CYA) attitude in which teams move toward a "contract negotiation" approach, rather than customer collaboration.

A tester with a CYA attitude will spend time making sure every requirement has a test, whether or not it does anything to actually help the quality of the software. Developers will CYA by adhering to the letter of the requirement, without bothering to think about whether or not it actually delivers value to the users—because if they're working in a CYA environment, trying to build what the customer actually needs can get them dinged for not building the software to spec. Business analysts and product owners will CYA by spending their time making sure that the scope and requirements line up perfectly, and often find themselves tempted to omit pesky requirements that don't align perfectly with the existing documentation, regardless of their value.

Software team members need to CYA most in an environment where change is seen as a bad thing. For a team that uses comprehensive documentation, it's easy to see change as a bad thing, because it requires so much work to revisit the scope, update the specs, alter the design, repair the traceability matrices, etc. This leads to a divisive environment, because managers in that sort of company will naturally try to find a "culprit" who can be blamed for all that extra work caused by the change. People on the team increasingly turn to "defensive documentation" to protect themselves when that blame inevitably comes around to them. This forces everyone on the team to CYA, so they can point to the part of the documentation that they were sticking to, in order to avoid a poor performance review or punishment.

The opposite of CYA is trust. A company that develops only the minimal documentation needed for the project has an environment where the team is trusted to do the right thing when a change happens. An agile team with a "we're all in this together" attitude, where if the project fails everyone shares the blame, doesn't need to CYA. It's easier for them to handle changes, because they don't need to maintain all of that unnecessary documentation. Instead, they can tackle the actual problem with face-to-face communication, and only write down what's necessary. And they can do this knowing that the company trusts that they're doing the right thing—*even if it causes the project to take longer*.

Better Communication for the Ebook Reader Project

Our ebook reader project could definitely have benefited from better communication. Remember the days of intense meetings where the business analysts carefully pieced together an extensive set of comprehensive requirements? The requirements didn't start out as a cynical CYA scheme. Everyone on the team genuinely thought that by arguing out every minute aspect of the software for days, they would cover all of their bases, and that would lead to the best possible product. Because they had spent all that time up front, they were able to stick to their guns and defend the original spec, even when it seemed like the end product might not be viable on the market. And if they'd been able to predict exactly what the market needed two years in advance, it would have worked out perfectly! Too bad it didn't work out that way—but at least nobody lost their jobs, because they could all point to the spec that they implemented precisely.

What would have happened had they used better communication from the beginning? How would the product have changed if instead of writing comprehensive requirements, the team had written down the **minimum amount of documentation** they needed to get started?

Figure 3-5. When the team relies more on face-to-face communication, and only uses the minimal amount of documentation needed to build the project, it's easier for everyone to stay in sync with each other.

They would have had to trust each other to make the right decisions along the way. This would have helped a lot when it came time to work on the ebook format, because they wouldn't have been tied to an outdated format specified at the beginning of the project, and they could have adopted the newer format instead. Even better, by the time they started work on the Internet storefront, it might have been obvious that it wasn't a good idea, and they could have simply abandoned it—which isn't an option if it's part of a specification that the team is on the hook for. Better communication would have let them keep the project up to date, and could have delivered a more valuable product.

Let's imagine that this happened for the ereader team. Now our team is much happier with the documentation that they're writing, because it's much less of a burden. They thought they'd save lots of time by communicating better and cutting out unnecessary documents. But what happens if even though they've done this, the project still isn't on track?

Somehow, that time savings never materialized. It seems like they're putting in more nights and weekends than ever before, trying to include all of the features that the product owner had promised in each timeboxed iteration. It seems that the more agile they get, the more work they have to do, and the more nights and weekends they spend away from their families. This can't be an improvement! Is there something they can do to fix this, before the team burns out for good?

Key Points

- Overly comprehensive documentation increases the risk of ambiguity, misunderstanding, and miscommunication between team members.
- Agile teams communicate most effectively when they *focus on face-to-face conversation* and rely on the minimum amount of documentation necessary for the project (Principle #4).
- Developers work with business users every day so that they can *deliver the most value* (Principle #5).
- Everyone on the agile team *feels responsible* for the project, and feels accountable for its success (Principle #6).

Project Execution—Moving the Project Along

Better communication and trust between everyone on the team is a great start. Once everyone gets along and knows how they fit into the project, they can start thinking about the biggest problem: actually doing the work every day. How does an agile team keep the project moving?

Principle #7: Working Software Is the Primary Measure of Progress.

A good team works to make sure that everyone—team members, managers, stakeholders, and customers—really understands where the project is at any time. But how do you actually communicate the status of a project? It's a much more difficult problem than it might seem at first.

A typical command-and-control project manager tries to keep the project on course and keeps everyone up to date with extensive schedules and status reports. But it's hard to capture the real "essence" of a project in a status report. The report itself is an imperfect communication tool: often, three different people can read the same status report and get three totally different impressions of where the project is. And status reporting can be highly politically charged for a project manager. Almost every project manager occasionally finds himself or herself under pressure to leave something off of a status report that will make a manager or team lead look bad—and it's always a piece of information that someone else needs in order to make a decision. So how do you report progress, if status reports aren't good enough?

The answer lies in working software. The minute you actually see the software working in front of you, you "get" it. You can see what the software does, and what it doesn't do. If a manager promised to deliver something that didn't make it into the software, it might be embarrassing—but it's impossible to not communicate that, because the software speaks for itself.

Figure 3-6. Working software is better than progress reports for giving everyone the latest update on the project's status, because it's the most effective way for the team to communicate what they've accomplished.

This is one reason why agile teams use iterative development. By delivering working software at the end of each iteration, and by doing a real product demonstration that shows everyone exactly what the team did, they keep everyone up to date on the progress of the software in a way that is almost impossible to misread.

Principle #8: Agile Processes Promote Sustainable Development. The Sponsors, Developers, and Users Should Be Able to Maintain a Constant Pace Indefinitely.

The ebook reader team isn't the first project team to work insane hours in order to meet an unrealistic deadline. In fact, the hard-and-fast deadline is the primary tool in the command-and-control project manager's toolbox. Whenever a deadline is approaching, everyone turns to nights and weekends as the first resort. An unrealistic deadline can be an underhanded tool to force more work out of a team by squeezing extra hours out of every week.

Except that in the long run, it doesn't work. It's well known that a team can crunch for a few weeks and get more work done, but after that their productivity typically falls off a cliff. This makes sense: people get tired and demotivated, and fatigue starts to set in. All of those errands and life events they pushed off have to force their way back in somehow. In fact, teams that work extreme amounts of overtime for an extended period actually deliver less work than teams that work normal, sane hours—and it's usually of lower quality.

This is why agile teams believe in maintaining a **sustainable pace**. They should plan on delivering work that can actually be done in the time they reserve for it. Iterative development makes this more realistic, because it's a lot easier to estimate how much software they can deliver in the next two, four, or six weeks than it is to estimate how much they can deliver in the next year and a half. By promising to deliver only what they can build, the team creates an environment where late nights and weekends are rare.[5]

Principle #9: Continuous Attention to Technical Excellence and Good Design Enhances Agility.

Poor estimates aren't the only cause of late nights and weekends. Most developers recognize that sinking, pit-of-the-stomach feeling that comes with the realization that a seemingly simple bit of coding turned out to be a nightmare to design. There go the next three weekends, which will now be spent tracking down bugs and patching up code.

---

5 This is a good example of the simplification we told you about in Chapter 1. Right now, we'll just tell you that "sustainable pace" means giving the team enough time to build the software so that they can keep sane hours, and not work nights and weekends. Later in the book, we'll go into details about exactly what a sustainable pace does to the team's working environment and the company's culture, and the effect that it has on the quality of the software they produce.

It's a lot faster in the long run to avoid a bug now than it is to fix it later. And it's a lot easier to maintain code that's well designed, because well-designed code is built in a way that's easy to extend.

The last two decades or so have brought us a revolution in software design. Object-oriented design and analysis, design patterns, decoupled and service-oriented architecture, and other innovations have given developers patterns and tools to bring technical excellence to every project.

But this doesn't mean that agile teams spend a lot of time creating large-scale designs at the start of every software project. Agile developers build up great coding habits that help them create well-designed code. They're constantly on the lookout for design and code problems, and take the time to fix those problems as soon as they're discovered. By taking a little extra time during the project to write solid code and fix problems today, they create a codebase that's easy to maintain tomorrow.

A Better Working Environment for the Ebook Reader Project Team

Your ebook team—and their spouses—would definitely have appreciated a sustainable pace. But the project itself would also have come out better. The team was doomed to late nights and weekends from the very first day of the project, because they simply didn't have the tools to create a realistic plan that would remain accurate a year and a half later.

What's worse, because the team laid out software design and architecture that was built to support a very detailed specification at the beginning of the project, they ended up with very complex code that was difficult to extend. This caused many of the little changes along the way to require large patches that left spaghetti code throughout the codebase. Had the team followed an iterative approach and delivered working software along the way, they could have planned each iteration so that they could keep a sustainable pace. A simpler, more just-in-time approach to the architecture could have allowed a more flexible and extensible design. Had they used better design, architecture, and coding practices, they would have ended up with code that's easier to maintain and extend.

Let's imagine that our ereader team has applied these new principles, and now they're a well-oiled software-producing machine. They're iterating and delivering working software regularly, and they're constantly adjusting to make sure they're always building the most valuable software they can. They're communicating well, and only documenting what they need to document. They're using great design practices, and building a maintainable codebase. And they're doing it all without having to work overtime. Our team has gone agile!

But the storm clouds are already gathering around the next project. A new project manager just sent out an invite to a giant meeting with everyone he can find. The meeting participants start to accept the invites, rooms get booked, and arguments about all of the requirements that need to be documented start flying around...and everyone on our newly minted agile team starts to get that "pit of the stomach" feeling.

They know what's coming. The first of the many specs, plans, and Gantt charts are just starting to circulate. How can they make sure the next project doesn't hit those same pitfalls they worked so hard to climb out of?

Key Points

- The most effective way to communicate the progress of the project is to *deliver working software* and put it in the hands of the users (Principle #7).

- Teams are most productive when they *work at a sustainable pace* and avoid heroics, shortcuts, and overtime (Principle #8).

- Software that's *designed and implemented well* is fastest to deliver because it's easiest to change (Principle #9).

Constantly Improving the Project and the Team

One of the most basic design principles—not just in software, but in all of engineering—is KISS ("keep it simple, stupid"). An agile team lives by this principle in the way they plan the project, build the software, and run the team.

Principle #10: Simplicity—the Art of Maximizing the Amount of Work Not Done—Is Essential.

Adding code to an existing project often makes it more complex, especially when you then add even more code that depends on it. Dependencies between systems, objects, services, etc., make code more complex and difficult to change: the dependencies increase the likelihood of one change cascading out to another part of the system, which then requires changes to a third part of the system, creating a domino effect of increasing complexity for every change. Using iteration and building the minimal documentation at the start of the project helps your team avoid delivering unnecessary software.

However, a lot of developers feel a little uncomfortable when they first hear phrases like "use iterative development," and "do the minimal amount of planning needed to start the project." They feel like it's too early to start the code for a project until they've made a lot of the design and architecture decisions and written them down—otherwise the team will write code today that they'll need remove tomorrow when the design changes.

This is an understandable reaction, because for many projects outside the realm of software development, this wouldn't make sense. It's not uncommon for a programmer who's new to agile to raise an objection like this: "If I'm having a contractor renovate my house, I want to see the complete blueprints first. I don't want him to have a quick discussion with me, and then start knocking down my walls."

This argument makes sense for home renovation. The reason is that when you're making a change to a house, the most destructive thing you can do is pick up a sledgehammer and break down a wall. But software projects are different from houses or other physical objects. Deleting code is not particularly destructive, because you can usually just recover it from the version control system. The most destructive thing you can do to your project is to build new code, and then build more code that depends on it, and then still more code that depends on that, leading to that painfully familiar domino effect of cascading changes...and eventually leaving you with an unmaintainable mess of spaghetti code.

Maximizing the amount of work *not* done means avoiding this mess—and the best way to do this is by building systems that don't have a lot of dependencies and unnecessary code. The most effective way to do this is to work with your customers and stakeholders to only build the most useful and valuable software. If a feature is not valuable, it's often cheaper for the company in the long run to not build it at all, because the cost of maintaining the additional code is actually higher than the value it delivers to the company. When teams write code, they can keep their software designs simple by creating software designs based on small, self-contained units (like classes, modules, services, etc.) that do only one thing; this helps avoid the domino effect.[6]

Principle #11: The Best Architectures, Requirements, and Designs Emerge from Self-Organizing Teams.

Overly complex designs are common in teams that do too much up-front planning. This isn't surprising when you think about it. Flip back to the picture of the waterfall process in Chapter 2. There's an entire phase dedicated to requirements, and another phase dedicated to design and architecture. Doing the best job possible while you're in the design and architecture phase must mean building the most awesome architec-

---

6 Here's another simplification. We'll talk a lot more about exactly how teams can build great code without creating large designs up front, what effect that has on their projects, and how they can do this while still embracing project changes later on.

ture the team can come up with. For a team that works this way, having few requirements and a simple design intuitively feels to them like they're short-changing the project. Is it any wonder that they come back with a large requirements document and a complex design? Of course not, because that's exactly what they're explicitly being asked to do, by having entire phases of their process devoted to those things.

A **self-organizing team**, on the other hand, does not have an explicit requirements or design phase. When a team is self-organizing, it means that they work together to plan the project (instead of relying on a single person who "owns" the plan), and they continually come together as a team to revise that plan. A team that works like this typically breaks the project down into user stories or other small chunks, and starts working on the ones that deliver the most value to the company first. Only then do they start thinking about detailed requirements, design, and architecture.

This makes the traditional software architect's job more difficult, but also more satisfying. Traditionally, a software architect sits in an office with a closed door and thinks abstractly about the problems that need to be solved. Obviously, many architects are not like this, but it's definitely not atypical for an architect to be somewhat disconnected from the day-to-day work of the team.

On an agile team, everyone shares responsibility for the architecture. A senior software architect or designer still has an important role to play—but it is no longer one where he or she can work in isolation. In fact, when a team is building the software piece by piece, starting with the most valuable chunks, the architect's job becomes more challenging (but often more interesting). Instead of creating one big design at the beginning of the project that covers all of the requirements, agile architects use **incremental design**, which involves techniques that allow them to design a system that is not just complete, but also easy for the team to modify as the project changes.

Principle #12: At Regular Intervals, the Team Reflects on How to Become More Effective, Then Tunes and Adjusts Its Behavior Accordingly.

A team isn't agile until they're constantly improving the way they build software. Agile teams constantly inspect and adapt—they look at how their projects have run, and they use that knowledge to improve in the future. And they don't just do this at the end of the project; when they meet every day, they look for ways to change, and they'll change the work that they're currently doing if it makes sense.[7] You need to be comfortable being brutally honest with yourself and your teammates about what's

---

7 Here's another simplification. Right now we'll just introduce the idea that agile teams inspect and adapt. In Chapter 4, you'll learn exactly how this works on a Scrum team, and what this has to do with self-organizing teams.

working and what isn't. This is especially important for teams that are just beginning down the road of agile development. The only way to become more capable as a team is to constantly look back at what you've done so far, to assess how well you're working as a team, and to come up with a plan for getting better.

This makes sense, and almost everyone agrees that it's a good thing to do. But looking back and taking stock of what went right and wrong is one of those things that many teams *genuinely* intend to do, but rarely actually get around to doing. One reason is that it's uncomfortable at first. It often involves looking at specific problems and mistakes, and very few people are comfortable publicly pointing out the mistakes that the other people on their team made. Over time, people on the teams get more and more comfortable talking about these things. Eventually, everyone starts to see this as more constructive than critical.

Another reason that teams don't do this reflection is that they never set aside the time to do it—or even if they set aside the time, getting a head start on the next project seems more important than thinking about the one that's done. Teams that start each project by reserving time both at the end of each iteration and at the end of the project to meet, review, assess, and come up with a plan for improvement are more likely to *actually meet* and talk about how they did. This helps them learn from their experiences and become more effective.

Key Points

- Agile teams *keep their solutions as simple as possible* by avoiding building unnecessary features or overly complex software (Principle #10).
- Self-organizing teams *share responsibility for all aspects of the project*, from conceiving the product to project management to design and implementation (Principle #11).
- By taking the time to *look back and talk about lessons they learned* after each iteration and also at the end of the project, agile teams constantly get better at building software (Principle #12).

The Agile Project: Bringing All the Principles Together

Agile is unique in the history of software engineering. It's unlike the waves of "silver bullet" methodologies over the years, which promised to solve your team's software problems through a combination of magic practices, brilliant software tools, and, not infrequently, large invoices from consulting companies.

One difference between teams that only get better-than-not-doing-it results and teams that get a much more substantial benefit from agile is that the team that uses agile more effectively recognizes that the practices aren't just a "menu" to choose from. The key to using these practices together is the mindset that the team brings to the project—and that mindset is driven by the agile values and principles.

Agile is different because it starts with values and principles. A team going agile has to look honestly not just at the way they build software, but also at the way they interact with each other and the rest of their company. By first understanding the principles, and only then applying a methodology—with the full understanding that it will take work, and a lot of assessment and improvement along the way—an agile team can be realistic about finding better ways to run their projects. This gives them a real path to increased agility, and lets them build and deliver better software.

 Frequently Asked Questions

I'm a "rock star" developer, and I just need people to get out of the way so I can build great software! Why do I need to think about things like task boards and burndown charts?

All great developers have faced the frustration of building a great piece of code, only to have to rip it apart and patch it up because someone who doesn't know anything about how code is built asked for a change at the last minute. To someone who really cares about the craft of programming, it's really frustrating to make unnecessary technical compromises rather than building the code correctly from day one, just because some non-developer couldn't be bothered to think about what they needed until halfway through the project.

That's why so many great developers are drawn to agile teams. Yes, it means that you need to care about planning, and get used to using planning tools like task boards and burndown charts. Agile methodologies are built on practices like that—and those practices are selected specifically because they are simple, and stripped down to the bare minimum that's necessary to effectively plan and run a project. One big pay-off that you get when you get involved with planning the project (and actually care about it!) is that you can help avoid those frustrating last-minute changes by asking the tough questions that need to be asked while the project's still being planned. This only works because effective agile teams constantly communicate with their users from the beginning of the project. A lot of good developers are sold on the idea of planning the first time they ask one of their users a tough question that triggers a change that would otherwise have come late in the project. Avoiding that same old aggravating, last-minute, rip-and-patch coding turns out to be a great sales pitch for adopting agile.

Agile planning is also about communicating with the rest of the team, and that can really help great developers improve. "Rock star" developers are always learning, but on a command-and-control team they're isolated from their teammates, so most of that learning has to be self-directed. A self-organizing team, on the other hand, does a huge amount of communication—but not those endless, useless status meetings that developers often hate being forced to attend. Instead, *team members decide for themselves what they need to talk about in order to do the project right*. Not only does this lead to better projects, it also means that if the developer sitting next to you has some knowledge that you could learn from, there's a good chance that you'll end up knowing it by the end of the project. For example, if the guy next to you was applying, say, a new design pattern to his work in a way that you hadn't seen before, you'll know by the end of the project whether or not it was a good idea. If it was a good idea, then you'll be able to add it to your toolbox. That's learning that happened automatically, without any extra effort on your part, all because the whole team is communicating effectively. That's one reason why developers who embrace agile often find themselves becoming technically better, and feel like they're constantly improving at the craft of programming.

I'm a project manager, and I'm still not clear on how I fit into an agile team. What's my role in all of this?

If you're a project manager, it's likely that you fall into one of three traditional project management roles:

- An "in the weeds" planner who gets estimates, builds project schedules, and directs the day-to-day work of the team

- A product expert, possibly playing a business analyst role, who determines the requirements, communicates them to the team, and ensures that they build software that satisfies them

- A supervisor who works with the senior managers and executives in your company to keep them informed of how their investment in the project is paying off

In Chapter 4, you'll learn about Scrum, the most common agile methodology, and about the roles found on a Scrum team. If you're a manager who gets your hands dirty and dives into the details with the team, then the role of Scrum Master is likely to be a good fit. The Scrum Master's job is to help the team plan, and to get roadblocks out of their way throughout the project so they can deliver the software. On the other hand, if your job is to understand what the company needs and communicate that to the team, then you're more likely to end up as a product owner. In that case, your job would be to manage the backlog, decide what features should go into each iteration, and answer the team's detailed questions throughout the project so that they stay on track and build the right software.

If you're a project manager who plays a supervisory role, you typically won't end up on an agile team, but that's OK. Instead, you'll have one of the most important roles to play as an agile champion, pushing your teams and your managers to adopt agile practices and promoting agile values. You'll recognize that when you have a backlog of features divided into iterations, along with the details that you have for the current iteration, you have at your fingertips the right level of detail that you need to communicate with your executives and senior managers. And the more that the project teams have a sense of their progress and how well they're meeting the project goals, the better a job they can do of giving you a realistic understanding of that progress. But to do this effectively, you'll need a good understanding of how agile teams work, so that you can speak their language and process the information they give you into a form that your executives can understand.

Wait a minute. If the whole team plans together, then does that mean nobody's in charge? That would be really impractical. How are decisions made?

That depends on what decisions are being made. If you're asking about resolving conflicts, then that should happen exactly the way it happens for your team today. Think about your current team, or the last project team you were on. Who was in charge? Who resolved disputes and disagreements that couldn't be resolved between team members? Who reviewed your performance? There are many, many ways that a company hierarchy can be created, and an agile team should be able to work within any hierarchy. However, agile teams tend to be better at resolving conflicts themselves, because they focus on communicating with each other, and they're aligned to the same goals much more effectively than other kinds of teams.

On the other hand, if you're asking about who decides what features will go into the software or how those features will be built, that's typically handled by people with specific roles on an agile team. On a Scrum team, the Product Owner has the authority to decide what features will go into the software. However, the team only has to accept those features that can fit into an iteration based on real information. You'll learn more about this in Chapter 4. The plan, however, is owned by the entire team, because they're self-organizing.

But just because the plan is owned by the team, that doesn't mean there isn't a boss. *Of course there's a boss.* If you're just going agile now, your boss in a year will probably be the same person as your boss today—the difference is that he or she believes in agile enough to give the team the authority to make project-related decisions, and will stand behind those decisions without trying to micromanage or second-guess them. That's the only way any of this can work in the real world.

Things You Can Do Today

Here are a few things that you can try today on your own or with your team:

- If you're in the process of building a project now, sit down with your team before you start working on the code and spend 15 minutes talking about what features you'll be building. Can you find any cases where two people have different ideas about what they're about to build?

- Write down a list of the features that you are currently working on. Try to organize them by value and difficulty.

- Take a few minutes and write down a list of all of the documentation that you and your team generate or consume. Can you spot anything that isn't actually used by the team to build the code?

- Next time you're working late, think about what caused you to have to stay late. Can you come up with something you and your team could have done to prevent it? Was a deadline too aggressive? Was extra work added at the last minute? Recognizing that this is a problem and taking the time to understand what's causing it is the first step toward fixing it.

 Where You Can Learn More

Here are resources to help you learn more about the ideas in this chapter:

- You can learn more about the values and principles of the Agile Manifesto and how it was created in *Agile Software Development: The Cooperative Game*, 2nd Edition, by Alistair Cockburn (Addison-Wesley, 2006).

- You can learn more about value, iteration, and other aspects of agile project management in *Agile Project Management: Creating Innovative Products*, 2nd Edition, by Jim Highsmith (Addison-Wesley, 2009).

- You can learn more about challenges teams face in going agile, and how they can overcome them, in *Succeeding with Agile*, by Mike Cohn (Addison-Wesley, 2009).

- You can learn more about getting past the command-and-control mindset in *Coaching Agile Teams*, by Lyssa Adkins (Addison-Wesley, 2010).

 ## Coaching Tips

Tips for agile coaches helping their team to work with the ideas in this chapter:

- Help the team to recognize that working very long hours causes them to build less code, not more, and they don't build it as well.
- Sit down with individual team members and talk about their jobs. What motivates them? What frustrates them? What drives the decisions they make?
- Ask individual team members to choose the three agile principles that most affect them, in either a positive or negative way. People will be surprised that their teammates chose different principles; this will help you find the common ground between everyone.
- Use the principles that everyone has in common as a starting point to figure out which practices best match the team's mindset.

CHAPTER 4

Scrum and Self-Organizing Teams

Grand principles that generate no action are mere vapor. Conversely, specific practices in the
absence of guiding principles are often inappropriately used.

—Jim Highsmith[1]

The board game *Othello* has the slogan, "A minute to learn, a lifetime to master." This applies really well to a team that's learning Scrum. The basic practices and mechanics of Scrum are straightforward, and not difficult to adopt. But understanding how Scrum's values can make those practices and mechanics result in better software can be more challenging.

The rules of Scrum are simple and easy to communicate, which makes it a great starting point for many teams adopting Agile. Here's the basic pattern for a Scrum project:

- There are three main roles on a Scrum project: **Product Owner**, **Scrum Master**, and **team member**. (We capitalize "Product Owner" and "Scrum Master" when talking about the Scrum roles.)

- The Product Owner works with the rest of the team to maintain and prioritize a **product backlog** of features and requirements that need to be built.

- The software is built using timeboxed iterations called **sprints**. At the start of each sprint, the team does **sprint planning** to determine which features from the backlog they will build. This is called the **sprint backlog**, and the team works throughout the sprint to build all of the features in it.

- Every day, the team holds a short face-to-face meeting called the **Daily Scrum** to update each other on the progress they've made, and to discuss the roadblocks

---

1 Jim Highsmith, *Agile Project Management: Creating Innovative Products*, 2nd Edition (Upper Saddle River, NJ: Pearson Education, 2009).

ahead. Each person answers three questions: What have I done since the last Daily Scrum? What will I do until the next Daily Scrum? What roadblocks are in my way?

- One person, the Scrum Master, keeps the project rolling by working with the team to get past roadblocks that they've identified and asked for help with. At the end of the sprint, working software is demonstrated to the product owner and stakeholders in the **sprint review,** and the team holds a **retrospective** to figure out lessons they've learned, so they can improve the way they run their sprints and build software in the future.

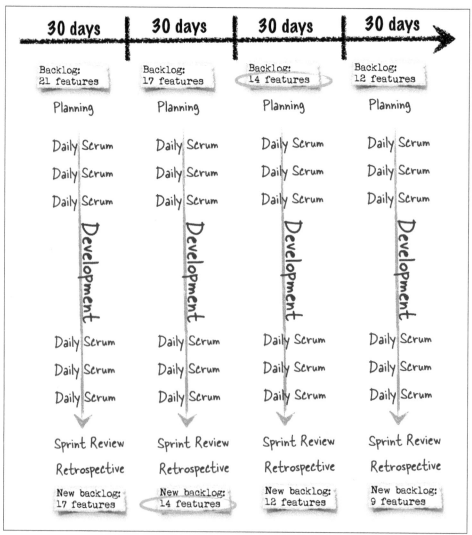

Figure 4-1. Basic Scrum pattern.

But for a Scrum team to become effective, they need to do more than just follow the basic Scrum pattern. Effective Scrum teams are **self-organizing**, as Ken Schwaber explains in *Agile Project Management with Scrum* (note the words that we emphasized in italics):

> For Scrum to work, the team has to deeply and viscerally understand *collective commitment* and *self-organization*. Scrum's theory, practices, and rules are easy to grasp intellectually. But until a group of individuals has made a collective commitment to deliver something tangible in a fixed amount of time, *those individuals probably don't get Scrum*. When the team members stop acting as many and adopt and commit to a common purpose, the team becomes capable of self-organization and can quickly cut through complexity and produce actionable plans.

The goal of this chapter is to help you "get Scrum" by building on the ideas from Chapters 2 and 3 to teach you the practices and patterns of Scrum. We'll use those practices to show you the ideas behind the principles of collective commitment and self-organization.

The Rules of Scrum

In *Agile Project Management with Scrum*, Ken Schwaber lays out the rules of Scrum that describe the basic pattern for a Scrum project. In fact, you can download the definitive rules of Scrum from *www.scrum.org* as a free PDF—it's an ebook called *The Scrum Guide*, by Ken Schwaber and Jeff Sutherland, the people who created Scrum and have helped spread it to the rest of the industry. These rules should be pretty familiar to you by now, because many of them were already described in Chapters 2 and 3. A typical Scrum project follows these rules:

- Each sprint starts with sprint planning done by the Scrum Master, Product Owner, and the rest of the team, consisting of a meeting divided into two parts, each timeboxed to four hours. The Product Owner's homework prior to sprint planning is to come up with a prioritized backlog for the product that consists of a set of items that the users and stakeholders have bought into. In the first part of the meeting, the Product Owner works with the team to select items that will be delivered at the end of the sprint based on their value and on the team's estimate of how much work they will be. The team agrees to give a demo of working software that includes those items at the end of the sprint. This first part is timeboxed (for a 30-day sprint it's timeboxed to four hours; for shorter sprints, it's proportionately shorter) so at the end the team takes whatever they've come up with so far and uses that as the sprint backlog. In the second part of the meeting, the team members (with the Product Owner's help) figure out the individual tasks they'll use to actually implement those items. Again, this part is timeboxed based on the length of the sprint (but often takes less time than that). At the end of sprint planning, the items they've selected become the sprint backlog.

- The team holds a Daily Scrum meeting every day. All team members (including the Scrum Master and Product Owner) must attend,[2] and interested stakeholders may attend as well (but must remain silent observers). The meeting is timeboxed to 15 minutes, so all team members must show up on time. Every team member answers three questions: What have I done since the last Daily Scrum? What will I do between now and the next Daily Scrum? What obstacles and roadblocks are in my way? Each team member must be brief; if an answer requires discussion, the relevant team members schedule a follow-up for immediately after the meeting.

- Each sprint is timeboxed to a specific length decided during sprint planning: many teams use 30 calendar days, but this length can vary—some teams choose two-week sprints, some choose one month (and again, the planning timebox should vary accordingly). During the sprint, the team builds the items in the sprint backlog into working software. They can get help from people who are not on the team, but people who are not on the team cannot tell the team how to do their jobs, and must trust the team to deliver. If anyone on the team discovers partway through the sprint that they overcommitted or that they can add extra items, they need to make sure the Product Owner knows as soon as they realize the sprint is in danger. He's the team member who can work with the users and stakeholders to reset their expectations, and use that information to adjust the sprint backlog to match the team's actual capacity. And if they find that they'll run out of work before the sprint ends, they can add more items to the sprint backlog. The team must keep the sprint backlog up to date and visible to everyone. In *very abnormal cases and extreme circumstances*, the Product Owner can terminate the sprint early and initiate new sprint planning if the team discovers that they cannot deliver working software (e.g., a serious technology, organizational, or staffing issue comes up). But everyone needs to know that terminating the sprint is rare, and has an extremely negative cost in terms of their ability to produce and deliver software, and seriously impacts the trust that they've built up with their users and stakeholders.

- At the end of the sprint, the team holds a sprint review meeting where they demonstrate working software to users and stakeholders. The demo may only

---

2 Does it seem unrealistic for your team to meet every day, maybe because people are spread between teams or have other commitments? Are you already starting to look for alternative approaches to the Daily Scrum, like replacing it with an online hangout or wiki page? That could be an indicator that your mindset needs to shift in order to get the best results from Scrum.

include items that are actually *done* done[3] (which, in this case, means that the team has finished all work on it and tested it, and that it's been accepted by the Product Owner as complete). The team can only present functional, working software, not intermediate items like architecture diagrams, database schemas, functional specs, etc. Stakeholders can ask questions, which the team can answer. At the end of the demo, the stakeholders are asked for their opinions and feedback, and are given the opportunity to share their thoughts, feelings, ideas, and opinions. If changes are needed, that's taken into account when the next sprint is planned. The Product Owner can add the changes to the product backlog, and if they need to be made immediately they'll end up in the sprint backlog for the next sprint.

- After the sprint, the team holds a sprint retrospective meeting to find specific ways to improve how they work. The team and Scrum Master (and optionally the Product Owner) attend. Each person answers two questions: What went well during the sprint? What can improve in the future? The Scrum Master takes note of any improvements, and specific items (such as setting up a new build server, adopting a new programming practice, or changing the office layout) are added to the product backlog as nonfunctional items.

And that's it. Simple!

Well, maybe not. If it's so simple, then why aren't we all doing Scrum? For those of us who are doing Scrum and following all of the rules, why do so many of our team members feel like we're only getting better-than-not-doing-it results? What's missing?

Narrative: a team working on a mobile phone app at a small company

Roger – team lead trying to go agile

Avi – the Product Owner

Eric – a Scrum Master on another team

---

3 The idea of *done* done—work that is really, truly done, and there's nothing else that needs to be worked on—is intuitive, but there are a lot of subtleties. This is another example of simplification, and we'll come back to this concept several more times throughout the book. Keep your eyes open for it! Now that you've seen a few of these simplifications, we're going to stop calling them out in footnotes, but we'll still use them throughout the book.

Act I: I Can Haz Scrum?

Hover Puppy Software is a small company that builds websites and mobile phone apps, and it's had a very good few years. Six months ago, their latest mobile phone app had enormous sales, and the CEO decided to invest the earnings back into the company by starting up a new project, a website called Lolleaderz.com that lets users create leaderboards and achievements for pet videos.

When the project first started up, the team lead, Roger, wanted to go agile. He was really happy to discover that his team was just as excited as he was at the prospect. Another team in the same company, the mobile phone team, had used Scrum to develop their wildly successful app, and the idea had spread around the company. One of the team members started calling Roger the Scrum Master, and the role stuck.

The first thing Roger did was look for a Product Owner, but it wasn't immediately obvious who that should be. Luckily for him, Hover Puppy is the sort of small company where everyone calls the CEO by his first name. Roger went to him and explained the situation, describing the Product Owner as the "king of the stakeholders" for the project. As it happened, one of the account managers, Avi, had just finished a project. The CEO introduced him to Roger, let them know that he was fully behind Scrum, and left it to them to figure out how to make it work.

The project seemed to go pretty well at first. Roger set up one-month sprints, and at the start of each sprint, Avi came up with a backlog of features to build. Roger set up a Daily Scrum meeting, and Avi blocked it out in his calendar so he could show up every day. The first sprint was great—everyone was getting along, and the team was making progress. At the end of that sprint, the team gave Avi a demo of a simple version of the website with a few features they'd all been planning. It seemed like this Scrum experiment was working.

Over the next few weeks, cracks started to show in the project, but it still looked like it was mostly on track. One account manager was working with one of her clients, a movie production company, to put ads for their upcoming summer blockbuster into each of the Hover Puppy websites. The team had promised Avi that they'd be able to give him a demo of this feature at the end of the sprint. But they ran into technical problems early on, and it ended up being pushed to the next sprint. Roger explained that Scrum teams always deliver working software, so if a feature's not done at the end of the sprint, it just gets pushed to the next one. But they weren't really sure if this was how Scrum was supposed to work.

Things seemed to get slower and slower with each sprint. By the end of the third sprint, Avi felt like he was spending more and more of his time working with the team, and had less time each day to do his real job of working with customers. At the beginning of the project, he thought he'd have control over what they did. Now he was starting to feel like he drew the short straw when he was chosen to be the Product

Owner for the Lolleaderz.com project. Roger got upset when he heard that Avi had started to complain to the other account managers that the team was hard to work with.

Worse, the team was really getting fed up with all of this Scrum stuff. Before Roger and Avi even got a chance to work though that problem, another minor crisis erupted when three of the developers pulled Roger aside and started to complain about the new Daily Scrum they had to go to. One of them said, "I've got a lot of work to do already to get this out the door, and these meetings are just wasting our time. Why do I need to sit through your daily status updates, and wait for you to give each person the next day's tasks? Can't you just email them to us?" Roger didn't have a great answer for that. He said that those were the rules of Scrum, and that was enough for the developers to keep going to the meetings. But none of them were particularly satisfied with that answer, and Roger was starting to wonder if the developers had a point.

One big blowup happened when Roger was planning the fourth sprint. Avi insisted that the feature that let users give "paws up" ratings to videos had to go in; otherwise they'd start to lose advertisers. But the database work for that feature was intensive, and needed their star database administrator (DBA) to make major changes to the data model, which meant that now he wouldn't have time to write the stored procedures. It looked like they were going to be a week late with the feature, but pushing it to the next sprint wasn't an option.

It was now six months and five sprints into the project. Roger felt like Avi was making increasingly larger demands of the team. Avi was frustrated that the project wasn't delivering a website that he could sell to his customers. The team was supposed to be done with the video tagging page and the social media feeds two sprints earlier, but they still hadn't delivered them. At the latest account managers meeting, Avi blamed the team for being late. Roger knew the project was at risk of getting cancelled.

Roger had had enough. The project that had started so well had turned into a monster. He felt like he was in over his head, but didn't know how to fix things. He went back to the books and websites where he'd learned about Scrum, and from everything he read it looked he was doing everything right—at least on paper. He had sprints, Daily Scrum meetings, and retrospectives. He was working with the Product Owner to prioritize the backlog, and he pulled the most valuable features from the backlog to work on during each sprint, working with the team to estimate them so they'd fit, and assigning them to developers.

Roger had just given the team the best pep talk he could: "I was just pulled into the CEO's office. He's not happy that we're behind, and Avi isn't happy either. Look, I'll protect you from this and take the heat for the problems. But we need to work on our estimates, because they were way off—and I really need you to make up for it by working the weekend to get this right."

This was the third time he'd asked them to work nights and weekends in the last two months. The project felt just like past projects that had gone off the rails.

So what went wrong? Can you spot the problem? What would you do if you were asked to take over as Scrum Master for this project? Think about the agile values and principles. Is there a way to apply them so the project might run better?

Everyone on a Scrum Team Owns the Project

Every Scrum project has a Product Owner, a Scrum Master, and a team. But not every project that has those roles assigned to people is an effective Scrum project. A Product Owner in Scrum acts differently than a Product Owner on a typical "big requirements up front" waterfall project. A Scrum Master does not do the same things as a command-and-control project manager, or technical team lead. When the Scrum Master, Product Owner, and team start to work together instead of separately, the project begins to look more like Scrum.

The Scrum Master Guides the Team's Decisions

How the Scrum Master does his job makes the biggest difference between traditional command-and-control project management and an agile Scrum team.

On a command-and-control project, the project manager is the owner and maintainer of the schedule and plan. He talks to the stakeholders, gets the requirements, breaks down the work, obtains estimates from the team, assigns tasks, and builds out a schedule. This is the approach that Roger took with the Lolleaderz.com project—he got the requirements from Avi, got estimates from the team, and assigned each person his tasks.

Team members on a command-and-control project have a natural CYA urge to wash their hands of project problems when they're caused by someone else's plan. If someone has exclusive ownership of the schedule and the plan, the rest of the team and the Product Owner are happy to let that person make those decisions.

That's one reason why Scrum doesn't have a separate role for a person who owns the plan. If a team has separate roles for owning the plan and following it, it's too easy for individual team members to say, "It's that guy's problem" when they run into trouble. And almost every project runs into trouble at some point, because almost all project problems either cause or are caused by planning problems. So the Scrum Master doesn't own the plan. He may help the team to create the plan. But more importantly, he guides the team's use of Scrum and its practices, and helps everyone feel like they own the plan together. The practices and values of Scrum help them all feel that sense of ownership.

The Product Owner Helps the Team Understand the Value of the Software

Imagine a conversation between the CEO and the Scrum Master about a project. The CEO asks what he's going to get with a $2 million investment in software over the next year. The Scrum Master tells the CEO that he's not sure yet; they'll have an update every month, and at the end of the project they'll have at least $2 million worth of software. No CEO in his right mind would ever approve that project. Why not?

The reason the CEO would never approve that project is that it's not based on a real **commitment**. Commitments are promises made by people to get certain things done, usually by a certain time. And a real commitment comes with an additional responsibility to alert everyone and come up with a solution when things change in a way that could mean that the promise won't be kept.

Most of us have been in meetings where a team member says that they didn't sign off on the deadlines they were committed to, so the fallout for not meeting the deadline isn't that person's fault. This happens because many inexperienced project managers make the mistake of thinking that once a task is written into a plan, the team is automatically committed to it.

Plans don't commit us. Our commitments commit us: the plan is just a convenient place to write those commitments down. Commitments are made by people, and documented in project plans. When someone points to a project plan to show that a commitment was made, it's not really the piece of paper that the person is pointing to. It's the promise that's written down on it that everyone is thinking about.

On a Scrum team, the Product Owner is the person who made the commitment to the company. He's the person who has to stand up and promise something specific that will be delivered at the end of the project. The Product Owner is keyed into the real business goals that the project is meant to fulfill. The more effectively he can get the team to understand those goals and feel committed to meeting them, the better the project will go. And when the project inevitably runs into trouble like technical problems, a change in the business, or people leaving the team, the Product Owner has to find a way to keep the team's understanding of goals current, and keep up their feeling of commitment. He makes day-to-day decisions based on business changes, and meets with the team every day to make sure they understand how the backlog and the goals of the project are changing.

The Product Owner doesn't just sit around and wait for the sprint to finish. The Product Owner's job is to own and prioritize the backlog, to be the voice of the business to the team, to help them understand what stories and backlog items are most important and most valuable, and to make sure that everyone understands what it means to be *done* done with a backlog item. During sprint planning, the team works collectively to choose the items to move from the product backlog into the sprint backlog based on their value and how much work they'll require, but the Product Owner is the one who guides them through this. And his job doesn't end there.

The Product Owner has a very active day-to-day role in the project. Like all good agile teams, Scrum teams rely heavily on face-to-face communication to understand exactly what they're building. The sprint planning that happens at the beginning of the sprint gives everyone enough information to get started, but that's not nearly enough time for the Product Owner to communicate to the entire team all of the details about what they'll be building. So during the sprint, the Product Owner works with all of the team members every single day, answering lots of detailed questions and giving them specific answers about what they'll be building and how users will use the features they're working on, as well as making lots of small decisions about how the product will work.

The Product Owner has the authority to make these decisions. (If he doesn't, he's the wrong person for the job! Scrum depends on the ability of the Product Owner to make decisions on behalf of the business, including accepting completed work.) But he doesn't have all of the information—there are usually many users and stakeholders, and they have valuable information and opinions as well, so the Product Owner also spends a lot of his time talking to them to get answers that the developers need. He also uses this as an opportunity to stay on top of any changes that happen, and to keep the product backlog up to date so it reflects the latest changes to what the company needs. That way, if there's a change to the relative value of different product backlog items, he can keep them prioritized so the team is ready for the next sprint planning session.

Everyone Owns the Project

Scrum teams like to use the fable of the pig and the chicken to help understand how commitments work:

> A Pig and a Chicken are walking down the road.
>
> The Chicken says: "Hey Pig, I was thinking we should open a restaurant!"
>
> Pig replies: "Hm, maybe; what would we call it?"
>
> The Chicken responds: "How about 'ham-n-eggs'?"
>
> The Pig thinks for a moment and says: "No, thanks. I'd be committed, but you'd only be involved!"[4]

---

4 From the Wikipedia page (*http://bit.ly/chicken-pig*) of "The Chicken and the Pig" (accessed July 26, 2014).

So on a Scrum project, who's an involved "chicken" and who's a committed "pig"? How is that different than an ineffective waterfall project? It all boils down to how the team members, project manager, and Product Owner act.[5]

Scrum teams often talk about roles in terms of pigs and chickens. That's shorthand for whether an individual person in that role is simply assigned to the project (a chicken), or if he or she is truly committed to its success (a pig). Think back to your own projects: did you always consider your own success or failure truly dependent on that project's success?

Figure 4-2. In the story of the pig and the chicken, the pig is committed to breakfast, while the chicken is merely involved.

---

5 Talking about pigs and chickens may seem a bit silly, but Scrum teams really do this. In fact, some older versions of the Scrum Guide actually included a section on pigs and chickens!

The fact is that the majority of people in their careers consider themselves chickens. They want to contribute to the project, but it's risky to have their actual success at work—reviews, raises, future career goals, continued employment—dependent on that project. It's also easy to forget that people work for money. Why do people do their jobs? What really motivates them? It's not necessarily success at the current project.

People on an *effective* agile team—all pigs—genuinely feel that in order for them to succeed, their project needs to succeed. But it's very easy for even an experienced Scrum team to fall back into a chicken mentality.

How many times have you, as a developer, chosen a technology for the project just because you want to learn it? As a project manager, have you chosen to work on agile projects because it makes you more marketable? Probably. We've all done this, at least a little bit. Everyone's self-motivated, and it's important to recognize that. But one thing that Scrum is asking you to do is: while you're working on a sprint, making the project successful is more important than any other *professional* goal[6] that you have. In other words, keep being a pig when you're on a Scrum team.

When all team members are pigs, it means that everyone is committed. And it also means that everyone will do any job, if that's what the project needs.

Here's an example to help you understand commitment. Let's say you're the CEO of a company, but you're also genuinely committed to the project. And let's also say that the project team is getting a little tired, and it's clear that they need coffee. If everyone else is working on something that just can't stop right now, then you'll go get coffee—and because you're genuinely committed, even though you're the CEO you feel like that's actually the best use of your time, because it's what the team needs right now.

On the other hand, every software project needs chickens. For example, every user is a potential chicken. How many times have you been frustrated by a feature of a browser, or word processor, or email client? Have you ever posted your feedback to a website or emailed it to a support team? That's one way to make yourself into a chicken. If the team listens to you and fixes the problem, you've helped add value to the product. The more involved a chicken gets, the more value he or she can potentially add.

When you're a chicken on a Scrum project, your opinion matters. You care about the outcome, and the team wants to hear what you have to say. But your job isn't tied to the project: you have other goals (like, say, selling the product, or supporting the

---

6 Just to be clear: a committed "pig" cares about the project's success more than he cares about anything else in his *professional* life. There are a lot of other things in his *personal* life—like his family, for example—that he usually cares more about. If that's not the case, it's actually a problem with the team's mindset, and it will interfere with sustainable pace.

product, or running the company). They're important goals, but they're not the same as the specific things that the project needs to produce.

This is why Scrum teams—and especially their Product Owners—cultivate relationships with their chickens. One of the most effective ways that they have to do this is to release working software to their users on a regular and predictable schedule. This keeps the chickens involved, and helps them see the influence that they have over the project.

How Product Owners, Scrum Masters, and team members can be better pigs

When a team member just does the tasks that are assigned to him by a project manager, but doesn't feel like it's really his problem when the plan runs into trouble, he's acting like a chicken. He doesn't feel a real commitment to the project, and more importantly, he doesn't feel commitment to the other people on his team. On the other hand, when that team member genuinely feels a sense of responsibility for getting the plan right and building the most valuable software possible for the company and for his team, he's acting like a pig.

The sad truth is that many companies expect team members to act like chickens, and not pigs. In fact, programmers often find that when they try to get involved with planning the project they're pushed away from the process, because planning and decision making is a privilege reserved for managers, not rank-and-file programmers. ("Who do you think you are, some sort of manager? Get back to the cubicle farm, lowly programmer!") When a company has that value built into their culture, it makes it very hard for a team to effectively adopt Scrum.

It's far too easy for a Scrum Master to inadvertently encourage the team to be chickens by becoming the owner—or "keeper"—of the plan. This is a very difficult habit to break for a command-and-control project manager who's learning to become a Scrum Master. It doesn't help that many project managers have found a lot of success in their careers being the "keeper" of the plan. It's easy for upper management to have one person to go to who's accountable. (Some people like to refer to that person as a "single, wringable neck.") It feels really good to be that person, because you feel useful and important, and that you've brought order to the chaos.

Planning is necessary. Taking planning out of the hands of the team isn't. When the Scrum Master breaks down the work for a sprint by himself, goes and gets estimates from the team, assigns work to them, and checks up on their status, he's acting like the "keeper" of the plan. He's also encouraging them to be chickens instead of pigs.

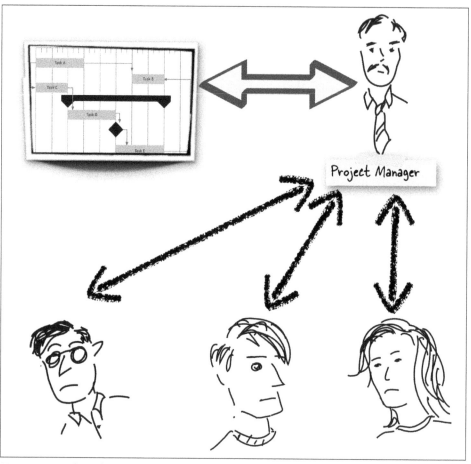

Figure 4-3. When the command-and-control project manager acts as the "keeper" of the plan, he encourages the team to be chickens.

Correcting a chicken attitude among the team is one of the most difficult barriers to Scrum adoption that Scrum Masters face. Teams often embrace the role of the command-and-control project manager because it takes the burden of having to think about the whole project off of their shoulders. But it's central to getting the project done quickly and well, because development teams that take a short-sighted approach to code build poorly designed, fragile systems. When the team takes short-cuts and cuts corners, they can get something that looks like it works out the door today, but they end up with a fragile system that's a nightmare to maintain down the road.

A Scrum Master can help encourage team members to be pigs by treating estimates as facts that have yet to be uncovered, not commitments to be wrung from the team. An estimate for a task is a fact because the team will spend a certain amount of time doing the work. The best estimates are real attempts to tell the truth about what will happen, not pie-in-the-sky, hopeful guesses that are used to please or placate a manager, or get out of the planning meeting faster.

A good plan is like a history that hasn't been written yet. At the end of the sprint, the team will be able to look back and say with 100% certainty exactly what they worked on and how long they spent on each task. The sprint will be behind them, and whatever happened during that sprint will be established information—facts on the record. If they've done a good job, then the plan at the beginning of the sprint will be very similar to the facts at the end. The more the plan looks like what will eventually happen, the more accurate it was.

This is a real change in mindset for many teams. People on a team that's used to treating a plan as a set of optimistic goals often find themselves struggling and failing to meet those goals. After all, it only takes one overly optimistic team member or manager to ruin everyone's plan (and the next four weekends), even if he thinks he's helping at the time. On the other hand, if the team treats the plan as their most realistic attempt at writing down what they think will actually happen over the next 30 days, they're much less likely to bite off more than they can chew—and much more likely to come in on time without cutting corners, taking shortcuts, and ending up with fragile code.

To many project managers, this is a new way of thinking about planning. Traditional project managers often see the plan as a way to motivate the team, and commit them to a deadline. They often see the plan as a way to get the team to do something, as if the team will just sit around doing nothing if not for the plan. A project manager that wrings aggressive estimates from the team and "ratifies" them at the start of the sprint will often feel comfortable using the plan later to bully the team. This is why an attitude of "plan the work, work the plan" can create a fracture between the project manager and the team.

On an effective Scrum team, instead of demanding estimates and then holding each person accountable for them, the Scrum Master works with the whole team in order to discover each estimate—not just the individual person assigned to do each task. A Scrum Master and team who work together to do the best job they can of predicting what will happen, and who keep working together throughout the project to keep that picture as accurate as possible, will give themselves the time to do the best work they can—and will end up delivering more valuable software as a result.

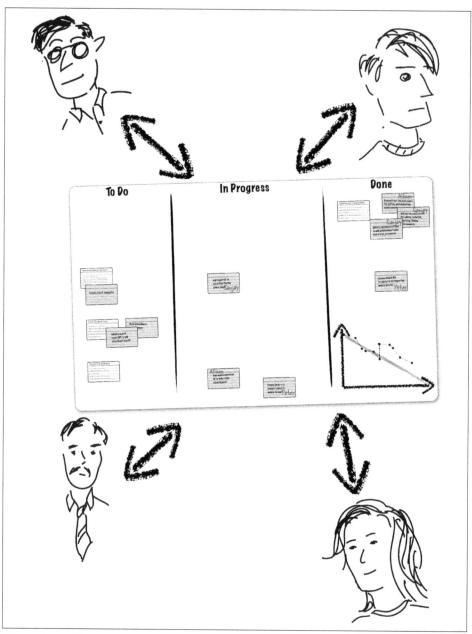

Figure 4-4. Self-organizing teams treat estimates and plans as facts that can be uncovered, not commitments that need to be wrung from the team.

Team members also feel more committed when they participate in assigning the work during a sprint planning session, rather than having the work assigned to them. In fact, if the team members really feel that sense of commitment, *the assignments don't even need to be made at the start of the sprint*. Effective Scrum teams can decide during the sprint who will do which tasks, based on which people are available and the skills that they can bring to the task. This is one of the keys to understanding how self-organizing teams work.

This means that on effective Scrum teams, the team members don't just commit to their individual tasks. Every single person feels a genuine commitment to delivering the most valuable software they can to their users and stakeholders. When everyone on the team shares this feeling, and agrees to deliver working software at the end of each sprint, we say that the team has made a **collective commitment**. Instead of committing to individual, micro-level tasks in a plan, the team is committed to delivering valuable items in the backlog. That *gives the team freedom to adjust the way they'll get the work done* as they discover new facts about the project. For example, if partway through the project Roger and the developers realize that they need to change the way something is built, Avi will trust them as long as everything in the sprint backlog is delivered. And if it turns out that they were wrong (which happens!) and they won't get everything in the sprint backlog built, they can talk to Avi about the things he cares about—the backlog items—without having to justify every little detail.

This is one of the fundamental reasons that Scrum works so well, and makes the difference between a highly productive Scrum team and one that's only gotten better-than-not-doing-it results.

No room for chickens

There is no room for a chicken on a Scrum team. Product Owners are part of the team, which means they need to be pigs, too. This does not always come easy to Product Owners, especially if they feel like they "drew the short straw" to end up assigned to a Scrum team. Most stakeholders naturally want to be chickens, because more distance is more comfortable. (Sometimes they do want to be pigs, even when it's not appropriate, because it will give them more authority to try to exert influence over the team. This is something that the Product Owner needs to sort out.)

There are ways that the Scrum Master and team can help encourage a genuine feeling of commitment in the Product Owner. The most important way is to *actually listen* to the Product Owner's opinions and ideas, and recognize that he or she brings real expertise to the project that the team needs.

Many programmers take the attitude that programming is the only important thing in a project, and that every other aspect of the project should take a backseat to the technical details. What's worse, many companies encourage this when they structure their teams around a core set of technical people. Separating project managers and

Product Owners from the technical team in a company's hierarchy encourages the developers to see everyone else as "outsiders," and to value their opinions less.

The Product Owner doesn't necessarily understand the technical details, but that's OK. On a Scrum team, everyone brings the specific skills and knowledge that they have, and does the tasks that are most appropriate for them. A Product Owner brings a real, deep understanding of the goals of the project to the table. The more that the Scrum Master and team engage the Product Owner, ask about those goals, and try to understand them from the Product Owner's point of view, the more committed the Product Owner will be to the project and the team.

Scrum Has Its Own Set of Values

Every company has its own culture that includes specific values. For example, some companies value separation of duties, where each person has a specific role to play, and is protected from having to be accountable for things that he or she can't easily influence or control. Other companies value transparency, where information is shared freely and even low-level employees can influence management decisions. Neither of these is the "right" way to run a company. Every individual company has a culture that evolves over time, based on the way it's managed and the decisions that are made.

Every methodology has values built into it. We learned in Chapter 3 that specific agile principles are often tied to (or implemented by) individual practices, and that those practices are an effective way for a team to bring each principle to the project. We've already seen that people on a team in a company that reserves decision making exclusively for managers will find it difficult to feel genuinely committed. The same goes for any value or principle: if it clashes with the company's values, it presents a barrier to adoption.

But in a company where the culture matches the agile values and principles, an agile team will be much more successful than a command-and-control team. (This is one of the sources of the "astonishing results" that some agile teams report.)

You might be surprised at just how well the agile values and principles match your company's culture.

A good first step in introducing agile to your company is to talk about the values, and how they might impact your company's culture. If you find that your agile adoption runs into trouble, finding the mismatch between agile values and company culture can help you smooth out the transition (or at least help you feel better by understanding why things went wrong).

Self-organizing teams work differently than command-and-control teams because they have different values. In *Agile Project Management with Scrum*, Ken Schwaber discusses the five Scrum values: **courage**, **commitment**, **respect**, **focus**, and

openness. Understanding self-organization starts with learning how these values are practical things that can be incorporated into your projects:

*Each person is **committed** to the project's goals*

That level of commitment can be achieved when the team has the authority to make decisions in order to meet those goals, and everyone has a say in how the project is planned and executed. The ebook reader team in Chapter 3 was originally given a requirement to build an Internet storefront. To make the product successful, they had to ignore that requirement in order to deliver a project that was much more valuable. This was only possible because they were allowed to make that decision with just the team, the Scrum Master, and the Product Owner. They didn't need to go through a bureaucracy to get it done.

*Team members **respect** each other*

When team members have mutual respect, they're able to trust each other to do a good job with the work they've taken on. But that respect doesn't always come easily to programmers and other technical people. Many programmers, especially highly skilled ones, often base their respect purely on technical ability. This can be a barrier to effective Scrum adoption. If a programmer doesn't respect the Product Owner, he won't listen to that Product Owner when they talk about the goals of the project.

A good Scrum Master finds ways to increase the team members' mutual respect for each other. For example, he may show the programmers that the Product Owner has a deep understanding of how the users think and what the company needs. As programmers start to understand how that knowledge is useful for the project to be successful, they start to value and respect the Product Owner's opinions.

*Everyone is **focused** on the work*

When a Scrum team member is working on a sprint, that's his only job for the duration of the sprint. He is free to do whatever work is needed to complete the sprint backlog, and handle any changes that are made to that backlog during the sprint. When every team member is focused on the sprint goals and given the freedom to do whatever work is needed to meet those goals, the whole team is able to organize itself and easily redirect whenever a change is needed.

On the other hand, a distracted team is a less effective team. There's a myth in the modern workplace that people—especially programmers—work best when multitasking, because they can move onto tasks for a second project when blocked on the first one. This is not how people work in real life! Switching between projects, or even between unrelated tasks on the same project, adds unexpected delays and effort, because context switching requires a lot of cognitive overhead. It takes a surprising amount of mental effort to put down your current work and pick up where you left off on another project. You end up having to review what you did last time just to remind yourself what problems you were trying to solve. Telling a team member to switch to a task on another project requires not just the time it takes to do that new task, but also the time it takes to switch to the task and back —which can be almost as much time as it takes to actually do it.

Don't buy it? Try this thought experiment. Say you've got two one-week tasks. And pretend that through some amazing bending of the laws of physics, multi-tasking doesn't add any overhead at all. You can switch between those tasks seamlessly, without adding a single second of overhead or delay, so those two tasks will take exactly two weeks. Even under these perfect (and impossible) circumstances, it doesn't make sense to multitask. If you don't multitask, you'll get the first task done at the end of the first week, and the second one done at the end of the second week. If you multitask, however, then you must have spent at least some time in the first week doing the second task, so it won't get done until sometime the next week. That's one reason why even if humans were good at multitasking (which we're not), it doesn't make sense to do it.

Multitasking isn't the only way that team members are distracted. They will often be required to attend useless meetings and extraneous committees, to perform activities that are irrelevant to the project, and to do support work for other projects. A good Scrum team is given permission to ignore these distractions without risking their careers or promotions.[7] (Support work for the current project that must be done now can be added to the sprint backlog—but only if something else is taken out to make it fit the timebox.)

The teams value *openness*

When you're working on a Scrum team, everyone else on the team should always be aware of what you're working on and how it moves the project toward its current goals. That's why the practices in the basic Scrum pattern are aimed at encouraging openness among the team members. Task boards, for example, allow everyone to see all of the work being done by each team member, and how much work is left to do. Burndown charts let each person gauge for him- or herself how quickly the sprint is meeting its sprint goals. The Daily Scrum, when done effectively, is an almost pure exercise in openness, because each person shares his or her tasks, challenges, and progress for the whole team to see. All of these things can help the team to create an atmosphere of mutual support and encouragement.

---

7 Does this advice seem unrealistic? Does it touch a nerve? If the team doesn't have permission to ignore distractions, then maybe they shouldn't be considered distractions. A distraction that can't be ignored is a requirement, and not a distraction at all. If you work on a team where ignoring a "distraction" can be a serious project problem, then your team's mindset may be a barrier to adopting Scrum. This gives you something to work on with your team.

Creating a culture of openness for a Scrum team sounds wonderful and positive, and it is. But it can often be one of the most difficult things for a Scrum team to do, because it's one of the most common ways for the values of Scrum to clash with the pre-existing culture of the company.

Many companies have a culture that discourages transparency, and replaces it with a rigid hierarchy that depends on opaqueness. Managers that establish a culture like this benefit from it in several ways. It's much easier in an opaque organization to tell a team to meet an unrealistic goal ("I don't care how you do it, just get it done!"), forcing the team to work overtime to meet it. And it gives the manager plausible deniability to CYA when the team inevitably fails to meet that goal ("It's not my fault they screwed up!").

This is why openness and self-organization can often be the untouchable "third rail" of a Scrum adoption. It's a central concept to getting a Scrum adoption right, but it also requires the company to treat the team differently than in the past. Being exposed to the details of development denies the opaque manager the cover to CYA. Many fledgling Scrum teams have found their adoption efforts undermined from above once opaque managers started to see how the sausage was made.

Openness is threatening to a cartoonish, pointy-haired, opaque manager. But realistically, it can also be a difficult thing for even a good team to adopt. Think about openness from the perspective of a developer who is seen as an expert in one part of the code, or a project manager who is the "keeper" of the plan, or a Product Owner who is the sole contact for many of the users and primary decision maker about what goes into the software. Each of these team members has every right to see those things as their contribution to the project. It can be very difficult to open those things up to the team, and encourage the other team members to share ownership and make changes without first getting permission.

This is a very natural way for individual team members to resist openness. But when they get past this and share ownership—including accountability when things go wrong—of all of those things with the whole team, everyone benefits, because it's the only way to trust each other and quickly deliver more valuable software.

Team members have the **courage** to stand up for the project

When you choose openness over opaqueness, you make the team stronger, rather than making yourself stronger at the expense of the team. It takes courage to do that, but when you do, you end up with a better product and a better work environment.

Scrum teams have the courage to live by values and principles that benefit the project. It takes courage to ward off the constant pushback from a company whose values clash with the Scrum and agile values. This requires vigilance on the part of every team member, especially the Scrum Master. But it also requires each person to be willing to trust that delivering valuable software will help him or her overcome resistance to these values. This requires courage too, especially when it comes time to sit down for a review with the boss. It takes courage to say to yourself, "Helping this team produce valuable software is more important to me than bragging rights from my own personal contribution."

So how would you build courage on a team? How would you get a team to believe in themselves, and believe that Scrum will not only help them build more valuable software, but that their company will see the value in their new methodology?

Key Points

- The basic pattern for a Scrum project covers the roles and practices of Scrum: Scrum Master, Product Owner, team, sprints, product and sprint backlogs, Daily Scrum meetings, reviews, and retrospectives.
- To really "get" Scrum, the team members need to go beyond just implementing practices, and actually understand *self-organization and collective commitment*.
- Teams talk about pigs and chickens to help them understand what it really means to be committed to delivering valuable software, and to truly feel ownership of everything the whole team produces.
- Teams need to truly understand and internalize the Scrum values of *commitment, respect, focus, openness, and courage* to become effective Scrum teams.

Narrative: a team working on a mobile phone app at a small company

Roger – team lead trying to go agile

Avi – the Product Owner

Eric – a Scrum Master on another team

Act II: Status Updates Are for Social Networks!

Back on the Lolleaderz.com team, Roger and Avi needed help—and they knew it. They also knew that there was another team at Hover Puppy that had a great experience with Scrum. Roger started talking to people on that team to see what the secret was, but he ended up more confused than before. It seemed like they were doing exactly the same things that the Lolleaderz.com team was doing: they also had sprints, Daily Scrums, retrospectives, a backlog, a Product Owner, and a Scrum Master. It seemed like both teams were doing exactly the same thing, but one team was getting great results while the other was slowly sinking. Roger and Avi sat down with Eric. Eric was Scrum Master on another team. He'd been having a lot of success with Scrum, and he was happy to help Avi and Roger to try to figure out what was giving them trouble.

The first thing Eric asked was, "Do you have a coach?" Roger wasn't sure what that meant. "You know, a mentor? Someone to help you get Scrum right? There's no way my team would have done as well as we did without one." This was the first time Roger really appreciated how good a salesman Avi was, because by the end of the discussion he'd convinced Eric to sign on as Scrum coach for the Lolleaderz.com team.

The following Monday, Roger and Avi wanted to make a big production of introducing Eric to the team at the Daily Scrum. Eric asked everyone to just go ahead the way they normally did—he'd watch the team work, and then try to come up with a few small suggestions. It was a good thing that he said that, because only half of the team was there for the introduction, anyway—they all knew that the lead developer always went first, and because he usually had the longest update, the rest of the team mostly arrived halfway through his status report.

For the rest of the meeting, team members took turns talking to Roger about their tasks. Everyone told Roger the progress they'd made on the tasks they were assigned. They asked Roger for their next assignments. During an update, one person pointed out that they were still waiting for the sysadmins to fix the configuration on one of the web servers, and asked Roger what he'd do to get it fixed. Roger added it to his list of roadblocks to clear for the team. Eric watched the whole thing without saying anything.

The next day, Eric watched through another Daily Scrum, which went the same way. He noticed that one of the team members reported that he was 95% done with his task. The same team member was 95% done with the same task previously. Afterward, he asked Roger about it. "Yes, it looks like that's going to slip. Don't worry, I'm on top of it. I've already updated the schedule. He's always late with tasks, so I added enough contingency to take care of it, and if it slips enough I'll make sure that gets reported to Avi and the CEO."

Eric set up a meeting later that day with Roger and Avi. He started out by explaining what he thought was the biggest problem. "Roger, you're just using the Daily Scrum as a way for you to manage your schedule. What happens if that team member keeps slipping? You just update your schedule, and now you've done your job, right? Except that updating a Gantt chart in a folder somewhere doesn't make the project any less late."

Roger did not like hearing this. Neither did Avi, because he used that schedule to update the rest of the project's stakeholders. Eric continued, telling Roger that he was using the Daily Scrum to get updates from the team. This made things even worse. "Of course I'm using it to get updates! That's what it's for, right?" Roger was beginning to have second thoughts about bringing Eric on as a coach.

Can you spot why Eric had a problem with Roger and Avi using the Daily Scrum to get status updates from the team, or maintaining the schedule based on those updates? If that's not what Daily Scrums are for, then why do Scrum teams hold them?

The Whole Team Uses the Daily Scrum

The Daily Scrum is one of the most effective tools that a Scrum team has at its disposal. This is because it does two very important things for the team. It functions as an **inspection** of the work that the team is doing, so they can adapt that work to deliver the most value. And it gives the team the opportunity to make decisions at the **last responsible moment**, giving them the flexibility to have the right person do the right work at the right time. When everyone on the team uses the Daily Scrum to limit the amount of planning they do to include only what's necessary to build the next increment of the software, the whole team starts to recognize it as a valuable tool and use it effectively.

Feedback and the Visibility-Inspection-Adaptation Cycle

A lot of developers who are new to agile are used to an entire world that revolves around programming. They come into work to a set of things that need to be built, and go home having built them. This is a very comfortable place for developers to be, because they can focus their jobs mainly on solving technical problems.

But every programmer knows what it's like to put a lot of time and effort into building out a solution, only to find at the end that there was an important part of the problem that they didn't understand—usually because it was never communicated to them.

This can be especially problematic on traditional, "big requirements up front" (BRUF) projects. Think about all of the steps a requirement has to go through on one of these projects before it gets to the developer. On typical BRUF waterfall project, planning works something like this:

- The project manager needs to scope out the work, often in some sort of business requirements or scope and objectives document.
- Managers need to sign off on the scope.
- A business analyst needs to review the scope, then talk to the users and other stakeholders to understand their jobs.
- The business analyst comes up with use cases, functional requirements, etc.
- The programmer takes the requirements and generates an estimate.
- The project manager takes the requirements and estimates, builds out a schedule, and reviews it with stakeholders and managers.

That's quite a chain of events that has to happen before the development even starts. It's no wonder that it's so rare for requirements to make it perfectly through that "game of telephone" into a developer's brain.

This isn't just a problem for BRUF waterfall teams. Even a team that is able to rely almost entirely on face-to-face communication will have problems with misunderstandings and incomplete communication. After all, face-to-face communication is very efficient, but also less precise (although often more accurate) than written communication. It's very easy for three people to have a great discussion and think they reached consensus, only to have three different impressions of what was discussed.

There's an old saying: "sunlight is the best disinfectant." That may be questionable medical advice, but it's very good advice for project teams. The best way we have for users to judge whether or not the team is building valuable software is to put working software in their hands as frequently as possible. That's called **visibility** (or **transparency**), and it applies to communication as well.

The Daily Scrum is an effective tool for visibility because it helps with these communication problems. When those problems happen, they come out in the work. Take the example of those three people who have three different impressions of the same discussion. What if all three of them now had to go off and do three separate tasks that get integrated at the end of a sprint? These issues, the small misunderstandings that cause incremental problems and friction along the way, pile up if they're not caught. And as they occur throughout a project, they lead to a steady erosion of the quality of the code that the team produces. A small misunderstanding here or there causes a defect or two, which has to be ripped out when it's discovered later, which requires a quick patch or a larger change. As this happens over the course of a long project, the quality of the codebase deteriorates over time.

On the other hand, think about the effect it would have if those three people took 15 minutes out of every day to sit down and ask each other three questions:

- What have I done since our last meeting?
- What am I planning on doing between now and our next meeting?
- What roadblocks are in my way?

When the team members describe their work to each other in the same way every day, a lot of the problems that are caused by inevitable miscommunication get caught before they become costly (and caustic!). When everyone on the team **inspects** what everyone else is doing, they come to conclusions together and maintain a common understanding of the project's goals and how they're meeting them.

During the Daily Scrum, when one person describes what he's working on, one of his teammates might have a suggestion for a way he can improve. If her suggestion is a good one, the work he does the next day will be better. She might also discover that he's working on the wrong task entirely, a problem that's most likely caused by miscommunication, which would also cause him to change his plans for the next day's work. These changes are called **adaptation**. The daily cycle of visibility, inspection, and adaptation allows teams to *continuously use feedback from their projects to improve how they build software*. This is one of the most important features of Scrum. Scrum teams make decisions based on experience and on actual, known facts from their projects.[8]

This kind of feedback is the way that Scrum teams cut out the "middle man" of a disconnected project manager who may be too distant from the work, reduce the damage caused by "game of telephone" communication, and save time while improving quality. This cycle is an important **feedback loop** that the team can use to keep the

---

8 Students of Scrum theory refer to this as an *empirical process control*—see p. 4 of the Scrum Guide (*http://scrum.org*) for more information on empiricism.

project on track, and to make sure that everyone is communicating and on the same page.

It's not always comfortable for programmers to play the role of "inspector" for all of their teammates' work. However, even the most introverted team members typically get used to it, and many eventually look forward to the Daily Scrum. That's because it's the most efficient way that Scrum teams have of managing their communication and building a shared understanding of their work.

The Last Responsible Moment

This is about the point where a smart, skeptical command-and-control project manager might be thinking something like this: "OK, we get it. Teams don't claim to know everything about their projects up front in Scrum. Communication and shared understanding are important for a team. But work actually needs to get done, and that work needs to be assigned to people. How does that actually happen? What are the mechanics of an actual programming task, DBA task, testing task, or other task ending up on a programmer's to-do list?"

There's a common technique used by Scrum trainers and agile coaches teaching their teams to run better Daily Scrum sessions by letting them fail.[9] When a team that's used to command-and-control management arrives for the Daily Scrum, they typically look to the project manager or Scrum Master for guidance. That's when he asks each of them for their status updates, and gives them their next assignments. This feels natural to a team used to having their assignments handed to them. An agile coach looking to help this team run more effective Daily Scrums might advise the Scrum Master, just this once, to stay silent. This will often lead to a minute or two of painful, awkward silence. Finally, someone will speak up and describe the work they did since the last meeting. If the team is lucky, the next thing that team member does is ask, "So what's my next task?"

This is the moment when the Scrum Master really distinguishes himself from a project manager. A project manager would proceed to hand the team member a pre-parceled task. The Scrum Master recognizes this as the chance for the team to have a collective "a ha!" moment, when they finally figure out exactly where task assignments come from. He might do this by asking a question like, "What do you think you should be doing next?" Or he might simply remain silent, depending on the team.

The point is that the team members themselves are the source of the task assignments. *Each person self-assigns her next task as soon as she's done with the current one.*

---

9 This technique, and other effective coaching techniques, is described by Lyssa Adkins in *Coaching Agile Teams.*

This is done during the Daily Scrum because it gives the rest of the team the opportunity to give input, and help course-correct. For example, if a developer assigns himself a complex database optimization task, the DBA might step in and suggest that he leave that task for later, and promise to do it next.

Wait a minute—can't we avoid bottlenecks by planning up front?

Command-and-control project management starts with the assumption that tasks on a development project must be done by a specific team member, typically because that person has specialized knowledge or skills (like a DBA with database optimization skills). This seems like an argument for planning up front: that person's tasks form a bottleneck in the schedule, and a team working on a deadline must plan around that bottleneck in order to avoid it.

Ironically, this actually turns out to be a very common source of project management problems. Very complex tasks are more difficult to estimate than simple ones. And tasks that require one specific person or resource carry more risk than tasks that can be done by any of several team members. So it shouldn't be a surprise that complex tasks that must be done by one specific, skilled team member—like that complex database optimization task—are the ones whose estimates are most likely to be incorrect. What's worse, project managers typically depend on that one skilled person for the estimate as well as the work.

We can't know everything in advance. There are some decisions that you need to make at the beginning of the project (Java or C#? Windows or Linux? Mac or PC?). And there are even some tasks that absolutely must be done by a specific person. But in general, Scrum teams do not make task assignments at the beginning of the project, or even at the beginning of a sprint.

In fact, they don't try to come up with a "final" sequence of tasks at all. The reason is that for most project tasks, and especially programming tasks, the team doesn't really know exactly how long they will take until they start working on them, and they often only discover dependencies when they crop up. It's very common for teams to discover missing tasks throughout a project. And it's also common for a task that seemed small to end up large, and vice versa. Of course, while it's common for teams to discover tasks that they missed during a sprint, that doesn't absolve them of the responsibility of developing as complete or final a task list as possible during sprint planning.

So instead of decomposing the work into tasks at the beginning of the sprint, sequencing the tasks, assigning each of them to team members before any work is started, and tracking to that plan, agile teams follow a simple rule for scheduling. They make all decisions at the **last responsible moment**.

Flip back to the Lolleaderz.com story. Roger and Avi ran into their problem in the fourth sprint because the DBA ended up taking longer to do one of those specialized tasks that seem like they absolutely must be fully and formally scheduled from day one. This is a common project failure mode caused by overplanning. The project manager assumes that a set of tasks will be done by a single person, usually an expert with specialized skills. Those tasks tend to be the ones with the greatest risk of slipping. When they inevitably slip, nobody else can handle those tasks, so it causes cascading delays—or, more commonly, overtime that leads the experts to do poor work (and possibly start looking for a new job!).

A Scrum team making decisions at the last responsible moment might handle this differently. Instead of assuming at the beginning of the sprint that the DBA will do all of those tasks, the tasks are written on index cards (or some electronic equivalent) and go up on the task board in the "to do" column. During the Daily Scrum, everyone can see them, and someone will typically point to them and ask if those are going to cause problems later in the sprint.

Open source teams have a saying: "given enough eyeballs, all bugs are shallow" (Linus's Law). The same thing applies to the plan, and the Daily Scrum is how the team gets eyeballs on it. When the team looks as carefully at the project work as they do at the source code, those eyeballs are much more likely to find the "bugs" in the schedule as well. It's much easier for a team to discover bottlenecks on the fly during a Daily Scrum than it is for a command-and-control project manager to figure them out up front. And when the team can see them coming, they have time to find a way around them. Because everyone is vigilant, they often discover that the last responsible moment for some tasks is much earlier in the sprint than it is for other tasks. This is the value of the visibility-inspection-adaptation cycle: it gives the group the opportunity to identify the potential problems and come up with a solution together.

So what would have happened if Roger and Avi had been holding more effective Daily Scrums? Instead of assigning work to the team, they could have used the time to get everyone on the team working together to identify schedule problems and self-assign tasks. They all might have realized early on—by working together and talking about it as a team—that they needed someone other than the DBA to start working on stored procedures in order to make it to the end of the sprint. Or, if that wasn't an option, they could at least have figured out that they'd bitten off more than they could chew, and set everyone's expectations earlier in the sprint about what working software would be delivered at the end of that sprint.

How to Hold an Effective Daily Scrum

Act like a "pig"
During this meeting, every team member is accountable to his or her teammates, and should explain what happened if a commitment that he or she made in the previous meeting wasn't met. Imagine yourself on a self-organizing team, where you truly feel accountable for the project. What do you need to know in order to

do your job every day? The most important thing you need to know is what you're working on. But if your team is truly self-organizing, you can't rely on someone like a command-and-control project manager to decide for you what that is. So you need some other mechanism to get your current assignment. That's the first thing that you get from the Daily Scrum: your next task. When it's your turn to answer the question about what you'll be doing between now and the next Daily Scrum, if you've finished all the work assigned to you so far, your job is to look at the tasks in the "to do" column and choose the one that makes the most sense for you and for the project. If it's not the right choice, someone else who's also acting like a genuinely committed "pig" will speak up.

Take detailed conversations offline

The goal of the Daily Scrum is to identify problems, not solve them. If a problem hasn't been resolved after a minute or two of discussion, schedule a follow-up meeting with anyone who feels they need to be involved. A lot of these follow-up meetings will be about who does what task. This is how teams self-organize: most tasks can be self-assigned, but some of them need discussion. It's only through inspection during the Daily Scrum that you can tell which is which.

Take turns going first

There's no single person who's the "keeper" of the schedule, and there's no single person who's more important to the project than anyone else. Obviously, some developers have more expertise than others. But good ideas can come from anyone, and if a junior person on the team has a good idea, don't dismiss it just because it didn't come from your top programmer. He or she may have spotted a serious problem with the tasks that the whole team needs to deal with. One way to keep everyone listening to each other for those good ideas is to have a different team member start the Daily Scrum each day.

Don't treat it like a ritual

Even though we hold these meetings every day—some Scrum teams even refer to them as "ceremonies"—everyone needs to be fully present and engaged every step of the way. It's easy to treat the three questions that each person answers— What have I done since the last Daily Scrum? What will I do until the next one? What's blocking my progress?—as a ritual that just needs to be adhered to for some reason everyone's forgotten. Rituals tend to fade over time, because people see them as perfunctory. These questions are the core of the Daily Scrum because those are exactly the things that the team needs to inspect every day in order to find the project problems early. For example, an effective way to spot a bottleneck caused by too many tasks that have to be done by a single person is to have each person answer the question about blocking progress, because the first person whose progress will eventually be blocked by the bottleneck will spot it earlier than anyone else.

Everyone participates

This includes testers, business analysts, and anyone else on the team—and the Product Owner, too. They're all genuinely committed. The Product Owner has an especially important job to do because he or she keeps everyone up to date on what tasks in the backlog are most valuable to the users and the company. The better the team understands the value they're delivering, the more accurately they can aim the software at the users. The Product Owner should also answer the three questions along with the rest of the team, because it's easy for the team to forget that he or she has an important job to do for the project too, and the answers help the rest of the team understand that job. (It turns out that talking to users, understanding their business, and managing that backlog really is a full-time job, and the developers respect that job more when they see that firsthand!)

Don't treat it like a status meeting

A typical status meeting is a great example of a "ritual" that we have to go through every week. Because we're all familiar with the ritualistic aspect of it, it's something we rarely question, or even think about. The status meeting is supposed to serve two purposes: keeping everyone on the team informed, and keeping management informed. But for most teams, this is really just a one-way communication, a bunch of individual two-person conversations between a single team member and a project manager. You can avoid this by making sure that each person in the Daily Scrum is really listening. (This means not checking email or cell phones, or doing work!) As the team members start to see the Daily Scrum as a way to catch problems early and avoid wasting developer time by going down the wrong path, it feels less like bureaucratic red tape, and more like a genuine developer-centric tool that they can use to make the code better.

Inspect every task

When you're looking for roadblocks, don't just look at what you're currently doing. Look several moves ahead by examining every item in the "to do" column to figure out if any of those items could have an impact. If there's a potential problem, it's better to bring it up with the team now and have it dismissed than to keep quiet and get burned by it later. That's why inspecting the tasks requires trust between everyone on the team. If someone—intentionally or unintentionally—doesn't accurately describe what they're working on and planning to do, the rest of the team could miss out on a potential roadblock, which will cause bigger problems if it's not caught early.

Change the plan if it needs to be changed

This is the "adapting" part of the visibility-inspection-adaptation cycle, and it's what puts the teeth in self-organization. Let's say the team identifies a roadblock during the Daily Scrum, and has a follow-up meeting where they realize that they made a serious miscalculation and won't be able to deliver a major feature that they'd promised. Does it make sense to keep working a plan that they know won't work? Of course not. The backlog and task board need to reflect the reality of the project, and if a problem is discovered, then the entire team must work together to fix the backlog and task board. This is where having a Product Owner who's a pig can come in very handy, because he or she can immediately start setting everyone else's expectations. Just remember, no matter how badly people will react to the change when they find out about it today, they'll react even worse if you don't tell them now, and they find out later.

Key Points

- In the Daily Scrum, each team member answers three questions: What have I done since the last Daily Scrum? What will I do between now and the next one? What are my bottlenecks?

- The team uses those questions to collaboratively inspect the project plan every day and adapt to changes that have come along in the project, and the answers give the team *constant feedback throughout the project*.

- Effective Scrum teams make decisions at the **last responsible moment** so that they can leave their options open, making it easier to adapt to changes.

- The Daily Scrum is *owned by the whole team*, not just the Scrum Master or Product Owner, and everyone participates equally.

Narrative: a team working on a mobile phone app at a small company

Roger – team lead trying to go agile

Avi – the Product Owner

Eric – a Scrum Master on another team

Act III: Sprinting into a Wall

After Eric, Roger, and Avi took a long lunch to really talk about how to use the Daily Scrum, Roger had an idea. At the next Daily Scrum meeting, he asked one of the junior developers to start the meeting by answering the three questions. When she asked Roger what her next task was, he just stayed silent. Nobody else said anything for about half a minute, and things got a little uncomfortable. Just as Roger started to wonder if this was really a good idea, one of the more senior developers spoke up. After a brief discussion that involved several other people on the team, the junior developer knew exactly what to do next. She pulled the index card for her task off of the "to do" column of the task board, wrote her name on the card, and taped it back up in the "in progress" column.

The rest of the Daily Scrum went really well. It seemed like all it took was that one discussion, and the team suddenly "got" it—they all started talking about each other's tasks, and only had to schedule two follow-up discussions to determine who would do what. Roger was pleasantly surprised that he didn't even have to go to one of them. The follow-up he did have to lead was with a developer who was 95% done with a task that had been 95% done for the last week. It turned out that there was a serious roadblock, and the developer needed help from someone but was afraid to ask for it because he didn't want to waste his teammates' time (and probably was a bit embarrassed, too).

A few Daily Scrums later, Roger was really happy when Eric pointed out that the team was starting to work together. And over the next week, he really started to feel like they were finally getting the real idea behind self-organization—and they were doing it together, as a team. Every day, the whole team worked together to choose the next day's work, and helped each other stay on track and solve problems. They were using the Daily Scrum to course-correct as a team, based on a daily review of the work they were actually doing.

Things seemed to be going great, all the way up to the end of the sprint. The team rolled out a new version of the working software, just like they had after the previous six sprints.

It was a disaster.

Avi came back from the next stakeholder meeting utterly crestfallen. He'd expected all of the account managers to be really excited about the new version of the Lolleaderz.com achievement editor that let users create their own achievements and share them on social networking sites. Plus, the team had updated the banner ad feature to allow each account manager to give customized pages to each of his or her accounts that showed up-to-date information on their page views and advertising costs.

Instead, most of the account managers were confused and caught off-guard. They felt like nobody had told them that so many things would change. Suddenly, each of them had dozens of voicemails from clients who were asking about these new features. In the past, they could rely on Roger's schedules to give them plenty of advance notice to start selling the new features. Now the world was changing quickly, and they felt like they didn't have time to keep up.

Avi had even worse news. Some of the stakeholders were asking for the old schedules back, and wondered if the team could hold off on releasing anything until the next quarter. It sounded like the company wanted them to stop using Scrum entirely and go back to their waterfall process. This was terrible!

Or was it? Eric heard the same news as Roger did, but instead of seeming despondent he seemed oddly optimistic. Why do you think he was?

Sprints, Planning, and Retrospectives

For some projects, sprint planning is easy—like when it's mainly a matter of finally getting around to building things in the backlog that people have been asking you to do for months. If there's a feature that your users keep demanding, and you make that a high priority, it's an easy win. That's when sprint planning is just common sense.

But sometimes sprint planning is more nuanced than that. Often, sprint planning requires you—and your whole team—to think about what your users need, and what they value, in a way that you never have before. When people talk about Scrum being hard, this is generally what they're referring to.

Luckily, effective Scrum teams have a not-so-secret weapon to attack this problem: the Product Owner. When the Product Owner really takes the time to understand what the stakeholders need and what will give them value, he can help the team aim each sprint at the problems that the company needs solved first. By giving the team visibility into that value, and helping them come up with a new plan for each sprint to deliver that value, he can help them turn a merely incremental process into a truly iterative one. And when the team is holding effective retrospectives at the end of each sprint, the Product Owner can help take the lessons the team learned back to the company so that everyone's expectations can stay in line with what the team can actually deliver.

Iterative or Incremental?

What is the value of each new release that's delivered at the end of each sprint?

If you plan out timeboxed sprints, stick to them so that when the time runs out the team stops all work, and have a team that delivers working software at the end of each sprint, you'll get a lot of benefit from that adoption. You'll get a routine checkpoint that helps you stay on top of the quality of the software. It allows your Product Owner, users, and stakeholders to see functionally complete versions, so you can all see how the features being built can fit together. This significantly lowers the risk of integration because it keeps the team from waiting until the end of the project to integrate features built by different people, only to discover that those features didn't quite work together.

Try this thought experiment to help understand integration problems. Let's say that two of your team members are working on different features of a program that have to save the user's current work to a file, but they do it differently. How many ways can you think of for those features to clash with each other? Here are a few to get you started: one feature might use a save icon, while another uses a file menu; or the two features could have entirely incompatible ways of accessing shared resources; or they could save files in incompatible formats; or they could overwrite shared data that the application manages; or there could be any number of other integration problems. Can you think of more potential problems that might arise in integration? If you've been building software for a long time, you don't need to use your imagination—you've probably seen similar things happen many times.

Bringing all of the development together at the end of each sprint instead of waiting until the end of the project can help the team recognize and even prevent many of those problems. There are other benefits to working this way as well: better communication, more involved stakeholders, and project status that's easier to gauge. When a team breaks a project into phases, it's called **incremental development**. Scrum sprints are another way to break your project into increments, which is why Scrum is an incremental methodology.

But Scrum is more than that. Scrum sprints are about more than just delivering working software on a timeboxed schedule. Scrum is also about understanding the value that the software delivers, looking at exactly how that value will be delivered, and changing course if there's a way to deliver more value. When methodologies and processes like Scrum work like that, it's called **iterative development**. That's why Scrum is both an incremental *and* iterative methodology.

Mike Cohn gives a good explanation of a key difference between iterative and incremental in his excellent book, *User Stories Applied*:

> An iterative process is one that makes progress through successive refinement. A development team takes a first cut at a system, knowing it is incomplete or weak in some (perhaps many) areas. They then iteratively refine those areas until the product is satisfactory. With each iteration the software is improved through the addition of greater detail.

> An incremental process is one in which software is built and delivered in pieces. Each piece, or increment, represents a complete subset of functionality. The increment may be either small or large, perhaps ranging from just a system's login screen on the small end to a highly flexible set of data management screens. Each increment is fully coded

and tested, and the common expectation is that the work of an iteration will not need to be revisited.[10]

We already have a term for taking a first cut at a system, knowing it is incomplete or weak in some areas, and iteratively refining those areas: the visibility-inspection-adaptation cycle. A Scrum team that's doing incremental development takes the same visibility-inspection-adaptation cycle that they already use for their Daily Scrums and applies it to the project as a whole. That's the goal of sprint planning, managing the sprint backlog, and holding retrospectives.

This is why the Product Owner is so important to Scrum teams, and why the role of Product Owner is called out as its own specific role in Scrum. It's the Product Owner's job to:

- Understand what the company needs most, and bring that knowledge back to the team
- Understand what software features the team can potentially deliver
- Figure out which features are more valuable to the company, and which are less valuable
- Work with the team to figure out which features are easier to build, and which are harder
- Use that knowledge of value, difficulty, uncertainty, complexity, etc. to help the team choose the right features to build in each sprint
- Bring that knowledge back to the rest of the company, so they can do what they need to do to prepare for the next release of the software

The Product Owner Makes or Breaks the Sprint

The Product Owner has a very specific job to do for the project. He or she owns the product backlog, and selects the highest priority items to ask the team to work on during the sprint. He works with the team during sprint planning to decide which of those items go into the sprint backlog (which is owned collectively by the team), and accepts those items that have been finished by the team on behalf of the company. This means that the Product Owner has to have a lot of authority—and a Product Owner who doesn't really have the authority to make those decisions (or who does, but is afraid to make them) is the wrong person for the job. It also means that the Product Owner has to have a really good sense of what's valuable to the company. He or she can talk to other people to figure out what items are more or less valuable, but

---

10 Mike Cohn, *User Stories Applied: For Agile Software Development* (Upper Saddle River, NJ: Pearson Education, 2004.

in the end it's up to the Product Owner to make the final decision about the priority of everything in the product backlog.

This is why it's so important that the team and the Product Owner agree from the very beginning of the sprint about what each of those items consists of. When they're planning out the sprint backlog together, they all need to agree on what it means for each item to be **"Done"**—not just done, but "Done." A backlog item is "Done" if it can be accepted by the Product Owner and delivered to the rest of the company. If each item doesn't have a clear, unambiguous definition of what it means to be "Done," there will be a lot of confusion and, almost certainly, heated arguments at the end of the sprint. But if everyone has a clear idea of what it means for each item to be "Done," the team always has a good sense of how far through the sprint they are at any time.

Sprints are timeboxed, often to 30 days (although some Scrum teams choose shorter sprint lengths, often two or three weeks). When the sprint ends, all items that are "Done" are accepted by the Product Owner. Any items that are not "Done" go back onto the product backlog—even if the team did a lot (or even most) of the work for them. This doesn't mean that team has to back out the work, delete source code, or undo anything. It just means that they don't get credit for having finished the item until it's actually "Done" and accepted by the Product Owner.

This is valuable because it makes sure that the team never gives the users the impression that they delivered value that wasn't actually delivered. It's always better to be conservative about what commitments were delivered. The sprint review is the only time that the whole team actually stands in front of their users and stakeholders to demonstrate what they've been working on for the last 30 days. If they didn't meet all of their commitments, everyone on the team has to look their users in the eye, and explain what they did and did not deliver. This is a very powerful tool for helping everyone to feel a real sense of collective commitment. This is also an opportunity for the users and stakeholders to ask the team questions, and that human interaction helps everyone connect and get a much better sense of what is really valuable—and they can start to build up a genuine feeling of trust. The more everyone meets and talks about the software like this, the greater the sense of trust, and the more freedom the team will have in the future to build the software. But even though the users and stakeholders are present and talking to the team, it's the Product Owner who actually accepts the work on behalf of the company.

In (hopefully) very rare cases, the Product Owner and the team discover that the sprint was either very badly planned, or that a serious change has happened that can't wait until the end of the sprint. In this case, the Product Owner has the authority to break the sprint, halt all work, and move all of the items from the sprint backlog back to the product backlog. This should be an extremely rare occurrence, because it can destroy all of that hard-earned trust between the team and their users and stakeholders.

Visibility and Value

Think about what motivates you when you're working. How often has something like this gone through your head at work:

- "Working with this technology will look great on my résumé" (if you're a developer)
- "If I prove myself on this project, I'll get to grow my team" (if you're a team lead)
- "Meeting this big deadline will get me that promotion" (if you're a project manager)
- "If I land that big client, I'll get a huge bonus" (if you're an account manager, Product Owner, stakeholder, etc.)

We all think things like that. And it's OK.

Every one of us has our own self-interest, and there's nothing wrong with that. But motivating each team member as an individual isn't the most effective way to bring a team together. On the other hand, when people work together toward a single goal, they can accomplish much more than they can on their own as individuals. So while we all have a basic need to get something out of our work, when each of us makes that thing our main concern, we get much less done than we do if we work together as a team.

Here's a good example of how self-interest can damage a project: let's say there's a team member who can dump his uninteresting or irritating tasks on someone else, usually a more junior member of the team. Most of us have seen this situation. For example, senior developers are often so busy building new software that they put off fixing bugs. It's not a coincidence that it's much more fun for them to build new features, especially if they get to learn new technology along the way. And for a developer doing this, it would be great to have a maintenance team of junior developers (possibly in another city where developers are paid less) who can fix all of those bugs. This is so common that many companies explicitly set their teams up this way, with an "A Team" set of experienced developers to build new features, and a maintenance team of less experienced developers to fix bugs and create patches for software that's been released.

This is a great, fun, and satisfying way to work for the senior developer who wants to use a "fire and forget" style of writing code, because he's confident that any bugs he makes will get fixed by someone else without him even having to think about it. But while this is fun way for one person on the team in the short run, it's a highly inefficient way for a team to operate in the long run. In almost all cases, the person who introduces a bug is the best person to fix it. He already knows the details of the code, and because he wrote it, it's already written in a style that's intuitive for him. Handing that bug off to someone else requires communication; sometimes just an email, but often additional documentation as well (like a bug report, or an updated spec). It also requires the person who's fixing it to spend time looking through the code to figure out what it does. A bug that would take the programmer who created it a few minutes to fix can easily take hours or even days for someone else, especially if he's more junior, and less experienced.

The "push off the grunt work" pattern is rarely found on Scrum teams because everyone on a Scrum team is genuinely committed. When a team has a culture where the more experienced developer does the "grunt work" in a few minutes when it's fresh rather than making a more junior team member spend hours on it later, that can be another source of the Scrum "hyper-productivity" and "astonishing results" that seem to elude many teams.

Any team (even non-agile ones) can try to capture this productivity by setting up rules preventing senior team members from dumping "boring" maintenance tasks on junior team members. But a truly effective Scrum team doesn't need to set up a rule for that, or separate rules for any number of situations. The reason is that on a Scrum team, everyone has a genuine feeling of ownership for every aspect of the project. If the senior team member feels that way, it would never even occur to him to "dump" these tasks—and, in fact, it wouldn't feel like dumping at all. He would be the logical person to do the work, so doing that work would feel like the most important thing for him to be doing right now (just like in the example of the CEO getting coffee).[11] The bug fixes and other maintenance tasks *would simply get added to the sprint backlog*, reviewed at the Daily Scrum, and like any other task it would get done by the right team member at the right time. (And the last responsible moment for fixing it is probably right now, because it's still fresh in the developer's head.)

On an effective Scrum team, everyone feels a true sense of ownership, not just of the code they build, but of the backlog, and of the work that everyone is doing to deliver working software. The sprint backlog represents a real commitment that everyone, even the most junior developer, feels that they've made to the users. That's what Ken Schwaber meant by "collective commitment" in the quote at the beginning of this chapter: that everyone on the team shares ownership of the backlog, and feels personally responsible for delivering the most valuable software that they can to the users—including all of the features, not just the ones that they're working on.

So how do you get that feeling of shared ownership embedded in the team, so that every single person—from the most junior developer to the senior technical lead to

---

11 In fact, someone on an effective Scrum team reading this will probably be confused or even a bit upset just reading about a senior person who "dumps" tasks on others, because it's such a foreign idea.

the Scrum Master and Product Owner—will voluntarily take on uninteresting or irritating tasks because he or she cares about the project?

Elevating goals motivate everyone on the team

Have you ever done volunteer work? Contributed to an open source project? Joined a club, or amateur sports team, or rock band, or church choir? Think about the last time you joined a group outside of your work or your family. Why did you do it?

You joined the group, and probably put a lot of effort and care into what you were doing for them, because you care about whatever it is the group was organized to do. If you were part of a voter drive, you care about getting people to participate in elections. If you were on a soccer team, you care about winning (and hopefully about playing well). So why should work be any different?

All of us are self-motivated. Minimally, we all work for money. If your job stopped paying you, you'd stop showing up. We have bills to pay, and many of us have families to feed. So paying us—and having a clean and safe office environment, giving us workable hours, and all of those other basic things that make up a work environment —is enough to get us in the door and at our desks during working hours.

But is it enough to get us to really care about building great software?

If you've ever worked on a team that isn't really motivated, you know that the answer to that question is "no." And the fact is, many of us have never worked on a team that's truly motivated. But if you have, you're probably thinking about that team right now, because it was likely the best work experience of your career. When everyone cares about building great software, things just seem to go better: people communicate more, argue less (although when they do argue, they do it much more passionately—and productively), and seem to just get things done.

Teams can be motivated by many things: getting an opportunity to work on a new technology or in a domain that they want to learn about, the possibility of a promotion, a performance bonus, working from home. Teams can be motivated by negative things, too: the boss will be mad, you'll get yelled at (or less money, or fired!). Those things, positive or negative, motivate people to work for themselves and their own interests, not to come together as a team.

When teams are motivated effectively, it's because they're organized around an **elevating goal**. In Chapter 16 of our book *Beautiful Teams*, project management author and expert Steve McConnell gave us this definition of what it means to have an elevating goal:

> If you're out digging ditches, that's not very elevating or inspiring. But if you're digging ditches to protect your town that's about to be attacked by an enemy, well, that's more inspiring, even though it's the same activity. And so the leader's job, really, is to try to

determine or frame the activity in such a way that people can understand what the value is.

Almost all software is built by teams, not individuals. For a team to work effectively, they need to be motivated together, not just as individuals. Teams are motivated best by elevating goals, which bring them together for a higher purpose that they all care about.

Delivering value can be a very effective elevating goal, one that can motivate the whole team. When a team has an elevating goal that they truly believe in, and they're given the room to decide for themselves how to accomplish it (and the freedom to take risks) they will work hard to use the tools they have available to solve any problem standing in the way of that goal.

Elevating goals are aimed at value, but the term "value" can seem abstract or disconnected. On an agile team, value has a very real and specific meaning: software is valuable if it makes your users' lives better. What happens if a senior vice president comes down to the team and says this: "Because of all your hard work over the last few months, we added 0.024% to our third quarter revenues. Great job, team!" That's not particularly motivating for most developers, not even ones who are paid with stock options.

On the other hand, what if that same person came down to the team and said this: "Wow, I used to spend three hours every day just sorting through these numbers. Your software is so easy to use and works so well that I can do it all in 10 minutes. Thank you!" That's much more motivating to most developers.

Developers—and by "developers" we mean all members of an agile team, even ones who don't necessarily write code—are highly motivated by *pride of workmanship*. We want to build software that's useful, and that people like and care about. We want our software to do a good job, and we want it to perform that job efficiently. We also want it to be built as well as it can be, which is why we spend so much time arguing about different designs, architectures, and technologies. These are things that teams actually care about. Making our users' lives better—which is the most direct way that we have of delivering value—can be a real, honest, elevating goal.

This principle is at the top of the list of principles behind the agile manifesto. Note the words that we highlighted:

> Our highest priority is to satisfy the customer through early and continuous delivery of *valuable software*.

The reason that this is our highest priority is because delivering value to our users is the most effective way that we have to motivate our teams—and that's the driving force behind good sprint planning.

How to Plan and Run an Effective Scrum Sprint

Starting with the backlog—which means starting with the users

Why do we plan delivering a specific feature this sprint, rather than pushing it off to the next one? Because we've worked together as a team to figure out which features are most valuable to our users. This is why the Product Owner is so important—it's his or her job to understand the users, and keep everyone on the team up to date on what they need most from the software.

Be realistic about what you can deliver

A lot of managers have a crazy idea that if you don't keep pushing developers, they'll slack off by committing to do as little work as possible, to give themselves long deadlines. On most teams, this is the opposite of the truth. Realistically, developers have a tendency to be overly optimistic—which is why most of us have seen many projects come in late, but rarely seen them deliver very early. Don't try to cram too many features into a sprint. (After all, the users only have to wait until the next sprint to get working software that includes the next set of features.) A good Scrum Master helps the team estimate the work and figure out what they can and can't include.

Change the plan if it needs to change

Take advantage of the Daily Scrum meetings to figure out if the team is really going to finish everything they've promised for the sprint. If the plan needs to be changed, it's the responsibility of the team to change it. If it becomes clear that the team won't be able to finish all of the work in the sprint backlog, then the team should move some of it (starting with the lowest value items) out of the sprint backlog and back into the product backlog—and the Scrum Master should make sure that everyone on the team understands the change. Users that are used to seeing working software frequently are generally less jarred by a sprint review that does not include all of the features they'd expected, especially if the Product Owner has done a good job of managing their expectations.

Get everyone talking about value

Effective Scrum teams tend to be full of people who understand what their users actually need, and what's valuable to them. The only way this can happen is if every person on the team understands what it will do for people who use it. How does it make their lives easier? What does it let them do that they couldn't do before? How much time and effort will it save them? These things really matter to agile developers. The more that you talk about them and make sure that they matter, the better the software will be.

Key Points

- Scrum is both **incremental** and **iterative**—it's incremental because it's broken down into consecutive sprints, but it's iterative because the team adapts each new sprint to changes that occur during the project.

- When effective Scrum teams say that they're *motivated by delivering value*, they mean that their most important goal is building software that improves users' lives.

- The Product Owner's job is to *keep the team motivated around value* by helping them understand their users, what they do, and what they need the software for.

Narrative: a team working on a mobile phone app at a small company

Roger – team lead trying to go agile

Avi – the Product Owner

Eric – a Scrum Master on another team

Act IV: Dog Catches Car

When Roger and Avi came to Eric with news of what had since come to be called the "stakeholder meeting from hell," they couldn't understand why he seemed optimistic. A few days later, the three of them left work early and headed to a nearby restaurant to talk it all through.

Eric started the conversation: "Why do you think all those account managers were upset?"

Neither Roger nor Avi really had a good answer. Roger started talking about how they'd done all of this work to become more agile, which in his mind meant being able to constantly adjust to a stream of feature requests, and build completely new products any time they were needed. Avi felt that he'd put a lot of work toward getting "plugged in" with the team, and was able to stream a whole bunch of great ideas from all of the account managers. They both felt that they'd given their stakeholders exactly what they'd asked for. "Look, I've got emails from each one of them asking for exactly what we delivered," Avi said. "How could they possibly get upset by any of this?"

This is when Eric explained why, as an agile coach, he was happy with what he saw, even though the project seemed to be running into trouble. He explained that before, they were like a giant cruise ship that required many nautical miles to make a turn. Now they were more like a fleet of highly coordinated speedboats. It took a lot more communication, but it meant they could turn on a dime. And Avi had gone from being overwhelmed and a little antagonistic toward the team to being a true team member and an effective conduit between the team and their users.

By helping the team to put an effective Daily Scrum in place, Roger empowered the team to self-organize around changing priorities. But a new problem emerged, and Eric explained that this happens to many teams who have made it past the first set of challenges in becoming self-organizing. A newly self-organizing team now has the power to change direction extremely efficiently. And a Product Owner who finds himself embedded in that team now has the power to set that direction.

Eric gave them a good analogy: "Have you ever seen a team of firemen practicing to aim a fire hose? When they're putting out fires, it just looks like they're pointing it at the flames. But they had to spend weeks or months learning how to effectively move it, and communicate with each other so they move in the same direction. Your team used to be a garden hose, and now they're a fire hose. It's like one of those cartoons where the character is being whipped around by a fire hose that's out of control—the two of you are scrambling to hold onto the end and point it in the right direction. Now it's time for you to learn how to move together and point the hose at the fire."

 Frequently Asked Questions

How do I deal with dependencies between tasks in my project plan?

The same way that you deal with them now—you talk to the team and try to figure out what they are.

This is a really common question for a project manager who's used to command-and-control, "big requirements up front" planning and to creating large Gantt charts at the start of the project. The idea of a self-organizing team, where each individual team member decides on his or her next task assignment just before starting work on it, sounds unrealistic. Often, this is because that project manager puts a lot of time and effort into identifying all of the dependencies between tasks. Project management textbooks—including ones that we've written!—have sections that explain the different types of dependencies (finish-start, start-start, etc.), and how to identify them and write them down when planning the project up front. So it's not unreasonable to ask where that dependency analysis fits into self-organizing teams.

Why do project managers need those dependencies at the beginning of the project? Because they need to define the project work, break it down into tasks, sequence those tasks, assign resources, and build out the project schedule. The only way to do that sequencing is to identify all of the dependencies between the individual tasks.

Say that a team member is working on a task in a large plan, and while he's working on it he discovers that it depends on another task. Uh-oh! Now the downstream tasks in the plan will all get pushed back because the task sequence didn't take that undiscovered dependency into account. This leads to cascading delays—one of the most common reasons project plans have to change. Even worse, if the team is working toward a fixed deadline, the project manager needs to make tough choices and have difficult conversations about cutting scope late in the project. No wonder project managers obsess about dependencies! This scenario of undiscovered dependencies throwing well-laid plans into chaos is common, which means that a seemingly complete dependency analysis can actually give a project manager a false sense of security about how much risk the team is taking on—and lead to delays that somehow always seem to come at the absolute worst moment. And the team also has that false sense of security, so they don't spend a lot of time thinking about dependencies once the project plan has been reviewed and distributed to the team.

Self-organizing teams also discover dependencies, but they do a much better job of it. The difference is that *they deal with dependencies at the last responsible moment*, when they have much better information about the tasks and can perform a more complete analysis.

This all sounds good in theory, but can it really work on a real project?
Think about the example from the previous chapter of the ineffective Daily Scrum run by a command-and-control project manager who assigns each team member's tasks every day. The project manager needs to know all of the task dependencies going into the meeting in order to make the task assignments. Compare that with the team that's truly self-organizing. When one team member assigns himself or herself a task, the entire team is watching and actively looking for dependencies during the meeting—as well as all of the previous and subsequent meetings. This is one of the reasons for the third Daily Scrum question each team member answers about roadblocks. Every one of those roadblocks is a dependency that the team is trying to discover, and every single team member spends time each day looking for those dependencies—so they discover those dependencies, and as a result prevent many of the cascading delays that command-and-control projects run into.

Why does this work? When a command-and-control project manager does the dependency analysis for a project during its planning phase, one of his most important tools is expert judgment. That's PM-speak for talking to the team and relying on their expertise to help flush out those dependencies. When a self-organizing team puts their whole plan under inspection during the Daily Scrum every day, they're using the same expert judgment, but now they have much better information because they do it together as a team every day. Doing that planning while the project is going on gives them much more visibility so they can make better decisions. The self-organizing team is much more likely to find a critical dependency because they're looking for it *during* the project, as opposed to the command-and-control team who have much less visibility and poorer information because they're doing that analysis weeks or months before the work begins. The higher visibility and better quality of just-in-time dependency analysis is an important source of productivity for effective Scrum teams.

I'm a little uncomfortable with this "last responsible moment" idea. Isn't it better to plan up front, even if that plan has to change?

Project managers often like to quote U.S. president and general Dwight D. Eisenhower, who said, "In preparing for battle I have always found that plans are useless, but planning is indispensable." Sitting down with the team and planning out your project gets everyone thinking about the details of the work the team will do and the specific problems that they'll have to work through to get the job done. Even if the estimates that the project manager and the team come up with aren't perfect, after a good planning session the team knows a lot more about the project, and everyone is better prepared for it. And when changes happen, the team can catch them—and learn from them, so in the future they can avoid whatever caused the planning problem. So why wouldn't you want to do all of the planning up front and get those benefits, especially if it's OK to change the plan when it needs to be changed?

A team that does its planning at the last responsible moment gets all of those benefits, and a lot more. It's not that the team doesn't do any planning up front. In fact, the opposite is true. The difference is that you save the up-front planning for the big things: the items in the product backlog. The product backlog contains items (often user stories) that the Product Owner and other non-technical people in the company can understand. Before the first sprint starts, the team and the Product Owner need to sit down and agree on the sprint backlog, which requires them to have a larger product backlog with story point estimates, so they have to have built that product backlog already. That's actually a lot of planning that the team does up front!

Can you give a real-world example of how Scrum sprint planning works?

Sure, here's an example that we've seen in real life. Let's say you're on a traditional project team that's working on a project with several new features, and also some performance tweaks. If you're planning this project, which would you have the team do first? Most teams will typically end up doing the new feature development first, leaving the performance tweaking until the end of the project. If you're a developer, there's a good chance that you'll find the new feature development much more interesting—tracking down and fixing performance problems can sometimes be a difficult and frustrating job, so it's not surprising that this kind of work often finds its way to the tail end of the plan.

But what if the users are really aware of the performance problems? What if those problems are getting in the way of those users doing their jobs, and faster software would make their lives much better than software with new features? Then the team *should* make the performance tweaks their top priority. In this case, a Product Owner that already spends time each week talking to the team about which features in the backlog are more valuable has a much better chance of ending up with those performance improvements getting done first.

Remind me again—what does this have to do with making decisions at the last responsible moment?

If the team does all of the planning up front, then they'll only prioritize the performance tweaks ahead of the new features if they happen to know from day one that it's a priority for the users. If the Product Owner hasn't made a habit of constantly talking to the team about what's valuable to users, and the team members haven't made a habit of listening to that, what's likely to happen if the Product Owner comes to them partway through the project with feedback that the users really need those performance tweaks done first? The project manager and the team are likely to push back, because that will be a large change that throws the whole plan into disarray. They'll also probably complain in private that the businesspeople they work with are always changing their minds, and will wish for a project where things don't change as much.

For a team like this, changes will still get done. But handling those changes is a lot more work for them, and tends to shake up the project. The reality is that almost every group of users has to deal with problems that constantly change over time— that's a fact of business, and a fact of life. It's unrealistic for a team to think that changes are out of the ordinary. This is why agile teams like to use the phrase, "*embrace change.*"

An inflexible "planning up front" attitude causes project changes to turn into a negotiation between the team and the Product Owner—and we already know that agile teams value customer collaboration over contract negotiation. In a negotiation, someone wins, someone loses, and everyone compromises. This is not an efficient way to run a project, and it leads to a lot of lost productivity.

On the other hand, when the team has a customer collaboration attitude, everyone works together, and everyone wins—there are no losers, because everyone naturally accepts the constraints that they have to work around together. Planning at the last responsible moment encourages this attitude because it helps the team avoid setting arbitrary constraints that they have to negotiate around later. This allows the team stay open to changes, and makes it possible (maybe not always easy, but possible) for them to reorder their work on the fly in order to meet changing goals (as opposed to planning the work and working the plan). And it makes it easier for the Product Owner to constantly engage the team about those goals.

Things You Can Do Today

Here are a few things that you can try today on your own or with your team:

- If you're working with a team that's already holding daily standup meetings, ask everyone to answer the three questions that are asked in a Daily Scrum.
- If you're working with a team that isn't already holding daily standup meetings, see if you can start holding one.
- Talk to your team about the last responsible moment. Write down a list of decisions that you and your team have made that you'll probably have to revisit because they were made too early.
- Talk to your team about items that might appear on a product backlog. What work do you know about that you aren't doing yet? Can you write down a list of those items?

Where You Can Learn More

Here are resources to help you learn more about the ideas in this chapter:

- You can learn more about self-organizing teams and how to manage projects in Scrum in *Agile Project Management with Scrum*, by Ken Schwaber (Microsoft Press, 2004).
- You can learn more about planning a Scrum project in *Agile Estimating and Planning*, by Mike Cohn (Addison-Wesley, 2005).
- You can learn more about the rules of Scrum from *The Scrum Guide* (Sutherland and Schwaber, 2011), which you can download from Scrum.org.

Coaching Tips

Tips for agile coaches helping their team to work with the ideas in this chapter:

- One of the most difficult parts of adopting Scrum is finding the Product Owner. If you're working with a team that wants to adopt Scrum, help them find the person who has the authority—and willingness—to make decisions on behalf of the business.

- Many agile coaches find that their Scrum teams run into problems because they've simply selected a Product Owner from within the team. Help them understand that the Product Owner needs to have the authority to accept features on behalf of the business.

- Is the team having a daily meeting that they call the Daily Scrum, but which is really just a status meeting that's held every day? This is an opportunity to help the team learn about the difference between command-and-control and self-organization.

- Help your Scrum Master to understand that she isn't responsible for telling every team member what to do every day, or tracking whether or not they've done it. Help the team to understand that the role of the Scrum Master is to ensure that they follow the rules of Scrum, and to knock down any impediments that are preventing them from doing so.

CHAPTER 5

Scrum Planning and Collective Commitment

Each developer must feel comfortable committing to the work she's signed up for. And since the team has a "we're all in this together" attitude, everyone needs to be comfortable with the overall commitment of the team.

—Mike Cohn[1]

You've learned the mechanics of Scrum, and how to use the basic Scrum pattern to get your team working together. But there's a big difference between Scrum theory and getting teams to actually build software on a live project. How do you set up your Scrum team to succeed? How do you get everyone to strive for the same goals? In other words, now that you understand what Scrum is all about—self-organization and collective commitment—how do you actually get your team to do it in real life?

In this chapter, you'll learn about the practices that many Scrum teams use for planning their sprints. You'll see how user stories can help you really understand exactly what your users need from the software, and you'll use story points and project velocity to get a good handle on how much work your team can do in a sprint. And you'll learn how to use two valuable visualization tools, burndown charts and task boards, to keep everyone on the same page.

You'll also learn why these practices and the basic pattern for a Scrum project aren't enough for your team to achieve "hyper-productivity" or "astonishing results." We'll revisit the Scrum values, and you'll learn how to assess if your team and company culture match those values—and what to do if they don't.

---

1 Mike Cohn, *User Stories Applied: For Agile Software Development* (Upper Saddle River, NJ: Pearson Education, 2004).

Figure 5-1. Product owners often find it challenging to get into their users' heads.

Narrative: a team working on a mobile phone app at a small company

Roger – team lead trying to go agile

Avi – the Product Owner

Eric – a Scrum Master on another team

Act V: Not Quite Expecting the Unexpected

The next day, the whole team met to talk about how they could start moving in unison and give the project a little more predictability. They talked about collective commitment, and what that really meant. Eric asked for a few of the team members to talk about times where they saw their software actually being used by a lot of people.

There was a lot of head nodding and smiling in the discussion—everyone seemed to get that they liked their jobs best when the software they built was used. Then he asked about a time when they found out that nobody was using the software. It turned out that the previous year, the team had spent four months building a user tracking and account management system, only to have a senior VP decide at the last minute that they'd just license a system to do that for them. Two people quit after that, and everyone felt awful. One of the lead developers who had worked a lot of overtime for that project seemed skeptical. "What's keeping that from happening again?"

Roger connected the dots for him: "We're happy when people use the software we build, and we hate it when we work on something that gets thrown out. So we just need a way to make sure that we're only building software that people will actually use."

From there, it was easy to get the team on board. Roger explained how sprint planning worked, and how Avi would work with them and their users so that only the most valuable things ended up in the sprint backlog. By the end of the meeting, Avi, Roger, and Eric all felt that almost everyone on the team was really starting to understand the idea of collective commitment, and genuinely wanted to build software that their users valued.

After the meeting, Eric, Roger, and Avi sat down to take stock. Roger and Avi started to congratulate each other on finally getting the team thinking together. And again, they were quite surprised by Eric's reaction. Rather than being optimistic, Eric looked concerned.

He said, "OK, you've got the team on board with sprint planning, and that's great. But that doesn't solve your bigger problem: how do you get the right features into the sprint backlog? Because if you don't get the most valuable things in there, you'll end up exactly where you are today—with users complaining about missing important things and being overwhelmed by things they didn't remember asking for."

Roger and Avi were skeptical, but that skepticism dissolved after their next sprint review with their users. Avi proudly brought up the latest version of Lolleaderz.com on their test server, and started to go through the new "Create an achievement" feature they'd been working on, where users could set up criteria for their friends to earn "achievements" by uploading specific videos. He set up an achievement he called "Got your goat!" by navigating through the new achievement editor: dragging the "goat" keyword out of a list, using the new toolbox widget to specify that it would be awarded after 500 page views, and decorating it with a pop-up animation using the graphics upload feature they built for it. At the end of the demo, the room was silent.

"Um, that looks like it was a lot of work," said one account manager. "So, uh, why did you build it?"

This was not what they wanted to hear at all! It turned out that all they needed was a simple feature to nominate your friends' videos to get a little star next to it. Somehow, the team had taken that simple request and turned it into a full-featured achievement criteria editor, complete with its own pseudo-scripting language and service infrastructure—and none of the account managers had any idea how to sell it to their customers. This a huge waste of the team's effort, but more importantly, now there were a bunch of new features in their backlog that were needed but not built.

This wasn't how it was supposed to go!

After the meeting, Roger and Avi went back to Eric, who was not at all surprised by the outcome. "So how do we fix this?" asked Roger.

Avi said that he was already trying his best to give the other account managers what they wanted. He'd been maintaining the backlog, organizing it by value, and bringing it to the team. How could he do any better? Roger didn't even know where to start, but he did know that if they didn't make any changes, they would keep getting the same results. Except this time, they'd given the team a huge pep talk and gotten them fired up about Scrum, and now they had a big disappointment for everyone. If they didn't make some sort of change fast, he felt that they might lose the team for good.

Eric said, "The trick here is to start to get into your users' heads. You need to know how they'll use the software. And even more importantly, you'll need a way to know at the end of the sprint whether or not you've built that software right. If you do that, your software will always be used, and your users will love it."

Roger was skeptical, because he knew from experience that users rarely seem to know what they want until they see it. And Avi was starting to get that "drew the short straw" feeling about his Product Owner role again.

Avi asked, "How do we get into their heads?"

User Stories, Velocity, and Generally Accepted Scrum Practices

Users and stakeholders hate unpredictability. Even if your team has genuinely made a collective commitment to build the most valuable software they can build for their users and stakeholders, if the working software that they deliver at the end of a sprint doesn't resemble the promise they made at the beginning, the users will be disappointed. In other words, it's not enough to deliver the most valuable software the team can build. You also need to make sure that there are no surprises when the people you're building the software for get their hands on it.

Avoiding those surprises—and pleasant surprises can be almost as damaging as unpleasant ones, if they set the future expectation that your team will always go above and beyond what they can normally deliver—generally boils down to two things.

First, the team needs to do a good job of setting expectations at the beginning of the sprint. And second, as the sprint progresses, they have to keep everyone up to date on all of the changes they discover during their Daily Scrum meetings. This is why it's valuable (but not required) to have users and stakeholders present in the Daily Scrum—but also why it's very important that they are only there to observe, and not to interfere. The Daily Scrum is the team's time to plan the next day's work, not answer questions from people who aren't on the team. Not all stakeholders will be able to attend the Daily Scrum; in some cases, none of them will. That's OK. It's great when stakeholders can make the time to attend, but it's not required. As long as the Product Owner is dedicated to keeping stakeholders in the loop about any changes the team makes to the plan, everyone will be on the same page when the end of the sprint rolls around.

But none of that matters if the team builds software that isn't useful.

Make Your Software Useful

Take one more look at that quote from Ken Schwaber at the beginning of Chapter 4. If you don't get collective commitment, you don't get Scrum. But what does that term, "collective commitment," really mean? What, as a team, are you committing to together?

Collective commitment means *genuinely trying to make your software more useful*. To make your software useful, you need to understand what it is that your users are doing. You have to truly care about helping them do whatever it is that they do—and you need to care about improving that aspect of their lives more than you care about any other aspect of the project.

This is built right into the Agile Manifesto. Think about what it means to build "working software"—how do we actually define "working"? It's trivial to make software that simply runs. It's not hard to build software that looks like it "works" but which drives the users crazy when they actually attempt to do their jobs with it. But building actual "working" software means building software that really helps the users get their work done. And the most effective way that we have of building working software is customer collaboration. This is another reason that we value working software over comprehensive documentation, and customer collaboration over contract negotiation.

Before agile changed the world of software development, teams routinely built software that was not useful, and we have plenty of evidence of this. Open up practically any academic textbook on software engineering written in the late 1990s or early 2000s, and you're likely to find a reference to the Standish Group's CHAOS report. The Standish Group started doing this report in the mid '90s in response to a perception—which happened to be true—that a huge number of projects failed (around a third of them were considered successful, as it turned out[2]). Their annual survey and study repeatedly found that project teams felt that many features in the software they built were not used. The 2002 study[3] put this figure at an absurdly high 64% (45% never used, 19% rarely used).

This may have been a shock to many in the academic community, but to a lot of software teams at the time, it was obvious. In fact, what the CHAOS report defined as "failure" was so common that many teams considered it a basic fact of software development. Teams would build software, throw it over the wall to their users, and hopefully some of what they built would stick. Many discussions (arguments) with users ended with a developer saying, "It's not a bug, it's a feature." This was a way for the developer to say that the software works exactly the way he intended it to work, and that the user needs to change his expectations to match it. This is a lousy way to treat users.

Roger and Avi ran into trouble with their achievement editor because they built a complex, over-engineered tool to solve a simple problem. This is a very common way for teams to build software that isn't as valuable as it could be. In fact, it's so common that there's a term for it: **gold-plating**. Teams gold-plate their software, or add extra features that were never requested and aren't needed by the users, with the best of intentions. Developers want to help, and they think that what they're building is really cool and will be very valuable. This is a very natural thing for an excited developer to do, and it's one of the main sources of those 64% of features that go unused.

Another contributor to that high number of unused features is the throw-it-over-the-wall mentality itself, because users feel like they have a limited time to work with the development team and will sometimes try to fit in as many feature requests as possible within that time. That can lead to stakeholders actually requesting features that are of little value when they're delivered.

Effective agile teams, however, rarely have this experience. It's rare for any feature of the software they build to go unused, much less two-thirds of them—so much so that people on those teams often see the conclusions of the CHAOS report as incorrect. In fact, it's not uncommon to hear the CHAOS report results snarkily referred to as "debunked" by some agile evangelists. So what are effective agile teams doing that allows them to build such useful software?

---

2 J. Laurenz Eveleens and Chris Verhoef, "The Rise and Fall of the Chaos Report Figures," IEEE Software vol. 27, no. 1 (2010).

3 *2002 CHAOS Report*, The Standish Group International Inc., 2002.

User Stories Help Build Features Your Users Will Use

Agile teams start by getting into their users' heads, and they have a very effective tool for doing that. A **user story** is a deceptively simple tool. It's a quick and simple description of a specific way that a user will use the software. Most user stories are between one and four sentences long—most teams have a rule of thumb that a user story has to fit on the front of a 3×5 index card.

Many teams write their user stories in a specific, Mad Libs–style, fill-in-the-blanks format:

- As a *<type of user>*, I want to *<specific action I'm taking>* so that *<what I want to happen as a result>*.

Here's a user story that the Lolleaderz.com team might have used as a starting point for the achievement feature.

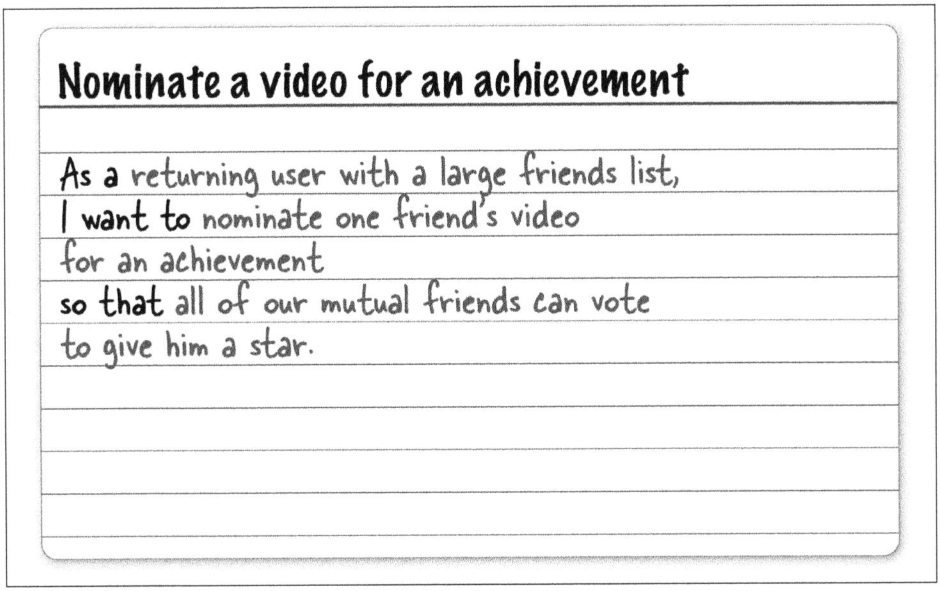

Figure 5-2. A user story written on an index card.

This user story is effective because it makes three important things obvious:

- Who the user is: "a returning user with a large friends list"
- What the user wants to do: "nominate one friend's video for an achievement"
- Why the user wants to do it: "so that all of our mutual friends can vote to give him a star"

It also has a title ("Nominate a video for an achievement"), which gives the team an easy way to refer to the user story when they're talking about it.

This is a lot of information packed into the user story. It means that there are many things that have to be built: user interfaces for nominating and voting, a way to store nominations and votes, an update to the system that displays the video to look for achievements and display a star, and probably several other things.

What's just as important is what isn't there. There's nothing about any sort of criteria editor (like the team added unnecessarily), or other unnecessary features. This is why a user story is an effective tool for fighting gold-plating. What happens if the team writes down user stories, goes over them with the Product Owner (and users, stakeholders, and anyone else who has a good opinion to share), and sticks to them? If they do this, they're a lot less likely to bloat the software with features that the users don't need and won't use.

User stories also give teams an easy way to manage their backlog. Many effective agile teams maintain a backlog that consists almost entirely of user stories. Because each user story is simple and written from the user's perspective, it's easy for the Product Owner to review the stories with the users and stakeholders in order to figure out which stories are the most valuable. And each story is very small, which makes it easier to add new ones or change their order at any time. When it comes time to start a sprint, the Product Owner and the team can pull some of the stories out of the backlog and designate them as to be delivered in this sprint.

The team can then discuss the stories with the Product Owner to make sure there is clarity on what the stories mean, and how they will know when each one is done. Most teams will then break the stories down into tasks and start to estimate how long those tasks will take. The tasks for each story would go in the "To Do" column of the task board to wait until someone can work on them. When a team member is ready to take a new task, he or she will select the next most valuable task they could do, write their name on it, and move it to the "In Progress" column to indicate that they are taking the task.

Conditions of Satisfaction

One way to be sure of what you're building is to be able to envision what it will look like when it's done. It's very satisfying for a developer to take a step back, look at what he or she just built, and feel like it's finished. **Conditions of satisfaction** are an effective tool for helping developers to know what the software will look like when it's complete, and to gauge how close they are to done. (Some teams refer to conditions of satisfaction as "acceptance criteria.")

Conditions of satisfaction, like user stories, seem really simple but accomplish a complex goal. Most teams define them for each user story by writing down some specific things that the user needs to be able to do with the software once the user story is written. Typically, the conditions of satisfaction can fit on the back of the same 3×5 index card as the user story. The Product Owner usually has a hand in writing the conditions of satisfaction or at least reviews them when they're written.

Conditions of satisfaction for the "achievements" user story might look like this:

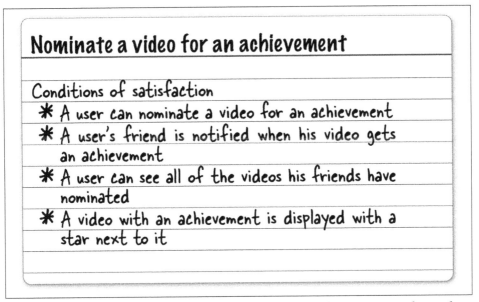

Figure 5-3. Conditions of satisfaction written on the back of the user story index card.

These conditions are valuable to developers because it helps them avoid declaring victory too early. It's not uncommon for a programmer to build many of the pieces of a feature, but put off the finishing touches until the end of the sprint. For example, he might build out the pages to do the nomination and modify the code that displays the video to add the star for achievements. But until he ties it all together so that every link is in place and all of the new code is fully integrated into the existing codebase, the feature isn't done—and it's a lot more efficient for him to finish building the story now while it's fresh in his mind.

Conditions of satisfaction help this by giving the team a concrete definition of "Done." This gives the team and the Product Owner a concrete, unambiguous way to figure out exactly when that story is "Done." To call the story "Done," all of the work it takes to understand it, build it, test it, and deploy it must also be done. The user story is "Done" when a user can open up the working software, and execute each of the conditions in exactly the same way that it would be demonstrated in the sprint review. Until the team member can do this, the user story isn't done, and he stays focused on that user story (remember the Scrum value about everyone being focused on the work?) until it's done. And as soon as it's done, he moves it from the "To-Do" column of the task board to the "Done" column. Done!

Story Points and Velocity

During sprint planning, your whole team works together to figure out how much work they can do in the sprint, so that they can set a goal for the working software that will be delivered at the end. But how, exactly, does the team do that?

There are practically as many ways to estimate how much work a team can do in a sprint as there are teams. One technique that has proven especially effective for Scrum teams over the years is to use **story points**. Story points are a way to understand how much effort you'll need to build a specific user story by assigning a number of points to it. The team comes up with those points by comparing the current user story to other stories your team has built in the past.

While there's no hard-and-fast rule about how many points to assign to each story, some teams assign between 1 and 5 story points to any user story. (The 5 value is arbitrary—other teams will give stories between 1 and 10 points, or use another number, as long as they use a consistent rule from sprint to sprint. Still other teams use numbers from the Fibonacci sequence, or exponential numbers. You can pick any scheme that works, as long as everyone on the team is comfortable with it.) One 3-point story should require about as much work as another 3-point story. As your team assigns points to all of the stories they work on, they start to see how many points' worth of stories they can complete (or "burn") in a sprint. If your team completes on average, say, 25 points' worth of stories in a sprint, then their **project velocity** is 25 points per sprint.

Teams tend to work at a pretty constant velocity when measured across many sprints. So while it's hard to predict what your project velocity will be before you start working with a team, you can use the velocity from past sprints to help you plan for the next one.

Now, anyone who's had to manage their retirement account has read the disclaimer, "Past performance is not a guarantee of future returns." The same goes for story points. Even if your team burned 32 points last sprint and 29 the sprint before, there's no guarantee that they will burn around 30 this sprint—in a given sprint, people will misjudge certain stories, run into unexpected technical problems, go on vacation, quit, or have other life events that interfere with the project. But despite that, story points and project velocity are a surprisingly reliable guide for most Scrum teams over time, and you can take advantage of that reliability when you plan your sprint.

A sprint planning session using story points might go like this:

1. Start with the most valuable user stories from the product backlog.

2. Take a story in that list—ideally the smallest one, because that makes a good baseline for comparison—find a similarly sized story from a previous sprint, and assign it the same number of points.

3. Discuss with the team whether that estimate is accurate—discovering additional problems, work, or technical challenges increases the estimate; simplifying factors, reusing existing code, or scaling back what needs to be built decreases the estimate.

4. Keep going through the stories until you've accumulated enough points to fill the sprint.

Don't overload your sprint backlog. It's OK to leave room in the backlog, but it's not OK to go beyond what your team has done in the past. If your team has an average velocity of 28 points per sprint, and you've already put 26 points' worth of stories into it, then you can only add a 2-point story or two 1-point stories. Because developers are very optimistic by nature—we have to be, because we're builders—the team will be tempted to add a 3-point story and just go over by one point. Don't give in to that temptation; it's a good way to disappoint your users at the next sprint review.

What about the first time you do this? It takes time to build up a history of stories, and to build up the common knowledge among your team about how big a 3-point story is. So for the first time through, just take a guess. Choose one story that seems to be about the middle of the road in terms of work, and arbitrarily assign it 3 points. Find the biggest story that's valuable, and assign it 5 points. Find the smallest one, and assign it 1 point. Use these as a starting point for estimating more stories and filling up your sprint. By the time you've gone through two sprints, you'll have plenty of stories to compare to, and a good idea of your team's average velocity.

Why story points work

Like user stories, story points are deceptively simple. They're very easy for teams to start using (although there are plenty of nuances to using them—which we won't cover here). But why are they so effective?

They're simple
> It's easy to explain to a new team member how story points work. Plus, the numbers tend to be low—in the dozens or hundreds, not thousands—which makes it easier for team members to get their heads around them.

They're not magic
> A lot of developers and project managers have seen many estimates turn out to be wrong, and develop the mindset that software development simply can't be estimated accurately. By basing story points off of real, live experience from this particular team, there's no mystery about where the number comes from.

The team is in control of them

When the boss tells you that you need to meet a certain numeric goal or metric, it feels like an imposition and adds to the pressure and stress on the team. But when the team decides themselves how to measure their own work, and *only uses that measurement for their own planning*, it becomes a valuable tool for them.

They get your team talking about estimates

When a new developer joins his first Scrum team, it might be the first time in his career that he's actually talked openly about estimates, or even had his opinion asked. Estimation is a skill, and the only way to get better at it is to practice—which, in most cases, means talking about how much effort certain tasks will need.

Developers aren't scared of them

Too many developers have had the experience of making an off-the-cuff estimate for a project manager, only to have that somehow turn into a hard deadline on a project schedule. That never happens with story points, because they're never turned into hours or dates—the only date, the end of the sprint, is fixed, and the amount of work promised for that date can be modified during the Daily Scrum as part of the visibility-inspection-adaptation cycle.

They help the team discover exactly what a story means

If you think that we're looking at a 5-point story, and I think it's only a 2-point story, we're probably not disagreeing on how much work is involved—we're disagreeing on exactly what that story means. If we talk it out,[4] it might turn out that I thought that the story required us to build a simple command-line tool, while you thought it needed a graphical user interface. It's a good thing we figured that out during sprint planning, instead of suffering a nasty surprise halfway through when our 2-point story turned out to be a 5-pointer!

They help everyone on the team become genuinely committed

Story points and velocity give everyone an objective "waypoint" that they can agree on: we burned 26 points last sprint; we agreed that this story was worth 4 points. If you're a chicken, you tend to back off from contributing to this—only to discover later that everyone moved on without you. The day that you realize that you had information that could have helped the team estimate a story at 3 points rather than 1 is the day that you start to care about sprint planning and keeping the estimates realistic—and that's how you become genuinely committed.

---

4 Score another one for face-to-face communication over comprehensive documentation!

Burndown Charts

A **burndown chart** is a way for anyone to see, at a glance, how the sprint is actually progressing when compared with the team's past velocity. Here's how to build a burndown chart based on story points (this also works with other units of measurement, like hours, but we'll use story points):

1. Start with an empty line chart. The x-axis has dates, starting with the first day of the sprint and ending with the last day. The y-axis has story points, ranging from 0 to 20% more than the total number of points in the sprint backlog. Draw the first dot on the chart: the number of points in the sprint, at day 0. Draw a straight line (called the "guideline") from the first point to the end of the project—zero points left when the sprint is complete.

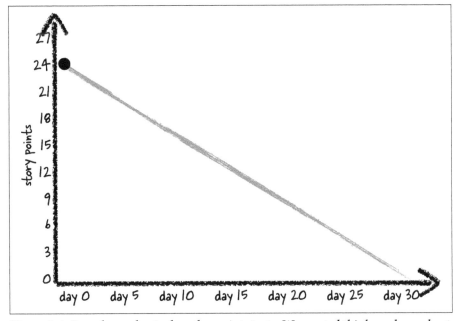

Figure 5-4. Burndown chart when the sprint starts. We created this burndown chart using story points, but you can also use hours, days, or another unit of measurement.

2. As soon as the first user story is finished and moved to the "Done" column of the task board, draw the next dot on the chart: the number of points left in the sprint, at the current day. As you finish more stories and burn more points off of the backlog, fill in more days in the burndown chart.

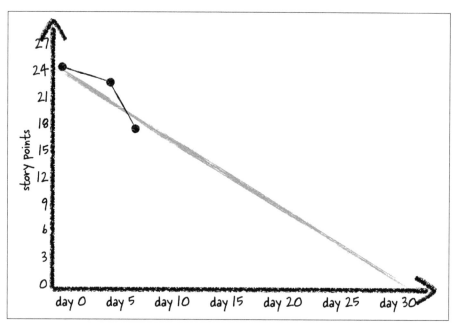

Figure 5-5. Two stories worth 7 points burned off

3. You might discover during a Daily Scrum that more work needs to be added. Sometimes you'll do this because the team is burning more points than they expected, and they'll finish early as a result. Or an important support task comes in, and the team and product owner agree that it needs to be added to the sprint, but they don't yet know how much work the team will need to remove to balance out the sprint. When you add the cards for that work to the task board, schedule a follow-up meeting to gather up the team, estimate the story points for each card, and add them to the chart. It's helpful to draw an extra line that shows where the points were added—and don't be afraid to write notes on the chart!

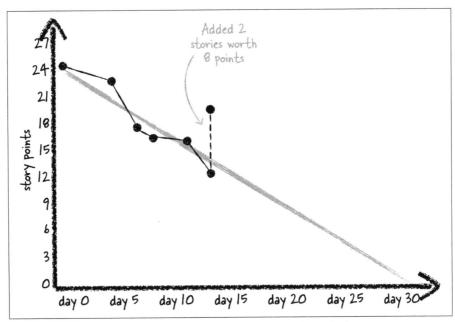

Figure 5-6. The Product Owner added stories halfway through the sprint.

4. As you get close to the end of the sprint, more and more points burn off the chart. Keep an eye out for a gap between the guideline and your actual burn-down, because that could mean you've got too many points left in the sprint and need to remove a user story.

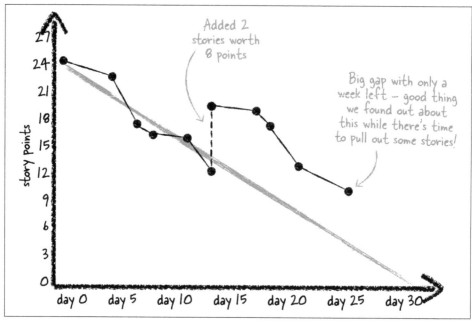

Figure 5-7. A gap between the burndown chart and the guideline tells you that there's a good chance you won't finish all of the stories by the end of the sprint.

There are lots of great software packages that let you manage your backlog, stories, and story points, and draw burndown charts automatically. However, many teams prefer to draw burndown charts by hand, and keep the chart on the same wall (often on the same whiteboard) as the task board. This lets everyone see exactly how the project is doing at any time. It's especially satisfying for the team if each developer gets to update the burndown chart after he or she completes a user story and moves the card to the "Done" column.

Planning and Running a Sprint Using Stories, Points, Tasks, and a Task Board

If you read the description of sprint planning in the Scrum Guide (*http://scrum.org*) (or in the beginning of Chapter 4), you'll see that you need to have a sprint planning meeting to come up with detailed answers to two questions:

- What will the team deliver in this sprint?
- How will the team do the work?

We just showed you how a team can use story points and velocity to figure out what will go into the sprint. That's a very common way for Scrum teams to handle the first half of sprint planning. But how do they actually plan out the work in the second half?

One of the most common ways for Scrum teams to plan out the actual work for the team is to add cards for individual development tasks. These tasks can be anything that the team actually does: write code, create design and architecture, build tests, install operating systems, design and build databases, deploy software to production servers, run usability tests, and do all of those other things that teams actually do every day to build and release software.

Here's how many teams do this:

1. The team holds the second sprint planning meeting. The Scrum Master starts with the first story, and leads a discussion with the team about exactly what they need to do to build it. Everyone works together to come up with a list of individual tasks that they think will each take no more than a day to complete. Each task is written on a separate card—some teams use different colored cards for stories and their tasks to make it easier to tell them apart—and the story card is grouped together with its task cards. This continues until all stories are planned. If the sprint planning timebox expires before all of the stories are broken down, each unplanned story gets a single task card for a task to plan out the story.

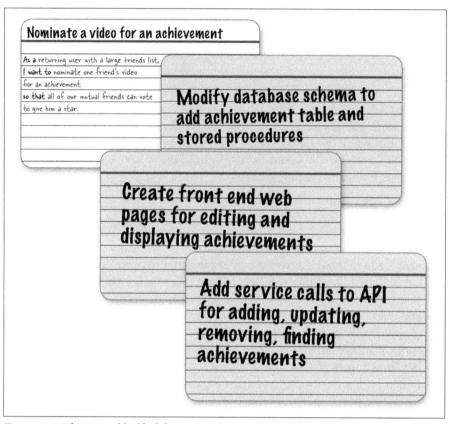

Figure 5-8. The second half of the sprint planning session is all about breaking the stories down into tasks that the team members will do during the sprint.

2. The stories and their tasks are grouped together and added to the "To Do" column of the task board.

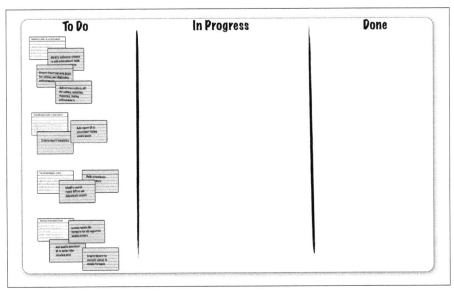

Figure 5-9. Each story card in a sprint is grouped together with the cards for its tasks and added to the "To Do" section of the task board.

3. When a team member finishes one task and is ready to move on to the next, he moves the task card for the completed work to the "Done" column. Then he pulls the task card for the next piece of work out of the "To Do" column, writes his name on it, and then puts it back on the board in the "In Progress" column. If the story is still in the "To Do" column, he moves it to "In Progress" as well (but doesn't write his name on it because one of his teammates might work on tasks for the same story).

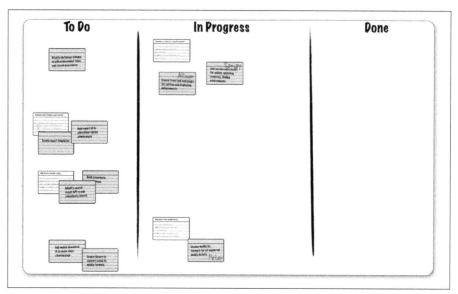

Figure 5-10. Each team member works on exactly one task at a time by writing his or her name on its card and moving it to the "In Progress" section of the task board.

4. As the sprint rolls along, the team moves tasks from "To Do" to "In Progress" to the "Done" column. It's pretty common for team members to discover that they need to do additional tasks to finish a story. When this happens, the new task is added to the board, and the team member points that out in the Daily Scrum so everyone is aware of what's going on, and can help spot potential problems.

5. Once a team member finishes the final task for a story, he pulls the story card off of the task board, verifies that all of the conditions of satisfaction are completed, and moves it to the "Done" column so that it's grouped with all of its tasks. (But remember—the story's not *done* done until the Product Owner accepts it as potentially shippable on behalf of the company!) If he discovers that one of the conditions of satisfaction hasn't been met, then there's still work to be done—so he moves the story back to the "In Progress" column and adds tasks to complete that work to the "To Do" column.

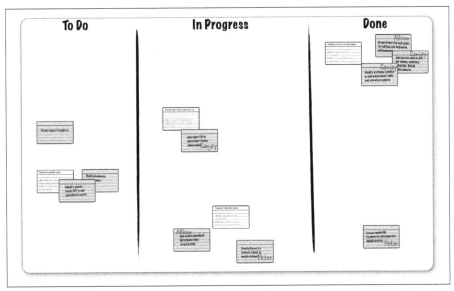

Figure 5-11. When a team member finishes a task, he or she moves it to the "Done" section of the task board and claims another task—and if all of the story's conditions of satisfaction are met, the story card is moved to the "Done" section too.

6. The sprint is done when the timebox expires. This means that there might still be story and task cards left in the "To Do" and "In Progress" columns. The stories go back to the product backlog so they can be prioritized in the next sprint planning session,[5] but the team can reduce the number of points based on the tasks that remain. The team does not get credit for completing a story until its card and all of its task cards are moved to the "Done" column.

Generally Accepted Scrum Practices

If you search Ken Schwaber's original book on Scrum, *Agile Project Management with Scrum,* you won't find any mention of user stories or story points. Many teams learned about them from other sources, like Mike Cohn's excellent book, *User Stories Applied.*[6]

---

5 There's actually some debate among Scrum trainers about moving incomplete work back into the product backlog and re-estimating the point value. There are some trainers who believe that is OK, while others teach that you should never change it (because this helps the team to get better at estimation). There are also some who feel it doesn't really matter either way, because it will all wash out in the end.

6 Mike Cohn, *User Stories Applied: For Agile Software Development* (Upper Saddle River, NJ: Pearson Education, 2004).

There are many great practices that teams use to improve how they use Scrum. This shouldn't be a surprise. The whole reason we have retrospectives is to find ways to improve what we're doing. If we decide that we're bound to what one person wrote in a book, and refuse to go beyond what's written in it, why bother finding ways to improve?

This is why many teams make use of additional tools and techniques, which Cohn termed **Generally Accepted Scrum Practices** (GASPs).[7] For example, many teams find that their Daily Scrum meetings are more effective when held as a standup meeting, where everyone stands until the meeting is complete. This is not a core Scrum practice, but it's accepted by many Scrum teams.

Remind yourself of the last principle in the Agile manifesto:

> At regular intervals, the team reflects on how to become more effective, then tunes and adjusts its behavior accordingly.

You and your team should keep this in mind when you hold your retrospectives. Try to find ways to improve, but don't reinvent the wheel. If you're running into a problem with Scrum, the odds are that someone else also ran into it at some point. If you have a good mentor (like Roger and Avi have Eric), he or she should be able to help you find a change or a practice that will help fix the problem.

 Key Points

- A user story helps the team understand their users by clearly explaining a specific need, and how the software will meet that need.

- Each user story has *conditions of satisfaction* to help the team know when the story is done.

- Teams use *story points and velocity* to estimate how many stories they can include in each sprint.

- Posting a **burndown chart** clearly where everyone can see it can help everyone on the team understand what's completed, what's left to build, and whether or not they're on track.

---

7 From "GASPing About the Product Backlog" (*http://bit.ly/GASPing*), accessed July 26, 2014.

Narrative: a team working on a mobile phone app at a small company

Roger – team lead trying to go agile

Avi – the Product Owner

Eric – a Scrum Master on another team

Act VI: Victory Lap

It was 11:30 p.m., and everyone was still at the office—but not for work. The team had just taken Lolleaderz.com live earlier that week, and there were already great reviews and a growing number of users. The CEO had caught wind of a little release party that Roger and Avi were planning, and he would have none of it. He brought in catering, a DJ, and an open bar. And Roger and Avi had had quite a bit to drink already.

Roger stumbled over to Eric, who was chatting with a few of the team members. "We couldn't have done this without you!"

Eric thought for a minute, and said, "That's really nice of you to say that. But think about what I did for you. I didn't actually do any of the work, right? I just pointed out some of the problems, gave you solutions that worked for me, and once in a while I let you run into some of those problems so you could see for yourself what was wrong."

Avi had come over. "Yeah, what about that? There were a couple of rough spots we got into. Why couldn't we avoid them? Not that I'm complaining—the results speak for themselves."

By now, most of the team and a few account managers had gathered around. Eric said, "If you hadn't had that terrible meeting with the other account managers, would you ever have gone ahead and put together the user stories? Would you know your project velocity, and be able to plan out your sprints?"

Roger thought for a minute. "So wait a minute. You're saying that the only way to learn is to run into trouble?"

Eric said, "I'd flip it around and think positive. The rough patches you run into give you a reason to work together and think about how to be more effective. You find a way to improve, you grow as a team."

There was a lot of head nodding, and a few "mm-hmms" from around the room. Finally, a voice came from the back. "That's what I want to hear!"

It was the CEO, and he looked pleased. "I see some really big things for this team in the future. Great work!"

Scrum Values Revisited

Roger, Avi, and the team ran into a lot of problems during the Lolleaderz.com project. For a lot of teams, those kinds of problems would have sunk the whole project and caused a CHAOS report-style failure. How did this team turn those problems into opportunities? How were they able to learn from them and succeed?

One big difference was that Roger and Avi had a secret weapon: an effective mentor, Eric, who could help them steer through the obstacles. The first thing that Eric did was to help Roger, Avi, and the rest of the team understand the Scrum values: commitment, respect, focus, openness, and courage. He talked about pigs and chickens, to help them understand what commitment really means. He helped them understand how to run a more effective Daily Scrum, and through that he was able to make sure they were focused. And he showed them that they could build up mutual respect by listening to each other. By improving how they plan and review their sprints and backlog using tools like user stories and velocity, Eric helped the team show everyone—including the other account managers and the CEO—what was going on with the project, which built up an attitude of openness across the team. And when the going got tough, Eric showed them that they had the courage to stick to the truth, even if it made people unhappy in the short run.

Every project has challenges and problems. When you're trying out a new methodology or practice for the first time, those problems can get magnified through lack of experience, misunderstanding, and regular old mistakes. A good mentor like Eric knows this. Instead of trying to prevent those mistakes, he took advantage of them to create learning experiences for the team. This is called *letting the team fail*, and it's a basic element of coaching.

Lyssa Adkins talks about this in *Coaching Agile Teams*:

> Let the team fail: Certainly, don't stand idly by while the team goes careening off a cliff. But do use the dozens of opportunities that arise each sprint to let them fail. Teams that fail together and recover together are much stronger and faster than ones that are protected. And the team may surprise you. The thing you thought was going to harm them may actually work for them. Watch and wait.[8]

---

8 Lyssa Adkins, *Coaching Agile Teams: A Companion for ScrumMasters, Agile Coaches, and Project Managers in Transition* (Boston: Addison-Wesley, 2010).

It's one thing to read words like courage, openness, commitment, focus, or respect, and agree that they sound like great ideas. It's quite another thing to walk into your boss's office and tell him that the team won't be able to deliver a feature because there's not enough time in the sprint. It's hard to have courage when your job is on the line.

You can't have a successful Scrum implementation without adhering to these values. And the truth is that while there are plenty of companies that have a culture that's compatible with Scrum, some companies do not. It's even possible that you work for a boss who demands a command-and-control style of project management, and will fire you if you try to create a self-organizing team.

Scrum teams learn from their mistakes—that's how they grow as a team. The team needs a culture where it's OK to make mistakes. That's why we collaborate so much as Scrum team members, and it's why respect is such an important Scrum value. But even if a team has a tolerance for mistakes and the ability to learn from them, they might be working in a company that doesn't accept mistakes. Software engineering innovator Grady Booch book, *Beautiful Teams*:

> One of the signs that I have for the health of an organization is that they're reticent to fail. Organizations that are totally anal and refuse to fail at all tend to be the least innovative organizations, and they're hardly any fun, because these people are so fearful of failing they take the most conservative actions. On the other hand, organizations that are freer in failing, not in a way that will destroy the business, but are given some freedom to fail, are the ones that are more productive, because they're not in fear for their life with every line of code.

So what do you do if you find yourself in an organization where failure means getting fired? Is Scrum even possible?

Practices Do Work Without the Values (Just Don't Call It Scrum)

Not every team in every company can self-organize from day one, and that's OK. If your company's culture doesn't match the Scrum values, then your job as a Scrum adopter is to help the people around you understand its values. The best way to do this is to lead by example: show everyone around you what it means to be open about your work, have respect for others on your team, and show courage when you run into problems. Finding a good mentor is a great way to show people that this can really work, and help people start to change their attitudes. Often, teams will bring in a consultant as a mentor because it's easier for their bosses to listen to someone from outside the company tell them that they need to make changes.

But sometimes, even if you do everything right, the prevailing culture of the company where you work might be too far away from the Scrum values. If that's the case, self-organization and collective commitment might simply be out of reach for your team.

And as Ken Schwaber showed us, if you don't get self-organization and collective commitment, you don't get Scrum.

And that's OK!

Even without the "heart and soul" of the values, and even without self-organization and collective commitment, Scrum still has some pretty great practices. They're very simple, easy to implement, and can generally be done inside the team without your asking permission (or apologizing later).

If you recognize that you're in an environment where you can put the practices in place but not the values, then you can still get better-than-not-doing-it results. And because it's better than not doing it, you should do it! Just make sure that you and your team recognize what you're doing, and where your boundaries are.

However, don't just adopt the practices and then call it a complete Scrum adoption. If you do, you'll set yourself up for a struggle later on. People in your company who have read about "hyper-productive teams" and "astonishing results" will question why you're not getting those results, and you won't have a good answer. Even worse, your team will probably get excited about Scrum, only to find that life has just changed slightly for them. In a sense, they'll get the message that this is the best that they can do, and if that's not much different than before, that can be frustrating and demotivating. These problems can poison future attempts to improve: by setting the bar too low, they assume that they're facing limitations outside their control.

In other words, by telling everyone, "You've done Scrum, congratulations!" you give the impression that Scrum is nothing more than renaming your status meeting to a Daily Scrum and your requirements to a backlog. That's dangerous for you, as an eager agile adopter, because the fundamental problems you were trying to solve in the first place by implementing Scrum still exist, so most people will assume that Scrum can't fix them—and, worse, that those are problems that exist everywhere and simply aren't fixable by humans. Think about how many times you've heard someone say something like, "Developers can't estimate," or "Software is always buggy," or "Projects always run late," as if those are basic facts of life that can't be changed.

The worst part is that when you constantly claim Scrum can solve problems that clearly haven't been solved and that people assume can't be solved, you start to come off as a pushy agile zealot. People will get sick of hearing about Scrum but not seeing any results. That hurts your career, and it ruins the idea of Scrum for all of the people around you.

There is another way!

Give your team new practices that they can do today, but also give them a vision of what they can accomplish tomorrow. Then they won't just assume that they're doing Scrum because they've adopted a few simple practices.

What if you openly acknowledge that you've put in place the Scrum practices, but you haven't started to work on self-organization or collective commitment *yet*? Instead of claiming that a "practices-only" Scrum implementation is complete, we can be honest with our teams that we're putting in place the practices, but that we still have a long way to go with the values, with self-organization, and with becoming genuinely committed to delivering value.

The first difference with that approach is that you haven't made any promises that you can't keep. You told people that you would make things a little better. So when they see better-than-not-doing-it results, instead of being disappointed that you haven't solved every problem the company will ever face, they're happy that your team is producing better software, and building it more quickly and easily. It's much easier to start talking about new values for the company if you have a track record of improvement, even small improvement. And from your boss's perspective, instead of criticizing him for not being "Scrum enough," you're giving him good results today and promising even better results tomorrow—if he'd just let the team go out on a limb with these new values.

Is Your Company's Culture Compatible with Scrum Values?

Not every company is ready to give up command-and-control project management and start self-organizing, and not every team is ready for collective commitment. The way to figure out if your team and company are ready is to evaluate whether the culture is compatible with the Scrum values. But how do the Scrum values translate into real-life practice?

Ask yourself each of these questions, and try to come up with honest answers. Discuss them with your team, and with your manager. If everyone is really OK with each of these things, then your company and team are ready for the Scrum values. If not, then those conversations will help you figure the right approach to bringing Scrum to your team.

To understand if you're ready for **commitment**, ask if you, your team, and your boss are OK with:

- Relinquishing control of the project, and trusting the team to decide what gets delivered?
- Not going off on your own and building something without talking to the rest of the team, and just integrating it at the end?

- Not having one "single, wringable neck?"[9]
- Listening to comments and feedback, and not telling people to mind their own business?
- Actually being *willing* to take responsibility? Does everyone on the team feel the same way?

To understand if you're ready for **respect**, ask if you, your team, and your boss are OK with:

- Trusting the team to do the right thing, and deliver each feature at the best possible date based on relative value and how the project progresses—even if it causes the project to take longer than you expect?
- Giving the team enough time to do the work, and not demanding overtime of them?
- Trusting the team to choose the tasks that are right for them and for the project, rather than relying on strict roles, RACI matrices, etc.?
- Not being able to ever say again that you don't know why the team decided to do something the way they did?

To understand if you're ready for **focus**, ask if you, your team, and your boss are OK with:

- Never asking anyone on the team to do work that's not part of the current sprint?
- Never asking anyone on your team to do work that the whole team hasn't agreed to take on ("but I need this done now!")?
- Putting what's most valuable to the company ahead of all other project or work concerns?
- Not being able to demand that team members work on specific tasks in a certain order up front?

To understand if you're ready for **openness**, ask if you, your team, and your boss are OK with:

- Listening to what other people have to say—and actually thinking about it?
- Thinking about project planning or users if you never have before?
- Thinking about technical details if you never have before?

---

9 Be a little careful with the phrase "single, wringable neck" because in many companies, that's the nickname for the Product Owner—the team may understand self-organization and collective commitment, but if the rest of the company doesn't, then as far as anyone outside of the team in concerned, that's his role.

- Thinking about what the programmer next to you is working on, and whether it really fits into the overall goal?
- The programmer next to you thinking about your work in exactly the same way?

To understand if you're ready for **courage**, ask if you, your team, and your boss are OK with:

- Not being able to blame lack of planning on your project manager?
- Not being able to blame poor requirements that don't hit the mark on your Product Owner or senior managers?
- Taking the time to really understand your users?
- Building something that isn't perfect, because what the users need most is something that's simply good enough?

If the answer to most of those questions is "yes," then your team, managers, and company probably have a culture that matches the Scrum values. On the other hand, if you've answered "no" to more than one or two bullets for any of the values, then that's a good starting point for a realistic and open discussion with your team and your boss. And if that open discussion sounds unrealistic, then you're definitely going to have to work on openness if you want to get the most out of Scrum.

 Frequently Asked Questions

Aren't backlogs and task boards basically the same thing as project schedules? Don't Scrum teams really just do the same thing that my team already does?

It's possible to use the tools and practices of Scrum in a way that's very similar to a traditional project. For example, some teams write user stories that are very similar to use cases. But a team that doesn't change the way they operate won't change their results—so teams that work this way don't make the shift in mindset necessary for Scrum, and as a result they don't get much of a gain in productivity (in other words, they get better-than-not-doing-it results).

One key difference between an effective Scrum team and many traditional project teams is that the Scrum team's plan doesn't then go on the shelf, only to be pulled out and get updated if the team goes off track. They inspect the plan for problems every day at the Daily Scrum meeting. But they do more than that. Many effective Scrum teams block out at least an hour every week to work with the Product Owner to update the backlog (some teams call it "grooming"). Product Owners discover new potential features all the time. During those weekly backlog sessions, the team works with the Product Owner to create new user story cards with conditions of satisfaction. They do their story point estimating to assign points to the new stories, and then work with the Product Owner to prioritize the new stories into the product backlog based on how valuable they are.

This gives the team two very powerful tools. One tool is that they get a lot of practice estimating work, so that when a change happens, they know exactly how to figure out its impact. They just go into "estimating mode" like they do every week.

The other tool this gives teams is the ability to constantly talk to the Product Owner about which stories are most valuable. If the team wants to have an effective conversation about this, they need to really understand the goals of the project. This is why elevating goals are so important: if the Product Owner has done a good job of keeping the team up to date on why their users need the software built, then it's much easier to figure out which stories in the product backlog are most valuable.

This all works because the team is used to constantly working with the Product Owner to understand the value of the each item in the backlog. And it works because the team members are constantly planning and estimating each of those backlog items. That way, when a change comes in, everyone on the team can jump into estimation mode, just like they do every week. And this is what planning at the last responsible moment really means: a team that's used to planning all the time, and that blocks out time to do that planning so it seems normal to them.

But don't programmers suck at planning—especially for software projects, which are inherently unpredictable?
This is probably the most common misconception about planning—or, worse, self-fulfilling prophecy. It's not that programmers don't suck at planning. The truth is that *everyone* sucks at planning, at least at first. If people were always great at planning, then businesses would always be successful, markets would always go up, and every marriage would last forever (after all, who plans for divorce on their wedding day?).

Planning is not the same as predicting the future. A lot of companies have teams and managers who believe in the myth of the perfect project plan, where developers can give perfectly accurate estimates, and project managers can always plan for every risk and add exactly enough contingency. Their plans change just as often as everyone else's do—probably more so, because they often put far too much detail into the plan at the very beginning, and the smaller details are much more likely to be wrong. No wonder their projects run into planning problems and we come away with the impression that programmers suck at planning, and that software projects are unpredictable!

Scrum teams plan more effectively because they plan from the top down. They lay out the broad strokes first, starting with a product backlog that contains just enough detail for the Product Owner and users to make decisions about what's most valuable. The team only starts detailed planning at the beginning of the sprint, and then only for those backlog items that they expect to include in the sprint. Most planning for day-to-day and hour-to-hour is left to the Daily Scrum. If some day-to-day or hour-to-hour planning needs to be done at the beginning of the sprint, the team will do it —but that's rare, so it doesn't need to take a lot of time, and the team can revisit those plans during the Daily Scrum.

Isn't it more effective to plan for everything up front, and then revisit that plan later?
Actually, it isn't. Many teams have found in practice that leaving decisions for the last responsible moment gives the team more flexibility, and helps them plan (or *not* plan) more effectively. This style of planning works well because it leaves the decisions to the people who are best equipped to make them, and doesn't require the decisions to be made until the time when they're best understood.

One important reason that so many large-scale plans fail is because planning at the lowest level from the start of the project is unrealistic, and requires developers to know information they simply don't have yet. This leads to the familiar CYA cycle where project managers blame the developers for poor estimates, and developers blame project managers for building poor plans. People get blamed, but nobody ends up facing real consequences—or everyone does, which means nobody is singled out. But in both cases, the real casualty is the quality of the software.

Scrum gives us freedom from the CYA cycle by only requiring planning at the level of detail that programmers have today, and allowing us to leave the details we don't know yet to the last responsible moment. We review, inspect, and adapt the plan every day, so that we can react quickly when (*not* if) the plan turns out to be wrong. In return, Scrum asks us all to be genuinely committed to delivering the most valuable software that we're capable of building.

Isn't it unrealistic to promise that you'll have working software to demonstrate at the end of each sprint? What if the team is working on something that can't really be demonstrated?
This is a good question that a lot of new Scrum teams ask. Some features, like new web application pages or additional buttons or changes in end-user behavior, are very easy to demonstrate. Just pull out the user story, fire up the software, and walk through each of the conditions of satisfaction. But some features are much more difficult to demonstrate. What do you do if the team spent a few weeks working on optimizing the database, or making service changes, or making other nonfunctional changes?

Every software change can be demonstrated somehow, and it's actually helpful for the programmers to find a way to do this. Let's say the sprint was focused on making database changes. The developers didn't just go into the database, make the change, and then move on without checking if the change worked—nobody actually programs that way! They wrote code to do some inserts, updates, changes, deletes, and whatever else they needed to do to make sure the database change worked correctly. And they probably also made changes to other parts of the codebase that used the database.

This is where the demo that the team gives to the Product Owner, users, and stakeholders during the sprint review can actually help them. It's pretty typical for developers to write throwaway code to check that the database changes worked. But if they know that they have a demo at the end of the sprint, they can take that opportunity to copy that throwaway code, paste it into a program (maybe a small console application, or maybe just a set of scripts that they check into their codebase), and spend a little extra time polishing it so that it can be demonstrated. This probably wouldn't take much extra time, but now they've got a way to test the change—which can come in handy later on if they need to make another change to the database, and now have some test scripts that they can reuse and build on.

The same approach is also very handy for other kinds of nonfunctional changes (meaning changes that don't necessarily change how users use the software, but which require changes to the code). A team that's working on performance changes can demonstrate before-and-after tests that show performance improvement. A team that made changes to the service architecture can demonstrate a simple program that shows the different kinds of data retrieved from the new service API. Every kind of change can be demonstrated somehow, and doing that demo leaves the team in better shape than otherwise. This is one of the ways that Scrum helps teams plan and improve.

When a team demonstrates nonfunctional changes, it generally consists of walking through the individual scripts, tests, programs, or other code that was written to test the change. The team needs to be careful to talk about their work in terms that the users understand—but it's often surprising how much more the users are capable of understanding than developers realize. But most importantly, this kind of demo gives the users and stakeholders an actual view into what the team has been building. Without the demo, from the outside it probably looked like the team had wasted a sprint not building anything. The demo helps the team show everyone why the software is taking as long as it is, and that's extremely valuable in helping the team set realistic deadlines in the future without getting pressure to shorten those deadlines from bosses who don't understand software.

When we have a bug in our production software, my team has to stop what they're doing and fix it, and I can't wait until the end of the sprint to do it. Isn't Scrum being unrealistic about support tasks?

All software teams deal with unexpected things that crop up all the time. Support is a great example of this. A team that works on a website may find a bug fix that needs to be pushed out to the users immediately, and has to scramble to get it done. If the fix can't wait until the end of the sprint, then the team only has one option—do it now.

An effective Scrum team is actually better at handling this than a team following a typical command-and-control, big requirements up front methodology. The reason is that the Scrum team already meets every day to look for changes and to adapt the plan to incorporate them. This team can handle the support issue just like any other issue or change that they run across. If it's one of those extreme situations where it absolutely can't wait until the next sprint, and the Product Owner agrees to this on behalf of the company, then they'll add it to the sprint backlog, prioritize it (probably at the very top), and use their planning tools—Daily Scrum, task board, burndown charts, user stories, story points, and velocity—to keep everyone in the loop and make sure that it gets done.

The big difference is that Scrum requires us to be honest with ourselves and our users about the impact that this change will have on the project. We can't pretend that adding this work comes without a cost. We'll see a bump up in the burndown chart, and it will be obvious to everyone that something else will need to come out of the sprint. Luckily, because Scrum teams are committed to delivering valuable software, users tend to trust them. And because the team has been demonstrating working software so frequently, the users have much more visibility into how the software is built, so they tend to be realistic about what can be done for a sprint.

It doesn't seem realistic to have a Product Owner who has all that authority to make decisions, all of those connections with customers and the company, and also so much free time to spend with the team every day. Doesn't that mean that Scrum can't possibly work?

Believe it or not, there are many effective Scrum teams across lots of different industries that work exactly like this. That's because their companies recognize that putting someone who has that much authority and seniority on a project team full-time gives them a huge advantage, and really cuts down on development work in the long run. Giving the team that lifeline to understanding the real value of the software they're building is the key to achieving those great results that so many Scrum teams report. Teams that talk about "astonishing results" are almost always at companies that placed enough value on their work to assign the right Product Owner to the team.

There's a real cost to this. Putting that great Product Owner on the team means that the company has to take him away from the work he's already doing—and, typically, the company still has to pay him the same amount of money. When a company trusts Scrum, their managers see that it delivers those results, in the form of a team that's able to stay in lockstep with the changing needs of the business. These managers will swallow the cost of assigning the Product Manager to that project if they recognize that it's worth that cost in the long run.

If that all seems very unrealistic in the company that you work for, then that's not as much a reflection on Scrum as it is a reflection on how much your company values the software that your team is building. Many companies explicitly tell their teams not to bother their important executives and businesspeople with day-to-day questions about the software that's being built. This is one of the most common ways that the Scrum values can clash with the values of the company.

This is also why so many companies choose a less effective, "big requirements up front" waterfall process. They're willing to make the teams put a lot more time, effort, and money into building out those documents so that they can reduce the amount of time that their businesspeople and executives spend talking to the teams. Working with a team every day is a lot of work; it takes much less work for an executive to read a document, make a few corrections, and then put up with software that isn't quite as good. And the company can often improve the situation by adding business analysts to make those documents better, and also adding extra quality engineers and testers to verify that the requirements were implemented. That's a lot of extra work to make up for not bothering an executive, but that's a fact of life in a lot of companies, and it's still possible to build good software that way (but then you're getting into CHAOS report territory, where the risk of creating features that aren't used goes up dramatically).

If the company values the software and the time of the team building it much less than it values the time and effort of the businesspeople, the cost-benefit analysis is pretty easy to do—and BRUF turns out to be a logical way to build software. If that's the kind of company you work for, then the way forward may be to help your managers and the rest of the company to understand the Scrum and agile values. And if that doesn't work, then at least you can start to put the Scrum practices in place and build a track record with better (but not astonishing) results.

I can see how sprint planning works once the team comes up with estimates, but I'm still not sure where those estimates come from. How do teams estimate tasks?

There are many different ways to estimate tasks. One of the most popular techniques that Scrum teams use is a technique called **planning poker**, another one of those generally accepted Scrum practices (GASPs).[10] It was invented by James Grenning, one of the people who created the Agile Manifesto, and made popular in Mike Cohn's book, *Agile Estimating and Planning*. Here's how it works:

> At the start of planning poker, each estimator is given a deck of cards. Each card has written on it one of the valid estimates. Each estimator may, for example, be given a deck of cards that reads 0, 1, 2, 3, 5, 8, 13, 20, 40, and 100. The cards should be prepared prior to the planning poker meeting, and the numbers should be large enough to see across a table. Cards can be saved and used for the next planning poker session.
>
> For each user story or theme to be estimated, a moderator reads the description. The moderator is usually the product owner or an analyst. However, the moderator can be anyone, as there is no special privilege associated with the role. The product owner answers any questions that the estimators have.
>
> After all questions are answered, each estimator privately selects a card representing his or her estimate. Cards are not shown until each estimator has made a selection. At that time, all cards are simultaneously turned over and shown so that all participants can see each estimate.
>
> It is very likely at this point that the estimates will differ significantly. This is actually good news. If estimates differ, the high and low estimators explain their estimates. It's

---

10 If you want to learn more about Planning Poker, we recommend reading the Planning Poker PDF (*http://bit.ly/plan-poker-pdf*) by its creator (and Agile Manifesto co-author) James Grenning.

important that this does not come across as attacking those estimators. Instead, you want to learn what they were thinking about.

It is very likely at this point that the estimates will differ significantly. This is actually good news. If estimates differ, the high and low estimators explain their estimates. It's important that this does not come across as attacking those estimators. Instead, you want to learn what they were thinking about.

—Mike Cohn, *Agile Estimating and Planning* (Pearson Education, 2005)

Planning poker is effective because it helps people take their expertise, opinions, and ideas, and combine them into one easily communicated number. The values on the cards aren't special (for example, in the past, some teams used cards with numbers from the Fibonacci sequence: 1, 2, 3, 5, 8, 13, 21, 34, 55, 89), but they're conveniently far enough apart so that it's easier to decide if a task will take 13 versus 21 hours, or a story will be 5 versus 8 points.

How do you handle global teams?

That's a great question, and a real challenge. Distributing your team in offices across the world poses very large challenges. They're not insurmountable challenges—many agile teams build great software even though they're not collocated (i.e., in the same room). But when you reduce face-to-face communication and rely on less reliable forms of communication, you always open your project up to more defects caused by the "game of telephone" effect.

One way that Scrum teams deal with this is to break their global teams up into smaller Scrum teams that are collocated. In addition to the Daily Scrum, they also schedule an additional daily meeting called the Scrum of Scrums, where members of each team get together and answer the three questions. They self-organize around their own backlog for the global project, and bring the new self-assigned tasks back to their teams. This is effective because it gives the entire global team their own, larger plan that is inspected every day.

The Scrum of Scrums approach is not a silver bullet, and does not solve all (or even most) of the problems of global teams. The hardest part about global teams is that it's very difficult to keep every single team member motivated with shared elevating goals, and as we saw in Chapter 4, that's the main way that team members become pigs and not chickens. While it's definitely possible to do it no matter how your team is distributed, it's much more challenging for the product owner to get that vision to everyone, because he or she has to do it across many time zones and over communications channels like teleconferences and email threads that are much less effective than in-person discussions and conversations.

OK, I get that the Daily Scrum keeps people working on the right tasks. But even well-meaning developers can get caught up doing things that aren't really the best use of their time. Can't Scrum teams still get sidetracked?

Yes, they can. In fact, Scrum founder Jeff Sutherland recently (as of the time we're writing this) published a paper[11] with Scott Downey called "Scrum Metrics for Hyperproductive Teams" that tackles exactly this topic. They worked with many Scrum teams to take a set of measurements so that they could figure out exactly how productive "hyperproductive" teams really are. They found that an effective Scrum team can deliver projects up to 400% faster than other, less effective teams. And keeping developers on track has a lot to do with getting that track record.

Sutherland and other Scrum thought leaders are constantly looking for ways to improve Scrum. One of the many interesting things in this paper is that a small tweak to the Daily Scrum aimed at keeping developers working toward the most valuable goals made a big difference in how well the team performed. The change that they made was to have the team answer different questions (their emphasis) about each item in the sprint backlog, starting with the first one ("Priority 1"):

- What did *WE* achieve yesterday on Priority 1?
- What was *OUR* contribution on Priority 1 worth in Story Points?
- What is *OUR* plan for completing Priority 1 today?
- What, if anything, is blocking *US* or has the potential to slow *US* down today?

The team works together to answer these questions. Then, instead of going from person to person, they go down the sprint backlog in descending value order, ending when they run out of items or when the Daily Scrum timebox expires.

So why does this work? One reason is that it keeps team members from disconnecting with the Daily Scrum ("yesterday I worked on my code, I'll work on my code until tomorrow, no roadblocks, move on [yawn!]"). And it keeps everyone focused on the highest value items. Even effective agile teams can inadvertently venture into CHAOS report territory if programmers start focusing on themselves and the tasks that seem most interesting to them, rather than on delivering the most valuable features first. These questions force the whole team to think about exactly that.

This gets back to the main point of the Daily Scrum—that it's actually a formal inspection meeting (just like inspections you may have learned about if you took a university course in software engineering), where the goal is to improve the quality of the team's planning and communication. It just happens to be a formal inspection that's interesting and engaging for the team.

---

11 Scott Downey and Jeff Sutherland, "Scrum Metrics for Hyperproductive Teams: How They Fly like Fighter Aircraft" (paper presented at the 2013 46th Hawaii International Conference on System Sciences, Maui, HI, January 7-10, 2013).

That's one of the best parts of Scrum: that it's constantly evolving, and that the top Scrum practitioners can contribute to make it better all the time.

 Things You Can Do Today

Here are a few things that you can try today on your own or with your team:

- If you don't use user stories yet, take one feature that you're currently building and write a user story for it. Bring it to the rest of the team—what do they think about it?
- Try planning poker today and block out time with your team to try estimating several tasks on your current project. You can print out cards or buy them (we get ours from Mountain Goat Software—or you can try their online planning poker game (*http://www.planningpoker.com*)).
- Once you've created an estimate, take over a whiteboard or put a large piece of paper on a wall and start creating a burndown chart. How long can you keep it going? Pay attention to what happens to the chart at the end of the project or iteration.
- Can you look at your last project or iteration and come up with a project velocity?

 Where You Can Learn More

Here are resources to help you learn more about the ideas in this chapter:

- You can learn more about Scrum and collective commitment in *Agile Project Management with Scrum*, by Ken Schwaber (Microsoft Press, 2004).
- You can learn more about user stories and generally accepted Scrum practices in *User Stories Applied*, by Mike Cohn (Addison-Wesley, 2004).
- You can learn more about planning a Scrum project in *Agile Estimating and Planning*, by Mike Cohn (Addison-Wesley, 2005).
- You can learn more about retrospectives in *Retrospectives: Making Good Teams Great*, by Esther Derby and Diana Larsen (Pragmatic Bookshelf, 2006).

Coaching Tips

Tips for agile coaches helping their team to work with the ideas in this chapter:

- One of the biggest coaching challenges is helping the team to really understand collective commitment. Look for cases where individual team members are hesitant to come up with an estimate or don't really take part in planning, or try to get the Scrum Master to do all the planning for them.

- Talk to individual team members about the goals for the project. Spot cases where people have "tunnel vision" and are only thinking about a particular feature or story that they feel that they "own." Encourage them to take on a task for another story or feature, and encourage other team members to take on tasks for this story or feature.

- Coach Scrum Masters to make all of the data available. Put burndown charts and task boards on a wall, and have the Daily Scrum in a visible area.

- Recognize the political dynamic: one reason it's uncomfortable for the team to make their true project progress public is that they probably have experience in the past with senior managers who got very angry when projects didn't appear to go perfectly. Your job *is not to solve this problem for them*; it's to help them recognize it, and understand where the culture of the company may need to slowly change in order to adopt Scrum more effectively.

CHAPTER 6

XP and Embracing Change

*People hate change... and that's because people hate change... I want to be sure that you get my point. People **really** hate change. They **really, really** do.*
—Steve McMenamin, *The Atlantic Systems Guild*, 1996 (from *Peopleware: Productive Projects and Teams*, by Tom DeMarco and Timothy Lister)

Have you ever noticed how often programmers complain about their users? Do a little web searching through programmer forums, and before long, you'll run across a thread where developers complain that their users don't know what they want before they ask for something to be built. It's a long-accepted part of programmer culture: users never ask for what they actually want, and they make your life hard when they change their minds all the time.

We saw earlier in the book that Scrum has an answer for this: work with the users to understand what's valuable to them, and deliver working software often, so that understanding can change over time. This gives project managers and business owners the ability to constantly revise the goal of a project, if that's what delivers the most value. But wait a minute—now the team has to make constant changes to code to keep up with those changes. Developers know from experience that when you have to make changes to code that was already written, it causes bugs. The more changes developers need to make, the more brittle the codebase gets. Aren't all of these changes going to make the software buggy and unstable?

This is one of the problems that XP sets out to solve. XP (or Extreme Programming) is an agile methodology. And just like Scrum, it's made up of practices, values, and principles. The practices are easy to learn, and they're highly impactful—they can change the way that you think about your work. But again, just like Scrum, that change only happens if the people on your team approach it with the right mindset.

In this chapter, you'll learn about the primary practices of XP, and how they can be applied (or misapplied) by a software team. You'll learn about the XP values and principles. And you'll learn how they help get each team member into the right mindset to build better code: instead of hating change, every person on the team learns to embrace change.

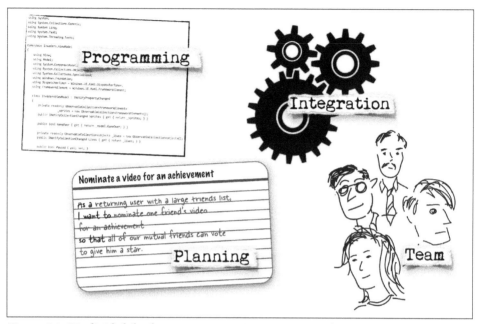

Figure 6-1. We divided the first 10 primary XP practices into four categories: programming, integration, planning, and team.

Narrative: a team working on a fantasy basketball website

Justin – a developer

Danielle – another developer

Bridget – their project manager

Act I: Going into Overtime

Justin always got a strange feeling in his gut when he was in the office late at night. It felt like he'd had too much coffee, even though he didn't really drink a lot of coffee. He never got that feeling when he was working late from home, only in the office.

"It's going to be one of those nights, isn't it?" said Danielle, Justin's teammate. Justin and Danielle had been friends in college. She was two years ahead of him in the same computer science program—one of the best in the country—and they'd even been lab partners in a chemistry class. She gave a reference for him when he applied for a job building online fantasy basketball game software at Chalk Player Online, a company that builds sports websites, and she was the first to welcome him onto the team.

The funny part was that he never intended to stay late. It's not that he had a problem working late. And his project manager, Bridget, had no problem with him working from home, especially if he was putting in a late night. But somehow tonight he found himself in the office past 10 p.m. once again, sending his girlfriend apologetic text messages and begging his roommate to walk his dog.

The funny thing is that Justin and Danielle had just been discussing how nice it would be to leave on time that night. But late in the afternoon, Bridget came to them with bad news: she'd had a meeting with the product managers for the software, and there was a big change that needed to be made to the code. When the project started out, it was only supposed to include NBA teams. But the product managers had decided that if they included teams in the European leagues when they launched, it would make a lot more money.

And now, Justin and Danielle are staying late. Again.

"This is really unfair," Justin said. "We checked and double-checked with them over three months ago that we'd only use NBA teams."

"You don't have to remind me. That meeting was my idea," said Danielle.

"And now they want us to add those teams after all. We're going to have to rip out a lot of code, and make a pretty big database change too." He paused for a second. "You know what? I blame Bridget. I'm so frustrated with her right now. She just doesn't get how hard this is going to be."

Danielle was looking over Justin's shoulder. She had a horrified look on her face.

"Bridget is standing right behind me, isn't she?"

"Yes, I am," said Bridget. "Look, I know this is a big change."

Justin said, "But it's not just that it's a change. It's that we told them what we were going to build. Months ago. They signed off on it. If they'd told us about the European leagues then, we'd have built something totally different. The system we built doesn't even have a way of representing a league, because we only had one."

"That was a basic assumption," added Danielle, "and changing it completely changes the way we design the system. We're going to have to rip out a lot of code, and that's going to create problems."

Bridget asked, "What kind of problems?"

"Have you ever fixed a car with duct tape and paperclips?" said Justin. "It's kind of like that."

The three of them looked at each other. There would be many late nights in the future.

The Primary Practices of XP

There are 13 **primary practices of Extreme Programming** that can help guide teams through the ins and outs of software development, and help them build code that lends itself to change. Unlike the practices of Scrum, many of the XP practices are specific to programming, and are aimed at addressing the most common problems that cause teams to build lousy code. In fact, there's so much of a focus on programming in many of these practices that people often have a mistaken belief that XP is only for advanced, highly skilled programmers.

In this chapter, we're going to talk about the first 10 primary XP practices. These 10 practices are divided into four categories—programming, integration, planning, and team—to make it easier to understand them, and to help you keep from falling into the "XP is only for rock star developers" trap.

Programming Practices

Two of the primary XP practices are aimed directly at programmers, and help those programmers write better code: test-first programming and pair programming. They're focused on several important aspects of software development. By writing automated tests before writing the code that gets tested, teams establish a higher level of quality in their software. Working in pairs, with two developers at a single workstation, helps get more eyes on the software to catch bugs before they're built into the code.

When a programmer does **test-first programming**, also known as test-driven development (or TDD), it means that before he writes code, he builds an automated test. Since the product code hasn't been written yet, the test fails. He knows that the code is working when the test passes. This creates a tight feedback loop that helps to prevent defects: write failing tests, build code to make them pass, find problems and learn more about how you'll solve them, then write more failing tests. These automated tests are usually called **unit tests**. The word "unit" makes sense: in almost every programming language, code is cleanly broken down into units (classes, methods, functions, subroutines, modules, etc.), and almost every language has at least one way of building and running automated tests that are tied to each of those units. By building the tests first, the programmer makes sure that each unit does what it's supposed to do.

Test-first programming makes sure each individual unit of code works, but it does more than that. It also helps the team prevent some of the most common—and most serious—problems that can make a codebase difficult to maintain. It's very easy to make a change to one part of the code, only to have a seemingly unrelated bug pop up in a completely unrelated feature because the developer didn't realize the two shared a dependency. When a programmer writes unit tests that are run every time the code builds, those automated tests help prevent dependencies from going undetected by immediately failing, and the tests help the programmer spot the problem before it's embedded in the codebase and too difficult to remove. Unit tests also help programmers write code that is easier to reuse; it's easy for a programmer to build a Java class, for example, that has a structure that makes it unintuitive to work with: confusing names, clumsy initialization, or other structural problems can easily sneak into anyone's code. When the programmer builds a unit test that has to use that class, the flaw can become obvious, and because the contents of the class haven't been written yet, the programmer can change it quickly. The unit test then becomes part of the codebase, so other developers can refer to it to see how the method was meant to be used.

The second primary XP practice that's focused on building code is **pair programming**. In a team that does pair programming, two developers sit together at a single workstation when writing code. In most cases, one programmer types, while the other watches—and they constantly discuss what's going on. Teams working in pairs inject far fewer bugs, because there are two sets of eyes looking to catch the bugs all the time. Pairing can also help reduce fatigue, because one programmer can take over typing when the other gets a little mentally tired. An effective pair programming team will discuss ideas and approaches, constantly brainstorm, and, as a result, be more innovative. They will also hold each other accountable for good practices: it's easy for one programmer to sweep a bad shortcut under the rug, but he'll be much less likely to take that shortcut when his pair partner is watching. We've spoken with developers on many different teams who told us that they've found that pairs build much more code—and much better code—working together than they would have if working separately.

Integration Practices

There are two primary XP practices that we put in the "integration" category. The first is the **10-minute build**: the team creates an automated build for the entire codebase that runs in under 10 minutes. This build includes automatically running all of the unit tests and generating a report of which tests passed and which failed.

Ten minutes may sound like an arbitrary length of time, but it makes sense from a team's perspective. If a build takes more than 10 minutes to run, team members are much less likely to run it often. Running the build often is very valuable to the team, because it makes problems immediately obvious. For example, the build runs the unit tests, so after the build runs, the team knows whether or not they've reached the level of quality they set up in the automated tests. In other words, it gives a relatively quick answer to the question, "Is our code working so far?" And because it's short enough that the team will run it often, everyone on the team has a continuously updated view of the quality of the code.

The other integration practice is **continuous integration**, and it's a practice built around tools that teams use to let many people work on a single set of source code files simultaneously. If you have a team, and everyone needs to work with the same files all the time, team members can't work on the same physical copies of the files at the same time—they'd constantly overwrite one another's changes. So the team will use a version control system that has a central (or decentralized) master set of files, which individual developers will **check out**, or copy into a private copy of the entire codebase that's only used by that programmer (often called a **sandbox**). The developer will work on the copy of the code in her sandbox, and periodically check it back into the repository.

The problem is that very often when a developer checks in her changes, she'll find that another of her team members made conflicting changes since she checked out her code. A lot of the time, those conflicts will show up immediately when she tries to build her local copy of the code, and it no longer compiles. But sometimes the problems are more severe, and the software no longer behaves correctly because of conflicting code that was checked in since her sandbox was last updated. These problems will all show up when she **integrates** the latest code from the repository back into her sandbox before checking in her changes.

And that's where continuous integration comes in: the team will constantly run the build and monitor for compiler errors or unit test failures. Many teams will set up a build server that periodically checks out the latest code from the repository, runs the automated build, and notifies the team if there are any errors. But setting up a continuous build server is only one part of continuous integration. Integrating continuously means that each team member constantly keeps his or her own copy of the codebase up to date. Team members periodically integrate the latest code from the repository back into their sandboxes. Teams that use pair programming will sometimes have a physical **build token**, like a stuffed plush toy or a rubber chicken (it's useful to make it something silly, so it's clear who has it), that they pass from pair to pair; when a pair gets the token, they take the next opportunity to integrate the latest code from the repository, fix any integration problems they find, then pass it on to the next pair. This ensures that integration problems are found and repaired as early as possible.

Planning Practices

XP teams use iterative development to manage their projects. Like Scrum, the XP planning practices are based on a larger cycle for long-term planning, broken into shorter iterations. In the **weekly cycle** practice, the XP team uses one-week iterations, and it works closely with the **stories** practice (which is identical to the user stories that you've already learned about). Each cycle starts with a planning meeting, where the team members review the progress they've made on the project, work with the customers to pick the stories for the iteration, and then break the stories into tasks that are estimated and assigned to developers.

This should sound familiar, because it's very similar to the Scrum planning meeting; in fact, many XP teams will adopt the exact Scrum planning practices (which accounts for the popularity of the Scrum-XP hybrid reported on the VersionOne State of Agile survey that you read about in Chapter 2). Once the planning is done, the team spends the first part of the iteration writing automated tests for the stories and tasks, and the rest of the iteration writing code to make the tests pass. However, instead of self-organizing, some XP teams will stack up all of the tasks for the iteration and have each developer take the next task in the stack when his current task is done. This helps ensure that developers don't cherry-pick their favorite tasks, and distributes the tasks evenly among all developers.

XP teams use the **quarterly cycle** practice to do long-term planning. Once a quarter, the team meets to take a look at the big picture. XP teams will talk about **themes**, or larger ideas in the real world that they can use to tie their project's stories together. Discussing themes helps the team figure out what stories will need to be added to the project, and keeps them connected to the real-world business problems that they're solving with the software. The team also steps back and talks about internal and external problems that they're experiencing, nagging bugs, and repairs that haven't been addressed yet. They take the time to reflect on the progress they've made so far, how well they're meeting their users' needs, and how the project is going overall. Some XP teams will use the same retrospective practice that Scrum teams use.

The final primary XP practice focused on planning is **slack**. This practice has the team add minor, lower-priority stories to each weekly cycle. These stories are broken down into tasks during the planning meeting, but those tasks are left for the end of the iteration. That way, if the team runs into unexpected problems, it's very easy for them to cut out those "slack" stories and still deliver complete, working software at the end of the cycle—and like all iterative development, XP teams only deliver software that's "*done* done" at the end of the cycle, which means that it works, all tests pass, and it can be demonstrated to the users.

Team Practices

XP isn't just about programming. It's about how teams work together, and it includes two primary practices that help teams gel that we grouped into a "team practices" category. The first is **sit together**, and it's pretty self-explanatory. Teams work best when they sit near each other, and have easy access to everyone else on the team. Many people don't realize that while programming as an individual is often done in isolation (when not done in pairs), working as a developer on a programming team is a highly social activity. Team members constantly consult each other about problems, ask each other for advice, and alert each other to problems. If the team sits together in an open workspace, this socialization is naturally encouraged. There's a lot of debate over just how open the workspace should be, because programmers also need to be shielded from distractions in order to work efficiently, and many programmers value the privacy of having a screen that can't be seen by people walking by. A popular solution to this is the "caves and commons" office layout, described by Steward Brand in his book *How Buildings Learn*.[1] In this layout, developers have private or shared offices that open out into a large common area with meeting tables and workstations for pairing.

The next primary XP team practice is **informative workspace**, where the team's working environment is set up to automatically communicate important project information to anyone who happens to be working in it. One popular way of making a workspace informative is to have a large task board and burndown chart posted prominently on a wall that everyone can see. By putting all of the information about the project in plain sight all the time, every single person on the team knows where the project stands, and that helps everyone make better decisions. Visible, always-in-your-face charts and other things that teams use to display data and make the workspace more informative are called **information radiators** because they automatically "radiate" current information about the project to anyone who happens to be nearby.

Large, visible charts aren't the only way to make a workspace informative. When team members have questions, run into problems, or raise issues, they have discussions. When those discussions take place in a shared workspace instead of closed conference rooms, the people around them overhear, and will absorb information about what's going on. When team members automatically absorb project information, whether it's from charts or from overheard conversations, it's called **osmotic communication**.While teams need to balance the value of that communication against the potential distraction of overheard discussions that can interrupt a developer's train of thought and slow down development, effective XP teams will find a good balance that helps keep everyone up to date.

Why are informative workspaces important? The idea is to help the team make better decisions, and to give them more control over how the project is run—just like task boards help Scrum teams. What's important here is that *the information is for the whole team*, not just for the team leads or managers. It's democratized, and spread out to everyone on the team without filtering. The more information about the project is shared, the more each individual on the team is able to influence the direction of the project.

---

1 Stewart Brand, How Buildings Learn: What Happens After They're Built (London: Penguin Books, 1995).

Why Teams Resist Changes, and How the Practices Help

Nobody likes writing code, and then having to change it because the person who asked for it changed his mind. Making changes late in the game can range from irritating to actually insulting—and even borderline disastrous, if you have to work weekends for the next month and a half because someone asked you and your team to build something, but didn't bother thinking it through all the way.

Figure 6-2. Every project manager recognizes the helpless feeling of needing a change and not being able to get the developers to make it, and every developer knows the anxiety of a seemingly innocuous code change ballooning into a monster that takes way too much time.

This is why developers often complain about how those annoying business users keep changing their minds. It's really common to hear complaints partway through a project like this: "Wait, you want that change? If I'd known that, I'd have built the code completely differently! Why can't you just tell us exactly what you want at the beginning of a project?"

And who can blame them? Teams resist these changes, especially late in the project[2], because it's work. And not just normal work—the worst, most irritating kind of work. Changes make you pick up something that you thought was finished, rip it apart, and rebuild large parts of it from the ground up. Moreover, it's not just the work of changing the code that's frustrating. Your whole team put a lot of mental effort into it, thinking through many problems and coming up with the most elegant solution you could find. Now you're being told to tear down your Taj Mahal, because someone really wanted an Eiffel Tower instead.

But there's more than one side to this story. The user or manager who asked for one thing and then changed his mind late in the project usually isn't doing it purposely to disrupt the team. We learned earlier in the book that fractured perspectives lead to poor project results, so let's try to look at this problem from his perspective. He needs software built so he can do his job, and that means he needs to work with the development team. Now he's being asked to come up with answers to questions that he may not fully understand: "Who should have access to this feature?" "How many simultaneous users will use this system?" "How much time is acceptable between when the 'Go' button is clicked and when the results are displayed?" "Do they need to choose these options and then make those selections, or vice versa?"

What started as a meeting where the user tried to explain his problem somehow ended up with him having to answer a seemingly unending stream of technical questions that he doesn't really know how to answer. And there's a ticking clock; he feels that if he doesn't give answers to every question, the team will delay the project—and blame him for the delay. (And, let's be honest, they probably will.) Everyone knows that building software is expensive, and he's not an expert in it, so he'll give the best answer that he can so that the meeting ends and he doesn't keep the team from moving forward and burning more budget.

How do we resolve this? Who's right?

The thing that agile methodologies—and XP in particular—do really well is admit up front that we don't know exactly what we're going to build, and that the most efficient way we have of figuring this out is to build it. They'll use working software instead of comprehensive documentation, because the most effective way they have of getting feedback from a user is to build part of the software first and get it into that user's hands.

So instead of setting your team up to try to shoot every change down, is it possible to create an environment where the team can actually handle those changes—gracefully, and without the disastrous weekend work or emotional strife? Nobody likes making changes, but maybe you can find a way to limit the impact each change has on the

---

2 Flip back to the principles behind the Agile Manifesto in Chapter 3. Do any of those principles apply here?

project, not only on the integrity of the code but also on the emotional state of the team and the users.

XP teams do this. They call it **embracing change**. An XP team doesn't just treat changes as a necessary evil; they recognize that the only way they can build the best software for their users is to get feedback often and respond to that feedback quickly. They expect change; it's on their calendar. It's not just bad news that always manages to show up, followed by a witch hunt to try to figure out who missed the requirement. Getting to the right mindset for XP means not just accepting changes, but explicitly asking for them.

Embracing change has two aspects: on the scope of the project, and on the codebase itself. The impact of changes on the code can be serious—a change that seems like it should be small can often surprise the team by requiring a frustrating and invasive rewrite. Teams will talk about "ripping out code" and plugging the hole with "duct tape, paperclips, and chewing gum." We'll delve into this aspect of embracing change in Chapter 7. For now, we'll concentrate on how XP teams embrace changes to the scope, functionality, and behavior of the software.

So how do the primary practices of XP help teams do that?

Planning

When teams plan iteratively, and deliver working software at the end of every iteration, they constantly get feedback. Everyone on the team knows that they're actively asking for that feedback—changes—and it's a lot easier to deal with changes emotionally when you're the one who asked for it in the first place.

Team

Problems are a lot easier to deal with when you've got people around you to help. When teams sit together, they pick up on problems a lot earlier. And an informative workspace helps make sure that everyone is thinking about the same problems. This gives everyone on the team *the ability to take control of those changes when they happen*, and not be caught off guard by an unexpected change. This gives the individual team members the autonomy they need to make choices that affect their code—and their lives.

Integration

One of the most frustrating problems caused by unexpected changes is how those changes ripple out through the entire codebase. If you're working on a change, it helps me, as your team member, to find about it early—that's why the team practices are really useful. But I'll still be caught off guard if a change you make to one part of the codebase causes an unexpected bug in the part that I'm working on. By continuously integrating (which is made easier because our build runs quickly), we'll find out about that problem very quickly, and fix it early—before it has a chance to surprise us and cause headaches later.

Programming

How does continuous integration help us find those changes? We've built a suite of unit tests that we run every time we integrate the code. So when you're integrating your change, you run all of the tests, including the ones for the part of the code I'm working on. If one of those tests fails, then we can work together—and even pair up—to fix the problem in both parts of the code.

If all of these practices are in place, then changes—even big ones—have a smaller impact. This helps the team learn that changes can be handled more easily.

Key Points

- When XP teams use **test-first programming**, they build **unit tests** first that express the behavior of the code that's about to be written, and then write code to make those tests pass. This creates a feedback loop that helps to prevent defects.

- Teams create a **10-minute build**, or an automated build that runs in under 10 minutes.

- Individual developers use **continuous integration** to constantly integrate changes from their teammates so everyone's sandbox is up to date.

- XP teams use iteration with their weekly cycle and quarterly cycle, and use stories in the same way that Scrum teams do.

- Teams add minor, low-priority cycles to each weekly cycle to create **slack**.

- When XP teams sit together, they periodically absorb project information through **osmotic communication**.

- XP teams work in an **informative workspace** that uses **information radiators** like wall charts to automatically communicate information to people who happen to work with it.

Narrative: a team working on a fantasy basketball website

Justin – a developer

Danielle – another developer

Bridget – their project manager

Act II: The Game Plan Changed, but We're Still Losing

Six weeks ago, Justin had thought that things were looking up. They'd just finished grinding out the first alpha release of the fantasy basketball site, complete with both the NBA and European leagues. But there had been problems.

"Problems is an understatement," he remembered Danielle saying. "This is buggy as hell." Everyone on the team was frustrated with the bugs, so they'd had a big meeting to discuss code quality. Bridget had said, "We need to do something about this... now!" People came up with suggestions: more design and code reviews, a big test event where they blocked out a few hours for all of the product managers to bang on the software at once, even hiring a full-time tester.

That's when Danielle told them about XP.

"We need to start doing this," she'd said. "These practices will fix our code problems."

Everyone on the team seemed to be on board, and Bridget agreed to put some real resources behind their XP adoption. She got the business to give the team a few weeks to get XP rolling, starting with a week-long unit test exercise. Because they didn't have any unit tests at all, the whole team took a week to write as many tests for as many parts of the software as they could.

Unfortunately, Bridget wasn't able to convince the office manager to let them sit together. But there was a wall near the coffee machine that didn't have anything on it, so Danielle made it more informative by posting a checklist of all of the primary XP practices, printed on a large sheet of paper in a big font. Right after she put up the checklist, she checked off the box next to "Informative Workspace." And after their week-long unit test exercise, she put a checkmark next to "Test-first Development." Justin set up a build server and had it check out the software from version control every hour, build the code, and run unit tests, emailing everyone the results. "Continuous integration"—check.

That was six weeks ago. They've been doing lots of work since then. So why did Justin feel like nothing really changed?

He and Danielle had just left a meeting with Bridget. It hadn't gone well. She was really angry that the fixes to the player stat management database were taking longer than they'd expected.

Right before the meeting, Justin and Danielle met privately and agreed that it wasn't remotely likely that they'd meet their deadline. But when they had the big team meeting and Bridget asked if they would be on time, they said yes, and absolutely reassured her that it would be. "Look, we'll apologize later," Danielle had said. Justin knew that they'd been cutting corners to meet the deadline, but it wasn't enough. They would still be late—but he agreed with Danielle that this wasn't the right time to let Bridget know. That would just end up causing more trouble for the project, which would delay it even more. He wasn't sure if that kind of trouble was why things went wrong with XP, but it certainly didn't seem to be helping.

Now he was taking a coffee break with Danielle, and he was a little hesitant to bring up these problems, but he really wanted to know if she felt the same way. "What do you think about our XP adoption so far?" he asked.

Danielle got an unhappy look on her face. "I don't know where we went wrong. These practices were supposed to fix our code, but I just spent four hours tracking down a bug in entirely new code that we wrote since we started doing XP. It seems like we're making the same old mistakes. Nothing's changed!"

"So where did we go wrong?" asked Justin.

Danielle thought about it for a bit. "Well, nobody's pairing anymore," she said. "We all started doing it at first, but after a few weeks it just seemed inefficient. I don't think anyone made the explicit decision to stop pairing. It's just that one person was on vacation, so that pair stopped working together."

Danielle was right, and it was an elephant in the room. The team had never actually talked about stopping their pair programming, but somehow it stopped. Test-driven development, too—Justin was writing just a few unit tests, and Danielle didn't feel like she had time to do them at all.

In fact, just a few days ago, Danielle had been feeling bad about abandoning pair programming, so she took a look through Justin's code. It was a mess. It was littered with commented-out blocks of code. There were huge methods that resembled spaghetti. Danielle wasn't afraid of being blunt, so she pointed it out to him. "What happened to that elegant code you used to write?"

Justin sighed, "I know! I'd love to write better code right now, but our deadlines are too tight. I just don't have time to think about it."

And Danielle understood—every minute felt critical, and Bridget made sure they knew every single day that failure was not an option. So even though both of them knew they could do better, the deadline was too tight and they just didn't have time.

"You know what? That's why we stopped doing pair programming. You and I were pairing until that big production bug fix came in," said Justin. "I had to jump on that, and you couldn't just sit around waiting for me, so you finished the database code we were working on. We just didn't have time to pair up. We don't have time to do any of this stuff!"

Danielle shrugged. "Maybe, maybe not." She got quiet for a minute. "Hey, can I be honest with you? I never really wrote unit tests first. I was programming as usual, and added tests after I finished each object. That wouldn't really make a difference, though. Would it?"

Justin thought about this for a minute. "So we're really not working much differently than we were before we started with XP, are we?"

The XP Values Help the Team Change Their Mindset

> Practices by themselves are barren. Unless given purpose by values, they become rote. Pair programming, for example, makes no sense as a "thing to do to check off a box". Pairing to please your boss is just frustrating. Pair programming to communicate, get feedback, simplify the system, catch errors, and bolster your courage makes a lot of sense.
>
> —Kent Beck *Extreme Programming Explained*, 2nd Edition

In the Scrum chapters, we showed you a quote from Ken Schwaber explaining that if you don't get collective commitment and self-organization, you "don't get Scrum." You saw how a team that tries to implement Scrum but doesn't "get" these things—going through the motions of implementing Scrum practices, but not self-organizing —usually ends up with only better-than-not-doing-it results.

There's a very similar pattern with XP. If you and your team resist change, push back against users who need the software to work differently than the team built it, and don't believe that it's realistic to build software that's easy (or even possible) to change, then you don't get XP. And if you and your team don't get simplicity—how simple design and code differ from complex design and code, where simplicity comes from, how your team's culture and climate affect its ability to produce simple code and architecture, and how simplicity prevents bugs—then you don't get XP. An important theme for the rest of this chapter is helping you to embrace change. In Chapter 7, you'll learn about simplicity and how it can help you design software that has fewer barriers to change. But before we can understand those things, it's useful to step back and understand where bugs come from.

So where *do* bugs come from, anyway?

Look in almost any software engineering textbook and you'll see the answer: **rework**.[3] Bugs come from many places, but the most common way that defects are injected into software—and that's the term you'll probably see in the software engineering textbook, *defect injection*—is through rework. The team built the software to do one thing, but then someone comes along and needs a change. The team has to do a lot of rework: ripping out old code, making changes to existing code, patching in new code. And this is easily the most common way that bugs are added to software.

But wait a minute. Can't we prevent those changes? Well, sure, in theory. And that same software engineering textbook has an answer: documenting the software requirements. If you do a really good job of gathering those requirements, writing them down, and reviewing them with everyone who needs the software, then you can prevent those changes from happening. The team can get a lot closer to software that meets all of the needs of the users, customers, and stakeholders. Of course there will be changes. But they'll be minimal.

In theory.

And you know what? This can work in practice, too. Many teams have built a lot of great software using thorough requirements.[4]

But this is a very rigid way of building software, because it only works if the people putting together the specification can actually figure out all (or, at least, enough) of the requirements at the beginning of the project. For the many situations where it works, there are just as many where it doesn't work. This is why projects that use requirements like this need change management systems, or some other apparatus for incorporating these changes.

This is where XP works better. It helps the team build the software in a way where changes will be much less damaging to the codebase. Rework and changes are fine— and even embraced—because the team builds the code to be changeable.

But even better, it prevents a big problem: the inability to incorporate really good ideas. It's very common for people on teams to have good ideas partway through the project. In fact, early versions of the software actually spark some of the best brainstorming. But when the team is using a "Big Requirements Up Front" (BRUF) method of development, that conversation ends badly:

Programmer: I have a great idea for the code!

---

3 Including our first book, *Applied Software Project Management*. And we weren't wrong. Traditional software engineering and project management brings a mindset of preventing changes, which is different from a mindset of embracing changes. But it's still a valid mindset, and not even necessarily incompatible with agile software development.

4 We have! And we're not even ashamed about it.

Team lead: That is a good idea. But it would cause too many changes. Write it up, and we'll reevaluate it when we groom the backlog in six months.

Programmer: But I can make this change in 10 minutes!

Project manager: It's too risky. We've seen how even a small change can cause bugs that ripple through the entire software. Don't worry, we're not telling you "no." We're just telling you "not now."

How frustrating. What will happen the next time this programmer has a great idea? There's a good chance he'll just keep it to himself.

A team that's afraid of making changes is a team that stifles innovation from the bottom up. That doesn't mean that they're a team that won't build software. They can build software, even good software. If you work with big requirements up front, you can accomplish the goal of meeting those requirements; that's actually a pretty good goal for a lot of teams. But it definitely has its downsides.

XP Helps Developers Learn to Work with Users

A lot of teams following a BRUF waterfall methodology find success with the first release, and often the second release too. This shouldn't be too surprising. Before the project starts, there's usually been a lot of discussion. There's a specific need that's well understood, and pressing enough to actually get the company to put money and resources behind the project. That means the first version of the requirements often reflect all of that discussion, and incorporate the best ideas that everyone came up with. In fact, usually the topic has been talked to death, and people are relieved that the team has actually started to build it. This is a great way of preventing changes and rework: because so much thought has gone into the requirements already, it's pretty likely that they don't need to be changed much. What's more, the second version probably mostly contains valuable features that the team just didn't have time to put into the first version. So it's a pretty common pattern for BRUF teams to have some early success, and build a first version of the software that works well and doesn't require many changes.

The problem is that when the project reaches the second, third, and fourth releases, people have been using the software. And we already know that delivering working software is a great way to elicit feedback from users (which, again, is why agile teams favor working software over comprehensive documentation). Now the users have some good feedback, and a lot of times implementing that feedback requires rework.

So what happens if the team built the software in a way that is difficult to change? They'll go through their planning, evaluate the requests, and determine that making those changes has a high risk of injecting defects into the code, which will cause the change to require a lot of time to implement. This will give them a very rational, well-deserved fear of changes. And it will force the users, clients, and stakeholders to find ways to change their requirements so that they can be implemented with the existing codebase. The great partnership that emerged in the first version of the software between the users and the team can easily turn into an antagonistic relationship—one that turns the requirement elicitation into a contract negotiation, and makes it difficult to have customer collaboration.

XP gives the team a way past this problem by providing practices which, if applied by a team with the right mindset, help them build a codebase that is easy to change. (You'll learn more about this in Chapter 7.)

But XP also changes the way that everyone on the team thinks about quality. Quality isn't just about avoiding bugs. It's about giving users software that meets their needs—even if that software isn't exactly what they originally asked for. Traditional BRUF teams separate the functional design (what the software does) from the technical design (how it's constructed). The functionality is written into a spec, which is then handed to the team to implement. If the programmers have questions, or if the functionality seems wrong, they can go back and ask the person who wrote the spec for clarification. Then a game of "telephone" happens—the spec writer asks the users, managers, and whoever else they elicited requirements from, and "translates" the results back into language that the programmers can understand. Interestingly, BRUF teams consider that to be very efficient, because it doesn't "waste" the developer's time by forcing him to talk to users. (And everyone knows that programmers don't have any social skills, right?)

The "trick" that XP pulls is forcing the developer to think like a user—starting with having the developer actually talk to the users. (What?!) If the developers don't have the skills to talk to the users, they'll start to build them. The XP practices actually help with this. For example, take test-driven development. The developers write tests first. This prevents bugs. But it also forces each developer to think, "What does this code have to do?" before writing it. A developer who gets into the habit of thinking about functionality like this before writing any code will start to ask the same thing when planning each weekly cycle.

XP also avoids the CYA inherent in a specification. It's straightforward for a developer to implement exactly what's in the spec as written, without ever thinking about whether it really meets the needs of the user. But if he's developed the habit of always asking "What is it supposed to do?" before writing code, he'll start spotting problems —and will feel comfortable demanding answers, because he needs those answers in order to write the tests. He won't just push that responsibility off onto whoever wrote a specification and handed it to him. When everyone on an XP team does this, they constantly ask for clarification from the users, and do their best to figure out what the software needs to do so that the users can do their jobs. They do this directly with the users, rather than through a single intermediary, which saves a lot of time.

In other words, BRUF lets you build what you *intended*. XP helps you build what your users actually *need*. And everyone is happier: the team members are happier because they can spend their time solving real problems instead of fighting with the code to make changes, and users are happier because they get what they want (and not what they thought they wanted six months ago). And what emerges is a whole team—including the users, customers, and stakeholders—where they don't have to commit to knowing exactly what they'll need in six months or a year, and instead concentrate on building the best software they can for the most important needs they know about today.

So how does XP do this?

Practices Only "Stick" When the Team Truly Believes in Them

The practices of XP help you concentrate on the quality of the code that you're building *before* you've put a lot of code in place. Where Scrum is all about making sure that your customers know what you can produce and what you can't, XP is about making it possible for you to make changes as quickly and as defect-free as possible. And that helps everyone on the team to develop an attitude toward quality that permeates all of the development work in your project.

This is a new way of thinking for many technical people, even very experienced "rock star" developers. It's often not hard to get the technical people on the team behind Scrum, especially a "better-than-not-doing-it" version of Scrum, if they feel like poor planning causes the problems on the project. And it's true that Scrum is a great way to improve the way that a team plans projects. But what happens when each individual developer looks at the XP practices, and discovers that those practices actually ask him or her to *change the way they code*?

Figure 6-3. A very common reaction to XP is that it sounds good in theory, but practices like pair programming and test-driven development "just won't work for our team." It's not necessarily an argument against those practices, as much as it is a feeling that this will be a difficult change.

One of the most basic facts about building software: there are an almost unlimited number of ways that you can write a program. Ask two developers to build exactly the same unit (class, function, library, or whatever applies to the language or framework being used), and it is highly unlikely that they'll both produce the same code. Is it too difficult to imagine that one of them might produce much better code than the other?

Obviously, programming skill has a lot to do with it. But skill isn't everything. And, in fact, many teams with very highly skilled developers have found themselves maintaining lousy code. Often, this lousy code happens when the developers are rushed to make a lot of changes that they hadn't planned for. And the end result is a lot of bugs... and a fear of changes and rework that permeates the team.

This is a pretty common reason that causes teams to turn to XP. And what a lot of those teams—and especially their managers—will focus on are the XP practices that are specifically aimed at catching and preventing bugs. Pair programming is a good idea, because it's like having a constant code review—and more eyes on the code means more bugs caught before they go in. Test-driven development means that the team will write and maintain tests to catch bugs that get added along the way, and continuous integration means that those tests will be run all the time. This all sounds like a great idea, right? And it will definitely catch more bugs.

A team that gets better-than-not-doing-it results with XP will find that pair programming prevents defects from getting into the software, and test-driven development and continuous integration catch defects when they're added. But a team like that will usually think of these practices as "nice-to-haves." The bare minimum that they have to do to get the project out the door is write code. There's always a tendency when teams get behind schedule to just do that bare minimum, and cut out all of those extra bells and whistles. They'll say things like, "We're running late, so we don't have time to write unit tests," or "It would be great if we had the capacity to dedicate two programmers to each task, but we just don't have that kind of manpower if we want to hit our deadlines."

This is not an unusual mindset for a team that first comes in contact with XP. The problem with this mindset is that these great practices end up being treated like going on a diet or exercising: things that are a really good idea, and if we didn't have such a busy lifestyle, we would definitely be doing them. But even for the people who do it religiously, if these practices feel optional, then when schedules get tight or projects run into problems, they'll get dropped.

This is also why it's counterproductive for teams to treat the XP practices like a checklist—or, even worse, try to assign a "percentage of XP we've put in place" value based on how many practices that they've adopted. This is treating the XP practices like the end itself, rather than a means to an end. This is a big, red, flashing warning sign that the team has a mindset that's not yet ready for XP.

A team that doesn't have the right mindset for XP will have to shift the way they think. That mindset shift can seem like a big deal to a team, especially if they don't really accept the idea that the practices are truly worth their time. So what causes a team to treat XP practices as "first-class citizen" practices that are vital for building great software, rather than optional add-ons that are a good idea, but not truly necessary?

An Effective Mindset Starts with the XP Values

Teams that have the right mindset always use great practices, and never need to be nagged to use them, because they *just know* that those practices lead to better software. Like Scrum, XP has five **values**. And like Scrum, these values help your team truly adopt XP, and avoid better-than-not-doing-it results. The XP values help get the team into a mindset where great practices seem like the obvious way to build great software. And conversely, getting into the right mindset for XP means understanding how its practices cause you to build great code.

The XP Values

Communication
> Each team member is aware of the work everyone else is doing.

Simplicity
> Developers focus on writing the most simple and direct solutions possible.

Feedback
> Constant tests and feedback loops keep the quality of the product in check.

Courage
> Each team member is focused on making the best choices for the project, even if it means having to discard failing solutions or approach things differently.

Respect
> Every team member is important and valuable to the project.

These all sound like great, abstract ideas. Who could disagree with them?

(You may find out shortly that *you* do... and that's OK, as long as you keep an open mind about them.)

Paved with Good Intentions

When a team starts their XP adoption, everyone is optimistic. They know there are problems with code quality, they're sick of the headaches and the bugs, and it seems like the XP practices will finally fix them.

Then real life creeps in. Intuitively, it feels very expensive having someone sit with you as you go through the thought process of writing code. If the only benefit to pair programming is an extra set of eyeballs to catch bugs, then there are more efficient ways to go about that. A code review after the code is written will probably catch almost as many bugs (and there's no reason you couldn't do one after a pair programming session). But if you're pressed for time because of a looming deadline, it's easy to convince yourself that a code review is almost as good as pair programing. "I'm sort of pairing, because I'm getting someone else involved!"

Almost every XP practice has a similar shortcut. You don't have to sit together; you can just have daily meetings. You don't need to have your team members continuously integrate in their sandboxes; you can just set up a server to do it automatically for you. You don't need to write tests first; you can do it after the fact, and still catch bugs when the tests fail.

All of those things are true. And in every case, it's better than not doing anything—so you'll get better-than-not-doing-it results.

Flip back to the quote from Kent Beck earlier in this chapter: "*Practices by themselves are barren. Unless given purpose by values, they become rote.*" This is similar to what Ken Schwaber said about Scrum, self-organization, and collective commitment: each XP practice does much more than simply bring extra eyeballs to the code, or get people to sit in the same room, or add tests to the codebase. They help the team bring the values of XP into the project.

That's why shortcuts that seem to do the same thing as the XP practices will only get better-than-not-doing-it results. They change the mechanics of how the team does their work, but they don't change the intent or the mindset of the team.

It's very common among teams that first encounter XP to skip past the values, because the practices seem more interesting. Many developers will literally open a book about XP, take a quick look at the XP values, and then flip straight to the section on the practices.

Practices are *concrete*. You can look at a practice and imagine yourself doing it, and you can understand the impact it has on your project. And practices are *isolated*— you can add an individual practice to your project without having to change the way that you think about everything that you and your team do.

Values are harder for teams to get their heads around. They're more abstract, and they affect the entire project and the way everyone thinks about it. You can technically add practices to your project without understanding the values (which gives you better-than-not-doing-it results). It's more difficult to understand the values without first having some experience with the practices.

This isn't unique to XP. It affects Scrum as well. It's very typical for an introductory Scrum training class to have one or two slides on the Scrum values, spend a few minutes talking through them, and then rush straight into the "meat" of the training —the practices. But we shouldn't be hard on the trainers about this. It's much easier to train people to learn individual XP or Scrum practices than it is for a trainer to use the values to change how they think. Most trainers know from experience that if they give a class that's focused on the values, they'll often get feedback from developers that it's "too theoretical" and doesn't give them practical information that they can use on their projects. And again, this is also an understandable reaction—it's hard to see why the values are practical until you actually understand them, and it's not immediately obvious why the practices don't really work without the values, so the developers are in a catch-22.

Flip back to the ongoing story about Justin, Danielle, and their fantasy basketball project. They barreled straight into adding XP practices before really taking the time to understand the XP values. Even though you don't have all of the details about how they did their work every day, see if you can spot ways that they went wrong with their attempt to adopt XP. Here are a few examples that we found:

Communication

Danielle and Justin didn't talk about dropping the practices they thought they needed. And they definitely didn't talk to Bridget about the real status of the work —which is fine with her, because when the project has problems, she'll be happy to blame them for not letting her know earlier.

Simplicity

Justin's code is looking increasingly complicated, even convoluted. He's capable of writing better code, but he just doesn't feel like he has time to do it.

Feedback

When they stopped pair programming together, Justin and Danielle basically stopped meeting at all. If Danielle had looked at his code earlier and given him some feedback, maybe it wouldn't be such a mess. And even though the workspace is more informative, the information that's being distributed isn't about helping people make better decisions about the project. Figuring out "how XP they are" doesn't actually make the software better.

Courage

When the team is "not remotely likely" to finish on time and they know it, it takes a lot of courage to tell the truth to everyone—especially if it means the messenger will be shot. Danielle and Justin don't have that kind of courage.

Respect

There's very little in professional life that's more disrespectful than expecting a team to deliver on an impossible schedule.[5] Bridget repeatedly set deadlines that were ridiculously aggressive. Even worse, she didn't feel the need to be around to see them through—like the time she called a meeting late on Friday and demanded that the team deliver a bunch of fixes by Monday morning, then had the team work through the weekend while she went on vacation. (That part wasn't actually in the story earlier in this chapter, but we have it on good authority that it happened.)

When the XP values aren't truly internalized by each person on the team, they're likely to get better-than-not-doing-it results (at best!). They'll talk about how some of the practices—most often, pair programming and test-driven development—"just won't work for our team." The team members won't really make an argument against those practices, as much as share a feeling that this will be a difficult change to make, and will favor a checklist approach that starts with other practices first.

---

5 Ironically, some managers fool themselves into thinking that teams thrive on this sort of pressure. [Ed: They get the team performance that they deserve.]

A good XP team has the right mindset when they really *get* the values. And when they do, something interesting happens to the way the team thinks about XP: the practices start to make sense.

For example, here's what often happens when a team starts doing continuous integration. A lot of teams avoid it at first, because they think that it requires them to set up a build server (which requires time, and a computer to run it on). But continuous integration can be done with nothing more than a build token, like a silly toy or stuffed animal. Imagine that a team that's new to XP starts doing this. The first person who receives the token takes a few minutes to integrate the code from the version control system back into her sandbox, does whatever testing she needs to do to make sure that the program still works, and then checks the code back into version control. The token is passed from developer to developer, and each time the developer integrates the code into her sandbox, tests, checks it back in, and then passes the token on to the next developer.

How will this help the team learn about XP values?

Often, the build token will repeatedly stop with the same developer for a long time, because that person feels like he just can't interrupt what he's doing right now. The rest of the team needs to find a way to communicate about this, and let that developer know that continuous integration is important to them—this will teach them about communication, and help them value it more. And that stubborn developer will learn about the value of respect, because he'll need to prioritize the team's continuous integration ahead of whatever current task he thinks is more important. There are other lessons about the values that can be learned by adopting continuous integration. The team can learn about feedback (when integrating today causes a big problem to come to light early, saving the team time down the road), courage (because if that problem is someone else's fault, you actually have to talk to them about it—and that's not always easy, especially for an introverted person), and more.

This is how adopting an XP practice helps shape the mindset of the team.

But you don't need to start adopting practices to learn if your team has an XP-compatible mindset. You can also play "Are you OK with?" for XP:

- Is the team actually OK with building software and throwing it out because they learned that it won't work? What about the boss?
- If the boss wants a tighter deadline, does the team truly believe that writing unit tests is the fastest way to meet it, even if it means writing more code?
- If a junior programmer takes on a task, is the rest of the team OK giving him the authority to finish it? What if they disagree with his approach? What if someone else thinks he can do it faster? Is it OK if the developer fails and learns from it?

So what do you do when your team doesn't quite "get" the XP values?

Narrative: a team working on a fantasy basketball website

Justin – a developer

Danielle – another developer

Bridget – their project manager

Act III: The Momentum Shifts

"Something really strange just happened, Justin."

Justin was deep in thought, working through his code for an algorithm to rank players by multiple stats. He stopped what he was doing, and looked up at Danielle.

"You know how when we were doing pair programming, it didn't really help much?"

"Yeah," said Justin. "First you would stare at me while I wrote code, then we'd swap. There was a lot of watching, but it didn't help. In fact, I checked the line counts to see how many lines of code we were adding per hour, and it basically cut our productivity in half. I think that's why we gradually stopped doing it."

"Well, I just had a really interesting pair programming session with Tyler," said Danielle.

"Tyler? The new kid? He just graduated from college like six weeks ago. I'm surprised anything interesting came out of that."

Danielle nodded. "I was surprised too. I only started pairing with him because I thought it would be a fast way to get him up to speed on part of the code. But when we went through the player data cache code—"

Justin interrupted. "Oh, man. That was painful to write."

"I know. And you know what? He asked why we weren't storing the keys and hashes along with the player objects."

Justin sat still, staring, for a few seconds. His jaw started to slack a bit. The system had a data cache that he and Danielle had written to fix some serious performance problems. It was very complex, so it took him a minute to think through the way their cache stored data. "Wait. Wait! Oh crap. That means we'll have bad data in the cache."

"Yes," said Danielle.

"And Tyler came up with that? The new kid?"

"Yes. We did a little testing, and found that this was a big problem. It was actually not too hard to fix once he spotted it, but it would have been a giant pain if we didn't catch it now. All we'd see is that once in a while, a player would have the wrong stats. We might not have even caught it before it was released to production."

Justin had a copy of the XP values that he'd printed out, tacked to the cube wall, and promptly forgotten about. He pointed to it. "You know, I hadn't really paid attention to these. But I think I just learned something about communication."

"And respect," said Danielle. "I'll definitely ask Tyler's opinion in the future. And I think I want to keep pairing with him."

Understanding the XP Principles Helps You Embrace Change

There's a gap between the values of XP and its practices. The values are broad—they give you a way to think about working together, but for people new to XP, it's sometimes hard to apply them to specific practices.

Luckily, XP has a set of **principles** that help guide you in applying the practices to your projects in the real world. These aren't the only principles that people on teams can live by, but they are the principles that XP teams use to help them get the job done.

Here's the list of XP principles. It seems like a long list—but keep in mind that XP isn't about memorizing these principles. The values of XP are broad, so the principles help fill in a lot of the details about how people on an XP team think about their problems. This makes them very important in helping you figure out if your team has the right mindset for XP.

Humanity
Remember that software is built by people, and there's a balance between the needs of each team member and the project's needs.

Economics
Somebody is always paying for software project and everybody has to keep the budget in mind.

Mutual benefit
Search for practices that benefit the individual, the team, and the customer together.

Self similarity
> The pattern of a monthly cycle is the same as a weekly cycle and the same as a daily cycle.

Improvement
> Do your best today, and stay aware of what you need to do to get better tomorrow.

Diversity
> Lots of different opinions and perspectives work together to come up with better solutions.

Reflection
> Good teams stay aware of what's working and what isn't in their software process.

Flow
> Constant delivery means a continuous flow of development work, not distinct phases.

Opportunity
> Each problem the team encounters is a chance to learn something new about software development.

Redundancy
> Even though it can seem wasteful at first blush, redundancy avoids big quality problems.

Failure
> You can learn a lot from failing. It's OK to try things that don't work.

Quality
> You can't deliver faster by accepting a lower quality product.

Accepted responsibility
> If someone is responsible for something, they need to have the authority to get it done.

Baby steps
> Take small steps in the right direction rather than making wholesale changes when adopting new practices.

The Principles of XP

These principles are useful to help you understand some of the specific practices that XP uses—and when you start exploring the practices, they help you understand the principles.

Just like with the XP values, it's tempting for people who are new to XP to gloss over the principles and skip straight to the practices. This is the path of least resistance for several reasons. You can add a practice without having to acknowledge that anything is wrong with your project. ("We're doing great, but we can do even better!") If you skip past the values and principles and jump straight into the practices, you can easily take a "checklist" approach to XP, adding each practice to a list and checking it off once teams are going through the motions for that practice. If your goal is to have a "complete" adoption of every XP practice, that approach works very well.

But if your goal is to help your team build better software, then the checklist approach to XP adoption will fail. You'll get better-than-not-doing-it results at best, and over time the practices will probably start to fade away as the team reverts to the way they'd always done things. That's a very familiar pattern for both XP and Scrum teams, and in the real world we've talked to many people on many different teams who have experienced it. Team members typically start to blame the methodology: "We're putting all of this effort into writing tests (or pair programming, or Daily Scrum meetings, etc.), and it's not buying us much. This methodology must not work."

The principles help us understand why this happens. Principles are about self-reflection. They force you to take a step back and *think about how you and your team do your jobs*. When you take the time to understand the values and principles, you start to learn where your team has problems. This is uncomfortable, and it's often a negative experience. For example, you might look at the principle of failure and realize that your team has a culture where failure is not an option. Even admitting that you ran into a problem will cause your boss to yell at you. Your team members may start to disrespect you as the person who always makes mistakes. There are many companies where simply admitting that you made a mistake will have serious professional consequences.[6]

This is why it's completely rational for people on many teams to ignore the values and principles, or pay lip service to them without actually making any changes. Put yourself in the position of someone who understands that their team's culture is at odds with the XP principle of failure. What happens if you raise the issue, and demand that people change the way they work? You might be able to change the culture of your team. Or your team members and your boss might get so mad at you that you get fired. We've seen the latter happen more often than the former. When you hear people say that agile is hard, this is one reason why.

---

6 A rookie mistake that some agile adopters make is to make fun of teams that "don't get it" and have an unsuccessful agile adoption. A principle or even a practice that works for one team could cause another team to be fired entirely. Try to be sympathetic when you run across teams who have trouble adopting agile.

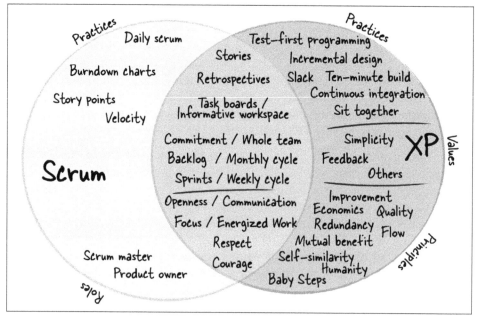

Figure 6-4. Scrum and XP are similar, but different.

XP Principles Help You Understand Planning

> Roles on a mature XP team aren't fixed and rigid. The goal is to have everyone contribute to the best he has to offer to the team's success. At first, fixed roles can help in learning new habits, like having technical people make technical decisions and business people make business decisions. After new, mutually respectful relationships are established among the team members, fixed roles interfere with the goal of having everyone do his best.
>
> —Kent Beck *Extreme Programming Explained,* 2nd Edition

It's not a coincidence that mindset problems stemming from a clash between the team and the methodology's values affects both Scrum and XP. Many of the values and principles of XP are shared with Scrum. But there are a lot of differences, too. Like roles—Scrum has the roles of Product Manager and Scrum Master, while a mature XP team doesn't have fixed roles. A useful way to learn about XP is to concentrate on the principles that it doesn't share with Scrum. That can be especially valuable when learning about how XP teams plan projects.

A lot of Scrum is about planning: planning the big picture using the product backlog, planning an iteration using the sprint backlog, and getting everyone on the team to collaborate on the plan using the Daily Scrum and other Scrum practices. XP uses similar iterative practices: the quarterly cycle is used to plan the big picture, the weekly cycle is used to manage iterations, and the team uses an informative workspace that contains tracking tools like a task board.

But planning and tracking an XP project is not the same as planning and tracking a Scrum project, and the principles help us understand why. Why doesn't an XP project have specific roles? This is where XP teams take **opportunity** and **diversity** very seriously. It's rare (although not unheard of) on a Scrum team for a Product Owner or Scrum Master to jump in and work on the software architecture and design, just like it's rare for a team member to take the lead in working with users or grooming the backlog. XP teams explicitly reject a separation of roles for two reasons. The first reason is that shutting someone out of a role means passing up an opportunity for him or her to contribute if he or she happens to have something to contribute. And the second is that anyone on the team might bring a fresh perspective, and that perspective could be the key to unraveling a tricky problem. Sometimes a highly technical developer has a very good idea for a user, or a project manager might have some valuable input on architecture—specifically because she's been thinking about the project from a completely different perspective than the people working on those aspects of it.

Understanding the principles in this way changes how you perform the practices. In the fantasy basketball project, Danielle learned that pairing with a brand-new developer who had never seen the code brought a completely different perspective. This is diversity at work: good ideas come from everywhere, even the new guy. That's why many XP teams rotate pair programming partners, rather than staying with the same pairs all the time. It brings **diversity** to the pairs and means bringing fresh eyes and fresh perspectives, which helps catch more problems and can spark innovation. And the principle of **humanity** comes into play as well: bringing different people in, and having them work together constantly, helps create an environment where everyone is giving feedback to each other all the time, and it helps each person learn to accept feedback and even criticism from their teams while still respecting them as people. And it helps give junior team members the courage to speak up when there are problems, even if they're paired with more senior team members. Principles like diversity and humanity combine with values like communication, respect, and courage to help a team make pair programming an effective tool for them.

Principles can also help us understand why XP doesn't have a specific after-action review practice, the way Scrum has retrospectives. XP places value on **improvement** and **reflection**, and XP teams constantly talk about how they're doing and how they can improve. But XP teams tend to be very conscious of "navel-gazing"—taking reflection too far and getting distracted from continuously delivering work. So XP teams tend to mix their reflection in with the work. This is something that pair programming is very good at: getting developers to talk about *what* they're doing *while* they're doing it. The principle of **baby steps** helps this a lot: instead of setting a large, overarching goal ("let's adopt all of the XP practices"), the team can take a small step toward it ("let's start pair programming, and we'll make sure we talk every day about how we're improving").

XP Principles Help You Understand Practices—and Vice Versa

XP teams use **stories**, and if you look at any story that an XP teams uses, it looks exactly like a story that would be used by a Scrum team. But while the practice is basically identical on both kinds of teams, you can learn a lot about how XP teams use those stories by applying the principles.

Figure 6-5 shows a typical story that an XP team might use on a project. XP, like Scrum, does not impose a universal format for user stories. In this case, the team decided to use a free-form sentence (rather than the "As a... I want to... So that..." format), and write the number of hours they thought it would take to implement the story on the front of the index card.

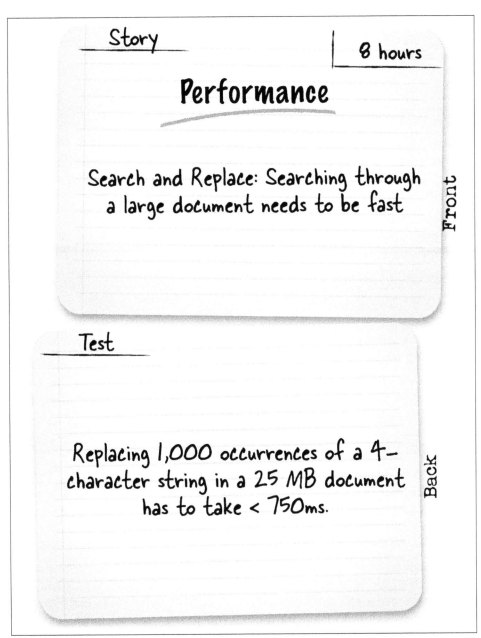

Story   8 hours

Performance

Search and Replace: Searching through a large document needs to be fast

Front

Test

Replacing 1,000 occurrences of a 4-character string in a 25 MB document has to take < 750ms.

Back

Figure 6-5. XP teams use the same stories as Scrum teams, but apply their own values and principles to them.

You already know how a Scrum team would use this story. It would be created as part of the backlog, incorporated into a sprint, and put on a task board. How would an XP team use the principles to integrate this story into their project? They might do very similar things. But they would also use the XP principles to help them understand how to incorporate the story into the project:

Economics
> The customers pick the stories for the team to build next. This keeps the project team focused on building only the highest-value stories.

Failure
> Stories are small and self-contained. The team can build a story and get it into the hands of the customer quickly, so if it's the wrong software they can work together to make whatever changes are needed.

Accepted responsibility
> A programmer read this card and estimated how long it would take to do. Now he's responsible for the work.

Communication
> Writing a story in users' language helps them to prioritize the work.

Quality
> Thinking about how you'll test the story up front helps you to deliver a higher quality product.

Because you already understand how user stories work, and how project teams use them, you can use that as a good starting point to help you understand these principles.

Feedback Loops

One way that XP and Scrum are similar is that both methodologies place a lot of value on **feedback**. We already saw how Scrum uses feedback loops to get continuous communication between the team and the customer. Scrum teams and XP teams share very similar values in **openness** (Scrum) and **communication** (XP). They have very similar ways of thinking about how people on software teams communicate.

But XP has more to say about feedback. XP teams aim for a very short iteration—the weekly cycle—to increase feedback and shorten the feedback loop. We learned with Scrum that to iterate effectively, the team has to take an active role in understanding what the users need and what's valuable to them. To keep feedback loops short, they continuously reflect on how the project is going. If there's a problem then the team will talk about it. Osmotic communication from sitting together helps spread that feedback around the team. When all of these things combine, the team can achieve **flow**, the XP principle that's about having a direct and efficient path through the project that delivers a constant stream of high-functioning, high-quality software.

You can see how many different pieces of XP—sit together, osmotic communication, feedback loops, communication, reflection—combine to help teams figure out an efficient and productive path through the project. But flow happens only when many moving parts work together: practices, principles, ideas, and, most of all, good software design and coding. When teams achieve flow, the whole team gets a feeling that they're releasing an uninterrupted delivery of software. As they communicate more and get more continuous feedback, they start seeing bottlenecks in the way they're building software, and they learn to work around obstacles together as a team. As they remove those bottlenecks, the flow becomes unencumbered.

Figure 6-6. When the team has the right mindset for XP, its practices feel like the most effective way to build software.

This isn't something that teams can achieve overnight. They need to spend time not just building software, but also talking about how they build software, and learning how each principle and practice can help them improve. And again, "baby steps" help the team feel comfortable setting a goal—like shorter feedback loops that lead to flow. The methodology as a whole becomes an adoption roadmap: the team can add practices one at a time, using the values and principles to guide each adoption. This week they might find a way to increase reflection, or find a way to improve their environment by sitting together, or pair more effectively. As long as the whole team is taking steps in the right direction, they know that they're improving how they plan, track, and execute the project. And this means that they're getting better every day—not just at XP, but at building software.

Key Points

- XP has five values that help teams get into the right mindset to avoid better-than-not-doing-it results.
- The XP value of **communication** means that every team member is aware of what his or her teammates are doing, and in constant communication with them.
- XP teams value **simplicity**, writing simple and direct solutions and avoiding complexity.
- By continuously testing and integrating, XP teams create **feedback loops** to keep their quality high.
- People on XP teams have the **courage** to make the best choices, even tough ones like throwing out bad solutions or doing more work in the short term to create a codebase that's easier to maintain in the long run.
- Every person on an XP team has **respect** for his or her teammates—and their managers and users.

Frequently Asked Questions

So what do I do first? How do I know what baby steps to take?

This is something that a lot of teams ask when they encounter XP, and there's no "one size fits all" answer. It depends on what your problems are. If you look at the first page of this chapter, you'll see a quote about how much people hate change. Don't underestimate that.

Adopting XP means making a change to how you build software. All of the excitement people have about the new practices can dissolve very quickly as soon as team members figure out that they need to do their work differently than they ever have before.

So what's the first step you need to take? Well, if you're looking at XP for solutions, then it stands to reason that you have problems that need to be solved. What are those problems? What XP practice can help with those problems?

If you have problems with bugs, try adding test-driven development first. If your team isn't communicating or people are surprised by changing requirements, add stories. But try one practice first—and don't just go through the motions. Sit down with the whole team and *talk about the XP values and principles.* Make sure that everyone understands what you're trying to accomplish with the practice. If every person understands the problem that you're trying to solve, and how it directly affects them, then you can measure how well the practice is working. This helps you tweak it if necessary—but, more importantly, it helps each person understand how that practice made their lives better. This helps them avoid the feeling that they're wasting precious time (which is what leads to practices slowly disappearing from the team).

Something's bothering me about pair programming—I can't really see doing it on my project. What gives?

When a team tries to adopt XP and eventually reverts to the way they were doing things before, pair programming is often the "canary in a coalmine" practice that disappears first. That often happens because it's the practice where a clash between the mindset of the team and the values of XP become most obvious. So if pair programming doesn't seem realistic for your team, think about each specific XP value. You can play a game of "Are you OK with?" about pair programing:

Communication
> Are you OK with talking to your teammates while you're programming? Are you OK with them talking to you? What about everyone talking about your code even if you're not around?

Simplicity
> Are you OK with someone pointing out that code you just wrote is too complex? Would you be willing to take the time to fix it now, rather than just put in a "TODO" or "TBD" comment? What if there's a looming deadline—are you still OK with that?

Feedback
> Are you OK with someone telling you—possibly bluntly, because programmers aren't always known for their tact—that your code isn't very good?

Courage
> Are you OK with watching someone else code and pointing out problems, even if it will cause an argument? What if you know that you might be wrong at least part of the time—are you OK being wrong about code? Are you OK with making mistakes in front of another developer, and having him or her notice? What if it's someone that you respect, or who's more senior to you?

Respect
> When someone does tell you that your code isn't great, are you willing to listen to him or her, and consider that they might be right, and you might be wrong? Are you OK with not holding a grudge?

If you and your team are not OK with these things, then that can help you figure out what you need to work on with your team before you adopt XP. What "are you OK with" question bothered everyone the most? Talk about it; figure out what's making people on the team uncomfortable. Set goals for yourself and your team to figure out how you might slowly chip away at that discomfort.

Or, worst-case scenario, if there's a mindset problem that simply will not allow you and your team to adopt pair programming, then find a different XP practice that you are OK with. But don't just adopt the "barren" practice—make sure that your whole team talks about each XP value, and really takes the principles seriously. After a while, there's a good chance that you'll come back to pair programming and discover that your mindset has changed, because you've taken baby steps with the other practices.

Why should my programmers write all those tests? I don't have extra headcount on my programming team to sit around and catch bugs. Isn't this why you hire cheaper QA people?
Test-first programming does a lot more than just adding tests and making sure that they're run. Are you uncomfortable with the idea of test-first programming or test-driven development? That's an indicator that you need to look at the values and principles. You'll probably find that you're not OK with one of them. You might have a problem with the XP principle of quality, which means that every person on the team is responsible for the quality of the project. You can't just throw the code over the wall to a tester, and make that person responsible for finding the bugs. Or maybe you're having trouble with redundancy—it seems like those tests add extra, potentially duplicate code to the codebase. Take a few minutes and actually look through the principles and values, and try to figure out what it is that's bothering you.

It's true that writing unit tests takes developers' time, and it's very common for developers who haven't written many unit tests to feel like it's a waste of their time, or beneath them.[7] But a funny thing happens when programmers start doing test-driven development. At some point, a unit test fails, and that failure uncovers a nasty little bug that would have taken hours to track down. After this happens a few times, a test-driven skeptic will often become a true believer. Many agile developers say that you become "test infected" when this happens, and test-driven development becomes the obvious way to build software.

One other thing to keep in mind: there's a lot more to test-first programming than meets the eye. In Chapter 7, you'll learn how writing unit tests first can have a profound impact on how the team designs their software. A team that does effective test-driven development will build better software, not just because they catch bugs, but because they build software differently than they do without writing tests first.

---

7 These developers are essentially saying, "I don't have time to go find bugs in our code—I'm too busy injecting them!"

Still not convinced? That's OK. You might just need to take a different approach to XP. Luckily, there are plenty of other practices that you can start with. Just like with pair programming, if you're having trouble convincing yourself or your team that test-first programming is the right way to go, then you can try a different baby step.

I'm a programmer, and this all feels very "loosey-goosey" to me. I typically get a ticket or a work item so that I know what I need to do every day. How do I know what I'm supposed to do next?

If you're used to working on a team where your project is tracked in a tracking system or on a Gantt chart, XP's approach to daily project work may seem very different to you. Every day you have a list of individual tasks to do, and you know that you're doing your job as you tick those tasks off. This is a comfortable way to work, because you always know that you're making progress. And it's comfortable for your boss and project manager, too—they can easily see the status of the project as tasks get checked off.

A developer who's used to working like that will often find a mature XP team difficult to work with at first. That's because in a command-and-control environment, someone else already took the requirements and broke them down into individual steps for you to follow—WBS items, work tickets, etc. This gives everyone a lot of structure, because all of those decisions were made at the beginning of the project.

An XP team doesn't do all of this up-front planning. They'll discuss themes and stories as part of their quarterly cycle, but they have very short, one-week iterations. Individual tasks are only planned on a week-by-week basis. This is the "extreme" part of Extreme Programming—that's an extreme way of making decisions at the last responsible moment, and to a developer who's used to having all of the decisions made very early, it feels like these decisions are cut extremely close.

Another way that an XP team may feel "disorganized" to someone used to a lot more structure: pairs are constantly switching, and people aren't planning ahead about who should do what task. The decisions about who does the work aren't even made until it's time to actually do the task. This is different from how Scrum teams function, with a daily meeting to review a sprint plan and assign tasks through self-organization. Because the XP team has such a short iteration and short feedback loops, they can leave the tasks in a pile and have each pair simply pull the next task off of the pile when they're ready for it.

How can you possibly expect a team to work well if each pair just pulls their next task off of a pile? Don't you need to plan out exactly who's doing which job, so that the person with the right expertise is doing it?

No. And, in fact, this is another area where XP works very well to help a team improve and evolve. At the beginning of the weekly cycle, the team looks at the stories that they're going to do, and they break those stories down into tasks. Because this is iterative development, at the end of the cycle they deliver working software that's "*done* done," and any partially completed stories are pushed to the next cycle. But they don't plan out who does each task. Instead, the tasks are left in a pile, queue, or other sort of collection. When a pair is done with their current task, they take the next one from the queue.

So does this mean that there's a rule that people have to take the next random task, even if there's someone else on the team better suited to do it? Of course not. The team members aren't robots. They'll do the job the best way they're capable of, making the smartest decisions they can along the way. But that's a decision that can be made just before the task needs to be done. It might make sense to swap pairs around so that someone who has a lot of relevant technical expertise pairs up with someone who wants to learn about it. That way, the next time there's a task that needs that expertise, the team has more options, because there are two people with that expertise.

There's a reason that XP doesn't have assigned roles. Here's what Kent Beck has to say about this in *Extreme Programming Explained*, 2nd Edition:

> After new, mutually respectful relationships are established among the team members, fixed roles interfere with the goal of having everyone do his best. Programmers can write a story if they are in the best position to write the story. Project managers can suggest architectural improvements if they are in the best position to suggest architectural improvements.

This reflects two important XP principles:

Accepted responsibility
Once the pair takes on the task, they commit to getting it done. If they run into problems, they'll do their best to deal with them. But they'll also ask for help from the rest of the team, even if that might bruise their egos a bit. (Hopefully, because they're sitting together, someone else will overhear their struggle and offer to help.)

Opportunity
Each new task is an opportunity for the developers doing the work to learn something new. If there's a technology that someone doesn't know, learning that technology becomes part of the task. This helps spread knowledge around the team, and it opens up more opportunities in the future.

There's one more idea that comes into play here: collective ownership. In addition to the 13 primary practices of XP, there are also 11 **corollary practices**:

Real customer involvement
Bringing customers into the quarterly and weekly planning sessions—and actually listening to them

Incremental deployment
Deploying small pieces of the system individually, rather than one "big shot" deployment (also, *believing* that a system can really be deployed this way)

Team continuity
> Keeping effective teams together

Shrinking teams
> As a team improves, they can get more work done more quickly; instead of adding work each week, remove a team member (and use that person to bring the XP culture to another team)

Root-cause analysis
> When something goes wrong, figure out what problem was, and then figure out why that problem occurred, and what caused that occurrence, and eliminate the problem further upstream

Shared code
> Every person on the team feels comfortable working on any piece of it, and everyone owns it collectively

Code and tests
> Only the code and the tests are maintained by the team; the documentation is generated automatically from the codebase, and history is kept alive as word-of-mouth team culture (because people rarely crack open dusty binders of old project plans, anyway)

Single codebase
> Don't manage multiple versions of the code

Daily deployment
> Push a new version of the software into production every day

Negotiated scope contract
> For a consulting company, instead of fixing the scope and negotiating time (and, often, sacrificing quality to meet the deadline), fix the time and have an ongoing negotiation of the scope

Pay-per-use
> This is another consulting-related practice—instead of charging for development work, charge the customer when they use the system; this gives real-time, constant feedback about which features are being used, and which aren't

We aren't going to talk about most of these corollary practices much in this book, but there's one of them that's relevant here: shared code. On an XP team, every single person on the project—even the project manager, if he or she is part of the team—has the right to edit any part of the codebase. Everyone owns everything, and they all have a feeling of ownership. This means that if a team member discovers a bug, they'll fix it, even if someone else injected it in the first place. This is different than how many traditional teams work, where each person is responsible for his or her own piece of the code.

(There is one more corollary practice that we'll talk a lot about: *root-cause analysis* and the *Five Whys* technique, which helps you to go beyond symptoms and fix the underlying problem when something goes wrong. We'll get back to this in Chapter 8.)

Breaking down these ownership barriers helps bring the whole team together, because when there's a problem they all feel an accepted responsibility for solving it. So if everyone feels responsible for the code, then everyone is equally capable of solving each task on the queue—or, at least, learning how to solve it. And the team feels like that learning process is part of the project, and worth their time.

There are really 11 corollary practices? Why are there so many XP practices?

If the number of practices in XP seems overwhelming, that's an indication that *you may have a checklist-oriented mindset* toward the XP practices—and we saw earlier how that kind of mindset can lead you to only get better-than-not-doing-it results. The corollary practices are there because they help solve problems that teams run into as they get better at building better software. One warning sign that you're taking a checklist approach is if you find yourself thinking, "How am I going to do all of these practices at once?" Remember the XP principles of baby steps improvement; if you take the time to understand what the practices do for you and your team, it will be easier to incorporate them and gradually improve how you and your team work together.

In Chapter 7, you'll learn about how the XP practices work together and have a big impact on the way that a team designs and builds code. As you read it, try to look for ways that the practices work together and reinforce each other. That will help give you the perspective to move beyond a checklist mindset and start to see XP as a whole system.

 Things You Can Do Today

Here are a few things that you can try today on your own or with your team:

- Give pair programming a shot, even if it feels a little weird at first. You don't need to commit to doing it forever; just try it for a few hours and see how it feels. You may find that it's a lot more comfortable than you expect!

- If you're a developer, try continuous integration. You don't even need to get the rest of your team on board with it (yet)—you can try it today. Next time you reach a breaking point in whatever you're doing, pull the latest code from the version control repository into your sandbox, and do whatever testing you need to do in order to feel comfortable that it's integrated. Do it again in a few hours. How often do you catch an integration problem that's easy to solve now, but would give you a headache later?

- Try test-driven development. Next time you create a new class (or module, or subroutine—whatever's considered a unit in the language that you're using), first build a unit test. Don't worry about making a complete test that covers every possible edge case; just create a simple test that runs, but which currently fails. You may need to spend some time learning how unit testing works with the language; this is a good exercise as well.

Where You Can Learn More

Here are resources to help you learn more about the ideas in this chapter:

- You can learn more about the practices, values, and principles of XP in *Extreme Programming Explained: Embrace Change, 2nd Edition*, by Kent Beck with Cynthia Andres (Addison-Wesley, 2004).
- You can learn more about unit testing and test-driven development in *Pragmatic Unit Testing*, by Andy Hunt and Dave Thomas (Pragmatic Bookshelf: Java version 2003, C# version 2007).

Coaching Tips

Tips for agile coaches helping their team to work with the ideas in this chapter:

- This is one of the most challenging aspects of agile coaching, especially for agile coaches who do not have a programming background. Focus on the XP values and principles, and help the team figure out for themselves how they impact the code.

- It's easy for teams to lose track of courage and respect. Help the team find examples where they were hesitant to give someone outside of the team a real view of the code quality. For example, did the team ever manipulate a demo to work around a known bug? Or change a bug report so that it seemed less severe than it was? Help them find ways to communicate this better.

- Where can the team do a better job communicating? Help them to find opportunities for creating information radiators.

CHAPTER 7

XP, Simplicity, and Incremental Design

I'm not a great programmer; I'm just a good programmer with great habits.
—Kent Beck, *creator of XP*

The goals of XP go beyond simply getting the team to work better. The larger goal of XP—of its practices, values, and principles—is to help teams **build software that can be extended and changed easily**, and to help those teams work, plan, and grow together in an environment that accepts and embraces these changes.

Adopting XP means more than just using pair programming for constant code reviews, or test-driven development to increase test coverage. Higher quality and getting along better with your teammates are great by-products of XP, and they help achieve the main goal. Those things are good, and they change the *way* that the team builds software, but *they don't fundamentally change the design of the software.*

It's worth repeating: an important goal of XP is software that can be changed easily. Teams can embrace change when they build software that is easier to change. This has a profound impact on how a good XP team approaches code and software design.

This also points to one of the keys to getting into the right mindset for XP: truly believing that practices you learned about in Chapter 6 like test-driven development, pair programming, and slack help you and your team to think about software design differently—and that leaving those practices out can lead you to build an inferior codebase that's difficult to change.

In this chapter, you'll learn how even smart programmers can build code with serious code and design problems. You'll learn about the final three primary practices of XP, and how they help you avoid those serious code and design problems. You'll learn about many great habits that XP team members develop (like Kent Beck talks about in the quote that begins this chapter). And you'll learn how all of the XP practices form an ecosystem that leads to better, more maintainable, flexible, and changeable code.

 ## Narrative: a team working on a fantasy basketball website

Justin – a developer

Danielle – another developer

Bridget – their project manager

Act IV: Going into Overtime, Part 2: Second Overtime

Justin usually intended to leave the office in time for the 5:42 p.m. train. Somehow that rarely happened. Today was no exception. And it always seemed to start the same way: a small bug to fix, or a minor tweak that he would want to put into the code, usually an hour before he wanted to leave. Somehow that small change would turn into a monster.

It always seemed to follow the same pattern. Partway through making a seemingly straightforward change, Justin would discover that it required him to change another part of the code. OK, no problem—he'd go ahead and change that code as well. But to get that second change to work, he'd need to make changes to a third and fourth part of the code. One of those changes might require him to jump to yet another part of the codebase, and then another, and maybe even another. Sometimes, by the time he finished finding all of the places that had to be fixed, he'd almost forget why he was making the change in the first place.

Once in a while, the change was so drastic that he just couldn't do it. He'd meet with Danielle and Bridget, and they'd decide that the changes required were so risky that they would destabilize the codebase. There was something particularly demoralizing about spending so many frustrating hours making a change, only to back it out and undo everything.

Tonight was no different. He was following the same change-upon-change-upon-change pattern. Justin remembered telling Danielle, "I promised my girlfriend I'd be home early, so I'm just going to do this one last thing." All he'd had to do was put an extra option in a drop-down box on the settings page. It was simple.

That was over five hours ago.

If he'd realized it was going to take this long, he would have logged in from home to get it done. Or, even better, he would have left it for tomorrow and not started in the first place.

Justin was trying to fix a drop-down menu that stored player configuration stats on the fantasy teams. All he'd needed to do was to add an option to a drop-down to let the user hide the ranking for the player. He got the item added to the drop-down, but the page kept giving its "You must select an item from the list" message whenever that new item was selected in the list. And it was taking him hours to get that seemingly simple bit of behavior to work.

When he debugged through the page validator code, he saw that it read the items from a cached copy of a database table, so he'd added a call to refresh the cache when the user clicked the "OK" button, and now the item was validating—which had required him to jump around the code and make three additional changes. And then there were three other pages that reused this same settings page, and he had to modify them as well.

All told, Justin had to make over a dozen different changes to the code, but he ended up with code that worked—thanks to a lousy, kludge[1] of a hack. He'd asked Danielle for advice, and she came up with a workaround for a nasty problem that he was having. "That cache refresh only uses the user ID number. Try creating a fake user class that only has its ID filled in, and returns null for everything else." It was ugly, but it worked.

Justin finally got his item added to the drop-down box. The familiar late-at-the-office feeling had set in long ago. He told Danielle, "Finally done. I'm going home. And I've been bouncing around so many parts of the code to get this stupid item in the box to work, I think I know what a pinball feels like."

She replied, "I know what you mean. I thought I would just make this one change to the login page, but to get it to work I had to change its code in three other places. Two of those changes required more changes to other classes, and one of those classes calls a service that's giving me a response that I don't know what to do with."

Justin asked, "Why is it always like this?"

Danielle said, "That's just how programming is. The real question is, are you really sure the code you just wrote works?"

---

1 A kludge (the "u" is usually pronounced "oo") is engineering slang for a quick-and-dirty solution that gets the job done but is ugly, clumsy, inelegant, and difficult to maintain. There's a bit more subtlety to this word than we can fit in a footnote. If you're not familiar with this idea, go and look it up right now.

She wished she hadn't asked the question. They stared at each other for a few uncomfortable seconds. "I'd better spend a few more minutes testing this." He put his headphones back on and started typing another apology text to his girlfriend.

Code and Design

In the story of the Chrysler Comprehensive Compensation (C3) project, Kent Beck needed to shift the team's cultural values away from creating clever code to creating simple solutions, a notoriously difficult task. One technique he used was the peer-pressure ritual. In one such ritual, the group formed a procession, placed a propeller beanie on the head of someone with an overly clever solution, and then spun the propeller on the beanie, commenting on the "cleverness" of the solution. The negative attention from peers caused people to move away from clever solutions; appreciation for simple designs drew them to simple solutions. True to people being different, not everyone on the team was "malleable" enough to adopt XP. One person did not enjoy the new working style with its requirements for conformity and close cooperation and eventually left the project.

—Alistair Cockburn, *Agile Software Development: The Cooperative Game,* 2nd Edition

XP teams build code that is easy to change. But how do they do this? It's not like anybody sets out to build code that's difficult to change.

In fact, a lot of developers—even really smart ones!—set out to do the opposite. They'll talk with their teams about building code to be reusable, and will spend a lot of time trying to design the perfect, most highly reusable components possible. But it's very difficult to plan for reuse, and far too easy to end up with code that's overly abstract and general, which has as much code devoted to building up a framework as it does code devoted to actually getting the job done. It's amazing how often today's really clever design for a reusable library turns into tomorrow's obstacle that the team has to work around, or is afraid to touch.

A lot of people assume that writing brittle code that's difficult to change is a rookie mistake. But more often, some of the best developers are the ones who build code that turns out to be difficult to change. (Very inexperienced developers rarely build up a codebase large enough to have much complexity.) It's not because the software that they built is necessarily poorly written, or even poorly designed. In most cases, it comes down to a matter of clever versus simple.

It's very natural for developers (especially smart ones) to try to solve not just today's problem, but also tomorrow's. Most of us have been in a planning session that never seemed to end because everyone could think of just one more edge case that would be difficult to implement. And the bigger the problem the team has to solve, the more work it takes to solve it.

Scrum teams avoid the endless planning problem by breaking the project down into sprints. They focus only on today's problems, and push everything else off to a future sprint. They make decisions about the planning at the last responsible moment. And when XP teams do their iterative planning using quarterly and weekly cycles, they're accomplishing the same thing.

Making decisions at the last responsible moment is not just a planning tool. It's also a very valuable tool for design, architecture, and coding. And it's the main means by which XP teams achieve the XP principle of **simplicity**.

If you've spent time as a programmer on a few different teams, odds are that you've seen code that's difficult to change. That code wasn't built to be difficult. It was built to do something—it's just that the thing it was built to do is different than what it needs to do now. And after a few rounds of repurposing, that code somehow became difficult. So why did the code end up that way?

Code Smells and Antipatterns (or, How to Tell If You're Being Too Clever)

Simplicity starts with knowing how not to do too much.

Here's an example of how complexity—a lack of simplicity—can affect a product. When one of the authors of this book was in college, he was given a gift of a kitchen appliance that was a combination of a blender, mixer, and food processor. It didn't do any of those jobs particularly well: it was a pretty good blender, a mediocre mixer, and an utterly unusable food processor. It also had additional problems that you wouldn't typically get with any of those appliances. For example, it had odd-shaped parts that were difficult to store and almost impossible to clean.

Nevertheless, for more than 10 years after college, he didn't buy a new mixer or food processor, because it seemed redundant. But because the hodgepodge appliance's food processor did such a lousy job, he avoided making any recipes that required a food processor. When he finally put the thing on a high shelf (he still couldn't bring himself to throw out a "perfectly good" electrical appliance) and bought the cheapest food processor at the local chain drug store, suddenly he could make a whole range of recipes that he hadn't been able to previously. And he wondered why it took over 10 years to get around to doing this.

This appliance was worse than useless. Instead of allowing its owner to make recipes that required a food processor, it basically *prevented* him from making them. But at the same time, its *mere existence* prevented him from buying another food processor, so for years he simply avoided any recipes that required a food processor. It's not that he didn't have the ability to make these recipes. It just somehow never seemed worth it to make the recipe because it was so much extra work to use the appliance. But for years it never even occurred to him to buy a new food processor, because he already had a "perfectly good" one. He *definitely* would have bought one had he not already had this appliance.

The reason that this appliance was so bad was because it was **complex**. Doing three jobs in one required extra parts, and required technical compromises that led to a design that was unintuitive and difficult to use (for example, it was very hard to get the mixer attachment on, because it wouldn't work unless it was seated perfectly). Replacing the hodgepodge with three **simple** components—say, a cheap blender, a cheap mixer, and a cheap food processor—would have cost less to begin with, taken up less storage space, and allowed for much more flexibility in the kitchen.

Problems like this are why simplicity is one of the XP values that we learned about in Chapter 6. XP teams recognize that this exact sort of complexity problem can affect project planning—just like we saw earlier in the book when our Scrum teams ran into trouble.

It's not hard, for example, to get most people to agree that for a team to be productive and get work done on a project, it's not useful for the project to have people who are sitting around idle with nothing to do. However, some command-and-control project managers take this idea to an extreme: they'll come up with a project plan that has every resource 100% allocated,[2] and require each developer to log every minute of his or her time against an approved task to make sure that all of the time is accounted for. Doing all of this extra tracking to achieve 100% allocation and verify that everyone is working all the time creates a lot of project management overhead: people need to keep track of their time and enter it (which doesn't sound like a lot of work in theory, but in practice can be time consuming and mentally taxing); managers need to create, update, and review the plans; and there are inevitably many meetings to "fix" problems because a developer only seems to be working 95% of the time.

This is a complex project management system—but more importantly, that extra complexity *doesn't actually add value to the project*. The team now spends approximately 20% of their time keeping track of and talking about what they do with the other 80%, which makes the whole project take longer. It seems like the team spends more and more of their time in status meetings, answering questions like, "What percent complete are you?" and, "Can you estimate how many more minutes you'll be spending on this task?"

An XP team uses iteration to make project planning decisions at the last responsible moment, just like Scrum teams. These practices are a much less complex way of planning projects. XP teams do not typically monitor everyone's time constantly, the way that the project manager in our example does, because monitoring everyone's time all the time doesn't actually help the project get done. Despite lofty intentions, the information that's collected from all of that monitoring is rarely used to make projections during the project, and is almost never revisited after the project is done. Worse, we

---

2 This particular sort of command-and-control project manager has a habit of referring to team members as "resources" all the time, even in casual conversation.

already know from earlier in the book that projects change over time. Planning for 100% allocation requires the entire team to make all of their project-related decisions at the beginning of the project; when any one of those decisions turns out to be wrong (and some always will—that's a normal part of running a project), it requires the entire team to revisit the plans, tasks, and allocation levels.

There's also a larger lesson in this example that can help you understand XP, and it has to do with recognizing patterns and using them to improve how you work.

If you've ever been on a team where a strict command-and-control project manager requires everyone to have 100% allocation, calls endless meetings to check everyone's status and ensure that allocation, and requires everyone to constantly update their tasks to meet that artificial allocation, then reading the last few paragraphs probably made you anxious and angry, and possibly gave you flashbacks to endless status meetings. This is because you recognized an **antipattern**: a pattern of behavior that a team exhibits that causes problems with the project. Recognizing the antipattern in project management gives you a way to call out the problem, and hopefully find solutions that will help simplify the way your project is managed—and let the team get back to building the product.

XP Teams Look for Code Smells and Fix Them

Code also has antipatterns, and just like with our project management antipattern, recognizing code antipatterns is the first step in stripping the complexity away from your codebase. When an antipattern specifically relates to the structure or design of code, it's called a **code smell**. XP teams are always on the lookout for these code smells, and develop the habit of fixing them when they find them, rather than letting them fester.

We're going to spend some time talking about a few of the most common code smells, so that you can better understand the mindset of an effective XP developer. This particular list isn't arbitrary; it comes from the experiences of many, many developers who discussed problems they've found in their own projects over the years. The terms "code smell" and "antipattern" first became popular with developers in the mid- to late 1990s, in large part thanks to the WikiWikiWeb (*http://c2.com/cgi/wiki*), the very first wiki, created by Ward Cunningham, one of the authors of the Agile Manifesto. The WikiWikiWeb was (and in some circles, continues to be) one of the most popular places for developers to discuss software design. The more people got together to discuss design and architecture problems they found in their projects, the more they found that there were common symptoms that they shared.[3]

---

3 We highly encourage every reader to read about many different kinds of code smells and antipatterns. In our opinion, one of the best sources for this information is still the original Wiki set up by Ward Cunningham (*http://bit.ly/code-smell*).

Many software engineers—including us—had an almost visceral response when first encountering these problems. It's a strange feeling to have a frustrating issue that you can't quite put your finger on perfectly described by a stranger. And that's actually a very important thing to keep in mind throughout this discussion: that these problems are *created by people*, recognized by people, and can be prevented or fixed by people. The symptoms might be technical in nature, but the root cause is a problem that affects the people on the team, so the solution will have to be both technical and team-oriented.

When we're holding training sessions for developers, the code smell that gets more people nodding their heads in recognition and agreement is **shotgun surgery**. This is what happens when you attempt to make a small change to one part of the code, but find that it requires changes to, say, two or three more seemingly unrelated or barely related parts of the codebase. You try to make those changes, only to discover that one or two of them require additional, also apparently unrelated changes. If the codebase is particularly smelly, it's not uncommon for a programmer to attempt a change that *should* be simple, make a dozen or more hops throughout the code, and eventually give up because his brain hurts from keeping track of the expanding trail of cascading changes.

When a developer digs down into the code that caused him to perform shotgun surgery, he'll often find code that exhibits another code smell: **half-baked code** (or half-baked objects, because this is not uncommon in object-oriented programming). Code smells half-baked when a programmer, in order to use one object (or module, unit, etc.), must also initialize other objects in a specific, prescribed way. For example, after initializing a particular library, a programmer always has to set certain variables to their default values, and must also initialize a separate library that it's dependent on. He only knows to do this because of documentation or sample code; failing to initialize it correctly will cause it to crash—or worse, exhibit unpredictable behavior.

Figure 7-1. Effective XP developers are in the habit of finding and fixing code smells like **very large classes** *and* **duplicated code***. These antipatterns have to do with the structure of individual units. We'll use gears as a visual metaphor for code in the figures in this chapter.*

Some code smells have to do with the way the code itself is written. When your code has **very large classes** (or, for non-object-oriented code, very large methods, or functions, or modules, etc.), it can be difficult to read and maintain. But more importantly, it's often an indication that it's trying to do too many things, and can be separated out into smaller units that are easier to understand. On the flip side, **duplicated code** is an identical (or almost identical) block of code that shows up in more than one place. This is a very likely source of bugs, especially if a programmer makes a change to three of the duplicates, but forgets to make that change to the fourth.

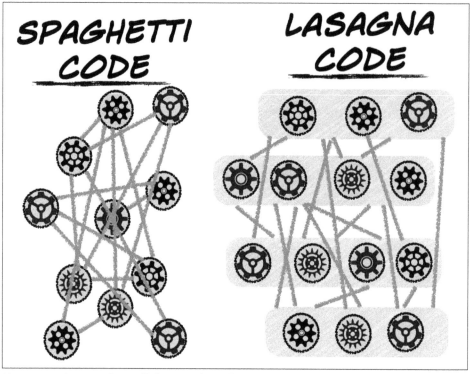

Figure 7-2. Some code smells have to do with the larger design of the system, and how the units interact with each other.

Other code smells concern the overall design of the code—how the individual units of code interact with each other. **Spaghetti code**, or code that has a complex and tangled structure, is one of the oldest code smells known to software engineering, dating back to at least the 1960s. You can often identify spaghetti code because it's decorated with scary or apologetic comments from other developers who previously tried and failed to detangle it. But its smelly cousin, **lasagna code**, might be a more insidious problem. Modern software design typically divides code into *layers* that each have a specific purpose or behavior that contributes to the whole design. However, when there are far too many layers, and those layers don't necessarily have a coherent pattern to them, it gets difficult to understand exactly what any one layer is supposed to do. This can be compounded by **leaks** between layers, where code, types, or ideas that should be contained within one layer find their way into neighboring ones.

Hooks, Edge Cases, and Code That Does Too Much

The code smells we just described are antipatterns that have to do with the *structure* of the code. There can also be problems with *what code does*. And effective XP developers understand that they need to be concerned with code behavior as much as code structure.

Here's a quick example. A team will anticipate a way that a unit of code—like a Java class—will be used in the future, and add a **hook**, or a placeholder to handle that future case. The hook seems "free" (because there's so little to it), but it really does have a cost: tying the team to a decision made today that could be put off until later. When it finally comes time to use the hook, the team has learned more about the problem that has to be solved, and the hook needs to change. It's frustrating for a team to discover that they made assumptions about how the hook would be used, only to realize they designed another part of the software around that hook. So now the hook is harder to change—despite the fact that it's empty!—because it's already used elsewhere in the code. A programmer who's in the habit of adding too many hooks forgets where those hooks are. She'll routinely run into trouble where she tries to use code she wrote a few weeks ago, only to discover that she never actually wrote the code, and instead will find a comment that says "TODO" where code should be. This is an antipattern: adding so many hooks that it's difficult to keep track of exactly what the code actually does.

Another antipattern that can make code difficult to understand is obsessing over edge cases. An **edge case** is a situation that happens rarely, and under a specific set of circumstances.[4] For example, a program that loads data from a file needs to handle the case where that file is not found. That program may also need to handle the case where the folder that contains the file cannot be found, possibly following different behavior than in the first case. There's also the case where the file exists but cannot be read from, or the case where the file is deleted partway through the read, or the case where the data in the file is in the wrong character set. A good programmer will be able to think of many, many edge cases just for the simple situation of loading data from a file. Where do you draw the line?

Many developers get bogged down in handling too many edge cases. There's a genuine need to handle edge cases, and many code situations require handling for several distinct ones. But every time additional code is added to handle each new edge case, the project has diminishing returns. There's a trap that some programmers are especially prone to where they spend as much time "bullet-proofing" their code against edge cases as they do writing the rest of the code. This is the point where edge cases become similar to overplanning, and start diverting effort. By its nature, code to handle edge cases is rarely run. If the code looks like a tangle of edge case handling, that makes it more difficult to understand, which makes it hard to change.

---

4 Some people use the terms *edge case* and *corner case* interchangeably. Others consider a corner case to be a very rare edge case (because a corner is where two edges meet).

Good developers tend to be the sort of people who obsess about details—and edge cases are exactly that sort of detail. And cleverness can turn a good developer into an edge-case-obsessed extremist. When this happens, team meetings are hijacked by a passionate but endless discussion of edge cases for a specific situation, where every programmer in the room suddenly develops a strong opinion that his or her favorite obscure edge case absolutely must be handled.

When developers overplan for edge cases or add too many hooks, they're being too clever. Instead of thinking about building code that's simple and easy to change, they're thinking about building code that's too complex, too abstract, or solves tomorrow's problems and not just today's.

This brings us to what we call the **framework trap**, an antipattern that stems from extreme developer cleverness. The framework trap is what we call it when a developer has to solve a single problem or perform a task, but instead of just writing code to do that one thing, he writes a larger framework that can be used in the future to solve similar problems or perform similar tasks.

Ron Jeffries, who worked with Kent Beck to co-found XP, described a simple way to avoid the framework trap: "Always implement things when you actually need them, never when you just foresee that you need them."[5] Some XP teams like to use the acronym YAGNI, or "You Ain't Gonna Need It," when they talk about this. When you try to foresee a need, and then you build extra code to meet that need, you're very cleverly falling into the framework trap.

---

5 From the Wikipedia page (*http://bit.ly/YAGNI-rule*) for YAGNI (retrieved July 6, 2014).

Figure 7-3. Brilliant web comic xkcd (http://xkcd.com/1319) shows what happens when developers fall into the framework trap.

Instead of solving that single, specific problem that needs to be solved today, clever developers like to aim bigger. They'll have thoughts along the lines of, "I can write this simple solution, but it will be even better if I build something that automates much of the work I just did so that nobody ever has to solve a problem like this one again." A developer who started out building a web page ends up with a framework that generates web pages. An attempt to solve a specific performance problem turns into a large, general-purpose cache. A simple program to download files on a schedule somehow acquires a scripting engine.

It's not hard to understand why developers go this route. Say that someone is thinking the following: "Had someone else built a framework for the job I'm working on right now, then I could just use it. So why not take a little extra time, put in the thought to abstract the problem, and come up with a more general solution?" That's actually a pretty noble sentiment, and it helps explain why so many teams fall into the framework trap.

Wait a minute, what's wrong with reusable frameworks?

Nothing's wrong with reusable frameworks, and there's certainly nothing in XP that precludes the use or the development of frameworks. In fact, one of our most popular books, *Head First C#*, teaches programmers how to use the .NET Framework, Microsoft's technology for building Windows applications. There are great frameworks on every platform for building web applications, rendering 3D graphics, building networked services, and doing many, many other things.

But that doesn't mean your project should set out to build a framework.

Let's talk about reusability for a minute, because the framework trap is our name for an antipattern related to building reusable code that XP teams learn to avoid. **Reusable code**—or code that is general enough so that it can be used in more than one part of the system—is one of those things that developers strive for. And it makes a lot of sense. Buttons in dialog boxes in your word processor work and look similar to each other. It would be very inefficient if the team that built the word processor coded each button from scratch; they'll write the code for the button once, and reuse it each time they need a button in a dialog. But the dialog buttons in your word processor work and look similar to the buttons in your browser's dialog boxes, and those are pretty much the same buttons as the ones in the dialog boxes in almost every other application. So the code for those buttons is (probably) somewhere outside any of those programs—your operating system provides libraries for basic buttons. The button code was written once, and reused thousands of times over. This is clearly a timesaver.

Programmers rarely build things from the ground up. They have all kinds of libraries that they use for reading and writing files, using network resources, drawing graphics, and almost any other thing that lots of programs do. This is a basic fact of programming. In fact, when a good programmer encounters a problem he hasn't solved yet, it's very common for him to first do a web search to see if there's a library to solve it. So once a programmer solves a problem that other people might run into, his first urge is often to figure out how to share his code for it.[6] This is a normal, productive way to think about building software.

---

6 We've done this ourselves. If you look on our website (*http://www.stellman-greene.com*), you'll see a few open source libraries that we've published so other programmers don't have to solve the same problems we did.

What's the difference between a library and a framework?

You know you're using a library if you can bring it into your project as a single independent part, without having to bring many other parts along with it. The difference is that a library is about *separating* code into small, reusable components. If the goal is to build simple code, then every component should do exactly one thing; a component that does many things should be separated into smaller, more independent units. This kind of separation is called **separation of concerns**, and effective XP developers recognize that it is an important element of code simplicity.

A framework, on the other hand, is about *combining* many small, reusable pieces into one large system. Learning C#, for example, usually means learning to use the .NET Framework as well as the syntax of the C# language. It includes libraries for accessing files, doing mathematical calculations, connecting to networks, and many, many other things (yes, including buttons). When you start building your program with C# and .NET, you get all of these things for "free" because they're part of the .NET Framework. It's generally not possible to separate them out. And it wouldn't really make sense to try to use one piece of the .NET Framework in a program that isn't written with .NET. Like most frameworks, many pieces have been combined into a large, all-or-nothing system.

Frameworks are much more complex than libraries, and a team that tries to build a framework when a library is more appropriate will often end up with overly complex design. This mistake is common when programmers see that other frameworks save them a lot of time, and want their code to do the same thing: "I didn't have to include any libraries to use this button in my .NET program, I just got it for 'free.' If I build a framework for my whole system, look at all of the things I can give other developers for 'free,' too!"

The downside of approaching a problem this way is that if you want to get all of those things for "free," you must use the entire framework. And this sometimes causes you to think about the problem differently. A .NET developer will naturally think about a problem somewhat differently from a Java developer (but not always too differently, because the frameworks for Java and .NET share many concepts), and very differently from a C++, Python, Perl, or Lisp developer. This is because when you have a set of tools to solve a problem, you think about the solution in terms of those tools. These are examples of languages and their frameworks (you typically don't think about building software in Java, Python, or Perl without also thinking about their standard libraries), so they don't place many restrictions on the way you think about the problem you're solving.

Figure 7-4. Building complex frameworks to solve simple problems sometimes feels like the right thing to do at the time (source: xkcd (http://xkcd.com/974/)).

Here's a common example of framework-oriented thinking. Teams use build scripts to automatically build their software. (In Chapter 6, we learned that on XP teams, these scripts run in under 10 minutes.) There are many tools for building scripts like this, and many of them include scripting languages. But for a framework-minded developer who works on several projects, it's not enough to write a separate build script for each project. It seems like there is far too much duplicated code between those scripts—and often, there is—so he'll write an entire build framework for all of the projects. ("If you use my framework, you don't ever have to write a build script. You'll get builds for 'free'!") So instead of having a small script for each project, there's a large framework that has to be maintained separately. This developer made a trade-off: he prevented a few dozen lines of build script from being repeated in several projects, but replaced it with a framework that consists of hundreds or even thousands of lines of code. When something goes wrong with the build (which, based on Murphy's law, usually happens at midnight just before a release), instead of troubleshooting a small build script, the developer who's trying to get the build to run has to track down a bug in a large framework. This is *not simple*.

Combining a lot of functionality into a large framework to solve a specific problem may work really well to solve that particular problem. When the problem itself changes, the framework makes it more difficult to respond to change.

In other words, by combining a lot of different pieces into a large framework, team members think that they're saving time, but what they're really doing is limiting their ability to respond to new information and needs. We call this the *framework trap*, and we can use it as an important idea for learning about simplicity and how it affects your project. The reason we like it as an example is that it captures an important aspect of a mindset that isn't always compatible with XP: a developer who prefers to combine behavior together into one large unit, rather than separate it into many small units.

Figure 7-5. A framework that seems like a good idea today can turn into a burden tomorrow.

Code Smells Increase Complexity

We've just described a bunch of code smells that XP teams habitually avoid. One thing that these code smells all have in common is that they *increase the complexity of their projects*. And the converse is true: if you find yourself having to remember how to initialize an object, or straining to remember a cascade of changes that you need to make, or giving up trying to pick your way through some painful spaghetti code, those are all indications that your projects' codebase almost certainly has a lot of unnecessary complexity. This is why XP teams strive to find and fix code smells as early as possible.

These aren't the only code smells, and they may not even be the most common ones on your projects. However, we chose these because after talking to many developers over the years, we've found that almost everyone recognizes at least one of these problems in their own code. These problems don't happen because of randomness, poorly skilled developers, or deliberate decisions caused by laziness or maliciousness. They're the result of bad habits that developers fall into, especially when they're pressed for time, or when they're forced to work around constraints (especially ones that *they put into the code* earlier in the project).

So what do you do when you find code smells in your project? Can they be prevented?

Key Points

- XP teams spot **code smells** (or **antipatterns** in their code) to avoid complexity and keep their design simple.

- Code smells like **half-baked code** and **very large classes** help teams spot individual units that can be simplified.

- Smells like **lasagna code** help them find problems in the larger design.

- An especially frustrating code smell called **shotgun surgery** happens when a developer tries to fix a problem, only to find that it requires a fix to other parts of the codebase, which themselves require additional fixes.

- Teams that overplan for edge cases, add too many hooks, or build large frameworks to solve individual problems are being too clever and end up with overly complex code.

- Even highly skilled teams can run into these problems when they have bad habits.

Make Code and Design Decisions at the Last Responsible Moment

[T]he shift to XP-style design is a shift in the timing of design decisions. Design is deferred until it can be made in the light of experience and the decisions can be used immediately. This allows the team to:

- Deploy software sooner.

- Make decisions with certainty.

- Avoid living with bad decisions.

- Maintain the pace of development as the original design assumptions are superseded.

The price of this strategy is that it requires the discipline to continue investing in design throughout the life of the project and to make large changes in small steps, so as to maintain the flow of valuable new functionality.

—Kent Beck *Extreme Programming Explained: Embrace Change,* 2nd Edition

We already know that Scrum teams make project planning decisions at the last responsible moment. This allows them to have a *much simpler plan*—often just a set of story and task cards on a task board, combined with a backlog. And it allows them to have much simpler project meetings, which can be timeboxed because only the relevant information is discussed.

To put it another way, Scrum teams *use the idea of the last responsible moment to bring simplicity to project planning,* and it helps increase productivity and lets teams make better decisions by avoiding project management antipatterns.

When it comes to planning the technical side of the project, XP teams do something very similar: they apply their core value of simplicity to architecture, design, and code. And just like Scrum teams, they do this by making decisions about architecture, design, and code at the last responsible moment. And much of the time, that moment happens *after* your code is written.

Does the idea of making code design decisions after the code is written seem odd? It doesn't seem odd to an XP developer, because XP teams are constantly **refactoring** their code: changing the structure of the code without changing its behavior. Refactoring isn't unique to XP; it's a common and very effective programming technique that XP teams have consistently adopted. In fact, most IDEs (programs that developers use to edit, run, and debug code) have refactoring tools built into them.

Here's an example of refactoring—and even if you're not a developer, you should be able to see how this refactoring made the code clearer and easier to understand. When we were writing our book on C# programming, *Head First C#*, we included the following block of code as a solution to one of the projects (a beehive simulator, hence all of the bee-related variable names) that we have our readers build.

```
                 foreach (Bee bee in world.Bees) {
                     beeControl = GetBeeControl(bee);
These four           if (bee.InsideHive) {
lines move a             if (fieldForm.Controls.Contains(beeControl)) {
BeeControl from              fieldForm.Controls.Remove(beeControl);
the Field form               beeControl.Size = new Size(40, 40);
to the Hive form.            hiveForm.Controls.Add(beeControl);
                             beeControl.BringToFront();
                     } else if (hiveForm.Controls.Contains(beeControl)) {      And these four
                         hiveForm.Controls.Remove(beeControl);                  lines move a
                         beeControl.Size = new Size(20, 20);                    BeeControl from
                         fieldForm.Controls.Add(beeControl);                    the Hive form to
                         beeControl.BringToFront();                             the Field form.
                     }
                     beeControl.Location = bee.Location;
                 }
```

Figure 7-6. *This was the original code snippet from one of the projects in our book on C# programming, Head First C#.*

During technical review, one of our reviewers pointed out that this code was too complex—he smelled a very large method. So we did something that most XP teams would do: we refactored this code to make it simpler and easier to understand. In this case, we took a block of four lines of code and moved them to a method that we named MoveBeeFromFieldToHive(). Then we did the same thing with another four-line block, extracting it into a method that we named MoveBeeFromHiveToField(). Here's how the code looked when it finally went to press (the two new methods appeared later in the code).

```
foreach (Bee bee in world.Bees) {
    beeControl = GetBeeControl(bee);
    if (bee.InsideHive) {
        if (fieldForm.Controls.Contains(beeControl))
            MoveBeeFromFieldToHive(beeControl);
    } else if (hiveForm.Controls.Contains(beeControl))
        MoveBeeFromHiveToField(beeControl, bee);
    beeControl.Location = bee.Location;
}
```

Figure 7-7. *We refactored the code by extracting two methods. The new code was simpler, which made it easier to see exactly what the code did.*

This is much clearer. Before the refactoring, if you wanted to understand what that code did, it required more knowledge about how the whole program was structured, so we had to add handwritten annotations to help readers understand two blocks of code. Moving those blocks of code into named methods made it more obvious how this code worked. In the refactored version, you can see exactly what those blocks do: one moves a bee from the field to the hive, and the other moves a bee from the hive back to the field.

This refactoring made a block of code easier to understand. But it also reduced the complexity of the entire project. It's not unreasonable to assume that somewhere else in the project, the programmer may need to move bees between the field and the hive. If these methods already exist, then it's much more likely that he'll use them—that's the path of least resistance. And even if he doesn't do that at first, if he smells the duplicated code later, he's more likely to do the quick refactoring to remove the duplicate code and replace it with method calls.

Fix Technical Debt by Refactoring Mercilessly

> Shipping first time code is like going into debt. A little debt speeds development so long as it is paid back promptly with a rewrite... The danger occurs when the debt is not repaid.

—Ward Cunningham, *Agile Manifesto author*

Poor software design and development adds up over time. Even great developers write code that can stand to be improved. The longer that design and code problems linger in the codebase, the more those problems can compound, which eventually leads to headaches like shotgun surgery. Teams refer to these lingering design and code problems as **technical debt**. An effective XP team leaves time in each cycle to "pay down" debt. This is a good way to use **slack**, the primary XP practice we covered in Chapter 6 in which the team adds stories and tasks to each weekly cycle as a buffer to absorb unexpected work.

Any good financial advisor will tell you that the best way to avoid money problems is never to get into debt in the first place. The same goes for technical debt. This is why XP teams **refactor mercilessly**, constantly smelling their code and looking for ways to simplify it through refactoring. As the programmers refactor, they learn more and more about how their code is used, and how that actual use differs from the way they'd expected it to be used. Through constant revision, each unit in the codebase gets increasingly better suited to the way it will actually be used. That iterative nature of constant coding and revision is something that a lot of teams don't necessarily plan for at the beginning of the project. But even though it takes extra time, refactoring mercilessly saves far more time than it costs, because a simple codebase is much easier to work with than a complex one.

When everyone on a team is in the habit of constantly refactoring, they build a code-base *that is much easier to change.* When the team members discover that they need to implement a new story, or more commonly, they discover that they misunderstood one of the stories and have to change the code, it's much easier to make the change to the code. They can embrace change—a primary goal of every XP team—because they're not fighting against the code to make the changes.

Isn't refactoring rework? And isn't rework one of the biggest sources of bugs?

Yes, this is rework. And yes, it's true that rework has a tendency to introduce bugs. If the users need a change late in the project, the team can accidentally inject bugs when they make it. But refactoring is a kind of rework that actually prevents bugs. Constantly refactoring throughout the project leaves you with a codebase made up of smaller, more *naturally reusable* units. The alternative—which is very familiar to most experienced programmers—is a codebase that is difficult to change.

Rework is traditionally a major source of bugs on waterfall projects. One reason is that as the design gets more complex, the code gets smellier, more brittle, and more difficult to change. But what if the act of refactoring causes developers to inadvertently introduce bugs? For example, what if a block of code does two different things, and the developer extracts it into a method that only does one of them? XP teams have an answer for this, too: test-first (or test-driven) development, one of the primary XP practices. When a programmer already has a set of unit tests for the unit being refactored, it's much safer to do the refactoring. And, in fact, the developer will feel much more comfortable doing more radical refactorings that would feel very invasive and risky without the tests. Because refactoring is, by definition, a change to the structure of the code that doesn't affect the behavior, the same unit tests should pass before and after the refactoring—and in the real world, the tests really do catch almost all of the bugs that would be introduced even in extensive refactoring.

Isn't it better to prevent this sort of problem by doing good design up front, at the beginning of the project? Isn't it safer to build the code right the first time?

Yes, it's safest to build the code right the first time. And that was one of the primary goals of software engineering—and especially of requirements engineering and project management—for many years. But it's also very, very unlikely that the code will be right the first time, because the team's understanding of the problem that they're trying to solve evolves as the project progresses and they write code. It's normal for the team's understanding of their project to change over time—that's a natural result of the team continuously delivering working software to the users (and we know that working software is a better tool for evaluating that problem than comprehensive documentation).

This is also why XP teams use iterative development, and why they include the *quarterly cycles* and *weekly cycles* among their primary practices. They give themselves enough time in every weekly iteration to account for building unit tests and do refactoring. And each delivery of working software helps the team work with their users to improve their understanding of the problem being solved and refine the stories. And by constantly looking for code smells and improving the design, they build and maintain a codebase that's easier to change.

But let's not be too hard on past teams who built software using big requirements and design up front. They didn't have mature tools—and by "tools," we mean both software tools and team practices that have been developed over the years—that make refactoring and unit testing easier. Even deployment and release were very difficult—just compiling code could take days or even weeks, and computers weren't networked, so software had to be copied to CDs, floppy disks, or even tape. These put a large minimum cost on rework, and it was much easier to make the case that it was worth writing documents and reviewing them extensively before starting to code.

Use Continuous Integration to Find Design Problems

We learned about the *continuous integration* practice in Chapter 6, and it's one of those mature tools that teams have at their disposal today. One reason that continuous integration improves design and prevents these design problems is that it allows the team to fail early when they introduce integration problems.

Figure 7-8. Continuous integration uncovers issues early.

A system that's designed to immediately report a failure as soon as it happens is called a **fail-fast system**. You want your system to fail quickly (hence the name, "fail-fast") if it needs to be fault-tolerant, and when it's important to discover the root cause of any problem as early as possible. Early failure provides a feedback loop that lets you apply that knowledge back to the project. This idea can be applied to the way that a team builds software, as much as it applies to the software that they build.

Failure is one of the principles of XP that we discussed in Chapter 6, and using continuous integration enables the project to fail fast when two team members add incompatible or conflicting code at the same time. Team members with a mindset compatible with XP will see integration failures as positive because failures help identify and fix problems early, when those problems are easiest to repair.

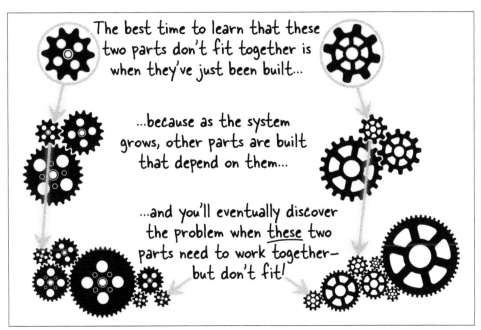

Figure 7-9. When design problems are caught early in the project, they're easier to fix, which prevents messy, kludgey hacks later on. That's one way continuous integration leads to better overall design.

Test-first programming helps the team naturally build small, independent pieces that are easier to integrate, so continuous integration is less of a burden for an XP team. The team constantly tests each unit to make sure the pieces work. When everyone on the team continuously integrates their code with the rest of the codebase, it prevents an individual developer from going off on his own and building a piece that doesn't quite fit.

Avoid Monolithic Design

Let's say that you're working on a software project, and you learn more about the problem that the software meant to solve partway through. That's a pretty familiar scenario for most software teams, and your team needs to be capable of making decisions at the last responsible moment in order to solve that problem.

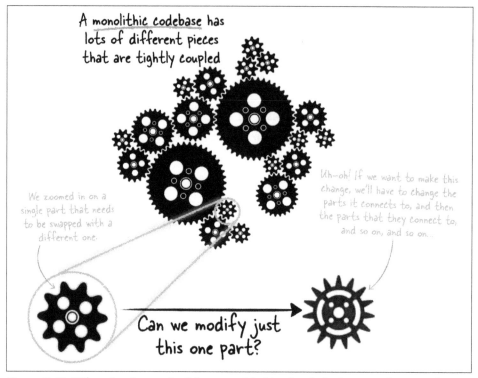

Figure 7-10. When developers don't have good habits that help them produce simple, decoupled code, they end up with code that has a monolithic design.

Traditional waterfall teams often have trouble with this scenario. Figuring out requirements up front, reviewing them with a large audience, and then building the code all at once naturally leads to code that's difficult to change. The team doesn't have a lot of incentive to design for change, because their changes are well controlled. The developers never develop habits (like constantly refactoring or spotting code smells) that cause them to build code that's easy to change.

This often naturally leads to **monolithic design**, or a software design made up of large, interconnected units that have many interdependencies and are difficult to separate.

Earlier in the book, we talked about how software is different than construction. In construction, the most damaging thing that you can do is take a sledgehammer and knock down walls. In software, deleting code doesn't cause much damage—you can just recover it from your version control repository. The most damaging thing you can do is write bad code, and then write more code that depends on it. Adding a dependency like that is sometimes called "coupling," because once those two pieces of code are tied together, it's difficult to change one without at least thinking about how the change will impact the other one.

Monolithic design often features **tightly coupled code**, where the typical unit has many connections to many other parts of the system. Trying to change highly coupled code is very frustrating—it's often the coupling that leads to shotgun surgery and many other antipatterns. It's those (often undocumented) connections between units that cause rework that produces bugs.

Just as code can be coupled, it can also be **decoupled**, by breaking the connections between units (or, even better, by never adding those connections in the first place).

Code smells and refactoring can help you to create decoupled code. Flip back to the refactoring example with the beehive code, where we extracted two methods from a block of C# code to move bees between a field and a hive. We saw that those two methods could be reused by another part of the codebase that also needs to move bees in the same way. But what if those methods are part of a larger unit that needs extensive initialization? If a programmer has good habits, when he tries to reuse those simple methods, he'll smell the half-baked code and refactor it to remove the extra initialization. Now it can be used in two different parts of the codebase, and it doesn't need to "know" how it's being called, because it's decoupled from the parts of the code that call it. And if it needs to be called from a third part of the codebase, it will be decoupled from that part as well.

A system is easiest to maintain when it's built with small, independent units: every part of the code is decoupled from every other part as much as is practically possible (which can be a surprising amount), so that there are very few dependencies between them. This is a major key to building a system that can be changed without a lot of rework. If your design is highly decoupled, then you'll rarely find yourself performing shotgun surgery or making changes to many parts of the system for a single change. And when you do, if you've developed the good habits to refactor today (not tomorrow) to remove those couplings, then you'll leave your codebase in a better, more decoupled state than you found it: with each unit performing only one task, and decoupled from unrelated units.

Incremental Design and the Holistic XP Practices

In Chapter 6, we talked about 10 of the 13 primary XP practices, dividing them into categories: programming, integration, planning, and team practices. There are three more primary XP practices, and we've come up with one more category for these three: *holistic practices*. The reason we saved them for this late in the discussion is that they only really make sense when taken together, and in context of everything we've talked about so far. We called them "holistic" because they are closely interconnected, and they don't work on their own—a team really can't do one without the others (as opposed to, say, pair programming or weekly cycles, which teams really can take on in baby steps).

The first holistic XP practice that we'll talk about is **incremental design**. Of all the primary XP practices, this one is the most difficult one for someone new to XP to understand. One goal of this chapter is to help you start to understand this practice, and how it affects the entire project and team.

You can find great examples of incremental design in many mature, high-quality open source projects, such as Linux, Apache HTTP Server, and Firefox. These projects are all designed around a solid, stable core; developers use a plug-in architecture (or some other way of separating code from the core) to build additional features, and only the most reused, most stable features are incorporated into the core. A design like this leads to highly decoupled code, and developers working on these projects are in the habit of constantly refactoring, writing many tests, and continuously integrating. (In fact, many of the practices included in XP originated with or were honed by developers working on these open source projects.)

Each of these open source projects is developed (for the most part) by programmers who add decoupled units that work independently, and are built to work with the project's core, and the codebase for the project seems to grow almost organically around that core over time. Each developer can typically add his or her own units independently of the rest of the team, and can rely on the fact that everyone has built highly decoupled code, so that the risk of new units clashing with existing ones is low. This doesn't happen in a vacuum, however; the team members are all very much aware of it. All of the additions happen on the same codebase, so these teams have both automated and manual continuous integration. (Some continuous integration and build servers available today actually originated with these projects.) And every developer is highly aware of code smells and antipatterns, and feels a great responsibility to fix them as soon as they're found. Refactoring is rarely left to the end of the project; each programmer feels a responsibility to add only the best code that he or she can, and relies on co-developers' eyeballs to constantly catch problems that he or she can fix.

As a result of these great practices and developer habits, the codebase grows **incrementally** over time; this is how a very large team distributed across many countries can build great software.[7]

---

7 You can learn more about how open source teams work in Eric S. Raymond's book *The Cathedral and the Bazaar* (O'Reilly, 1999). You can learn a lot about the day-to-day behavior of open source teams from Karl Fogel's book, *Producing Open Source Software* (O'Reilly), which you can download for free from *http://producingoss.com/* (but which we recommend buying from O'Reilly to support his excellent work).

At its core, incremental design is about *making code design decisions at the last responsible moment*, avoiding one of the most common traps that developers—even advanced, highly skilled developers—fall into: trying to build everything at once.

Teams that fall into the "build everything at once" trap have developed bad habits that lead to monolithic or convoluted software design. For example, they might focus on solving problems bigger than, and tangential to, their immediate ones (doing things like focusing on more than edge cases instead of focusing on the specific thing each unit of code needs to do) or overthink future cases and add too many hooks, or build large, abstract frameworks to solve small, concrete problems. What do all of these things have in common? They're examples of teams making too many design decisions too early in the project.

On the other hand, when the team has developed the habits that lead them to build decoupled code made up of small, solid, independent units, they don't need to come up with the complete design up front. They can come up with a high-level design, without having to think of every possible scenario that might not fit into it. They can be confident that when they discover an edge case that isn't handled, they'll have the tools in place to deal with it later. This frees people up to think about the problem in the way they would naturally think about it, and to build the code piece by piece as they learn more about the problem they're tackling. This is the idea behind incremental design, and it results in a highly flexible, adaptable, and changeable codebase. But it only works when *every developer truly believes* in making design and code decisions at the last responsible moment. Everyone on the team needs to believe that it's faster to build a small, decoupled piece of the system today, and trust themselves to fix it tomorrow if it isn't quite right.

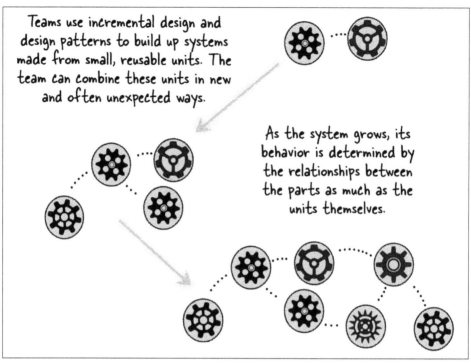

Teams use incremental design and design patterns to build up systems made from small, reusable units. The team can combine these units in new and often unexpected ways.

As the system grows, its behavior is determined by the relationships between the parts as much as the units themselves.

Figure 7-11. Incremental design leads to more robust, more maintainable systems.

This isn't just about how the programmers design and build the code. It's also about the team's climate: how they interact, the environment they work in, and most importantly, the attitude that they have.

Many teams are put in a position where they are not given enough time to do their jobs. Or, worse, they are made to feel like they don't have time, despite the fact that their deadlines are artificial—and possibly fabricated by a boss or project manager who thinks that impossible deadlines are a good motivator. On a team that has a mindset like this, any work that they do that doesn't immediately add code to the codebase feels extraneous.

When you don't feel like you have time to do your best work, *it almost doesn't matter how good your habits are*. The more time and schedule pressure that you feel, the more likely you are to throw out great practices like refactoring, test-driven development, and continuous integration. You won't refactor, for example, because you have code that works, and you feel like you don't have time to make it better. Your code will run with or without unit tests, so every minute you spend writing those tests feels like a minute that you don't spend adding features. We know in our heads that these practices make you build code faster; but when we're under extreme pressure, we feel in our guts that *we just don't have time for them*.

Consider a developer who's on a team that is under a lot of pressure by the boss. Maybe he promised users that they'd have a complete product but agreed to an unrealistically short deadline, and he wants to meet the deadline by putting pressure on the team to skip unit tests, and to avoid refactoring, and to basically not do anything at all that doesn't directly add features to the code. On a team like this, it's common for developers to encounter code smells and think, "I don't have time to think about this! I just need to get this new feature in as quickly as possible and move on to the next one." They will naturally produce highly coupled code (because taking the extra few minutes to decouple it feels like extraneous work, and *I just don't have time to think about it!*). Their boss is a barrier to effective adoption of XP, and a team working for a boss like this is likely to build smelly code that's difficult to maintain, and difficult to change. Their projects will almost certainly be late, and some may even fail entirely.[8]

XP has an answer for this, too, and it brings us to the last two holistic XP practices: **energized work** and **whole team**.

Teams Work Best When They Feel Like They Have Time to Think

> Software development is a game of insight, and insight comes to the prepared, rested, relaxed mind.
>
> —Kent Beck *Extreme Programming Explained: Embrace Change,* 2nd Edition

Energized work means establishing an environment where every team member is given enough time and freedom to do the job. This keeps them in the mental space where they can develop and use good habits that lead to better, more naturally changeable code. This, in turn, lets them produce much more code, and deliver more valuable features (and features that are more valuable) to the users and customers, in a shorter period of time.

Software development is almost entirely a mental exercise.[9] Every good developer has spent hours staring at a problem and gotten nowhere, then had an epiphany later about exactly how to solve the problem while eating dinner (or taking a shower, or riding a bike, etc.). Every software project relies on a series of small innovations like that, one after another.

It's widely known that it takes time (usually between 15 and 45 minutes) for a developer to get into a state of "flow," a state of high concentration in which she's highly

---

8 Flip back to Chapter 5 and find the quote from Grady Booch about innovation and fear of failing. Here's a good example of a team that is no fun at all.

9 Does it seem weird to you that programming is almost entirely mental? Here's a quick experiment to prove it to yourself. Think of a piece of code that took hours to write. Now retype it. It'll go much faster. Typing, the physical part of writing code, is clearly not the most time-consuming part.

productive.[10] Interruptions and distractions can pull a developer right out of this state. But when she is put under pressure to deliver code as fast as possible yesterday, it's almost impossible to get into this state. She's so worried about pushing the code out the door that she feels like she doesn't have time to think.

Disrespect, unrealistic artificial deadlines, and other bad behavior from the boss can lead to an **unenergized** environment, or a working environment where people don't feel like they have the ability to make decisions, and don't have the mental space to make good decisions or innovate.

When managers create a climate where development work is always behind, and the team is held to arbitrary, unrealistic deadlines, they'll cut corners when building the code. This usually means throwing out many of the great practices that XP brings. But more importantly, it means that the developers rarely get to the mental state— "flow"—that's necessary for bringing simplicity to the project.

XP teams strive to create the opposite kind of workspace: an energized environment. Giving the team an energized environment means helping every person on the team to feel like he or she has *autonomy*. Everyone can decide how their work should be done, and feels like they have the freedom to make changes—not just to the code, but also to the whole plan for the project, and the way that the project is run. The way XP teams do that is with some of their planning-oriented practices: by using weekly cycles so that they don't arbitrarily make decisions up front that can be decided later, and by using slack to add lower-priority work that can get moved to the next cycle. These practices increase the team's feeling of autonomy by giving them more flexibility in the plan. And autonomy can also come from the codebase itself: by avoiding antipatterns and building a codebase that's not difficult to change, the team opens up choices for themselves later in the project.

In Chapter 3, we learned about the agile principle of **sustainable pace**: agile processes promote sustainable development. The sponsors, developers, and users should be able to maintain a constant pace indefinitely. Can you see how the XP principle of courage is needed in order to maintain a sustainable pace?

Many XP practitioners use the terms "energized work," "40-hour work week," and "sustainable pace" interchangeably, and it's why XP teams create an environment where they can do energized work by establishing sane working hours. There's actually a long history behind the 40-hour work week—historically, labor organizers demanded "eight hours labor, eight hours recreation, and eight hours rest."[11] By the

---

10 You can read some of the best writing on how developers achieve and sustain flow in *Peopleware: Productive Projects and Teams,* 3rd Edition, by Tom DeMarco and Timothy Lister.

11 You can read more about the history of the 40-hour week and 8-hour day in the excellent Wikipedia article for the topic (*http://bit.ly/8-hr-day*) (retrieved April 6, 2014).

1950s, and after countless productivity studies and charts that showed productivity decreasing and quality problems increasing when work weeks expanded past 40 hours, many industries had adopted this principle as well. XP teams know that when they set a sustainable pace, and allow everyone on the team time for a life outside of the office, the quality of the work goes up along with the happiness of the team members.

Team Members Trust Each Other and Make Decisions Together

> People need a sense of "team": We belong. We are in this together. We support each others' work, growth, and learning.
>
> —Kent Beck *Extreme Programming Explained: Embrace Change*, 2nd Edition

Great teams can accomplish much more working together than the same number of people can accomplish working individually. Why is that? When you bring people with the right skills and perspectives together, and when you give those people an environment that encourages open communication and mutual respect, you help innovation to thrive. People on the team have ideas that spark more ideas in others.

The **whole team** practice is about helping the individuals on the team come together as a whole. When they encounter obstacles, they work together to overcome them. When there's an important decision that affects the direction of the project, that decision is made together. Everyone on the team learns to trust the rest of the team members to figure out which decisions can be made individually, and which decisions need to be brought to the rest of the team.

On a whole team, every team member is part of the discussion of what features are valuable to the users, what work the team will take on, and how the software will be built. If every team member is trusted to make coding decisions that will deliver the most value, then there's little risk of individual programmers spending extra time building extra code that doesn't accomplish the goal.

The flipside of trust is understanding that everyone makes mistakes. When the "whole team" dynamic is working, a team member isn't afraid to make those mistakes, because he knows that the rest of the team will understand that mistakes happen, and that the only way to move forward is to make those inevitable mistakes and learn from them together.

The XP Design, Planning, Team, and Holistic Practices Form an Ecosystem That Spurs Innovation

A whole team that has an energized work environment will design better software than a disconnected team in a stifling environment. Innovation may sound like a lofty concept, but it's a practical, day-to-day reality on an effective XP team. Developers who regularly achieve a state of flow and work in an informative workspace that encourages osmotic communication often find themselves feeding off of each other's ideas. And designing software incrementally gives each developer the freedom to write new code with few constraints—that's like giving a blank canvas to an artist. The team's great habits will help them avoid and fix antipatterns, so that when they grow the codebase incrementally they don't restrict themselves in the future.

When a team with great habits has a manager who trusts them, even more good things happen. A great manager trusts the team to understand the value that they're delivering, and gives them a climate where they can focus on creating the best product without having to meet an unrealistic timeline. A team with a manager like this works faster, and is more likely to build a highly changeable product that will do a great job of meeting the users' needs.

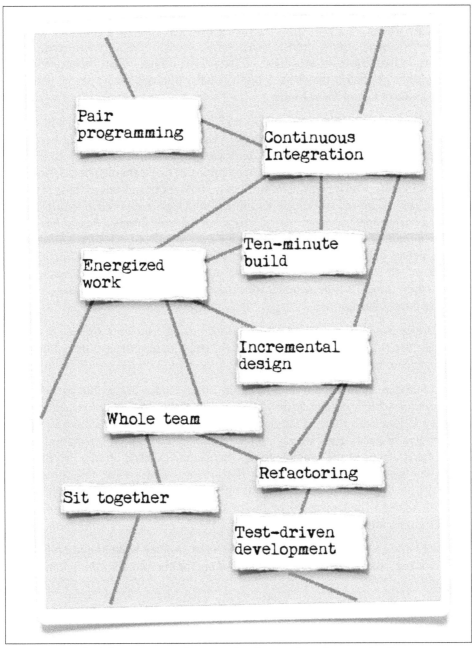

Figure 7-12. All of the practices relate to each other, and reinforce each other.

We waited until Chapter 7 to introduce the holistic practices because they make much more sense when combined with the other primary XP practices, and a team won't really "get" them without a mindset that's compatible with the XP values and principles. A team that just looks at individual practices and implements them one by one will probably get better-than-not-doing-it-results, but they won't see a profound impact on the design of the software.

On a good XP team, where everyone has truly internalized the principles and values, the practices form an *ecosystem* where they reinforce each other. Testing first helps the team to build small, independent, decoupled units, which make any code problems and antipatterns easier to refactor and eliminate. The team members sit together and work in pairs, which helps them work as a whole team, and causes them to have a more focused, energized working environment, which gives them time to think about the design. They integrate continuously, so when one pair injects a defect that affects a different part of the software it causes unit tests to fail fast. This lets the team fix code problems quickly and before those problems are buried under additional layers of code, which leads to a cleaner codebase. Continuous integration is made easier because they have a 10-minute build, which also makes it easier for the team to focus and have fewer interruptions.

To a developer with the right mindset for XP, this all feels very simple. In fact, it seems like you're just building software the way you should, and all of these things are happening automatically.

A team that doesn't have that mindset, on the other hand, will run into barriers with XP adoption—they'll get buried in implementing the individual practices, and feel like they're done with their XP implementation once everyone is technically writing tests, coding in pairs, using weekly cycles, or using a continuous integration server. Those are straightforward, tangible things that can be checked off of a list. But then there's this gap between implementing the practices and getting this "ecosystem" effect that an XP team may read about, but never really achieve—just like Scrum teams that might implement all of the practices, but never see those astonishing results or hyperproductivity.

How does a team get into the right mindset? How do they make the jump between implementing practices, and fundamentally changing the way they design and build software?

Incremental Design Versus Designing for Reuse

Andrew: So, designing for reuse isn't always a great thing?

Auke: It's not really a very suitable approach for software development. What you typically do in open source is that you start by building something for one use first. Then, somebody else takes it and starts modifying to their needs. And he can reuse it. And once you've done that—use and reuse—you know what the commonality is, and you can refactor out the common functionality.

That pattern you see quite a lot. Design for reuse is too static. It doesn't work that way and is a very poor fit. It may be something to strive for, but is not feasible in the foreseeable future. Use-use-reuse is a much better fit.

—Interview with Auke Jilderda, *Beautiful Teams* (Chapter 8)

Throughout this book, we've talked about how a team can start to get themselves into the right mindset for a methodology by adopting its practices. At first, they might just get better-than-not-doing-it results. But as they get used to the practices and start to understand how they fit together, the way that everyone on the team thinks about building software starts to shift. This was true for Scrum, and it's also true about XP. And a key to getting into the XP mindset lies with incremental design.

The Unix toolset is a classic example of incremental design, and that's what allowed thousands of developers to contribute small and large pieces to it over the course of many years. The Unix tools consist of many small pieces[12] that were developed independently, mostly by programmers who were trying to solve a specific problem (and not trying to build a large, monolithic operating system). We can use the Unix toolset to learn about how incremental design can let many different people—many of whom have never met—contribute to a single large, robust, high-quality system that has continued to grow incrementally for decades.

Here's an example of how the Unix tools work. Let's say that you have a bunch of large text files with a lot of data—maybe they're addresses for a mailing list, or configuration files for an operating system, or numbers that need to be crunched. You need to quickly come up with a way to transform them (for example, to pull out just the name and phone number, or alter certain sections of the configuration in a specific way, or find data values that match a pattern). How would you do this?

You could write a program that reads the data from the file, processes the lines, sections, strings, etc., and generates the output. But if you're familiar with the Unix tools (like `cat`, `ls`, `cut`, `awk`, `sed`, etc.), you already know that they're built to handle problems like this. You'd write a script—or even just a command that you'd execute on the

---

12 You can see a comprehensive list of the Unix tools on Wikipedia (*http://bit.ly/unix-utils*) (retrieved July 27, 2014).

command line—that reads the data from the file, does the transformations, and writes the output to another file.

Say you have a large, comma-delimited address book file of addresses called *addr.txt*. It has eight columns: name, title, email address, phone number, mailing address, city, state, and US zip code. You want to find the name, title, and phone number of every person in Minnesota. If the full name and title are in the first two columns, the phone number is in the fourth column, and state and zip code are in the last two columns, then this Unix command will produce the right output and write it to *output.txt*:[13]

```
egrep ",MN,[0-9]{5}([-][0-9]{4})?$" addr.txt | cut -d, -f1,2,4 > output.txt
```

So were Unix tools built by people who wanted to make it easy to process address books? Obviously not. The Unix tools were *based on a philosophy of simplicity*: each tool produces output that every other tool can use as input, and every tool does one straightforward, specific job. The cut tool reads each line of the input, cuts out certain fields or columns, and pastes them into the output. The grep tool checks each line in the input and only prints that line to the output if it matches a pattern. But these two tools—especially when combined with the other Unix tools—can do an almost unlimited number of tasks. For example, a system administrator might combine them with tools like find (which finds files in the filesystem) or last (which tells you what users were on the current machine recently) to perform many complex system administration tasks.

These tools are a fundamental part of what made Unix the most popular type of operating system for Internet services and business systems. And over the years, a general design for system tools emerged, along with a system administrator culture among people who use those tools every day. New tools and new uses for those tools have evolved over time. For example, file compression became more widespread in the 1980s and 1990s. When the gzip tool was added to the Unix toolset in 1992, there was a straightforward pattern for adding it. Before the first line was written, it was clear how it would get its data in and out (pipes), how it would be executed (from the command line), even where documentation would go (man pages). The toolset could easily expand, and because all of the tools are decoupled and independent of each other, the ability to compress and decompress files could be added without requiring any changes elsewhere in the system.

Over the last four decades, the Unix toolset has continued to expand in this way. Thousands of developers contributed individual tools, or made improvements to the existing tools. The Unix system grew in a natural, almost organic way. And along with

---

13 Are you really bothered by the fact that there are many edge cases that aren't handled by our example, like how it assumes all of the addresses are in the United States, or it doesn't account for a header row or quoted strings with embedded commas? Try not to focus on the edge cases; this is just a toy example.

---

it, a culture and knowledge base grew. This allowed people who use Unix to perform more and more complex tasks, which in turn helped them find new ways that the system needed to grow.

When Units Interact in a Simple Way, the System Can Grow Incrementally

The Unix tools all follow a very strict pattern about input and output. The | character in the command line above is a pipe—it's used to take output from one tool and feed it as input into another. The < character pipes input from a file, and the > character pipes output to a file. The standard Unix tools all produce output that works with these pipes—that's part of a **contract** that each of those units adheres to. The contract between Unix tools is very simple, which makes it easy to extend the whole Unix system. As long as each additional tool adheres to the same contract, it will fit in with the others.

An important tool for helping a team build a system using incremental design is to have a very simple contract between the units of that system. How do those units communicate with each other? Do they pass messages? Call functions or methods? Access services on the network? The more simple and consistent the unit-to-unit communication mechanism is, the easier it is for the team to add units.

So how do you make a contract simple? The same way you make units simple: make decisions about how units communicate at the last responsible moment. And we already have a tool to help with this: test-first programming. When a developer builds unit tests first, it helps her strip out complexity by forcing her to use that unit before it's written. She can use the same unit testing tool or framework to write simple **integration tests** that test how multiple units communicate with each other—and she'll write those tests before she adds the code to communicate. For example, if there's an interaction between units where the output of one unit is passed as input into another, whose output is then fed into a third, she'll write a test that simulates that interaction—how they *integrate* together.

The reason this helps keep the contract between units simple is that it becomes clear very quickly if that contract is complex. With a simple contract, this sort of integration test is very easy to write. But when the contract is complex, the integration test is a burden: the developer will find herself having to initialize many different, seemingly unrelated objects, clumsily translating data from one format to another, and having to jump through hoops to get the units to communicate. And just like with writing unit tests, writing these integration tests first will help avoid those problems before they get built into the software.

Great Design Emerges from Simple Interactions

We use the term "emergence" when complex behavior arises from simple systems. Emergence is common in nature: individual ants have simple behavior, but a whole ant colony has much more complex behavior that arises out of the interactions between individual ants; the whole of the ant colony is greater than the sum of the ants.

When a system is designed so that its behavior seems to emerge from the *interactions* between the individual units working together, in a way that doesn't seem to originate from one single unit, it's called **emergent design**. Systems built using emergent design almost always consist of small, independent, decoupled units (like Unix tools, or ants). Those pieces are combined to perform complex tasks, and the behavior of the system comes as much from the interactions between those units as it does from the individual units themselves.

There's rarely a deep hierarchy of units calling other units; instead, the system will use messages, queues, or other ways for units to communicate without requiring a central control system. Again, the Unix tools are a good example of this.[14] Input is piped out of one tool and into another, which makes them easy to chain together. This leads to a very linear usage: the first tool is called, then the second, then the third. It's possible to create a more complex interaction between the tools, but they lend themselves to a simple, shallow call structure (as opposed to a deep, nested call hierarchy with layers of units that call each other).

When a system is designed like this—with simple units that interact in a simple way—something interesting can happen. It can start to feel to the team like the *behavior* emerges from the system as a whole, not just the individual units. Complex behavior often doesn't seem to have a single source at all. This is a lot like the way that an ant colony's behavior doesn't seem to originate with any individual ants. The team has this real, palpable feeling that each part of the system is simple, and that the behavior of the whole system emerges from the interactions between those units.

To people who have spent years building the Unix toolset, this feeling of emergent behavior is familiar. You can start to see a *very* basic kind of emergent behavior from the combination of parts in the simple address book example: cut only knows about extracting characters from a line, and grep only knows how to match patterns, but somehow they combine together to process addresses without a specific command to tell the system what an address is, or how to process it.

---

14 Ants are also a good example of decoupled units that use simple communication—in their case, with phero-mones—that causes complex behavior to emerge from the whole system.

XP teams that are firing on all cylinders find themselves naturally building software and systems using emergent design. This starts with simplicity: each unit is designed for a specific use. Test-first programming ensures that the unit stays simple and only has that one use. The programmer writes the tests to make sure that it performs that one function, and then writes the code—and when the tests pass, he stops writing it, so that no extra behavior is added, and there's no code that's there for no reason. All of the code in the unit is necessary.

The team avoids deep call stacks, where one unit calls another, which calls a third, and so on. Instead, the program's call structure looks flat and wide, which reduces dependencies between units. These interactions are kept as simple as possible: when one unit needs data, it gets it from one other unit—or, even better, from a message on a queue, so it doesn't even need to know where that input came from. To keep the system simple, the team avoids multi-stage, complex interactions between many units (just like Unix tools only pipe data in from one tool and out to another).

New design emerges when the people on the team discover changes that need to be made. To add new behavior to the system or change the way it works, they need to change the individual units, or change the way those units interact. But because each unit is decoupled, and the interactions between them are simple, these changes tend not to cascade throughout the system. If the code smells bad—say, the programmer finds himself doing shotgun surgery, or runs across spaghetti code or half-baked objects—that's a giant warning sign that unnecessary complexity has worked its way in, and he knows (and, more importantly, he *feels*) that it's worth taking the time to refactor it out into simpler units.

A system built using emergent design can grow for years, while staying maintainable and easy to change. Teams that are good at XP have the tools to keep the codebase simple, and they work in a way that encourages them to continually monitor the code for complexity and refactor it out. This in turn lets them comfortably make changes, which allows more design to emerge. It's a virtuous cycle that leads to simple, stable, very high quality code—and, as a result, teams find that it's much faster to build and maintain software this way. When the system needs to be maintained (to fix a bug, or to make a change), there's rarely a large, overarching modification that touches many different parts of the code.

And because the team members know how flexible the system is, and what they can and can't extend, they get better at making decisions at the last responsible moment. They find that as a team, they have an increasingly good sense of when a specific design decision can be made tomorrow—which in turn helps keep the code simple today. The team is more relaxed, and team members work better together. They produce high-quality code very quickly, and, when they need to change the code, it can be done easily, and without creating bugs.

In other words, teams keep their code simple, which allows them to embrace change.

And that's the point of XP.

Narrative: a team working on a fantasy basketball website

Justin – a developer

Danielle – another developer

Bridget – their project manager

Act V: Final Score

Danielle and Justin were pair programming together when Danielle realized something. "Did you realize this is the first time we've paired together in almost three months?"

It was almost a year since Danielle first told the team about XP. They'd been releasing every week, but this past weekly cycle was special. The company had announced a promotional campaign with one of the major television networks, and the team just pushed the code for it into production. Danielle and Justin were taking a few minutes to look back at the last few cycles, the way they always did.

Justin said, "You're right. We used to pair all the time, but we've rotated partners so many times that I think I've worked with every single person on the team."

Danielle asked, "When's the last time you had to work late?"

Justin thought for a minute. "You know what? I'd have to check my phone to see the last time I texted any apologies. It's been a while."

"I think it's because we're getting better at this," said Danielle. "I know I'm writing much simpler code than I did even six months ago."

"You're right. When I first read about test-driven development, it seemed really theoretical to me. Now it just makes sense," said Justin. "We used to have all of these arguments about it with the whole team, trying to convince each other that it was worth the time. I can't remember the last time I had to argue with anyone about that."

Danielle said, "It's funny, I don't feel like I'm doing things all that differently."

Bridget was walking by, and had stopped to listen in on the discussion. "It feels different to me," she said. Justin and Danielle looked up. They hadn't noticed her standing there. "My job used to mainly be about finding ways to convince the product managers to give us more time. We were always running late, and it seemed like everything they asked for would take months."

Justin asked, "It's not like that anymore?"

"Not at all! I used to say 'no' all the time. Now I say usually 'yes,' even when what they're asking for sounds really big. You guys made my job much easier."

"I guess that's why you don't yell at us anymore," said Danielle. "And I guess that's why we're not putting in weekends trying to make up for lost time."

Bridget looked at Justin and Danielle for a minute. "Wait a minute, so you guys could be putting in more work for me?"

Justin thought she was joking. Danielle wasn't sure. "I think maybe we're not done learning yet," she said.

 Key Points

- Developers fix code smells by constantly **refactoring** their code, or improving the code structure without changing its behavior.

- By refactoring mercilessly, XP teams avoid **technical debt**, or code problems that are known but have not been fixed.

- A good way that XP use **slack** is to make sure there's enough time in each weekly cycle for refactoring and paying down technical debt.

- Continuous integration helps teams find integration problems early when they're easier to fix.

- When the team refactors, pays down technical debt, and fixes code problems, they end up with a codebase that's easy to change.

- XP teams practice **incremental design** by creating decoupled code that consists of small, independent units.

- Teams incrementally build only the units that are needed for the immediate problem being worked on, and trust themselves to make good code decisions at the last responsible moment.

- **Energized work** lets XP teams create an environment where each person on the team can work at a sustainable pace and feels like there's enough time to do the job right.

- XP team members trust each other, and feel like they're members of a whole team.

 Frequently Asked Questions

Incremental design sounds really theoretical. Does anyone actually build software this way?
When people say that something is "theoretical," what they often mean is, "I haven't tried it yet, and it seems difficult."

Nothing in XP is theoretical. Every practice in XP is a specific skill that programmers need to learn, practice, and get better at. The better they get at those good practices, the more they turn those practices into great habits, and the better they get at writing code. The values and principles are real, practical ideas that help you and your team improve those skills, individually and together.

That's why XP takes practice. Just like you can't simply buy a guitar, music, and a "How to Play Guitar" book and become a great musician overnight, you can't just start doing XP practices and expect to be great at them. But if you keep practicing, you will get better. Just like with music, if you keep making the same programming, design, and planning mistakes over and over again, you won't learn, and you won't improve.

Whenever I add technical debt items as slack, they never get done. How do I make sure we fix technical debt?
If you find that your team rarely gets around to doing the items in the weekly cycle that were added as slack, then you're putting too many items into each weekly cycle. Slack items aren't optional. They're just items that won't prevent the team from releasing working software that's "*done* done" at the end of the iteration. They're still important items, and most of the time they should get done. If not, then try removing items when you're planning the weekly cycle.

On the other hand, if it's the technical debt items in particular that aren't getting done, then your team may have a mindset problem when it comes to actually fixing those items. In fact, there's a trap related to technical debt that a lot of teams fall into. They'll identify technical debt items, but instead of fixing them as soon as possible, they'll add them to a backlog using index cards, spreadsheets, tickets, or another tracking mechanism. Once the technical debt is identified, it's given a lower priority than development of new features. Somehow, the team never really gets around to fixing technical debt, as if simply "acknowledging" that it's there and tagging it for future repair is good enough.

A team that doesn't fix technical debt treats it like a natural byproduct of development. To that team, it's more important to get a new feature delivered—even if it takes a hack or a kludge—so that the project can keep rolling forward.

And you know what? There's nothing wrong with the attitude that delivering valuable software is more important than making beautiful technical solutions. The reason that effective XP teams constantly fix technical debt is because it makes it easier to keep delivering valuable software in the future.

If you're a programmer with this mindset, fixing technical debt while you're adding more code, constantly refactoring as you go, feels like a very important and pressing thing to do. Everyone on your team knows that it's worth taking the time to fix the technical problem as soon as it's discovered because it makes the codebase easier to change (just like it's worth it to pay off your credit cards every month—you can survive by not doing it, but over time, the debt becomes crushing). That's why XP team members give themselves enough time in the weekly cycle—and *genuinely feel* like they have enough time—to fix the problems.

If you find that your technical debt is piling up, then you should discuss it with your team. Try to figure out if it's not getting fixed because of external pressure to add more features. Or maybe it's because you and your teammates don't really feel like it's the most important thing for you to be doing right now. Or it could be because developers on your team get rewarded with respect and attention for delivering "sexy" new features, and feel like they won't get any recognition for fixing "plumbing." If it takes the same effort to add new features as it does to fix technical debt, but you're going to get a bigger raise because the boss knows you built the new feature that the users love, it's rational to push technical debt far down on the priority list. Whatever the reason is, being open about it and discussing it with each other will help.

Some of the XP principles sound fishy. Did they just put "self-similarity" in there because it sounded impressive, or because it was created in the 1990s when everyone was talking about self-similarity, fractals, and chaos theory?

Absolutely not. It's easy to dismiss a principle if you haven't seen it used effectively to improve a team and their understanding of XP. But every single one of those principles really does help you understand XP better. Self-similarity is no exception.

Self-similarity means that the same patterns appear at different scales, from very large to very small. There is a great deal of self-similarity in good software design. Software that is solid, reliable, and easy to use is often made up of layers that are solid, reliable, and easy to use. Those layers are made up of units that are solid, reliable, and easy to use. And when you crack open one of those units and look at the code, what do you think you'll find? That's right: code that's solid, reliable, and easy to understand.

There's self-similarity in energized work: teams achieve flow when individual developers can get into the "flow" mindset. And there's self-similarity in planning: a developer plans out tests, and then builds the code; a team plans out the features, and then runs the weekly cycle; they'll plan out themes, and then run the quarterly cycle.

So do you need to look for self-similarity in every aspect of your work? Of course not, it's just one principle. But it helps you notice patterns that will give you a better understanding of how your own projects work. And every other principle does the same thing for you. So don't dismiss them—they're valuable tools that can help you understand. If they seem extraneous, then try to think of how they apply to the work you're doing. That will help you get further in your adoption of XP.

I read on the Internet that test-driven development is dead. Is that true?

Test-driven development is a tool. Saying that test-driven development is dead is like saying that screwdrivers are dead. Many teams use test-driven development every day and find a lot of success with it. As long as teams are doing test-driven development, it's still alive and kicking.

However, there's a deeper level to the "is test-driven development dead?" discussion. One reason that people—especially people who have a lot of experience with agile and XP—raise that question is because they've found that there are teams who go beyond using TDD as a tool and treat it as a sort of orthodoxy. They focus on the tests as an end in and of itself, rather than a means to an end of building better software. They'll fall into the framework trap, putting many hours into creating extensive and complex testing frameworks. Test-driven development is supposed to help the team keep the codebase simple; when it adds complexity, something's gone wrong.[15]

Others who make the "is TDD dead?" argument have found that some XP practices (especially TDD and pair programming) seem to generate a lot of emotional resistance from some teams who aren't familiar with them.

The goal of a team using XP is not to write unit tests, any more than the goal of a team following a waterfall process is to write specifications. The goal is to build working software, and both TDD and specifications are a means to that end.

There's one other thing that may help you understand this debate and the ideas behind it a little better. Throughout Chapter 6 and Chapter 7, we've been using the terms "test-driven development" and "test-first programming" interchangeably. This is a very common usage for both terms, and for many years the terms were considered synonymous—and we felt that this was a reasonable simplification to help you understand the concepts. But some people consider test-first programming to simply refer to the fact that you write unit tests before you write the code for the unit, and use test-driven development to refer to the wider design approach.

Do you need to write tests first to build well-designed code? Of course not—many teams have built great code without using TDD. But is TDD a valuable tool for build-

---

15 Do you find yourself building complex unit tests? Do you artificially achieve 100% test coverage, possibly by creating highly reflective test cases or creating very complex mock objects? Do you end up with unit tests that are difficult to change? Are some of your unit tests commented out because someone needed to make a change that broke the test, and it was too complex for him to understand and fix? If you answered yes to any of these questions, you may be creating unit tests that make your codebase more complex instead of simpler.

ing well-designed code? Absolutely. If you haven't done test-driven development, it's easy to come up with *hypothetical* reasons not to do it ("I like to sketch out what I'm building and see how it will hang together; otherwise, I have nothing to write tests for, so clearly I need to make compromises when it comes to TDD!"). But the fact is, many teams use TDD exactly as prescribed,[16] and many of those hypothetical reasons disappear when you make an earnest attempt to use it.

It's actually worth having a look at the article that launched much of the "Is TDD Dead?" discussion—and, importantly, Kent Beck's response[17] that he posted on Facebook, which does an excellent job of explaining exactly how TDD helps you solve programming problems and create better software designs:

RIP TDD

April 29, 2014 at 11:10am

DHH has consigned TDD to the scrapheap of history *http://david.heinemeierhansson.com/2014/tdd-is-dead-long-live-testing.html*. I'm sad, not because I rescued it from the scrapheap of history in the first place, but because now I need to hire new techniques to help me solve many of my problems during programming:

- Over-engineering. I have a tendency to "throw in" functionality I "know" I'm "going to need". Making one red test green (along with the list of future tests) helps me implement just enough. I need to find a new way to stay focused.

- API feedback. I need to find a new way to get quick feedback about my API decisions.

- Logic errors. I need to find a new way to catch those pesky sense-of-test errors I'm so prone to making.

- Documentation. I need to find a new way to communicate how I expect APIs to be used and to record what I was thinking during development.

- Feeling overwhelmed. I'm really going to miss how, using TDD, even if I couldn't imagine an implementation I could almost always figure out how to write a test. I need to find a new way to take that next step up the mountain.

- Separate interface from implementation thinking. I have a tendency to pollute API design decisions with implementation speculation. I need to find a new way to separate the two levels of thinking while still providing rapid feedback between them.

- Agreement. I need to find a new way to be precise with a programming partner about what problem I'm solving.

---

16 Including us. We're in the habit of always doing test-driven development when we write our own code.

17 A very small number of readers might not recognize the sarcasm in Kent Beck's Facebook post. Explaining a joke removes the humor, but just to be clear, he's explaining how now that TDD is supposedly dead, he'll need to find a replacement that does all of the valuable things it used to do for him.

- Anxiety. Perhaps what I'll miss most is the way TDD gives me an instantaneous "Is Everything Okay?" button.

I'm sure I'll find other ways to solve all these problems. In time. The pain will fade. Farewell TDD, old friend.

—(Kent Beck's Facebook page (*http://bit.ly/beck-fb*))

So what's the verdict? There are some teams who tried to use test-driven development and have found it very useful. Others have found it difficult to adopt. The best way for you to decide for yourself is to actually try it out. If you do try it—and we very much encourage you to do so—then one way to get good results is to be very careful not to fall into the framework trap when building out your unit tests.

Kent Beck was responding to an essay by David Heinemeier Hansson (known as DHH in the Ruby community), creator of Ruby on Rails and an important thinker in the agile community, called "TDD is dead. Long live testing."[18] DHH does a good job of identifying some important hallmarks of unit tests that fell into the framework trap:

> Test-first units leads to an overly complex web of intermediary objects and indirection in order to avoid doing anything that's "slow". Like hitting the database. Or file IO. Or going through the browser to test the whole system. It's given birth to some truly horrendous monstrosities of architecture. A dense jungle of service objects, command patterns, and worse.
>
> I rarely unit test in the traditional sense of the word, where all dependencies are mocked out, and thousands of tests can close in seconds.

Does that description sound at all familiar? It should—it's very similar to some of the code smells that you learned about earlier in this chapter. Unit tests are susceptible to exactly the same complexity problems that can affect any code. If you find yourself building very complex unit tests, then it's possible that you're falling into the same trap that DHH is correctly calling out.

DHH also identifies an important feature of TDD:

> It didn't start out like that. When I first discovered TDD, it was like a courteous invitation to a better world of writing software. A mind hack to get you going with the practice of testing where no testing had happened before. It opened my eyes to the tranquility of a well-tested code base, and the bliss of confidence it grants those making changes to software.
>
> The test-first part was a wonderful set of training wheels that taught me how to think about testing at a deeper level, but also some I quickly left behind.

This is a great reason for you to try TDD. It really does help you think about testing at a deeper level, just like it does all of those things that Kent Beck listed in his Face-

---

18 David Heinemeier Hansson, "TDD is dead. Long live testing. (*http://bit.ly/tdd-dead*)" (April 23, 2014).

book post. Is it the only way to accomplish those things? No. But it's very effective, and that's why it's an important part of XP.

 Things You Can Do Today

Here are a few things that you can try today on your own or with your team:

- If you're a developer, try refactoring your code. You might already be using an IDE that has refactoring tools built into it. Can you find a small way to change the structure of the code that you're currently working on that will simplify it without changing its behavior?
- Go to the WikiWikiWeb (*http://bit.ly/code-smell*) and read through the page of code smells. Can you spot any of these in your code? If you can't, look harder.
- Is it easy to check out your codebase from your version control system and build it? If you need to follow many different steps, try to find a way to automate that with a build script. Every step you take toward simplifying the checkout and build process makes your life easier in the long run.
- Did you try test-driven development yet? No? Try it. Take a user story or feature that you've been asked to deliver. Before you start building the code, write just one or two tests for a single unit that you're going to have to build. You don't need to build a complete suite of tests yet. Just build one or two, and then build code that makes them pass.

 Where You Can Learn More

Here are resources to help you learn more about the ideas in this chapter:

- You can learn more about simplicity, incremental design, and the other holistic XP practices in *Extreme Programming Explained: Embrace Change,* 2nd Edition, by Kent Beck with Cynthia Andres (Addison-Wesley, 2004).
- You can learn more about refactoring in *Refactoring: Improving the Design of Existing Code,* by Martin Fowler, Kent Beck, John Brant, and William Opdyke (Addison-Wesley, 1999).

- You can learn more about flow and how to build a more energized working environment in *Peopleware: Productive Projects and Teams*, 3rd Edition, by Tom DeMarco and Tim Lister (Addison-Wesley, 2013).

 **Coaching Tips**

Tips for agile coaches helping their team to work with the ideas in this chapter:

- Does your team fall into the framework trap? Do they try to solve large, abstract problems instead of small, specific ones? Help them recognize that this is complex thinking. The mindset shift from complexity to simplicity is one of the most important ways to help a team adopt XP.

- Talk about YAGNI ("You Ain't Gonna Need It") with the team. Help them find at least one piece of code that they don't actually need. Many teams build entire features that were never requested, and are never used. Did your team do that?

- Recognize when team members are uncomfortable with a practice like test-driven development or pair programming, and help them get past their discomfort. Avoid long philosophical debates about the merits of the practice, and instead concentrate on finding specific problems that the team is having which the practice can help. Experience is the best way to get past defensiveness and discomfort—sometimes all it takes is a team member spending an hour or two trying it out.

- Some practices—especially test-driven development—attract a single team member who is highly enthusiastic about it, but whose well-meaning excitement can feel like bullying or zealotry to the rest of the team. Help that team member remember that it took him or her time and effort to learn that new skill, and that other people on the team aren't there yet. Patience is one of the most difficult things to coach, so be patient with yourself as well.

CHAPTER 8

Lean, Eliminating Waste, and Seeing the Whole

Lean is a mindset—a mental model of how the world works.
—Mary and Tom Poppendieck, *The Lean Mindset: Ask the Right Questions*

So far in this book, you've learned about Scrum and XP. Each of those methodologies has practices that you and your team can put in place, and values and principles that help everyone on the team reach an effective mindset. You can tell that you're on a team doing Scrum because you're attending a Daily Scrum, using sprints, and working with a Product Owner and Scrum Master. The same goes for XP: if you're refactoring mercilessly, doing test-driven development, continuously integrating, and doing incremental design, your team is using XP.

But one thing that XP and Scrum have in common is that if you and your team don't understand their values and principles, then you'll end up going through the motions and getting better-than-not-doing-it results. As Ken Schwaber pointed out, if you don't understand collective commitment and self-organization, you don't "get" scrum, and the Scrum values help you understand those things. Ditto for XP: without understanding its values like simplicity and energized work, you'll end up treating the practices like a checklist—your team won't truly embrace change, and you'll end up with complex software that's difficult to maintain.

Lean is different. Unlike Scrum and XP, Lean doesn't include a set of practices. Lean is a mindset, and just like with the mindset for Scrum or XP, Lean comes with values and principles (which, in Lean terminology, are called "thinking tools"). The mindset of lean is sometimes called *lean thinking*. The term "lean" has been applied to manufacturing for many decades; it was adapted for software development by Tom and Mary Poppendieck in the first decade of the twenty-first century. We'll use the capital-L term "Lean" to refer to this adaption of lean ideas to agile software development.

In this chapter, you'll learn about Lean, the values that help you get into the lean thinking mindset, and the thinking tools that help your team identify waste and eliminate it, and see the whole system that you use to build software.

Lean Thinking

Lean is a mindset. This is an interesting idea—giving a name to a mindset—and it's very useful.

We saw earlier in the book that to effectively adopt Scrum, a team needs to have a specific mindset. And we saw that the Scrum values of commitment, focus, openness, respect, and courage help the team get into that mindset. We also saw that XP requires a mindset of its own, and that an XP team uses the values of simplicity, communication, feedback, respect, and courage in the same way.

So it shouldn't be surprising that Lean comes with its own set of values, and that a team looking to adopt lean thinking starts with those values.

The Lean values are:

Eliminate waste
Find the work that you're doing that doesn't directly help to create valuable software and remove it from the project.

Amplify learning
Use feedback from your project to improve how you build software.

Decide as late as possible
Make every important decision for your project when you have the most information about it—at the last responsible moment.

Deliver as fast as possible
Understand the cost of delay, and minimize it using pull systems and queues.

Empower the team
Establish a focused and effective work environment, and build a whole team of energized people.

Build integrity in
Build software that intuitively makes sense to the users, and which forms a coherent whole.

See the whole

Understand the work that happens on your project—and take the right kind of measurements to make sure you're actually seeing everything clearly, warts and all.

Each value comes with *thinking tools* to help you apply the values to real-world situations for your team. Each of these thinking tools is roughly analogous to an XP principle—they're used in exactly the same way. As we explain these values, we'll show you their associated thinking tools and how you use them to help your team get into the Lean mindset.

You Already Understand Many of These Values

An organization will get what it values, and the Agile Manifesto does us a great service in shifting our perception of value from process to people, from documentation to code, from contracts to collaboration, from plans to action.

—Tom and Mary Poppendieck, *Lean Software Development: An Agile Toolkit*

Does it surprise you that you've already encountered many of the Lean values and thinking tools? It shouldn't. Lean is an important part of agile. When the Poppendiecks were adapting ideas from lean manufacturing to software development, they borrowed from other parts of agile, including XP. But more importantly, the manufacturing ideas that they used have been an important part of engineering and quality management for decades. Ken Schwaber drew on many of the same quality ideas when developing Scrum—we saw this when learning about how the Daily Scrum is a formal inspection.

Because this book covers several agile methodologies, we've already covered some important parts of Lean. We'll go through them here—the only reason they don't take up much space in this chapter is because you've learned about them in depth already. They're still core elements to lean thinking.

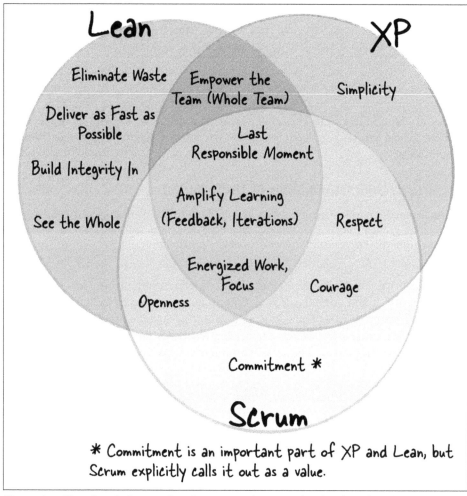

Figure 8-1. You already know a lot about Lean, because there's a lot of overlap between the values of lean thinking and the values of Scrum and XP.

Take another look at the list of Lean values. At least one of them should jump out at you: *decide as late as possible*. Both Scrum and XP heavily rely on the idea of making decisions at the last responsible moment. This Lean value is exactly the same idea. Scrum teams apply this idea to planning. So do XP teams, and they also apply it to design and coding. Lean practitioners do this too—in fact, this value even has a thinking tool called *the last responsible moment*, which is identical to the concept that you've already learned about.

There's another value that you've learned about already: **amplify learning**—and you know that you've already learned it because its first two thinking tools are **feedback** and **iterations**.These are exactly the same concepts that you learned about with both

Scrum and XP. This value also has two other thinking tools: *synchronization* and *set-based development*. Synchronization is very similar to continuous integration and collective ownership in XP, and we'll cover set-based development in just a minute.

Finally, you've also learned about the value **empower the team**, and its thinking tools **self-determination**, **motivation**, **leadership**, and **expertise**. These ideas are almost identical to the ideas behind the XP practices of whole team and energized work—especially avoiding long days and long nights because they have a severe and negative impact on the software. You learned in Chapter 4 that Scrum teams also value this, as part of the Scrum value of **focus**. A team whose members have control over their lives will build better software. And you'll learn later that an important aspect of seeing the whole is sharing information about the project with everyone, including managers—this is exactly why Scrum teams value *openness*.

Commitment, Options Thinking, and Set-Based Development

Here's something we said back in Chapter 4—it's worth reading again:

> Plans don't commit us. Our commitments commit us: the plan is just a convenient place to write those commitments down. Commitments are made by people, and documented in project plans. When someone points to a project plan to show that a commitment was made, it's not really the piece of paper that the person is pointing to. It's the promise that's written down on it that everyone is thinking about.

So what does that really mean? It means that when you make a plan, first you make the commitment, and then you write it down.

Now have another look at Figure 8-1. We added a footnote to commitment about how it's part of Lean and XP, because even though it's only explicitly called out in the Scrum values, commitment is an important part of both the XP mindset and lean thinking. But Lean goes further and adds nuances to the ideas of commitment: **options thinking**, or seeing the difference between something that you're committed to and something that you have the right (but not the obligation) to do; and **set-based development**, or running a project in a way that gives you more options by having the team follow several paths simultaneously to build alternatives that they can compare.

Scrum teams commit to delivering value, but give themselves options for how to do it

Teams *should* make commitments,[1] right?

For example, when a Scrum team member is asked about delivering a specific feature in a few months, he can't just tell the users and managers, "This is Scrum, so I don't

---

1 There's a great resource for learning about options thinking. It's a graphic novel called *Commitment*, by Olav Maassen, Chris Matts, and Chris Geary. You can thank David Anderson for recommending it to us!

have to commit to anything beyond the end of this sprint. Talk to me two months from now." Instead, Scrum teams use a product backlog, so that they can work with the business to understand what's valuable. They make a commitment to deliver valuable software at the end of this sprint, the next sprint, and every sprint for the next few months.

Contrast this with a command-and-control project manager who creates a very detailed project plan that commits people to working on specific tasks months ahead of time. When a team makes a commitment up front to deliver a specific feature with a lot of detailed planning, that gives everyone the illusion that everything is under control. The project manager can point to a specific task that a developer is going to be working on, say, Tuesday at 10:30 a.m. four weeks from now; that gives everyone a feeling that the team has already thought through all of the options and committed to the best path. The problem is that they haven't *really* committed to anything. They don't have enough information to have done that. In fact, there's only one thing that they actually know in this situation: that whatever the plan says the programmer will be doing on Tuesday at 10:30 a.m. four weeks from now is almost certainly wrong.[2]

So instead of planning each task in detail and committing to those detailed tasks, Scrum teams self-organize, and collectively commit to delivering value. And instead of committing to having a specific developer perform a specific task at, say, Tuesday at 10:30 a.m. four weeks from now, they leave decisions to a later responsible moment (probably a Daily Scrum meeting in four weeks).

However, the Scrum team *does not make a commitment to deliver specific backlog items until the sprint has started.* And even after the sprint has started, the Product Owner can take items out of the sprint if they no longer make sense. By making a smaller commitment—to deliver value—instead of committing to specific backlog items, they leave those decisions and commitments to a later responsible moment.

When the sprint starts, the items in the sprint backlog may *feel* like commitments to the team, because they were discussed during the sprint planning session and put on the task board. But they're not commitments. They're **options**. You know that they're not commitments because the Product Owner can remove them from the sprint. And if the team discovers near the end of the sprint that it won't be "*done* done" by the end of the timebox, they'll push it to the next sprint. This is one reason that Scrum works so well: it separates true commitments (delivering valuable working software at the

---

2 If you have a background in finance, you may recognize that when it comes to options thinking, there is a lot of overlap with the world of financial services. Traders and portfolio managers buy and sell options, or instruments that give one party the option to buy or sell an underlying stock or commodity (like oil or wheat) on a certain date at a specific price. This gives them the ability to pursue a strategy to buy that stock or commodity without having to completely commit to owning it. In other words, they can keep their options open.

end of a timeboxed sprint) from options (delivering a specific feature at a specific date).

Getting people to think about options instead of commitments can be difficult, because it's not always easy to think clearly about what it means to commit. Nobody likes being forced to make a commitment on the spot. Most of us have been in a meeting where a boss demands a date from a team member, and the team member shifts uncomfortably in his seat and gives a non-committal, non-answer. This situation happens when bosses or project managers feel like they've been "burned" by a team that made a commitment and then failed to meet it. Their gut reaction is to micromanage the team by demanding many commitments from individual team members about many short-term tasks. This creates an environment where developers are afraid of making commitments.

How do projects get to the point where bosses and project managers feel like they don't trust the team, and that they've repeatedly failed to meet their commitments? This happens because even though individual people may shy away from commitments (especially under pressure in front of the boss), *teams have a tendency to overcommit*. Sometimes this is due to heroics—like an overeager developer who promises more than he can deliver. Other times, it's because commitment is rewarded: it's practical for someone to commit today and apologize later for unforeseen circumstances that knock the project off track. ("There's no way we could have predicted that!") In a company with a culture of blame and CYA, the commit-and-apologize-later approach, while not particularly effective for delivering software, is often the most effective way to get a higher salary or to keep your job.

It's worth repeating the main idea here: bosses often have a tendency to demand commitment, and teams often have a tendency to overcommit.

Incremental design, set-based development, and other ways to give your team options

A task on a Scrum task board goes through three states: to do, in progress, and done. When a task is in the "to do" column, it's still an option, not a commitment. And even while the task is in progress, the team can decide at a Daily Scrum to change direction if it makes sense. In Chapter 4, we talked about how a Scrum team doesn't spend a lot of time modeling and tracking dependencies between tasks, because those dependencies are mainly useful for projecting out a schedule. Instead, the team is free to add and remove tasks on the task board every day during the Daily Scrum. These tasks are options, not commitments: tasks don't have due dates, and there's no such thing as a "late" task that causes the rest of the project to blow a deadline. This encourages options thinking on the team, because they've only committed to the goal, and can change the tasks at any time to meet that goal more effectively based on any new information that they've uncovered.

Here's an example of how Scrum teams use options thinking. Let's say during sprint planning a Scrum team broke a story down into four tasks based on assumptions that they made about storing data in a database, and they included a database design task that would probably have to be done by a DBA. Two weeks into the sprint, a developer discovers that the data they need is already in the database in another format, and it makes more sense to build an object or service than gather the data into a form that the rest of the system can use. To the Scrum team, this is good news! They can pull tasks off of the task board at the next Daily Scrum, freeing up time in the sprint to add another backlog item or clear some technical debt.

In contrast, for a traditional waterfall team, discovering that a task should be done by someone else can be much more difficult to handle: now the project manager has to reallocate resources because the DBA is no longer needed for this task, and that can throw off many project dependencies and ripple through other projects. This is a problem if those project plans contained many commitments that now must be renegotiated. The project manager will be tempted to go back to the team and demand that they use the database anyway. Or a technical architect may feel like the team committed to using his design that depended on the database, and now that commitment is being broken.

Many developers recognize the feeling of being asked to make unnecessary or even counterproductive technical compromises by someone who is not close to the project, like that project manager or technical architect. From the developer's perspective, the team is being asked to compromise the integrity of the software. From the project manager or architect's perspective, the developer is breaking a commitment. Everyone has a cause to see the other person as a "bad guy."

The real problem is that the design should never have been committed to in the first place—if everyone saw it as an option rather than a commitment, the team would be free to build the best software, and the project manager and architect would not have to change their plans or feel slighted.

So how do you get both the boss and the team members to make fewer commitments, and treat more "final" decisions as options?

XP gives us a good answer to this question: incremental design. When a team builds simple components, and each of those components does only one thing, that lets them combine those components in lots of different ways. The team uses refactoring and test-driven development to keep those components as independent as possible.

In other words, decoupled, independent components create options.

When new thinking arises, or a new requirement is discovered, if the components are very large and there are a lot of dependencies between them, the team will spend most of their effort ripping apart that code and performing shotgun surgery. But an XP team that used incremental design has kept their options open. They'll add only

---

the minimal code that they need to meet the new requirement, and they'll keep refactoring and continue to use test-driven development. The team will add as few dependencies as possible, which will continue to keep as many options as possible open to them in the future.

So XP and Scrum teams practice options thinking in how they plan their work and design their software. But is there something that teams can do to explicitly build options into their project?

Yes, there is. When teams practice **set-based development**, they spend time talking about their options, and change the way that they work in order to give themselves additional options in the future. The team will do extra work to pursue more than one option, trusting that the extra work will pay for itself by giving the team more information so that they can make a better decision later.

Let's say that a team has a business problem that has a number of possible technical solutions—for example, our Scrum team that discovered partway through the sprint that they don't need the DBA to modify the database. What if the team doesn't know whether the object-based solution is better than the database solution? This is very common in software projects. You often don't know which solution is best until you build them both—or, at least, until you *start* building them.

When developers are tackling difficult problems, they don't really understand what's involved in solving them until they get their hands dirty. Every developer recognizes the situation where they started working on a "simple" problem that turned out to be much more complicated or subtle than they expected. This is a fact of life for software teams. If the team made a commitment because they assumed that a problem was simple, discovering that it's much more complex than expected gives the team two choices: break the commitment, or deliver hacky, kludgey code and rack up technical debt.

Set-based development will help our Scrum team cope with the fact that they don't know which of the two solutions will work out best. Instead of choosing one path (building the data model) or the other (creating an object-based solution), *the team adds tasks to the task board to pursue both options*. This may seem like it might be wasteful at first, but it can actually save the team a lot of effort in the long run. If one of those approaches truly leads to a much better solution, while the other one leads to a hacky solution with lots of technical debt, then it's worth it for the team to pursue both options—at least long enough for developers on both paths to think through their solutions. This gives them much more information to make a better decision, and the responsible moment for making that decision is *after* they've spent time working on the problem.

Another example of set-based development that teams use regularly is **A/B testing**. This is a practice commonly found when developing user interfaces and improving user experience, and has been used with a lot of success at Amazon, Microsoft, and many other companies. In A/B testing, the team builds two or more solutions—for example, two different layouts or decision paths for a web-based user interface (an "A" layout and a "B" layout). The team will then randomly assign either the A or B option to beta testers—or, for some projects, to live users—and monitor their usage and success rates. Companies have found repeatedly that while it takes more time and effort to build two different complete solutions, it's well worth it in the long run because they can take measurements and prove that one of those solutions was more successful. Not only that, but often the less successful solution still has useful lessons, like features that they can later incorporate into the final product.

These examples show how teams use set-based development and options thinking in the real world. More importantly, they show you how the ideas that you've already learned in Scrum and XP give you a foothold for learning about Lean and lean thinking.

Key Points

- **Lean** (or **lean thinking**) is the name for a mindset, and like other agile mindsets it has values to help you understand and adopt it.

- Lean is a mindset, not a methodology, which is why it doesn't have practices that help you run projects.

- There are values shared between lean thinking and the larger world of agile: *decide as late as possible* (or making decisions at the last responsible moment) and *amplify learning* (using feedback and iterations).

- The Lean value **empower the team** is very similar to the Scrum value of focus, and the XP value of energized work.

- **Options thinking** means understanding the difference between options and commitments, and making decisions about your project that give you as many options in the future as possible.

- When a team uses **set-based development**, they explore more than one option at a time and choose the best one—like when they do **A/B testing** to test multiple user interface options on a sample user population and choose the features that work best.

Narrative: a team working on a mobile phone camera app at a company that was bought by a large Internet conglomerate

Catherine – a developer

Timothy – another developer

Dan – their boss

Act I: Just One More Thing...

"Come on, everyone. Buck up and do it."

Catherine was sick of hearing that from her boss. She had just finished a meeting with him, and he was not happy with the team's progress on a new feature he'd asked them to add. Two of the developers had run into a problem that would cause it to take longer, and he wouldn't give them more time to finish. He hadn't exactly said that they would face consequences if they didn't get it done when he expected it done, but it was clear to everyone that delays were a bad thing.

Catherine was much happier last year, when she worked at a small company with just one programming team. They all worked on a single product, a mobile phone app that added features to the phone's camera. The team was small, but they were highly innovative, and everyone knew how to work well together.

They were also very highly regarded by the rest of the industry. So it only seemed natural that a large Internet conglomerate would express interest in buying the company. Catherine and her teammates had been very excited about this, because they'd read all about that company's relaxed working environment, fridges full of soda, flexible work hours, and other perks. When the deal finally went through, they all got big bonuses (she paid off her student loans!), and the whole team moved to their new, beautiful offices downtown.

"How did we end up this way, Timothy?" asked Catherine, walking out of her boss's office. "This used to be fun. What happened?"

Timothy was a programmer, and had been on the team almost as long as Catherine. "I don't know, Catherine," he said. "It seems like everything takes twice as long as it should."

"I don't mind working longer hours," said Catherine. "But it feels like no matter how long or hard we work, we're always behind."

"I know," said Timothy. "And we'll never get out from under it all."

"Hey, Cathy! Tim! Do you guys have a minute?"

Catherine and Timothy looked at each other. "This doesn't sound good," she said. Their boss, Dan, was calling them back into his office.

"I just got off the phone with one of senior managers at our company's social networking site, and I've got great news." (Somehow, all new requests for the team were "great news.") "He had an idea for integrating their social network data with our camera app. I want you guys to get on it immediately. I'll send you an email with a list of features we need to add, and make sure they get into our next sprint."

Timothy said, "OK. We're halfway through the sprint. What should we remove?"

Catherine shot him a dagger of a stare. She knew this wouldn't end well.

Dan had been looking at his screen while talking to them. He slowly looked up at Timothy. "Don't you think you've got enough resources to get it in this cycle, Tim?"

Timothy started to respond. "Well, uh, no, we've got four other features, and one of them is already behind—"

Dan cut him off. "That's an excuse. I don't see anyone staying late or working real hard these days. I was here at 6 this morning, and nobody else was here. You're telling me we can't put a little more time in? This isn't a big request. I could code it myself in a day."

Catherine knew where this was heading. She'd heard this whole exchange before, and it didn't end well last time. They'd barely gotten that other "great news" request from Dan into the software, and they only got it there by skipping the unit tests and racking up technical debt. And the users noticed—their four- and five-star online reviews dropped to two and three stars after that release.

"Just tell everyone to buck up and do it. It'll be quick, and we'll get a lot of recognition for it in the company."

Creating Heroes and Magical Thinking

There's a school of thought among many managers that if you set very high goals for people, it will motivate them, and they'll work hard to meet those goals. If you give each individual team member aggressive goals and a tight timeline, everyone will rise to the occasion. There's a gut feeling that this "rugged individualism" approach to building teams will eliminate bureaucracy. Each person is individually empowered to solve his or her own problems, and that leads to a highly effective team of problem solvers.

The rugged individualist manager congratulates heroics. The developer who stays late, works weekends, and brings complete solutions back to the team gets the most recognition, and rises to the top of the team. The hero developer rises to the top not because of teamwork, not because of making the whole product better or improving how the team builds software, but because of what he did, alone, after hours.

This is counterproductive. It's traditional thinking, but time and time again teams have found that this "individualist" thinking leads to worse software. Why is that the case?

The best software is created when teams work together. We've already seen a heavy focus on teamwork in both Scrum (with self-organization and collective commitment) and XP (creating an energized environment where the people come together as a whole team). Many agile teams in the real world have seen over and over again how improving their teamwork and giving themselves sane, relaxed working conditions helped them build better software.

So why do so many bosses gather groups of "rugged individuals" instead of building real teams of people who work together and collaborate?

Try to put yourself into this manager's shoes for a minute. It's easy for you to look at the team as a sort of "black box" that creates software. You'll tell the team what to build, wait for a few days, and somehow software appears. If one of your developers is especially good at working on his own, and is willing to work late nights and weekends, he'll immediately stand out to you as someone who can push software out the door. This person is a gift to you as a manager: pile work on him, and it gets done. You'll reward that person, and maybe others will step up to the plate and work the same way.

It seems like the more pressure that you put on the team, the more work you'll get out of them. The more that you reward the late-night workers and the people who can scramble the fastest through the chaos, the more software gets built. And how do you put pressure on people? You'll make sure that they know that there's always more work to be done, and that whatever is currently being worked on needs to get out the door as fast as possible.

It's important for us to be charitable to this boss, even if he's created a distinctly unenergized work environment where every team member feels like he or she doesn't have time to think, and just needs to get work done now. We've got the luxury of having seen from XP exactly how this causes the team to build software that's poorly designed and difficult to change. This boss, on the other hand, doesn't think that way.

This boss uses *magical thinking*.

When a manager has magical thinking, anything is possible. The team can take on any project, no matter how big. Every new project is "just a little feature" or "no big deal, my team can handle it" because a trained group of smart people can accomplish anything. No matter how much work they've taken on this week, next week they can take on even more. You can always add an extra task to the team's plate, and it will somehow get done without affecting any of the other work. If it means that the team needs to pull a "power week" where they work an extra 20 hours, or a few developers have to work over the weekend, that's OK—they'll get the job done. Like magic.

It's not just managers who have magical thinking. There's a symbiosis with the hero—he's willing to work overtime to pull off "miracles" for recognition, a leadership position, and possibly a higher salary. He becomes the measuring stick against which all other team members are valued. The boss doesn't really look very closely at how the software is actually designed and built, or how many poorly constructed stopgaps are turned into long-term solutions. So the number of hours worked per week becomes the main measure of how valuable a team member is.

Magical thinking feels good. You feel like you've solved a big problem, whether you're a manager "motivating" a team or a hero team member who worked very hard to get software out the door. But software built with magical thinking causes more problems than it solves long term: technical debt piles up, software is never "*done* done," and quality and testing are always considered "nice-to-haves": bugs are injected often and usually found by users after the software has been released. And eventually the team slows to a crawl because they spend more and more time fixing bugs and maintaining lousy code than they do building new features.

With both Scrum and XP, we've talked about how the best software is produced most quickly by teams who are given enough time to do the work (through timeboxed iterations), the ability to focus on one task at a time, and an environment of collaboration where they can help each other get over obstacles. This is why agile does not thrive alongside magical thinking or hero developers.

So how do we avoid magical thinking?

This is one of the main goals of Lean. Instead of treating the team as a black box, lean thinking helps you understand exactly what the team does day by day and week by week to build software. A Lean mindset has you look beyond the team, and clearly see what happens before the team starts working and after they deliver—because magical thinking happens there, too. Lean thinking helps you strip away the little white lies that bosses tell teams, that managers tell each other, and that we tell ourselves—lies that keep us from building the best software we can, as quickly as possible. Lean attempts to get rid of those falsehoods, and helps teams work together to think about how to provide real value rather than just burn effort.

Eliminate Waste

It's not always easy to see waste, or even recognize that you and your team spend hours or days doing something that has no practical value for the project. The Lean value **eliminate waste** is about finding project activities that don't add value and eliminating them.

Most teams don't really think about how they build software. There's usually a "way we do things here" that's shared between team members, and which new people pick up when they join the team. It's unusual for most of us to stop and take stock of how we actually get software from concept to production—in fact, it's almost strange to even think about how the team works. Everyone is used to the way things are done. If you always start a project with a big spec, then it would seem strange to the team to try to build software without one. If everyone always uses a build framework that was written three years ago, then your next project will almost certainly use it, too.

Your job, if you're on a team, is to get software out the door, right? Nobody really has time to stop and question the meaning and purpose of life, or of specifications.

In XP, we learned that when teams get into the habit of constantly refactoring their code, they end up with much more flexible designs. The same idea applies to thinking about the way your whole team works in general: if you get into the habit of continuously "refactoring" the way you run your project, you'll end up with a more flexible and capable team.

So how do you "refactor" the way the team runs projects?

The first step in refactoring code is looking for antipatterns. In lean thinking, antipatterns for running projects are called **waste**. That makes sense: waste is anything that your team does that doesn't actively help them build better software.

Think about the last few projects that you worked on. Can you think of things that your team did that didn't actually help the project? What about things that everyone was expected to do, never got around to doing, but still feels bad about skipping? Did you have to write a specification that never got read? Or were you handed a spec but never actually used it? Did you intend to write unit tests or do code reviews, but somehow they never got done? Maybe you did code reviews, but they were done just before the release—so people were hesitant to bring up any issues for fear of delaying the production release, and any issues that were found were merely tagged for repair later.

There's often a lot of work that gets done on a project, but doesn't actually cause the software to get better. For example, a project manager may put a lot of time and effort into a large Gantt chart or other project plan that never accurately represents reality, because it's based on estimates and early information that have changed significantly between when the plan was written and when the team starts working on building software. What's worse, that project manager may put a lot of work into updating the plan after the fact so that it's up to date for periodic status meetings. Clearly that won't help the software, because by the time the plan is brought up to date the software is out the door. Now, maybe this project manager doesn't intend to put effort into something that isn't used by the team. It could be that a senior manager might freak out if the plan says anything other than "100% on time and under budget." Everyone—including the project manager—might be perfectly aware that it's not helping the project.

This is an example of waste: work done by a project manager on a plan that never reflects reality, and isn't actually used by the software team. Not every project plan is like this—not even on waterfall projects. Plenty of waterfall projects have effective planning (or, at least, planning that's as effective as can be done in an inefficient organization). But if you've been a project manager or developer on a project like this, you'll recognize this antipattern. It will be clear to you that it's waste.

When you take a hard, objective look at what you and your team actually do every day, you can start to spot all kinds of waste. Maybe you've got a binder of specifications that's never been opened, and is gathering dust on a shelf. The work that went into building those documents is waste. If you spend a few hours a week sitting through code reviews that focus entirely on superficial errors or personal preferences but don't affect design or catch real bugs, then that's waste. Some waste happens before your project even begins, like writing an extensive statement of work that the team needs to spend a day reviewing but which gets thrown out when the work starts. Are you spending hours debugging deployment problems that could be taken care of with scripts? That's waste too. Useless status meetings where people take turns reciting their individual status so a project coordinator can write it into meeting minutes that are never looked at? Waste.

A Scrum team—even one that gets better-than-not-doing-it results—that replaces the useless status meeting with a Daily Scrum has eliminated that waste. And you've seen throughout this book how the other examples of waste that we just listed can also be eliminated.

If something is waste from a software development perspective, that doesn't mean that it's not useful. It's just not useful for building software. Maybe a senior manager needs that project plan so that she can convince shareholders to keep funding the project. Or maybe the meeting minutes are required for regulators. A statement of work may not be useful for the team, but it could be a required part of a contracting process. Those things may all still be required, but they're *not useful for the project itself*. That makes them waste.

The Lean value of eliminating waste starts with **seeing waste**, the first thinking tool for this value.

It's often hard to see wasteful activities as waste because they're almost always someone else's priority: a project manager who's not part of the team, a contracting officer, a senior manager. Some waste is accepted by the team—maybe everyone knows that the budgeting process is time consuming and doesn't include any activities that directly result in the software being built. Other waste is so familiar that it's essentially invisible—like your team is spread out across three different, disconnected parts of the floor, so it takes an extra five minutes to walk over to your teammate and have a discussion.

The Poppendiecks came up with an idea called the Seven Wastes of Software Development. Like much of Lean, this is adapted from ideas developed at Toyota in the middle of the last century. They discovered that these ideas can help you and your team to see the waste on your software project:

Partially done work
> When you're doing iteration, you only deliver work that's "*done* done" because if it's not 100% complete and working, then you haven't delivered value to your users. Any activity that doesn't deliver value is waste.

Extra processes
> An example of an extra process is the project management antipattern from Chapter 7, where the team spends 20% of their time giving status and creating estimates that aren't used for anything other than updating a status sheet. All that extra effort going through the process of tracking and reporting time doesn't create any value.

Extra features
> When the team builds a feature that nobody has asked for instead of one that the users actually need, that's waste. Sometimes this happens because someone on the team is very excited about a new technology, and wants an opportunity to learn it. This might be valuable to the person who improved their skillset, and that might even be valuable in the future for the team. But it doesn't directly help build valuable software, so it's all waste.

Task switching
> Some teams are expected to multitask, and often this multitasking gets out of hand. Team members feel like they already have a full-time job (like building software), plus many additional part-time tasks added on (like support, training, etc.)—and every bit of work is critical and top priority. The Scrum value of Focus helped us see that switching between projects, or even between unrelated tasks on the same project, adds unexpected delays and effort, because context switching requires a lot of cognitive overhead. Now we have another word for this: waste.

Waiting

There are so many things that professional software developers have to sit around and wait for: someone needs to finish reviewing a specification, or approve access to some system that the project uses, or fix a computer problem, or obtain a software license... these are all waste.

Motion

When the team doesn't sit together, people literally have to stand up and walk to their team members in order to have a discussion. This extra motion can actually add days or even weeks to a project if you add up all of the time team members spend walking around.

Defects

Test-driven development prevents a lot of defects. Every developer who is "test infected" had that "a ha" moment where a unit test caught a bug that would have been very painful to fix later, and realized that it took a lot less time to write all of the tests than it would have to track down that one bug—especially if a user discovers the bug after the software is released. On the other hand, when the team needs to stay late scrambling to fix bugs that could have been prevented, that's waste.

Do some of these things that we're calling "waste" seem like they're useful? Even when something is waste, it's usually useful (or, at least, it seems useful) to someone. Even the developers' seat layout that's spread across the floor inefficiently probably helped the office manager who planned it to solve a different organizational problem. What seeing waste does is help you understand those motives, and lets you objectively evaluate whether they're more important than getting your project done efficiently.

Even when they're useful to someone, all of these things are wasteful *for building a product that delivers value to the users and the company.* Lean thinking involves clearly seeing activities done by people inside and outside of the team that do not add value to the specific goals of the project.

The framework trap in Chapter 7 is a good example of waste that the team has trouble spotting. If the developers build a large framework to address a problem that can be solved with much less code, that framework is waste—which is ironic, considering that the original purpose of the framework was to avoid waste by automating repetitive tasks or eliminating duplicate code. Even worse, that framework often becomes an obstacle in the future, because the team needs to either extend it or work around it whenever they need to add features that aren't explicitly support by it. That extra effort is also waste.

A team that can see waste clearly can see that the framework prevents value from being added to the project. That team understands that waste affects how they do their work every day, and clearly sees that waste in their daily work—and even when that waste is deemed necessary for the company, they see it as waste because it doesn't add value to the product.

Use a Value Stream Map to Help See Waste Clearly

In *Lean Software Development*, Mary and Tom Poppendieck recommend a simple pencil-and-paper exercise to help you find waste. It's called a **value stream map**, and you can build one for any process. Like many techniques used in conjunction with Lean, it originated in manufacturing, but it makes sense for software teams as well.

It shouldn't take you more than half an hour to build a value stream map for your project. Here's how to do it. Start with a small unit of value that the team has already built and delivered to the customers or users. Try to find the smallest unit possible—this is an example of a **minimal marketable feature** (MMF), or the smallest "chunk" of the product that the customers are willing to prioritize. Think back through all of the steps that the unit went through from inception to delivery. Draw a box for every one of these steps, using arrows to connect the boxes. Because you're drawing the actual path that a real feature took through your project, this will be a straight line—there are no decision points or forks in the path, because it represents the actual history of a real feature.

The concept of a minimal marketable feature is important here. Luckily, it's a concept that you've already learned about. When the Product Owner of a Scrum team manages items in the backlog, those items are typically MMFs. An MMF often takes the form of a user story, requirement, or feature request.

Next, estimate how much time it took to do the work for the first step, and how much time elapsed before the next step to start. Repeat this for each of the steps, and draw lines underneath the boxes to represent the work and wait times.

Figure 8-2 shows an example of a value stream map for a real feature going through a traditional waterfall process.

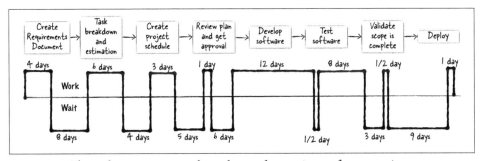

Figure 8-2. This value stream map shows how a feature in a software project moves through a traditional project management cycle. A team can use it to see more clearly where time is wasted.

The value stream map clearly shows how much wait time was involved during the process. It took a total of 71 days from the time the team started work on it to the time that it was deployed. Of those 71 days, 35.5 were spent waiting rather than working. That waiting time could be caused by many different things: the requirements document may take a long time to circulate to all reviewers, or an estimation meeting had to wait because everyone's schedule was booked, or plans are always reviewed by a committee that only meets once a week. The value stream map shows the cumulative effect of those delays on the feature, without bogging you down with the details of why those delays happened. Seeing the overall impact helps you delve into which delays are waste, and which ones are necessary for the project.

To the team, it may not have seemed like they were waiting a long time for the plan to get approved, because they were probably working on another feature during the waiting time. But the customer who needs the feature doesn't necessarily know about all of the other priorities that the team is focusing on. And, to be honest, he doesn't really care—all he knows is that for his feature, a total of 71 days elapsed between the time the team started building it and the time that it was delivered.

Imagine how the boss might react when he sees how much waiting was involved, especially if he had to deal with the increasingly impatient and angry customer. If the team can find a way to cut down on waste and reduce the waiting time, they can significantly improve the delivery time for future features. That will make the customer happier, which will make the boss happier too. And that's how visualizing the waste makes it easier to convince everyone—especially the boss—that *something* needs to change.

Gain a Deeper Understanding of the Product

> Perceived integrity means that the totality of the product achieves a balance of function, usability, reliability, and economy that delights customers. Conceptual integrity means that the system's central concepts work together as a smooth, cohesive whole.
>
> —Mary and Tom Poppendieck, *Lean Software Development: An Agile Toolkit*

When your team has a lean thinking mindset, it means more than just thinking clearly about how they do their work, and seeing waste. It also means clear thinking about the software product that they're building, and how that product delivers value to the users. When the team thinks about how that product delivers value, they're thinking about *integrity*. This leads us to the next Lean value: **build integrity in**. A software team that has a lean thinking mindset always thinks about how they build integrity into their software.

There are actually two aspects to this: internal and external integrity. The software needs to have integrity from the users' perspective (external), but it also needs to have integrity from the perspective of the developers (internal). Lean includes two thinking tools to help us understand internal integrity: **refactoring** and **testing**. These are exactly the same things that you learned about in Chapter 7. In fact, a very effective way to build a system with a high degree of internal integrity is to use XP, especially test-driven development, refactoring, and incremental design.

In this chapter, we'll concentrate on external integrity—what makes software more valuable to users. That means understanding how the users think.

This can seem very abstract. Luckily, Lean has two thinking tools to help you get your brain around integrity. The first tool is **perceived integrity**, or how well the product meets the needs of the person using it—and how well the person immediately sees that his or her needs are met.

Every good product is built to solve a problem or fill a need. Sometimes that need is matter-of-factly and businesslike: an accounting firm needs a tax and accounting system that includes changes to this year's tax code, so that their clients' deductions are legal. Other times, that need is harder to put your finger on: a video game needs to be really fun.

If software is buggy and crashes a lot, it clearly has a perceived integrity problem. But once you get past the software simply working, perceived integrity can be more subtle. There's a major news website, for example, that has repeatedly had perceived integrity problems over the years. For a long time, it was difficult to copy text from articles and paste it into documents or emails. At first, attempting to click and drag to copy and paste would cause the website to pop up a definition of the word that the user clicked on. Eventually that definition feature was disabled, and users were allowed to copy and paste. But a redesign of the website blocked text selection entirely, and attempting to select text would cause the website to pop up a related article in a different window.

This website's clicking, selecting, copying, and pasting behavior was inconsistent and frustrating. It may have had a real purpose: news organizations often want to prevent people from copying their intellectual property and pasting it into emails, and would prefer that users use the "Email this article" feature to share the articles. However, this didn't change the fact that the website did not work the way that the users expected it to. This is an example of poor perceived integrity.

The second thinking tool to help you understand integrity is **conceptual integrity**, or how well the features of the software work together to form a single, unified product. When you and your team understand the perceived and conceptual integrity of your software, you can make it more valuable to your users.

There's a great example of how conceptual integrity affected an entire industry: the evolution of video games over the course of the first decade of the twenty-first century. In the late 1990s, the majority of people who were playing video games were pretty savvy. There were far fewer casual video game players, and many of them were frustrated because they'd buy the latest game only to discover that it was way too hard for them. On the other hand, the hardest of hardcore gamers routinely complained that many new games were too easy.

Video games became increasingly popular over the following decade. And as they did, the industry found ways to design games for both audiences. How did they do this?

The first thing they had to realize was that casual gamers and hardcore gamers need conceptual integrity in their games. Fun, casual games like *Tetris*, *Angry Birds*, and *Candy Crush* need to slowly increase in difficulty over many levels. Casual gamers value this steady increase in difficulty, combined with a continual feeling of accomplishment. If *Angry Birds* started with five easy levels, and then confronted the player with a level that was extremely difficult, people would stop playing because there would be an obvious break in conceptual integrity. A break like that is called *dissonance*.

Hardcore gamers don't like games with a slow, steady learning curve or being constantly rewarded for progress that they didn't earn. They often get more satisfaction from "grinding," or being required to engage in repetitive and often frustrating tasks before getting rewarded with progress.

A fun video game shouldn't have a frustrating level; a "grinding" video game shouldn't have an easy level. Games like *Flappy Bird*, *Super Meat Boy*, and many of the *Final Fantasy* games are lauded by hardcore gamers for their difficulty, and for the number of times that many levels need to be repeated before it can be mastered. An easy level in a grinding video game would cause as much dissonance to a hardcore gamer as a nearly impossible level in a relatively easy game would for a casual gamer.

Teams building video games ran into a lot of trouble with conceptual integrity as the video game industry grew over the first few years of the twenty-first century. There were many games that got poor reviews because they were seen as too easy by hardcore gamers, or too difficult by casual gamers. Those teams learned to include features in their games that improved conceptual integrity for both of these audiences. For example, most games aimed at both markets now have a difficulty setting. If your character keeps dying, a game will prompt you to lower the difficulty. A hardcore gamer would never choose this option—and a game with good conceptual integrity won't continue to ask him if he wants an easier game, because simply asking that question is incongruous with a difficult game. But there is also recognition in the industry that casual and hardcore gamers represent two distinct markets, and there are many games that are marketed to only one group or the other.

All of these developments are about increasing the value that the game brings to the player by understanding how he or she plays the game, and designing games with conceptual integrity in their difficulty level. Video game teams changed the way that they work, making changes to how they design games in order to improve conceptual integrity. It is now very common for software teams to decide at the beginning of the project whether they're building for casual gamers, hardcore gamers, or both. They'll include testing tasks that target the intended audience, and work with their marketing departments to make sure that the games are marketed to the right audience. These are examples of how a team can change the way work is done in order to increase conceptual integrity.

See the Whole

When you work on a software team, you don't work in a vacuum. How your team and your company are structured can have a big impact on how you do your work. And there are all sorts of barriers and stumbling blocks in any organization that can impact your projects as well. For example, you may need to get half a dozen specification approvals from managers before you can start working on a new feature of your software. Maybe a few negative comments from a user cause a product owner to panic and start scheduling your weekends for you. Your boss could fall in love with an overly complex workflow in a ticketing system, and now you need to push every ticket through eight phases before you can start working on it. These are just a few examples—you can probably think of your own examples of inefficient activities that are baked into the way you and your team work.

We saw earlier how these things are waste, but we also saw that sometimes they serve a purpose that may not benefit your project, but are needed by the project or the company. For example, you and your team may waste time (from the project's perspective) filling out reports that don't help the project, but if they're required by a regulator then they're worth it to the company. How do we know which activities are genuinely useful?

That's where the next Lean value comes in: **see the whole**. To really understand whether your team is working efficiently and effectively, you need to take a step back and understand the whole system, because you need to see the whole *objectively*: it's easy to become emotionally invested in a solution. For example, say a project manager created a timesheet system that requires every developer to fill out a daily timesheet in 15-minute increments. She might be really happy with the constant status updates that she's getting. But she might not be aware of how taxing it is on the team —and it's a lot easier to convince her to give up those extra updates if you can show that they're costing the team, say, 5% of their productivity.

But while recognizing the nature of the system that the team works in may sound straightforward, it isn't always easy to do. Each person on a team may feel good or bad about a project depending on how satisfying it was to work on, or how they see their individual contribution. For example, a developer might find a project very satisfying if she solved an interesting coding problem. A project manager will be more satisfied with a project if the team came in ahead of every deadline—but if the developer had to give up her nights and weekends to meet that deadline, she might feel like the project was less successful.

This is why Lean teams take **measurements**—another Lean thinking tool—so that everyone can see the project the same way. There are many things that a software team can measure, and choosing the right measurement helps the team get a better picture of the project. They'll take different measurements depending on what problem they want to solve. Everyone on the project has a different perspective, and taking objective measurements helps get everyone to see the project on the same terms.

For people who haven't spent a lot of time measuring a system—especially the system that a team uses to build software—this can seem very abstract. Let's make it concrete with an example.

Users care very much about how responsive teams are to their needs. Businesspeople and users want their requests to make it into the software quickly. They're much happier when a team can give them one new feature a month than when they have to wait three months for all three features. This is why both Scrum and XP use iterations, and it's why agile teams use shorter feedback loops.

Imagine that you're a business owner paying for a software project. How do you know if you're spending your money wisely? Let's say that you've gotten a steady flow of status reports from your project manager telling you that the project is coming in on schedule and under budget, and that everything is going very well. He has many dashboards, reports, and completed tasks on project plans that are full of green dots to show how each of the past four releases has been almost entirely on track.

This sounds like incontrovertible evidence that the project team is building software very well, and is delivering features that the users requested. Even more, the project manager can point to buffers in the schedule, a tidy risk register, and a ticketing system to show that the project is fully under control, and that allowances have been made for known and unknown risks in the future. As the boss, this gives you a warm, fuzzy feeling: you have control over the project, a good idea of how it runs, and a way to handle unexpected problems that pop up.

But what if you hear from several of your customers who use the software that they made simple requests months ago, and still have not seen them added as features to the software? What if you're starting to lose customers because they're switching to a competitor that they perceive as more responsive to their needs? Would you say that the project is a success? Clearly there's a serious problem, and you need to work with the team to fix it.

How would you work with the team to get them to respond to the most important requests more quickly? Let's say that you try to confront the team, but they point to their positive status reports and tell you that the project is going just fine for them. How do you get them to see the problem?

An objective measurement can help with this. Many teams will measure **lead time** for each feature. This is a measurement of the average time elapsed between when a feature is requested and when it's delivered.

Here's how to calculate it. Any time a user makes a request, record the start date. When a version of the software is released that includes that request, record the end date. The amount of time elapsed between the start date and the end date is the lead time for each request. Add up the lead times for all of the requests in the release and divide by the number of features to calculate the average lead time for the release.[3]

If you ask all the team members what they think the average lead time will be, what do you think they'll say? If the team releases software every month, they'll probably guess that it's between one and two months. That could be an acceptable lead time—most of your users could be satisfied with that, and maybe you just heard a few "squeaky wheel" stories from especially disgruntled users.

But what if the lead time turns out to be a lot longer than your users will accept? What if it takes six months for even a simple user request to make it into the software, and this is not acceptable? Is it the team's fault? Is it something that you're doing? Or is the long lead time an unavoidable side effect of how your business is run? You don't know yet. But now you know that there's a problem, and because you took measurements, you can help the team understand that there's a problem too.

Now when you confront your team about the complaints, if the project manager points to the status reports and tells you that there are no problems, you can point to the objective lead time measurement and *prove* to the team there is a problem after all. This is much better than just saying, "I'm the boss, fix it," because now there's a clear, objective goal that everyone can work toward. It's not an arbitrary decision, and it's not magical thinking.

Find the Root Cause of Problems That You Discover

Taking measurements and seeing the objective truth about your project and your team is only the first part of seeing the whole. The second part is understanding the **root cause**, or the actual reason that the problem is happening.

Back at the end of Chapter 6, we said that we'd get back to root-cause analysis, because in addition to being an important part of lean thinking, it's also one of the corollary practices of XP teams. XP teams and Lean teams both utilize a technique called **Five Whys** to figure out the root cause of a problem. Like much of lean thinking, this technique originated with Japanese auto manufacturing, but has found a

---

3 There are other ways to calculate lead time—for example, you can calculate it so that large features are weighed more heavily than small features. We chose a very simple method of calculating lead time for this example to make it clear how measurements can help this team.

home among agile teams. In this simple practice, the team members ask why a problem happened, and when they answer the question they continue to ask why (usually around five times) until they discover a root cause.

In our example, the team can use the Five Whys technique to find the root cause of their long lead time by asking questions like this:

- *Why is the average lead time so long?* Because it's taking over six months for most users' feature requests to make it into the software.

- *Why is it taking over six months for users' requests to make it into the software?* Because those feature requests are almost always pushed back to make room on the schedule for last-minute changes.

- *Why are there so many last-minute changes?* Because before the team can release software to the users, they need to do a review with senior managers, and those senior managers almost always ask for basic, foundational changes.

- *Why do the senior managers almost always ask for basic, foundational changes?* Because they all have very specific opinions about how the software should look, how it needs to function, and sometimes even the technical tools that should be used to build it, but the team doesn't hear those opinions until after they've built all of the code and have demoed it to the senior managers.

- *Why doesn't the team hear those opinions until after they've built all of the code and given a demo?* Because the senior managers are too busy to talk to the team early in the project, so they'll only attend the final demo—and send the team back to the drawing board after the software is finished.

Aha! Now we know why it takes so long for the team to respond to user requests. Taking measurements and looking for the root cause helped us to see that this wasn't the team's fault at all. It turns out that the team finishes many of the features, but when they give the demo to the senior managers, they're asked to make a lot of changes. Maybe it turns out that these changes are necessary, and those managers had good ideas. But even necessary changes require that this particular project manager do an impact analysis, update her project plan, and reschedule the changed features for a later release. This is what led to the very long lead time that was measured. And it gets worse—some feature requests were already scheduled for the next release; now they need to be bumped to the *following* release to make room for the changes made by the managers. And it turns out that those requests' especially long lead times caused some of the users to switch to the competitors.

Understanding the root cause of the long lead times gives us several potential solutions. The team can build software more iteratively, and ask the managers to attend demos at the end of each iteration, rather than at the end of each major release. Or the managers can delegate their approval to someone (like a Product Owner) who stays more involved with the project and meets with the team more often, and trust that person to make the right decisions. Or the team and managers can keep building software the same way and live with the long lead times, but bring in account managers to work with the users and clients to manage their expectations.

To sum up: the team started with a problem—not responding quickly enough to users' feature requests. By taking measurements and looking for the root cause, they were able to *see the whole*. They understood where their project fit in with the rest of the company, and could identify several possible fixes that would lead to a long-term solution. And most importantly, the team and the boss now both have the same objective information, and can make decisions together.

Deliver As Fast As Possible

There's one more Lean value: **deliver as fast as possible**.

When you read that, what comes to mind? Do you think of a pushy boss or project manager prodding the team to work late and get code out the door? Does "deliver as fast as possible" mean cutting out tests, low-priority features, and anything else that is deemed "extraneous" or low-priority? Maybe it makes you think of a heroic developer working late nights and weekends or putting in quick-and-dirty hacks to get an important feature out the door. This is where most managers' minds go when they hear the phrase, "deliver as fast as possible," and many developers, testers, and other software engineers think the same thing.

Agile teams know that those things cause your team to deliver more slowly, not more quickly. This idea is why we have the agile principle of promoting sustainable development ("The sponsors, developers, and users should be able to maintain a constant pace indefinitely"—this is one of the principles that you learned about in Chapter 3). Taking shortcuts, cutting corners, and working very long hours costs more time and money than it saves. Teams deliver better work more quickly when they have time to do things right.

But while this is true, it's also abstract and somewhat high-minded. The Scrum principle of Focus and the XP practice of Energized Work help to make it more concrete. Scrum and XP gave us insight into how to realistically achieve this optimal pace for delivery with iterations and flow. Lean takes this idea further by giving us three thinking tools to help teams deliver as fast as possible: pull systems, queuing theory, and the cost of delay.

The purpose of **queuing theory** is to make sure that people are not overloaded with work, so that they have time to do things the right way. A queue is a list of tasks, features, or to-do items for a team or for an individual developer. Queues have an order, and are typically first-in, first-out—meaning unless someone explicitly changes the order, the item that has been on the queue the longest is the next one that a team member will pull off of the queue to work on. Queuing theory is the mathematical study of queues, and one of the areas of queuing theory involves predicting the impact that adding queues early in a system can have on its outcome. Lean tells us that making a team's queue of work public, and making it central to the decision-making process, helps teams to deliver more quickly.

Key Points

- When managers believe that teams can do the impossible, and ignore real-world constraints or project realities, they're using **magical thinking**.

- Teams with a lean mindset work to **eliminate waste** by finding any activities that don't directly contribute to building a valuable product and removing them.

- Any activity that doesn't directly add value to a project is **waste**, and Lean teams strive to see waste for what it is and eliminate it from their projects wherever possible.

- Mary and Tom Poppendieck came up with the **Seven Wastes of Software Development**: partially done work, extra processes, extra features, task switching, waiting, motion, and defects.

- **Build integrity in** is another Lean value that includes **perceived integrity**, or how well a product meets its users' needs, and **conceptual integrity**, or how cohesively a product's features work together.

- The Lean mindset helps teams **see the whole**, or objectively understand the way the team works, including its flaws; **measurements** help you keep an objective view of your project and your team.

- **Deliver as fast as possible** means getting rid of any wasteful activities that delay your work and cause bottlenecks.

Use an Area Chart to Visualize Work in Progress

How do you know if you're delivering as fast as possible?

Lean thinking gives us an answer to this question: measurement. And an effective way to measure how your team delivers valuable products is to use a **work-in-**

progress (WIP) area chart. This is a simple diagram that shows how the minimal marketable features are flowing through your value stream.

If you've created a value stream map, then you can build a WIP area chart, which is an area chart that shows how features, products, or other measures of value flow through every part of the value stream. This works best if you use MMFs, because they represent the minimally sized "chunk" of value that's created.

Let's take a look at an example of a value stream map that shows how a web development shop handles most of their MMFs.

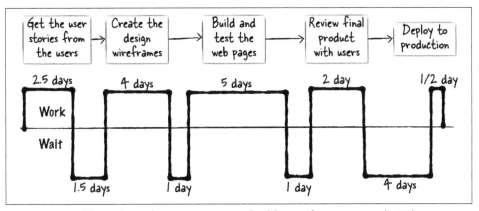

Figure 8-3. We'll use this value stream map to build a work-in-progress (WIP) area chart.

The goal of the WIP area chart is to show a complete history of the **work in progress** —all of the valuable features that the team is currently working on. The chart will show us how many MMFs were in progress on any date, and how those MMFs broke down across the various value stream stages. The work in progress *is a measurement of features, not tasks*. In other words, it shows the number of features or parts of the product that are being worked on, not the specific tasks that the team does to produce them. Back in the Scrum chapter, you saw how features relate to tasks when the team broke stories down into tasks that moved across a task board. A story is a good way to represent an MMF because it's a small, self-contained "chunk" of value that's delivered to the user. The story would appear in the WIP area chart; the tasks that the team uses to build the story don't.

To build the WIP area chart, start with an x-axis that shows the date, and a y-axis that shows the number of MMFs. The chart has a line for each of the boxes in the value stream map. The lines divide the chart into areas for boxes in the value stream map.

There are no MMFs in progress before the project starts, so there's just a single dot at X=0 at the lefthand side of the diagram (day 0). Let's say that when the project starts, the team starts working with the users on nine user stories, and they're using those user stories as MMFs for their project. Then a few days later, they add three more stories. You'll draw a dot at 9 for the first day, then another at 9 + 3 = 12 when those new MMFs were added, and you'll connect them.

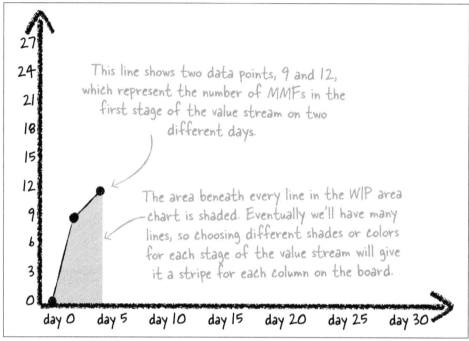

Figure 8-4. Start building up the WIP area chart by creating a line chart of MMFs (like user stories) in the first stage of the value stream, and shading the area underneath it.

A few days later, the programmers start working on creating the design wireframes for four of the stories, so those four stories have progressed to the next stage in the value stream. The total number of MMFs in the system is still 12, but now they're divided into 8 still being worked on—or **waiting**, because the value stream map tracks both work and wait time—in the first stage of the value stream, and 4 in the second stage. So you can add dots at 4 and 12 to represent this.

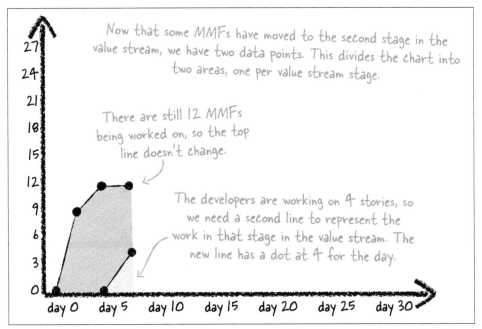

Figure 8-5. When work progresses to the next stage in the value stream, a new line for that stage is added to the WIP area chart, dividing it into two areas. The top line still represents the total number of MMFs in in progress, and the space between it and the new line represents the number of MMFs in the first stage.

As MMFs move through the value stream, the total number of tasks grows, and over time the WIP area chart acquires stripes for each stage in the value stream map.

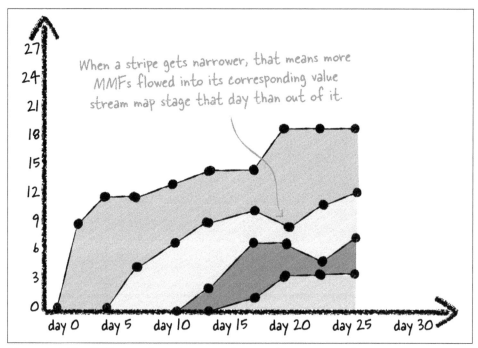

Figure 8-6. The WIP area chart shows you how work in progress changes over time.

What happens when MMFs are completed? If you keep them on the chart, eventually the number of "done" MMFs grows to a size that dwarfs all of the other columns. This makes the active MMFs resemble a ribbon on top of a mountain.

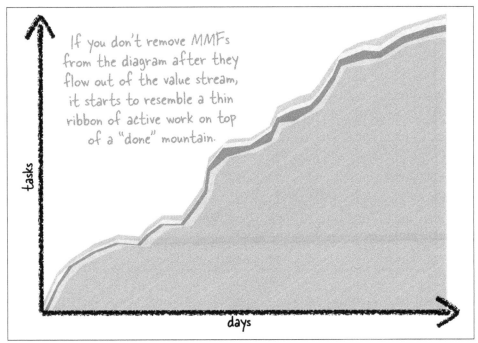

Figure 8-7. When a team wants to show the boss how much work they've accomplished, they'll leave the "done" tasks on the chart because it looks impressive. Unfortunately, that makes it a lot more difficult to use the chart to measure work in progress.

This is showing growth, not flow. And while it makes for a great status report item to impress a senior manager—because it shows that the team has gotten an enormous amount of work done—it's not particularly useful for managing flow. Removing the "done" work from the diagram gives a clearer visualization of how value flowed down the value stream over time.

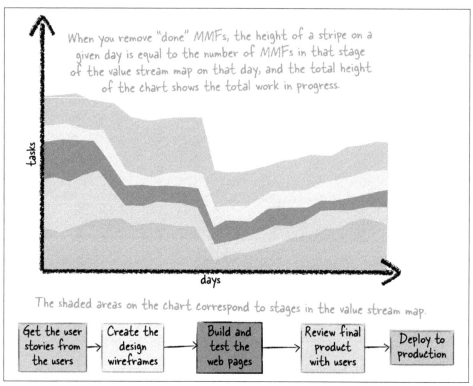

Figure 8-8. It's useful to remove the "done" tasks from the chart, and use different shades for each stripe to make it easy to figure out which columns they correspond to.

This is why most WIP area charts do not include completed tasks. That way, if your project stabilizes over time, your WIP area chart looks stable too.[4] When a MMF moves from one stage in the value stream to the next, the stripe for the old stage it moved from gets thinner, and the stripe for the new one to gets thicker. This makes it easy to spot trends—like when many MMFs move from one column to another (or out of the value stream entirely) at the same time.

---

4 Did you look at this chart and wonder why we aren't calling it a cumulative flow diagram, or CFD? In Chapter 9, we'll explain the difference between a WIP area chart and a CFD.

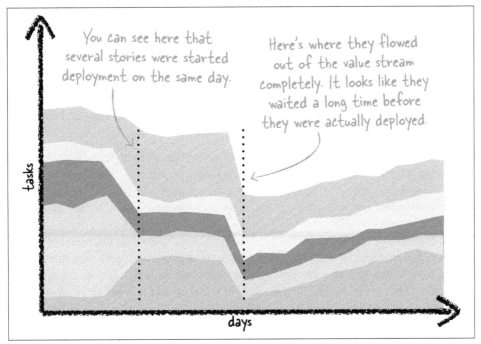

Figure 8-9. The WIP area chart helps you see how the work flows through the value stream, and makes it easier to spot delays and other potential waste—like stories that took a very long time to deploy to production.

Control Bottlenecks by Limiting Work in Progress

An important idea that uses queuing theory is called the *theory of constraints*, introduced by a physicist turned management guru named Eliyahu M. Goldratt. One of the ideas behind the theory of constraints is that a particular constraint (like work piling up behind an overburdened team) limits the total amount of work that can get through the system. When the constraint is resolved, another constraint becomes the critical one. The theory of constraints tells us: *every overloaded workflow has at least one constraint.*

When a constraint causes work to pile up at a specific point in a workflow, people will often call it a **bottleneck**. Removing one bottleneck from the system—maybe by changing the process or adding people—will cause work to flow more smoothly. The theory of constraints tells us that there will still be another critical constraint or bottleneck somewhere else in the system. However, we can reduce the total amount of waste by systematically tracking down the critical constraint and eliminating it.

What does it feel like to work on a team that has to deal with one of these constraints on a day-to-day basis? In other words, what does it feel like when you and your team are the bottleneck?

When you're the bottleneck in the system, you're always expected to multitask, constantly switching between your normal full-time job and many smaller part-time ones. Keep in mind that plenty of healthy teams usually have many tasks due at the same time but don't call it "multitasking"; people typically use the term "multitasking" in order to mask the fact that the team is simply overloaded. Splitting the work up and telling the team to multitask often keeps you from recognizing that you simply have more work than time, especially when you consider the extra time and cognitive effort required to switch between tasks.

For example, a team that already has 100% of their time already devoted to development work may have a boss with magical thinking who asks them to "multitask" and spend several hours a week that they don't have on support, training, maintenance, meetings, or other work. It's difficult for them to necessarily see that they have more work than time, especially if that extra work is added a bit at a time. They'll just start to feel overloaded, and because it's called "multitasking" they won't necessarily realize why they feel that way; it will just feel as if they have many part-time jobs that they're having trouble keeping up with. We can help that team by applying queuing theory to gain insight into the problem. Now we know that more and more of their work is piling up in a bottleneck somewhere in their workflow, and that growing pile of work is weighing on them.

Pull Systems Help Teams Eliminate Constraints

> And I have a philosophy that I live by. Everybody that works with me knows this; it's on the wall: "If stupid enters the room, you have a moral duty to shoot it, no matter who's escorting it."
>
> —Keoki Andrus, *Beautiful Teams* (Chapter 6)

A **pull system** is a way of running a project or a process that uses queues or buffers to eliminate constraints. This is another concept that originated with Japanese auto manufacturing, but has since found its place in software development. Car manufacturers—specifically Toyota in the 1950s and 1960s—started to look at their warehouses of parts, and tried to find ways to reduce the number of parts that they needed to have lying around. After a lot of experimentation, they discovered that even if you had almost all of the parts needed to assemble cars available in the warehouse, a shortage of just a few parts could hold up the entire line. Entire assembly teams would end up waiting for those missing parts to be delivered. The **cost of delay** became important: if a part was in short supply, a delay in getting that part to the assembly line was very expensive; if the part was abundant, the cost of delay was low.

Teams at Toyota found that they could reduce their costs and deliver cars much more quickly if they could figure out which parts the teams needed right now, and deliver only those parts to the line. To fix this, they came up with the Toyota Production System (or TPS)—this was the precursor of lean manufacturing, which the Poppendiecks adapted to create lean software development.

At the heart of TPS is the idea that there are *three types of waste that create constraints in the workflow* and must be removed:

- *Muda* (無駄), which means "futility; uselessness; idleness; superfluity; waste; wastage; wastefulness"
- *Mura* (斑), which means "unevenness; irregularity; lack of uniformity; nonuniformity; inequality"
- *Muri* (無理), which means "unreasonableness; impossible; beyond one's power; too difficult; by force; perforce; forcibly; compulsorily; excessiveness; immoderation"

Anyone who's been on a poorly managed, poorly run software project—especially one that used an ineffective process—is intimately familiar with the ideas of futility, unevenness, and unreasonableness. This is true of ineffective waterfall processes, but anyone who's been on, say, a team that was only able to get better-than-not-doing-it results (or worse) by forcing Scrum or XP practices on a team with the wrong mindset will also recognize these things.

Do any of these things feel familiar?

- It takes a very long time to get everyone to sign off on a specification, and in the meantime developers are sitting around waiting for the project to start. Once it does start, they're already late.
- It takes management forever to secure the budget. By the time the project is given the green light, it's already late.
- Halfway through development, the team recognizes that an important part of the software design or architecture needs to be changed, but that will cause very large problems because so many other things depend on it.
- The QA team doesn't start testing the software until every feature is complete. They find a major bug or a serious performance problem, and the team has to scramble to fix it.
- The analysis and design take so long that by the time coding begins, everyone needs to work nights and weekends to meet the deadline.
- A software architect designs a large, beautiful, complex system that's impractical to implement.
- Even the smallest change to a specification, a document, or a plan needs to go through a burdensome change control process. People find ways to work around the process by putting even sweeping, large-scale changes into a ticketing or bug tracking system instead.

- The project is running late, so the boss adds extra people to the team for the last few weeks. Instead of making the project go faster, this move creates confusion and chaos.[5]

Think back to your own projects that ran into problems because of things that you knew were stupid. They may have been stupid rules that you had to live with (or work around) that were imposed by a boss or were part of your company's culture. Maybe there were stupid, unnecessary deadlines that were arbitrarily set in order to motivate you.

These things aren't random. Take a minute to look back at the definitions of muda, mura, and muri. Then look at the list of familiar project problems, as well as the problems you've seen on your own projects. See if you can fit each of these problems into one of these three categories. Were there things you had to do that were futile, useless, or superfluous? This is muda—work you had to do that didn't add value. What about times when you were sitting around idle, anxiously waiting for someone to get back to you so you could get your work done? This is mura—unevenness, or work that happens in fits and starts. Those times that you had to stay late or work weekends because you were expected to do more work than was humanly possible? That's muri—overburdening, or being expected to do unreasonable or impossible things.

Even though there are many differences between software development and car manufacturing, the Poppendiecks recognized that these ideas from lean manufacturing also affect software projects. So it stands to reason that if software teams face problems similar to those in manufacturing, the solutions that worked for manufacturers will also work for software teams. For manufacturing, that solution is a pull system (also known as "just-in-time production").

The manufacturing team at Toyota in the 1950s, led by engineer Taiichi Ohno, recognized that it was difficult to predict in advance which parts would be in short supply in the future—it often seemed like different parts were in short supply. This was an important root cause of waste (muda, mura, and muri). So they came up with a system where stations on each assembly line would *signal* that they're ready for more parts, with a team set up to deliver parts based on those signals. Each station would have a small queue of parts that they needed. Instead of having a warehouse that pushed parts onto a line, they had a line that pulled parts from a warehouse, and only took parts when the queue got low.

---

5 In *The Mythical Man Month*, Fred Brooks gave us Brooks's Law: "Adding manpower to a late project makes it later." Think about that while you're reading about muda, mura, and muri.

This is called a *pull system* because it consists of independent teams or team members that pull only those parts that they need (rather than having a large stockpile of parts pushed on them and routinely topped off). Toyota and other car manufactures found that it made their entire assembly process much faster and cheaper, because it cut out a huge amount of waste and waiting time. In fact, every time a specific bit of waste was identified, they were able to make a small change to their process in order to eliminate it.

Pull systems are very useful for building software—maybe not surprisingly, for exactly the same reason that they're useful in manufacturing. Instead of having users, managers, or product owners push tasks, features, or requests down to a team, they'll add those requests to a queue that the team pulls from. When work backs up and causes unevenness partway through the project, they can create a buffer to help smooth it out. The team may have several different queues and buffers throughout their project. And as it turns out, this is a very effective way of reducing waiting time, cutting out waste, and helping users, managers, product owners, and software teams decide on what software is built.

Here's a very simple example of how a pull system might solve a familiar problem: the software team that has to wait until every single feature is written into a large specification that must then go through a cumbersome review process. Maybe the process is a way to get all of the perspectives from every person; it may just be a way to provide CYA to bosses and stakeholders who are afraid to make a real commitment; or it might just be how the company always did business, and it never occurred to anyone that it's wasteful. What would it look like if we replaced this with a simple pull system?

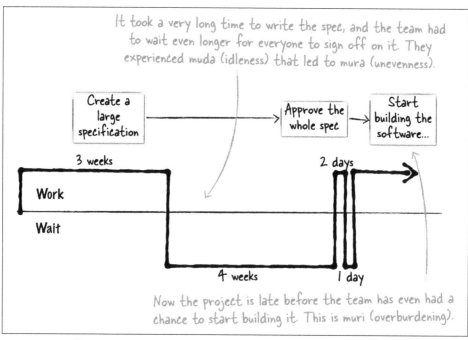

It took a very long time to write the spec, and the team had to wait even longer for everyone to sign off on it. They experienced muda (idleness) that led to mura (unevenness).

Create a large specification → Approve the whole spec → Start building the software...

3 weeks | 2 days

Work

Wait

4 weeks | 1 day

Now the project is late before the team has even had a chance to start building it. This is muri (overburdening).

Figure 8-10. This value stream map shows the waste that happens when the team is waiting for a large specification to be created and approved.

This is a very familiar problem, and in the real world many teams have found ways to work around it. For example, the designers and architects might do "prework" based on an early draft of the spec, and their best guess as to what they'll eventually be building. But while the team will find ways to eliminate the waste from the project—"shooting stupid when it enters the room"—they can only do so much. There will still be waste, often a lot of it, especially if they guess wrong and now have to undo some of the prework.

A pull system is a better way to remove this unevenness and prevent the overburdening.

The first step in creating a pull system is to break the work down into small, pullable chunks. So instead of building a large spec, the team can break it into minimal marketable features—say, individual stories, and maybe a small amount of documentation to go with each story. Those stories would then be approved individually. Typically, when a spec review process is held up for a long time, it's because people have problems with some of the features. (Can you see how breaking the work down into smaller MMFs gives the team more options? That's options thinking.) Approving individual MMFs should allow at least a few features to get approved quickly. As soon as the first MMF has been approved, the team can start working on it. Now the team doesn't have to guess. Instead, there's a real discussion of the work that needs to be done. There may be a real reason for the approval process (like a regulatory requirement, or a genuine need to get everyone's perspective); now the team can get a real sign-off before starting the work.

This is how all the parts of lean thinking—seeing the whole, identifying the waste, and setting up a pull system of eliminate the unevenness and overburdening—can come together to help a team improve the way they do work. But that's just the beginning. In the next chapter, you'll learn about how to apply the mindset of Lean to improve the way your team builds software.

Key Points

- A **minimal marketable feature** (MMF) is the smallest "chunk" of value or functionality that the team can deliver, such as a story or a user request—something that might end up on a Product Owner's backlog).

- A **value stream map** is a visual tool to help Lean teams see the reality of how their project works by showing the entire lifespan of an MMF, including the working and waiting time at every stage.

- Understanding the **root cause** of a problem helps you see the whole; the **Five Whys** technique is an effective way to do that.

- A useful tool to help your team **deliver as fast as possible** is a *WIP area chart*, or a visual tool that shows how MMFs flow through your project's value stream.

- There are three important wastes that constrain your workflow: **muda** (futility), **mura** (unevenness), and **muri** (unreasonableness and impossibility).

Frequently Asked Questions

This seems like some useful information about how to run projects, but I'm still having trouble seeing how it impacts my day-to-day work. How can Lean help me in my job?

Most of the time, we don't want to hear people say that something is "theoretical" or "academic"—when someone says that, it's usually an indication that they don't see an immediate practical application. However, in many ways it's actually true about Lean, because *lean is a mindset*. It doesn't include practices that your team does every day, any more than the Agile Manifesto or the Scrum or XP values do. But just like the Agile Manifesto and the Scrum and XP values, Lean is extremely valuable for getting you and your team into the right mindset to build software better and build better software.

Back in Chapter 2, we introduced the idea of a fractured perspective, and throughout the book you've seen many examples of how that fracture leads to teams getting better-than-not-doing-it results at best, and complete project failure at worst. Lean thinking helps you take a bird's-eye view not just of your project, but of your whole team, your company, and the rules, policies, and culture that cause you and your team to run into serious project problems.

Flip back to the beginning of this chapter and look at the lean values one more time. These values are all about helping you look beyond the work that you're doing right now.

Once you start looking for waste, you start seeing it everywhere ("eliminate waste"). You'll stop seeing the way you build software as a set of discrete tasks, and start to see it as a system ("see the whole"). You'll use tools like "Five Whys" to go beyond fixing individual problems in the work that you and your team did, and recognize systematic problems that affect your project over and over ("amplify learning"). Every single Lean value changes the way that you look at your project, your team, and your company. This will help you get to a larger perspective.

In Chapter 9, you'll learn how to take this new perspective and use it to make real, permanent changes to improve how you and your team build software.

You said that "muri" can translate to "impossible," but isn't that just being negative? Anything is possible given a sufficiently motivated team, right?

If only that were true. Here's a thought experiment to help show you that some things really are impossible.

Imagine that the CEO of your small startup walks into your office and tells you that your biggest client is obsessed with Brooklyn. He dumps a package of toothpicks and popsicle sticks on a table, and tells you that if you and your team can have a perfect scale model of the Brooklyn Bridge made out of toothpicks and popsicle sticks by the time the client gets here, that client will triple the company's business and make you all rich. If you don't have it done perfectly, he'll take his business to your main competitor, and the company will fold.

The client will be here in less than an hour. Everything is on the line. Nothing is impossible! You'll save your company, right?

Unless you happen to be a civil engineer who's also a virtuoso with glue, you'll fail. Some tasks are simply not possible, no matter how much motivation you have.

Some people manage their teams by assuming that motivation is all that you need to accomplish any goal. Management like that—what we called magical thinking—is dangerous. When you're on a team that's being run as if you can do anything, you'll routinely run into expectations that are impossible to meet. Often, it's because of unrealistic or unreasonable deadlines. But sometimes the problem you're solving is technically impossible (or, at least, extremely unfeasible without a very large amount of work—like if your codebase is in terrible shape and full of code smells).

This is *muri*. Have another look at the definition that we gave earlier: "unreasonableness; impossible; beyond one's power; too difficult; by force; perforce; forcibly; compulsorily; excessiveness; immoderation." Lean thinking helps you identify muri, and it helps you see that any effort that you and your team spend trying to do the impossible is waste. The most effective way to eliminate this waste is to eliminate the magical thinking that caused your team to attempt the impossible in the first place.

 Things You Can Do Today

Here are a few things that you can try today on your own or with your team:

- Identify all of the MMFs on your project. How are they managed? Do you write user stories on cards or sticky notes and put them on a task board? Do you have individual requirements in a specification? Find a larger feature or story and see if you can break it down into smaller chunks.
- Look for waste in your project. Write down examples of muda, mura, and muri.
- Find any MMFs that you and your team completed already and create a value stream map for them. See if you can get your whole team to do it together. Then create a value stream map for another MMF. What are the similarities and differences between the two value streams?
- Find a bottleneck that your team routinely hits. (Your value stream map can be very helpful for doing this.) Have a discussion about what you can do to alleviate it in the future.
- Look at the dates that you and your team are currently committed to. Have you *really* made the commitments that you think you've made? Are there options to deliver something different, while still meeting those commitments?

Where You Can Learn More

Here are resources to help you learn more about the ideas in this chapter:

- You can learn more about Lean, the values of lean thinking, and value stream maps in *Lean Software Development: An Agile Toolkit,* by Mary and Tom Poppendieck (Addison-Wesley, 2003).

- You can also learn more about Lean and value stream mapping in *Lean-Agile Software Development: Achieving Enterprise Agility,* by Alan Shalloway, Guy Beaver, and James R. Trott (Addison-Wesley, 2009).

- You can learn more about MMFs by reading about how to break down or decompose user stories in *User Stories Applied,* by Mike Cohn (Addison-Wesley, 2004).

- You can learn more about options thinking in *Commitment,* a graphic novel about managing project risk by Olav Maassen, Chris Matts, and Chris Geary (Hathaway te Brake Publications, 2013).

Coaching Tips

Tips for agile coaches helping their team to work with the ideas in this chapter:

- Most people on software teams have never encountered a mindset with a name. Helping them to understand that Lean is a mindset, rather than a methodology, is a good first step toward helping the team adopt lean thinking.

- Getting comfortable talking about waste is one of the most difficult parts of lean thinking. While most coaches agree that teams should stay positive and not negative, a "gripe session" can be helpful when it comes to helping teams learn to identify waste—especially when it comes to unreasonableness and impossibility.

- You can keep the discussion of waste positive by helping them find examples of things that are waste from the *project* perspective, but which are vitally important *to the company*. That will help put them in the right frame of mind to identify waste without judging it negatively.

- Part of your job as coach is to avoid friction between the team and the company. If the company has a mindset where even bringing up problems with senior managers can cause serious consequences for the team, that can cause serious problems with your agile adoption. If possible, *gently* work with managers to help them recognize their own magical thinking.

- Another way to stay positive is to help both teams and managers separate the process or system from the people working within it. Waste, inefficiency, feedback—these are all things that have to do with the process, and are not judgments about the people who make it work.

CHAPTER 9

Kanban, Flow, and Constantly Improving

Kanban is not a software development lifecycle methodology or an approach to project management. It requires that some process is already in place so that Kanban can be applied to incrementally change the underlying process.
—David Anderson, *Kanban*

Kanban is a method for process improvement used by agile teams. Teams that use Kanban start by understanding the way that they currently build software, and make improvements to it over time. Like Scrum and XP, Kanban requires a mindset. Specifically, it requires the lean thinking mindset. We've already learned that Lean is the name for a mindset, with values and principles. Teams that use Kanban start by applying the Lean mindset to the way they work. This provides a solid foundation which, combined with the Kanban method, gives them the means to improve their process. When teams use Kanban to improve, they focus on eliminating the waste from their process (including muda, mura, and muri—the wastes of unevenness, overburdening, and futility that we learned about in Chapter 8).

Kanban is a manufacturing term, adapted for software development by David Anderson. Here's how he describes its relationship to Lean in his 2010 book, *Kanban*: "The Kanban Method introduces a complex adaptive system that is intended to catalyze a Lean outcome within an organization." There are teams that apply Lean and lean thinking to software development without using Kanban, but Kanban is by far the most common—and, to many agile practitioners, the most effective—way to bring lean thinking into your organization.

Kanban has a different focus from agile methodologies like Scrum and XP. Scrum primarily focuses on project management: the scope of the work that will be done, when that work will be delivered, and whether the outcome of that work meets the needs of the users and stakeholders. The focus of XP is software development. The XP values and practices are built around creating an environment conducive to development, and developing programmer habits that help them design and build code that's simple and easy to change.

Kanban is about *helping a team improve the way that they build software*. A team that uses Kanban has a clear picture of what actions they use to build software, how they interact with the rest of the company, where they run into waste caused by inefficiency and unevenness, and how to improve over time by removing the root cause of that waste. When a team improves the way that they build software, it's traditionally called *process improvement*. Kanban is a good example of applying agile ideas (like the last responsible moment) to create a process improvement method that is straightforward and easy for teams to adopt.

Kanban has practices that give you a way to stabilize and improve your system for building software. The latest set of core practices can be found on the Kanban Yahoo! group (*http://bit.ly/kanban-yahoo*):

> First follow the foundational principles:
>
> * Start with what you do now
>
> * Agree to pursue incremental, evolutionary change
>
> * Initially, respect current roles, responsibilities & job titles
>
> Then adopt the core practices:
>
> * Visualize
>
> * Limit WIP
>
> * Manage Flow
>
> * Make Process Policies Explicit
>
> * Implement Feedback Loops
>
> * Improve Collaboratively, Evolve Experimentally (using models/scientific method)
>
> It is not expected that implementations adopt all six practices initially. Partial implementations are referred to as "shallow" with the expectation that they gradually increase in depth as more practices are adopted and implemented with greater capability.

In this chapter, you'll learn about Kanban, its principles and how they relate to Lean, and its practices. You'll learn how its emphasis on flow and queuing theory can help your team put lean thinking in practice. And you'll learn about how Kanban can help your team to create a culture of continuous improvement.

Narrative: a team working on a mobile phone camera app at a company that was bought by a large Internet conglomerate

Catherine – a developer

Timothy – another developer

Dan – their boss

Act II: Playing Catch-Up

Catherine and Timothy were getting sick of Dan. They understood that there were deadlines, and that the work they were doing was important. And they even recognized the kind of pressure that he was under to deliver. But it seemed like every little project, no matter how small, ended up in "Intensive Care Unit mode," which was what Dan called it when he started to micromanage them.

Their current project was no different. They were working on a new feature for their phone camera app that turns their friends' faces into old timey "Wanted" posters. It was supposed to be a simple project that integrated their camera app with their parent company's social networking system. And as usual, they found a bunch of bugs during testing that would cause them to miss the deadline.

"I'm pretty sure we wouldn't have any trouble getting this done on time if he would just let us do our jobs," said Timothy.

"I know what you mean," said Catherine. "It's like he's meddling in every little thing I do. Speaking of meddling, it's after seven and starting to get dark out. We're late for his evening status meeting."

It was "crunch time," which is what Dan called it when there was a deadline they weren't going to make. That meant it was always crunch time.

Catherine and Timothy walked over to Dan's office and sat down. Their other teammates were already there, and nobody looked happy. Dan was already in full-on micromanagement mode.

"Look, we're in intensive care on at least three projects. Tim, Cathy, we'll start with yours."

Catherine said, "We're making progress—"

Dan cut her off. "You're not making progress. This project is falling apart. I've given you enough time to do it your way, now we need to do it the *right* way."

Timothy replied, "But there was that bug that had to be fixed."

"It seems like there's always that bug. You guys just can't seem to get these projects done on time. I'm going to have to jump in here, because you're not giving this project enough urgency."

"Hold on," said Catherine. "It's not a coincidence that we always end up here. There's a lot of waste that happens along the way."

"What do you mean, waste?" asked Dan. "That sounds really negative. We need to stay positive if we want to be successful here." (Dan always talked about staying positive, even when he was berating people who worked for him.)

"Well, like the way it takes weeks to get everyone to agree on any change to a user interface. About halfway through that discussion you tell us to get started on it, and it seems like we spend more time changing that code than we spent writing it in the first place."

Timothy said, "Right. Or the way we're always surprised that the QA team finds bugs. Somehow it happens every time, but we never give ourselves enough time to fix them."

Dan started looking angry. "Look, that's just the way software projects work. Stop pointing fingers and blaming people. It's my fault, or the QA team's fault."

Catherine was fed up. "Look, Dan, that's enough."

Everyone looked at her. She almost never raised her voice like that.

"We're not blaming anyone. There are problems that seem to happen over and over again. We have these meetings twice a day, and we sound like a broken record. We need to talk about problems that happen over and over again. They're always the same problems, and we act surprised every time."

Dan seemed a little taken aback that she was yelling back at him. He stood up, stared her down for a minute, then sat back down in his chair again. "You know what? All of those things are great to think about next time. Right now, we're going to just have to put a little more time and urgency into it. This is crunch time."

The Principles of Kanban

Let's take a closer look at Kanban's foundational principles:

- Start with what you do now
- Agree to pursue incremental, evolutionary change

- Initially, respect current roles, responsibilities, and job titles

That first principle—starting with what you do now—has a different focus from everything you've read so far in this book.

We've spent a lot of time comparing agile methodologies to traditional waterfall projects. Scrum, for example, gives you a complete system for managing and delivering your projects. If you want to adopt Scrum, you need to create new roles (Scrum Master and Product Owner), and you need to give your team new activities (sprint planning, Daily Scrum meetings, task boards). This is necessary for adopting Scrum because it's a system for managing your project and delivering software.

Kanban is *not* a system for managing projects. It's a method for improving your process: the steps that your team takes to build and deliver software. Before you can improve anything, you need a starting point, and the starting point for Kanban is what you do today.

Find a Starting Point and Evolve Experimentally from There

The thing about habitual problems is that they're habitual.

When your team does something on a project that will eventually lead to bugs and missed deadlines, it doesn't feel like a mistake at the time. You can do all the root-cause analysis that you want after the fact; faced with the same choice, the team will probably still make the same decision. That's how people are.

For example, let's say that a programming team always finds themselves delivering software to their users, only to repeatedly have awkward meetings where users can't find the features they think they were promised. Now, it's certainly possible that these developers are incredibly forgetful, and that they always forget one or two of the features that they discussed with the users. But it's more likely that they have a recurring problem with how they gather their requirements or communicate them to the users.

The goal of process improvement is to find recurring problems, figure out what those problems have in common, and come up with tools to fix them.

The key here is the second part of that sentence: figuring out what those problems have in common. If you just assume, for example, that a developer simply can't remember all of the things the users asked for, or that the users constantly change their minds, then you've effectively decided that the problems are unfixable. But if you assume that there's a real root cause that's happening over and over again, then you stand a chance of finding and fixing it.

That's where Kanban starts: taking a look at how you work today, and treating it as a set of changeable, repeatable steps. Kanban teams call steps or rules that they always follow **policies**. This essentially boils down to a team recognizing their habits, seeing what steps they take every time they build software, and writing all of those things down.

Writing down the rules that a team follows can sometimes be tricky, because it's easy to fall into the trap of judging a team—or an individual team member—on the results of a project: if the project is successful, everyone on the team must be good at their jobs; if the project fails, they must be incompetent. This is unfair, because it assumes that everything in the project is within the control of the team. Lean thinking helps get past this by telling us to see the whole, which in this case means *seeing that there's a bigger system in place*.

That's worth repeating: *every team has a system for building software*. This system may be chaotic. It may change frequently. It may exist mainly inside the heads of the team members, who never actually discussed a larger system that they follow. For teams that follow a methodology like Scrum, the system is codified and understood by everyone. But many teams follow a system that exists mainly as "tribal" knowledge: we always start a project by talking to these particular customer representatives, or building that sort of schedule, or creating story cards, or having programmers jump in and immediately start to code after a quick meeting with a manager.

This is the system that Kanban starts with. The team already has a way to run their project. Kanban just asks them to understand that system. That's what it means to start with what you do now. The goal of Kanban is to make small improvements to that system. That's what it means to pursue incremental, evolutionary change—and why Kanban has the practice **improve collaboratively, evolve experimentally**. In lean thinking, part of seeing the whole is taking measurements, and measurements are at the core of experimentation and the scientific method. A Kanban team will start with their system for building software, and take measurements to get an objective understanding of it. Then they'll make specific changes *as a team*—later in this chapter, you'll learn exactly how those changes work—and check their measurements to see if those changes have the desired effect.

The Lean value of amplifying learning is also an important part of evolving the system that your team uses to build software. Throughout this book you've learned about feedback loops. When you collaborate to measure the system and evolve experimentally, those feedback loops become a very important tool for gathering information and feeding it back into the system; the Kanban practice of **implementing feedback loops** should make sense to you, and should help you to see how Kanban and Lean are closely linked.

Amplifying learning also factors into the Kanban principle of initially respecting current roles and responsibilities. For example, say that a team always starts each project with a meeting between a project manager, a business analyst, and a programmer. They may not have written down a rule for what goes on in that meeting, but you probably have a good idea of what goes on in it just from reading those job titles.

That's one reason why Kanban respects current roles, responsibilities, and job titles—because they're an important part of the system.

A common theme between all of these principles is that Kanban only works for a team when they take the time to understand their own system for building software. If there was one right way to build software, everyone would just use it. But we started this book by saying back in Chapter 2 that there is no silver bullet—there's no single set of "best" practices that will guarantee that a team builds software right every time. Even the same team, using the same practices, can have success with one project but fail miserably in the next one. This is why Kanban starts with understanding the current system for running the project: once you see the whole system, Kanban gives you practices to improve it.

Wait a minute. So Kanban doesn't tell me how to run my project?

No, it doesn't.[1] Kanban asks you to start by understanding how you currently run projects. That could be Scrum, XP, better-than-not-doing-it Scrum, an effective waterfall process, an ineffective waterfall process, or even a haphazard, "fly-by-the-seat-of-your-pants" way of doing things. Once you figure out how your team currently builds software, Kanban gives you practices to help improve it.

So if you already have a way of building software, why do you need Kanban?

Most teams manage to deliver *something*. How do you know if the team is wasting a lot of time or effort? Are they doing work that delivers a lot of value? Or are they being asked to work in a way that habitually causes problems or makes it hard to deliver valuable software?

When we have a system in place—no matter what that system looks like—it doesn't occur to most of us to question it. Even if you're using Scrum or XP, you could be wasting a lot of time and effort without even knowing it. Habitual problems are very difficult to spot. Everyone can be following the rules and doing the right things. But just like behavior can emerge from a system, waste can emerge from the way many different people work together.

We saw an example of this in Chapter 8, where a team finds themselves with a very large lead time, even though everyone is constantly working and nobody is slacking off or intentionally waiting to do work. But even though everyone is constantly working, to the person who requested the software, it looks like there are very big delays—

---

1 Kanban isn't a project management method, but that certainly doesn't mean that Kanban isn't for project managers! In fact, David Anderson posted a series of blog posts that explain exactly how project managers fit into Kanban, and offers a "Project Management with Kanban" class through the Lean Kanban University. We recommend reading his posts (*http://bit.ly/DJAA-kanban*) to learn more about this.

and nobody on the team even noticed, because they feel like they're doing everything that they can do to get the work done as quickly as possible.

This is the kind of problem that Kanban solves.

Stories Go into the System; Code Comes Out

> Systems thinking looks at organizations as systems; it analyzes how the parts of an organization interrelate and how the organization as a whole performs over time.
>
> —Tom and Mary Poppendieck, *Lean Software Development*

The first step in improving a system is recognizing that it exists. This is the idea behind the Lean principle *see the whole*. When you see the whole, you stop thinking of the team as making a series of individual, disconnected decisions, and start to think of them as following a system. In Lean, this is called **systems thinking**.

Every system takes inputs and turns them into outputs. What does a Scrum team look like from a systems thinking perspective? You can think of Scrum as a system that takes project backlog items as its input and produces code as its output. Many Scrum teams have a project backlog that consists entirely of stories; these teams can almost think of themselves as "machines" that turn stories into code.

Clearly these are teams, not machines, and we certainly don't want to fall into the habit of thinking of people as machines or cogs. But there's value in thinking about the work that you do as part of a greater system. If you apply systems thinking to your Scrum team, it makes it much easier to see when you're doing work that doesn't directly (or even indirectly) help turn stories into code. And by recognizing that all of Scrum is a system, you can understand how it works better and make improvements to it. This is the kind of thinking that leads to improvements such as Jeff Sutherland's changes to the questions in the Daily Scrum that you learned about in Chapter 5. That's a good example of systems thinking applied to Scrum that leads to incremental, evolutionary improvements.

Kanban asks you to start by understanding the system that you and your team use. And even if you don't follow a methodology with a name, you can still apply systems thinking to your own team to figure out how you work.

Every software team follows a system, whether they know it or not

It's easy to see how a team that follows Scrum is using a system. But what if your team doesn't have anything like that? Maybe you just dive in and start working on software. It certainly feels like you don't run your projects the same way every time. So you don't really have a system, right?

The funny thing about people—especially on teams—is that we *always* follow rules. They may not be written down, and we often make them up if they don't exist. But humans intuit rules all the time, and once a rule gets into our heads we have a tough time shaking it. And even if you don't think you follow rules, when a new person comes onto your team, you definitely recognize when that person breaks an unwritten rule.

And Lean even gives us a tool to take unwritten rules and turn them into a system: a value stream map. When you take an MMF (that's the minimal marketable feature we learned about in Chapter 8—like a story, requirement, or user request, for example) and draw out the value stream map that it followed on its path to becoming code, you've written down a description of a path through your system.

When you work on a team that follows many unwritten rules, it's likely that one MMF follows a very different path from another. But because humans naturally intuit and follow rules, it's also pretty likely that you can map out a small number of value streams that cover the majority of the MMFs that your team turns into code. If you can do this, then you can build a very accurate description of the system that you and your team follow. The first step in that system is deciding which value stream the MMF will flow down.

It's worthwhile to have a system that works the same way for everyone, even if there are many different possible paths that an MMF can take. Once you understand how the system works—in other words, once you see the whole—you can start to make real decisions about which paths are wasteful, and make incremental, evolutionary changes to the way you and your team build the code.

Kanban is not a software methodology or a project management system

One of the most common pitfalls that people run into when learning about Kanban is to attempt to treat it as a methodology for building software. It isn't. Kanban is a method for process improvement. It helps you understand the methodology that you use and find ways to make it better.

Take a minute and just flip forward a few pages in this chapter. You'll see pictures that look like task boards. *These are not task boards.* They're called kanban boards. The way that you know they're not task boards is that *they don't have tasks on them.* They have **work items**. A work item is a single, self-contained unit of work that can be tracked through the entire system. It's typically larger than an MMF, requirement, user story, or other individual scope item.

One difference between a task board and a kanban board is that while tasks flow across a task board, *work items are not tasks*. The tasks are what the people do to move the work items through the system. In other words, the tasks are the "cogs" of the machine that push the work item through. This is why you can use systems thinking to understand your software workflow without dehumanizing people by thinking of them as cogs in a machine. It's the tasks that are the cogs; the people are still unique individuals with their own personalities, wants, and motivations.

The columns on the kanban board may seem similar to steps in a value stream; however, many Kanban practitioners distinguish value stream maps from kanban boards. They will map the state of work items in the workflow separately from the value stream, something that they call **workflow mapping**. The difference is that value stream mapping is a Lean thinking tool to help you understand the system that you work in; workflow mapping is how the Kanban method determines the actual steps that each work item goes through. (You'll learn more about how to build a kanban board later on in the chapter.)

Here's an example of how task boards do one thing, while kanban boards do another. Scrum is focused on helping teams self-organize and meet their collective commitments. By the time the task board is in play, the team has selected backlog items—work items—to include in the sprint, and broken them down into tasks. As the tasks flow across the task board, the work items start to move from the "To Do" column to the "Done" column. To the team, it feels like they're making progress.

A typical kanban board only shows those larger work items, not the individual tasks. And while the task board only "sees" the work items when they're To Do, In Progress, or Done, the kanban board will have a bigger picture. Where do the work items come from? How does the Product Owner know what work items to put in the project backlog, and how to prioritize them? After the team completes the work item, is it tracked by a production team to make sure that it's been deployed properly? The work item has a larger lifecycle that extends beyond the team that's building it. The kanban board will have columns for the steps that a work item goes through before and after the Scrum team gets their hands on it.

What's more, the kanban board can help show problems that never appear on the task board. Many Scrum teams are very good at building the software that they're asked to build, but still find themselves with disappointed users. Maybe the work items they're building aren't the right ones that satisfy the customers' needs. Or maybe there's a very long lag before or after the team works on the work items, maybe due to a lengthy review or deployment process. Even though these problems are completely out of the team's control, they'll often be blamed for them. The kanban board will help with this.

So while Kanban is not a system for project management, it has a very important relationship with the project management used by the team. Kanban is intended to improve and change the process in use on the project and that this can and will affect how the project is managed. Typically, Kanban is used to improve predictability of flow, and this will affect planning and scheduling on the project. Extensive use of

Kanban and its metrics is likely to have a significant knock-on effect on the method of project management.[2]

In the next part of this chapter, you'll learn about the practices of Kanban, how to build a kanban board, and how to use to make incremental, evolutionary improvements to the *whole* system.

Improving Your Process with Kanban

We already know that Kanban is an agile method that's focused on process improvement, and is based on Lean values and lean thinking. Kanban was formulated by David Anderson, who first started experimenting with the ideas of Lean while working at Microsoft and Corbis. And like much of Lean, the name "kanban" originates with ideas developed at car manufacturers in Japan. But what's so agile about Kanban? How is it different than traditional process improvement?

Software teams have been doing process improvement for about as long as people have been building software. In an ideal world, process improvement works very well: the team gets senior sponsorship for the effort, takes measurements, identifies problems, implements improvements, and then starts over again to identify more improvements. Eventually, the improvements help the entire organization first let them make their process repeatable, then managed, and finally bring it under statistical control. There have been many companies that have reported extensive success doing this.

If you're a developer who has lived through a typical process improvement effort, you're probably ready to put this book down in frustration after reading that.

The term "process improvement" often conjures up Dilbert-like images of endless committees and binders full of process documentation, because typical process improvement is very different from the ideal. In a typical process improvement effort, a large company decides that their programmers are not producing software efficiently enough (or that they need a process certification for contracting or marketing purposes), so they hire a consulting company to spend a lot of time (and money) drawing many flowcharts of the existing and desired development processes, and training the teams to use the new ones. Then the teams spend about 10 minutes trying out one of the new processes, find that it's unnatural, awkward, and difficult to work with, and stop using it. But because senior managers sponsored the whole process improvement effort, politically the teams have to look like they're using it, so they fill out whatever paperwork the new process requires (like scope documents and statements of work) and produce the compulsory artifacts (like code review meeting

---

2 Thanks to David Anderson for helping us with the wording of this paragraph.

minutes and test reports that are mostly empty and boilerplate). For every successful process improvement effort—and yes, there are a few—there are many neutral or failed efforts whose main by-product is a deep dislike of the term "process improvement."

There's one big difference between Kanban and traditional process improvement. In traditional process improvement, the decisions are typically sponsored by senior managers, made by a committee (like a software engineering process group), and handed down to the teams through their bosses. In Kanban, the improvement is *left in the hands of the team*, and this is one reason that agile teams have found success with Kanban. The team members themselves find the problems with their workflow, suggest their own improvements, measure the results, and hold themselves accountable to their own standards.

So how does Kanban help a team improve their own process?

Visualize the Workflow

The first step in improving a process is understanding how the team currently works, and that's what the Kanban practice **visualize** is about. This sounds simple, but it's much more challenging than it sounds—and it's where many traditional process improvement efforts go wrong.

Imagine that you're a programmer, and your boss comes to you and asks, "How do you build software?" Your job is to write down how you do your work. So you start up Visio (or Omnigraffle, or another diagramming application) and start building a flowchart that shows all of the things that you do every day. Then you realize that while everyone always talks about holding code reviews (or testing your code before you commit, etc.), you don't actually do it every time. But you think that it would be a good idea, and you definitely do it *sometimes*, so you add it to your diagram. This is human nature. It's easy to justify the addition to yourself—if it's a good idea, then writing it down may help make sure that you do it all the time.

This will thoroughly screw up a process improvement effort.

One reason is that it masks a real problem. If the step that you've added to your diagram is a good idea, the fact that it now appears on a diagram makes it seem like you're already doing it. Nobody will think to ask, "Why aren't we doing it?" Why would they? You're doing it already! What if there's a reason that you're not doing it every time—say, code reviews always get cancelled because only senior team members are allowed to do code reviews and they're always busy? You'll never discover that and try to fix the underlying problem, because everyone will look at the diagram, see that code reviews are always happening, and focus their improvement effort elsewhere.

In Kanban, visualizing means writing down exactly what the team does, warts and all, without embellishing it. This is part of lean thinking: a Kanban team takes the Lean principle of *see the whole* very seriously. When the team has the right mindset, it *just feels wrong* to tinker with the workflow while you're trying to visualize it, because that would interfere with seeing the whole. The value of *decide as late as possible* is also important here: you don't have all of the information about how you build software yet, so there's a later responsible moment to make decisions about how you'll change it.

Like other agile methodologies, doing the practices of Kanban helps you get into the Lean mindset and adopt lean thinking. The better you accurately, objectively visualize the workflow, the better you embed the values of *see the whole* and *decide as late as possible* into your own thinking.

So how do teams visualize the workflow?

Use a kanban board to visualize the workflow

A **kanban board** is a tool that teams use to visualize their workflow. (The K in the methodology name *Kanban* is typically uppercase; the *k* in *kanban board* is usually lowercase.) A kanban board looks a lot like a Scrum task board: it typically consists of columns drawn on a whiteboard, with sticky notes stuck in each column. (It's more common to find sticky notes stuck to kanban boards than it is to find index cards.)

There are three very important differences between a task board and a kanban board. You already learned about the first difference: that kanban boards only have stories, and do not show tasks. Another difference is that columns in kanban boards usually vary from team to team. Finally, kanban boards can set limits on the amount of work in a column. We'll talk about those limits later on; for now, let's concentrate on the columns themselves, and how different teams using Kanban will often have different columns in their kanban boards. One team's board might have familiar To Do, In Progress, and Done columns. But another team's board could have entirely different columns.

When a team wants to adopt Kanban, the first thing that they do is visualize the workflow by creating a kanban board. For example, one of the first kanban boards in David Anderson's book, *Kanban*, has these columns: Input Queue, Analysis (In Prog), Analysis (Done), Dev Ready, Development (In Prog), Development (Done), Build Ready, Test, and Release Ready. This board would be used by a team that follows a process where each feature goes through analysis, development, build, and test. So they might start off with a kanban board like the one shown in Figure 9-1, with sticky notes in the columns representing the work items flowing through the system.

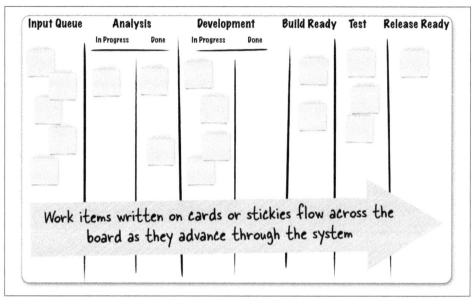

Input Queue	Analysis		Development		Build Ready	Test	Release Ready
	In Progress	Done	In Progress	Done			

Work items written on cards or stickies flow across the board as they advance through the system

Figure 9-1. An example of how work items written on sticky notes flow across a kanban board. David Anderson used a board with these columns in his book, Kanban, but kanban boards have different columns depending on how the people on the team actually do their work.

The team would then use the kanban board in a way that's similar to how a Scrum team uses a task board. The Kanban team holds a meeting (usually daily) called "walking the board," in which they discuss the state of each item on the board. The board should already reflect the current state of the system: every item that completes a current step should already have been advanced to the next column by having its sticky note pulled up and moved into the next column. But if that hasn't been done yet, the team will make sure that the board is up to date during the meeting.

It is important to understand that a kanban board visualizes the underlying workflow and process in use. Any examples given here or in other texts (such as David Anderson's *Kanban*) are merely examples from real contexts. In general, you should never copy another kanban board; rather, you should develop your own by studying your own workflow and visualizing it. Copying an existing process definition out of context would be the antithesis of the Kanban Method's evolutionary approach to change. If the method requires you to start with what you do now, then you should not start by copying something someone else is doing.[3]

---

3 Thanks to David Anderson for helping us out with the wording here.

Let's go back to our example from Chapter 8, in which a team was trying to cope with very long lead times and disappointed customers. If you flip back to the initial description of the team, it's basically a summary of the initial workflow that the project manager described to the boss. Here's a quick recap:

1. Team gets a feature request from a user

2. Project manager schedules features for the next release

3. Team builds the feature

4. Team tests the feature

5. Project manager verifies that the tests pass

6. The feature is done and included in the next release

The paragraphs in Chapter 8 are one way to communicate this workflow, and this numbered list is another way, but a visualization is a much more effective tool to do that. Figure 9-2 shows what the project manager's "happy path" version of the workflow looks like on a kanban board.

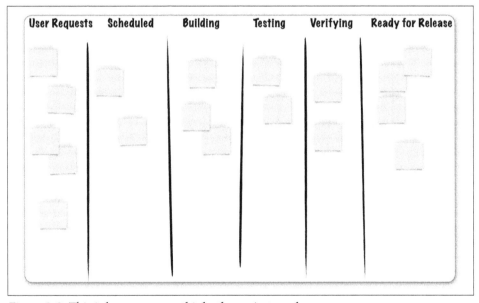

Figure 9-2. This is how everyone thinks the project works.

But that's not what's happening in real life. In Chapter 8, the team used Five Whys to learn more about their workflow. Afterward, it looked more like this:

1. Team gets a feature request from a user

2. Project manager schedules features for the next three-month release

3. Team builds the feature

4. Team tests the feature

5. Project manager verifies that the tests pass

6. *Project manager schedules a demo with senior management*

7. *If senior management wants the team to make changes to the feature, the project manager does an impact analysis on the changes, and the feature moves back to step 1—if not, it moves on to step 8*

8. The feature is done and included in the next release

Now we know that there's an extra step, where senior managers can optionally make changes to features and bump them to future releases after the team thought they were done.

We'll modify the kanban board to represent this better understanding by adding a column called "Manager Review" for those features that are waiting for the demo with the senior manager.

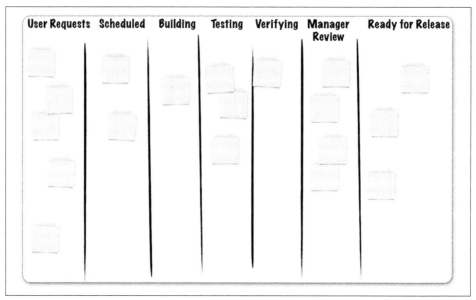

Figure 9-3. This kanban board gives a more accurate and realistic picture of how the project is run.

Now we have a more accurate visualization of the team's workflow. If we keep the kanban board going over the course of a release, it becomes very obvious where the problem is. The work items pile up in the "Manager Review" column, and keep piling up until the end of the release, as shown in Figure 9-4.

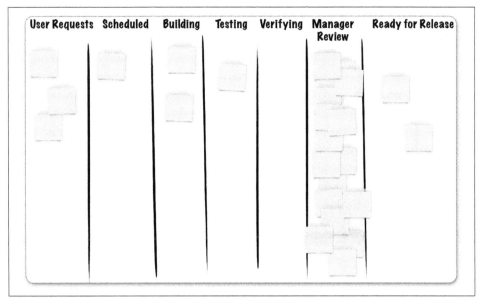

Figure 9-4. When you use a kanban board to visualize the workflow, problems caused by unevenness (mura) become easier to spot.

But what about the work items that were bumped to a future release to make room for the managers' changes? We especially care about those work items, because they're the ones that were causing some users to switch to the competitors. Sometimes work for those work items has already started, and needs to keep going even when they're bumped. When work items are bumped after the manager review, they end up going right back to the beginning of the process. Let's make sure these are represented on the kanban board—we'll add a column at the beginning of the board called "Bumped by Managers" and move those stickies back there (we put a small dot on each of the bumped stickies to make them easier to spot as they flow across the board a second time).

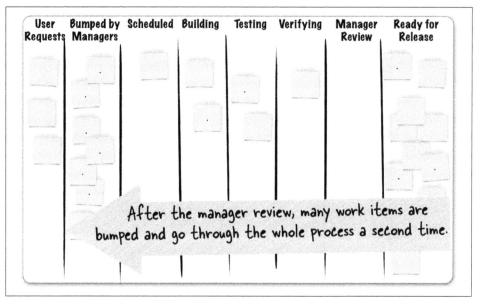

User Requests	Bumped by Managers	Scheduled	Building	Testing	Verifying	Manager Review	Ready for Release

After the manager review, many work items are bumped and go through the whole process a second time.

Figure 9-5. The kanban board makes the waste more obvious when you can see stickies go through the workflow more than once.

This is a pretty good visualization of the process that this team is following. Now we can see exactly what's gone wrong with this project, and why the lead time keeps getting worse. Some people on the team probably had a pretty good idea that this was going on, but now it's made clear to anyone who looks at the board. And more importantly, it becomes objective and explicit evidence that the way the senior managers review the features is a major cause of the lead time problem.

Limit Work in Progress

> We would never run the servers in our computer rooms at full utilization—why haven't we learned that lesson in software development?
>
> —Mary and Tom Poppendieck, *Lean Software Development: An Agile Toolkit*

A team can only do so much work at a time. We learned this with both Scrum and XP, and it's an important part of lean thinking as well. When a team agrees to do more work than they can actually accomplish by the time they'd agreed to deliver it, bad things happen. They either leave some of the work out of the delivery, do a poor job of building the product, or work at an unsustainable pace that will cost dearly in future releases. And sometimes it's not obvious that a team has taken on more work than they can handle: each individual deadline may seem reasonable for the work being done, but if each person is expected to multitask on multiple projects or tasks at the same time, the team slowly becomes overburdened, and the extra effort required for task switching can eat up as much as half of their productivity.

Visualizing the workflow helps the team see this overburdening problem clearly, and that's the first step toward fixing the problem. Unevenness and overburdening—which we learned about in Chatper 8—become clear on the kanban board when stickies always pile up in one column. Luckily, queuing theory doesn't just alert us to the problem; it also gives us a way to fix it. Once unevenness in the workflow has been identified, we can use it to control the amount of work that flows through the whole system by placing a strict limit on the amount of work that is allowed to pile up behind it. This is what's behind the Kanban practice **limit work in progress**.

Limiting work in progress (WIP) means setting a limit on the number of work items that can be in a particular stage in the project's workflow. A lot of people tend to focus on moving work items through the workflow as fast as they can. And for a single work item, that workflow is linear: if you're a developer and you're done with the design for a feature, and your workflow says that the next thing you do with it is build it and then send it on to a tester, the next thing you're going to do is build the code for it—and it's easy to become fixated on getting that feature built and sent on to the tester as quickly as possible because it was the last thing you were working on.

But what if the test team is already working on more features than they can test right now? It doesn't make sense to jump into development for this feature if it will just end up waiting around because nobody's ready to test it. That would cause overburdening for the test team. So what can be done about it?

For this, Kanban goes back to lean thinking—specifically, the principle of options thinking that you learned about in Chapter 8. One reason that a Kanban team uses a kanban board is because it shows all of your options. If you're that developer who just finished the design for a feature, it's easy to think that you now have a commitment to work on the code next. But working on the code for that particular feature is an option, not a commitment. When you look at the whole kanban board, you'll see many stickies that you can work on next. Maybe there are other stickies in earlier columns for other features that need to be designed, or ones in later columns for features with bugs that the testers found that need to be fixed. In fact, most of the time you have many options that you can choose from. Which do you choose first?

Setting a WIP limit for a step in your workflow means limiting the number of features that are allowed to move into that step. This helps limit the team's options to make that decision easier in a way that will prevent overburdening and keep the features flowing through the workflow as efficiently as possible. When you finish designing that feature, for example, and you see that the workflow is already at its limit for writing code, then you'll look for other options and work on them instead—and the test team won't get overburdened. (Think about this for a minute: can you see how this will reduce the average lead time for a feature? If so, then you're starting to get the hang of systems thinking!)

Let's go back to the team that used Five Whys to find the root cause of their lead time problem. Once we created a kanban board for them, the overburdening became clear: stickies started piling up in the "Manager Review" column. So to limit the work in progress for this team's workflow, we just need to find a way to place a strict limit on the number of features that pile up before the managers hold a review session.

In Kanban, once you recognize a workflow problem like this, the way that you deal with it is to **set a WIP limit** (or work in progress limit). To do this, the team needs to meet with the boss and the other senior managers and convince them to agree to a new policy. The new policy would set a WIP limit that says that only a certain number of features are allowed to pile up in the "Manager Review" column on the kanban board. The kanban board and lead time measurements give the team and their project manager a lot of objective evidence to help convince the managers to agree to this.

When we set a WIP limit on a column, it's no longer a sinkhole that collects a pile of work items. Instead, it becomes a **queue**, or a stage in your workflow where work items are managed in a smooth and orderly way.

There is no hard-and-fast rule that says how large the WIP limit should be; instead, teams will take an evolutionary approach to setting WIP limits. Kanban teams typically choose a WIP limit that makes sense and that everyone can agree on, and then use measurements to adjust it experimentally. For our team, let's say that each release typically has 30 features, and that the senior managers feel comfortable that they can meet three times over the course of the release, so we'll choose a WIP limit of 10. We'll do that by adding a number 10 to the "Manager Review" column on the kanban board, as shown in Figure 9-6.

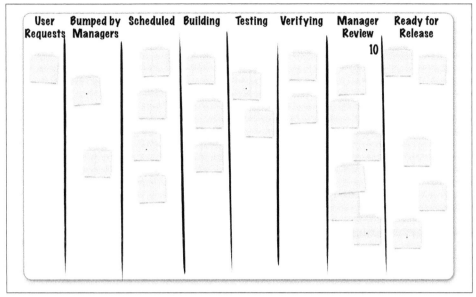

User Requests	Bumped by Managers	Scheduled	Building	Testing	Verifying	Manager Review 10	Ready for Release

Figure 9-6. The number 10 in the Manager Review column is its WIP limit.

What happens when the tenth work item flows into the Manager Review column, causing it to hit its WIP limit? After that limit is reached, the team no longer pushes any more work items into that column. There's probably other work that they can do. If all of the development is done, they can help the QA team start testing the software. Maybe there's technical debt that they can start fixing—if there aren't stickies somewhere on the board for these items, there should be. The one thing that they *don't* do is push more features into the "Manager Review" column. That's the agreement that they've made with the senior managers: as soon as this column hits its WIP limit, the managers will hold the review meeting, and work will pile up behind it until that happens.

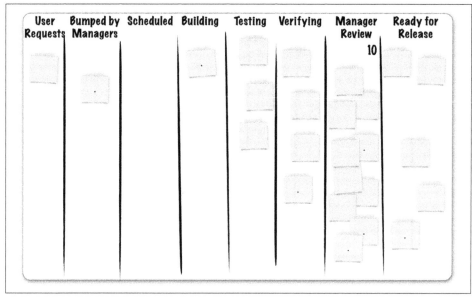

Figure 9-7. When a column reaches its WIP limit, no more stickies can be moved into it, even if the work for those stickies is done. The team shifts their focus to work on work items in other columns that have not yet reached a WIP limit.

Once the managers honor their agreement, hold the review meeting, and clear the logjam, the work can progress. The WIP limit causes the managers to give their feedback much earlier, and the team can immediately make the adjustments they need. If it looks like features are going to get bumped, the managers know at the beginning of project instead of the end. Now it's less disruptive to the team because they're not pushing so much work that's already been done into a "Bumped" backlog. The work they're doing becomes valuable immediately, rather than getting stale sitting in the "Bumped" backlog until it's no longer as relevant to the company (or until it makes customers so mad that they switch to a competitor).

The reason that this is effective is that *the cycle of manager review and team adjustment is a feedback loop*. When this feedback loop is too long—for example, when it's the length of the whole release—the information that's fed back into the project becomes disruptive, not helpful, because it causes the team to react by shelving a bunch of work that they already did. It causes waste.

Adding a WIP limit to fix the overburdening causes the average time a work item spends in the system to get much shorter. Now the managers hold their review multiple times over the course of the project, which allows the team to make their adjustments earlier. And that lets the managers use that information to change the priority of the features early enough in the project so that valuable work isn't wasted.

Even better, the team and the managers now have control over the length of the feedback loop. For example, if the managers find that this information is valuable, they can agree to shrink the WIP limit to six features, which will cause them to meet more frequently, and give earlier feedback to the team.

Why not make the WIP limit 1 and meet all the time? Aren't shorter feedback loops better?

Not if the team spends more time holding review meetings and dealing with feedback than they do actually getting work done. Like any tool, WIP limits and feedback loops can be abused. When a system has a feedback loop that's too short, it ends up in a state that's called **thrashing**. This is what happens when too much information is fed back into the system, and there isn't enough time to respond before the next batch of information is fed back.

Visualizing the workflow with a kanban board helps the team see the feedback loops, and experiment with WIP limits to find an optimal feedback loop length that provides frequent feedback that the team can respond to, but which allows them enough time to respond to that feedback before the next batch comes in.

Teams should also avoid sending the same items through the feedback loop many times, because this can clog the system. Once again, the kanban board makes it clear when this happens. For example, on our team's board, when managers have feedback and need it to be redone, they'll send it back to the backlog. This causes a team member to pull the sticky off of the board and move it back to an earlier column. The team can keep track of stickies that were moved backward on the board by adding a dot or other mark on them. This is a clear indicator that the feedback loop is going to be repeated for this feature. When the feature comes back through the workflow, it will end up in the "Manager Review" column again and take away one of the WIP limit slots. That has the effect of clogging up the feedback loop.

The team can avoid this problem by removing the extra loop from the workflow and making it more linear for most of the features. What if the team can convince the managers to agree to one feature review, and only choose some features to be bumped back into the backlog? If the managers can trust the team to accept their feedback for most of the features and not require an additional review for them before the feature is released, the team can add an extra development and testing step after the review.

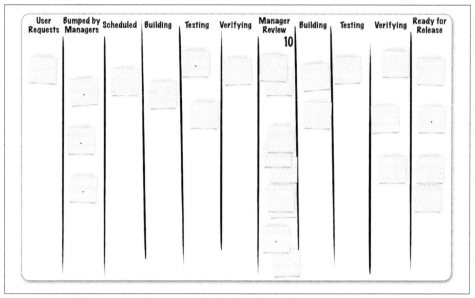

Figure 9-8. Adding extra columns to the kanban board—and preventing many stickies from being bumped back to an earlier column—gives the team more control over the process.

This workflow looks longer on the kanban board. But because we used objective evidence of lead time measurements and experimentation with WIP limits to evolve the workflow like this, we can be confident that it's actually faster. And we can keep measuring lead time and visualizing the workflow to prove to the team and the managers that even though there are more steps, it's faster for each feature to get through the workflow and included into the release. But while those measurements are useful for continuing to improve the project and to convince the managers that the project is improving, you probably won't need them in order to convince the team. They'll be convinced by their own results, because after unevenness and overburdening are removed, the project *feels faster*.

Key Points

- Kanban is a method for process improvement, or a way to help teams improve the way they build software and work together as a team, that's based on the Lean mindset.

- Kanban teams *start with what you do now* by seeing the whole as it exists today, and pursue incremental, evolutionary change to improve the system gradually over time.

- The Kanban practice *improve collaboratively, evolve experimentally* means taking measurements, making gradual improvements, and then confirming that they worked using those measurements.
- Every team has a system for building software (whether or not they recognize it), and the Lean idea of *systems thinking* means helping the team understand that system.
- A **kanban board** is a board way for Kanban teams to visualize their workflow.
- The kanban board has columns that represent each stage in the workflow of a work item, with stickies in the columns to represent each work item in the system that flow across the board as they advance through the system.
- Kanban boards use work items, not tasks, because Kanban is not a system for project management.
- When Kanban teams **limit work in progress** (WIP), they add a number to a column on the kanban board that represents that maximum number of work items allowed in that stage in the workflow.
- Kanban teams work with their users, managers, and other stakeholders to make sure that everyone agrees that when a column is at its WIP limit, the team will focus their work elsewhere in the project and not advance any more work items into that workflow stage.

Measure and Manage Flow

As teams continue to deliver work, they identify workflow problems and adjust their WIP limits so that the feedback loops provide enough information without causing thrashing. The **flow** of the system is the rate at which work items move through it. When the team finds an optimal pace for delivery combined with a comfortable amount of feedback, they've *maximized the flow*. Cutting down on the unevenness and overburdening, and letting your teams finish each task and move on to the next one, increases the flow of work through your project. When unevenness in the system causes work to pile up, it interrupts the work and decreases the flow. A Kanban team uses the **manage flow** practice by measuring the flow and taking active steps to improve it for the team.

You already know what it feels like when work is flowing. You feel like you're getting a lot accomplished, and that you aren't wasting time or stuck waiting for someone else to do something for you. The personal feeling of being on a team with a lot of flow is that every day, all day, you have the feeling that you're doing something valuable. That's what everyone is striving for.

You also know what it feels like when work doesn't flow. It feels like you're mired in muck, and that you're barely making progress. It feels like you're always waiting for someone to finish building something that you need, or to make a decision that affects your work, or to approve some ticket, or somehow always find some other way to block your work—even when you know that nobody is intentionally trying to block it. It feels uncoordinated and disjointed, and you spend a lot of time explaining to other people why you're waiting. It's not that you're underallocated; your project team is probably 100% allocated, or even overallocated. But while your project plan may say that you're 90% done, it feels like there's still 90% of the project left to go.

And your users know what it feels like when work doesn't flow, because their lead times keep going up. It seems like the team takes longer and longer to respond to their requests, and even simple features seem to take forever to build.

The whole point of Kanban is to increase flow, and to get the whole team involved in increasing that flow. When the flow increases, frustration with unevenness and long lead times decreases.

Use CFDs and WIP Area Charts to Measure and Manage Flow

The kanban board is an important tool for managing flow specifically because it visualizes the source of the problem, and lets you limit work in progress where it will be most effective.   When you look for the work that piles up and add a WIP limit to smooth it out, you're taking steps to increase the flow. The WIP limit works because you're helping the team focus their effort on the specific part of the project that's blocking work from flowing. In fact, *that's all that a WIP limit does*—it changes which work items the team is currently working on, and causes them to work on the ones that will even out the flow and clear up unevenness and workflow problems before they start to form.

But how do you know that you're actually increasing flow when you add WIP limits? Once again, we can go back to lean thinking, which tells us that we should take measurements—and an effective tool for measuring flow is a **cumulative flow diagram**, or CFD. A CFD is similar to a WIP area chart, with one important difference: instead of flowing off of the diagram, the work items *accumulate* in the final stripe or bar. And while the WIP area charts that you saw in Chapter 8 have stripes or bars that correspond to states in a value stream map, the CFDs (and WIP area charts) in this chapter have stripes that correspond to the columns on a kanban board.

The CFDs in this chapter have additional lines on them that show the average **arrival rate** (the number of work items added to the workflow every day) and average **inven-**

tory (the total number of work items in the workflow). The CFD can also show the average **lead time** (or the amount of time each work item stays in the system, just like we talked about with work items in Chapter 8). Not all CFDs have these lines; however, they are very helpful in understanding the flow of work items through the system.

The key to managing flow with a CFD is to look for patterns that indicate a problem. The kanban board can show you where the unevenness, loops, and other workflow problems are today, and helps you manage your flow on a day-to-day basis by adding WIP limits. The CFD lets you look at *the way your entire process is performing over time*, so you can take steps to find and fix the root cause of any long-term problems.

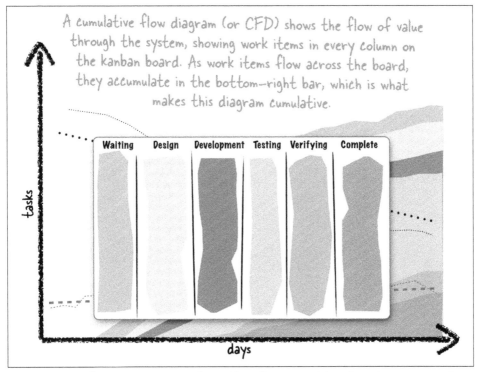

Figure 9-9. Kanban teams use cumulative flow diagrams with stripes that correspond to the columns on the kanban board. A cumulative flow diagram (CFD) is like a WIP area chart, except that instead of flowing off of the end of the chart, work items accumulate so all of the stripes or bars continue to go up over time.

How to build a cumulative flow diagram and use it to calculate the average lead time

To build a CFD, start with a WIP area chart. But instead of gathering data from a value stream map, you'll gather the data from the number of work items in each column on the kanban board.

Next, you'll need two additional pieces of data that you'll add to the diagram every day: the arrival rate and the inventory. To find the arrival rate for each day, count the number of work items that were added to the first column. To find the inventory for each day, count the total number of work items in every column. Add a dot to the CFD each day for the arrival rate and inventory, and connect them to create two line charts overlaid on top of the WIP area chart.

Most teams that use CFDs don't draw them incrementally on a wall; they use Excel or another spreadsheet program that supports charting. One reason—aside from ease of managing data—is that the spreadsheet can automatically add a linear trendline to the arrival rate and inventory line charts. These trendlines are very useful, because they can tell you whether or not your system is stable. If they're flat and horizontal, the system is stable. If one of them is tilted, then that value is changing over time. You'll need to *add WIP limits to stabilize your system*, and you'll be able to tell that the system is stable once those lines flatten out.

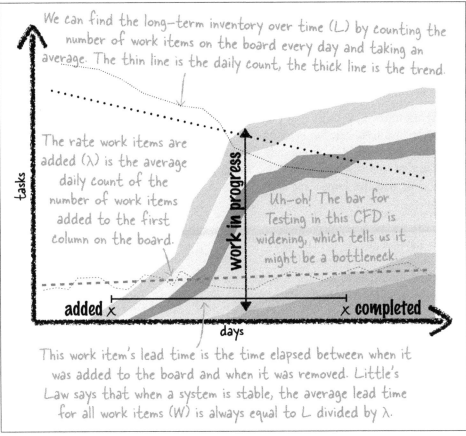

The thin line is the daily count, the thick line is the trend.

Figure 9-10. This is an example of a CFD that also shows the arrival rate and inventory. The total size of the work in progress at any given time can be found by measuring the difference between the top of the chart and the top of the "done" stripe. The horizontal solid black line shows the lead time for a specific work item in the system. We can't calculate the average lead time yet because the system is not stable—the long-term inventory and arrival rates have tilted trendlines, which means they aren't constant.

If you look at the hand-written notes in Figure 9-10, you'll see that we assigned letters to these values: we used L for the average long-term inventory, λ (that's a Greek lambda) for the average arrival rate (or the number of work items added every day), and W for the average lead time (or the average amount of time a user is waiting for the team to finish a work item request).

Take a look at the inventory line in the CFD—that's the thick dotted line near the top. It's trending downward, which tells us that the total inventory is going down over time. It shows that many work items flowed out of the system and were never replaced. But if you look on the bottom, the arrival rate is increasing.

If we keep tracking this project, what will happen? Will the inventory fill up again? Will there be another release that empties work items out of the system? If more features arrive than leave, then over the long term the inventory will trend upward—and the team will feel it. They'll slowly have more and more work to do, and will feel like they have less time to do it. It's that "mired in muck" feeling that happens when the system isn't flowing.

Luckily, we know how to fix that problem: add WIP limits. The team can use experimentation and feedback loops to find WIP limit values that work for their system, and if they get them right eventually the rate that work items arrive will balance out with the rate that the team can finish them. The long-term inventory trend will be flat, and so will the long-term arrival rate. And once that happens, the system is **stable**.

And when a system is *stable*, there's a simple relationship between these values called **Little's Law**—a theorem that's part of queueing theory—named for its discoverer, John Little, who first proposed it in the 1950s, and who is considered by many to be the father of marketing science And even though there's a Greek letter involved, you don't need to know a lot of math to use it:

$$L = W \times \lambda$$

In English, this means that if you have a stable workflow, the average inventory is *always* equal to the average arrival rate multiplied by the average lead time. That's a mathematical law: it's been proven and if a system is stable, it is always true. And the reverse is true, too:

$$W = L \div \lambda$$

If you know the average inventory and the average arrival rate, *you can calculate the average lead time*. In fact, calculating the average inventory and arrival rate is pretty straightforward: just write down the total number of work items on your kanban board every day, and write down the number that were added to the first column that day. We show those on our CFDs using thin dashed or dotted lines. If your system is stable, then after some time you can find the average daily inventory and the daily arrival rate, which we show as thick straight lines. Divide the average inventory by the average arrival rate and you get the lead time.

Stop and think about that for a minute. Lead time is one of the best ways that you have to measure your users' frustration level: deliver quickly and your users are pleased; take a long time to deliver, and your users grow increasingly frustrated. And long lead times are good indicators of quality problems, as David Anderson pointed out in his book, *Kanban*:

Longer lead times seem to be associated with significantly poorer quality. In fact, an approximately six-and-a-half times increase in average lead time resulted in a greater than 30-fold increase in initial defects. Longer average lead times result from greater amounts of work in progress. Hence, the management leverage point for improving quality is to reduce the quantity of work in progress.

Your lead time is determined entirely by the rate that work items arrive into your system, and the rate that they flow through it—and WIP limits give you control over the flow rate.

So what does this mean? It means that when your system is stable, you can cut your customers' lead time down *simply by not starting work on new features*.

Use a CFD to experiment with WIP limits and manage the flow

One of the core ideas of Kanban is that once you visualize the workflow, you can measure the flow, make your system stable, and actually take control of your project's lead time by managing the rate that you start work on new work items.

This may seem a little abstract. It's helpful to think about how you'd apply a CFD to a very simple system that most of us are familiar with: a doctor's office. Let's say that you had to visit a particular doctor several times to get a series of tests and discuss the results. You notice that if you have an appointment with the doctor in the morning after the office first opens, you don't have to wait very long. But if your appointment is later in the day, you have to sit in the waiting room for a long time—and the later the appointment, the longer the wait. Clearly this system is not stable. How would you use a CFD to stabilize it?

The first step would be to visualize the workflow. Let's say that every patient starts out by taking a seat in the waiting room. Eventually, a nurse calls the patient back to one of the exam rooms, where she gets weighed and has her blood pressure and temperature taken. Then she waits for the doctor to see her. In this office, there are five exam rooms and two doctors, and they're almost always occupied. More importantly, that means there can never be more than five patients in the exam rooms, or two patients seeing doctors. Those are WIP limits, imposed by the real-life constraints of the system.

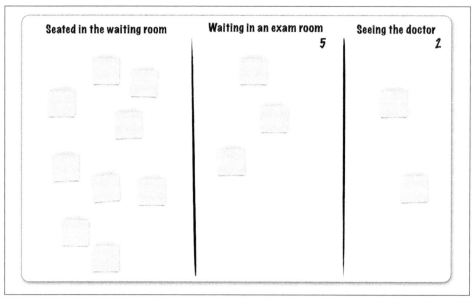

Seated in the waiting room	Waiting in an exam room 5	Seeing the doctor 2

Figure 9-11. A kanban board for a doctor's office. The first column shows the patients who are currently in the waiting room, the second column shows the patients in the exam rooms, and the third shows the patients currently being seen by a doctor. There are five exam rooms and two doctors—these are natural WIP limits, so they're visualized on the board as well.

These doctors don't like the fact that their patients later in the day always complain of long wait times. What's worse, they feel more and more rushed to get the patients out of the office at the end of the day, and they're worried that they may not always be making the best medical decisions because they're under pressure to move patients through the office as fast as they can. Can Kanban help these doctors reduce their patients' waiting time and provide better care?

Let's find out. We'll start by building a CFD for a typical day. We'll have the office staff count the number of patients who walk into the office every 15 minutes. This gives us an arrival rate—literally the number of patients who arrived in the office. And we can count the inventory for each 15-minute interval by counting the total number of patients in the waiting room and the five exam rooms. Every time someone arrives, they'll add a sticky to the first column on the kanban board. When a patient moves from the waiting room to an exam room, they'll move the sticky to the second column. And when the doctor sees the patient, they'll move the sticky to the third column. Once the doctor is done with the patient, the sticky comes off the board. The office staff can record the counts of the stickies in the columns for every 15-minute interval.

Now they have all of the data that they need in order to build a CFD.

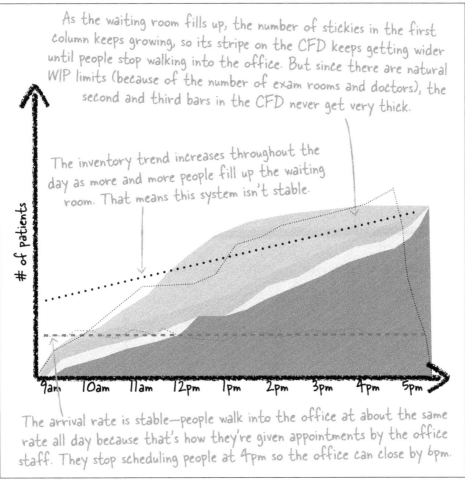

As the waiting room fills up, the number of stickies in the first column keeps growing, so its stripe on the CFD keeps getting wider until people stop walking into the office. But since there are natural WIP limits (because of the number of exam rooms and doctors), the second and third bars in the CFD never get very thick.

The inventory trend increases throughout the day as more and more people fill up the waiting room. That means this system isn't stable.

# of patients

9am 10am 11am 12pm 1pm 2pm 3pm 4pm 5pm

The arrival rate is stable—people walk into the office at about the same rate all day because that's how they're given appointments by the office staff. They stop scheduling people at 4pm so the office can close by 6pm.

Figure 9-12. This CFD shows the flow of patients through the doctor's office. The waiting room gets more and more full throughout the day. Can you guess why the bar for the third column disappears between 12:15 p.m. and 1 p.m.?

This system isn't stable yet. The arrival rate is stable, because the office staff books patient appointments so that they arrive at a constant rate. They don't want to stay late, so they stop booking appointments at 4 p.m. People do run late for their appointments, but the trend for the arrival rate is flat so this must be pretty constant throughout the day.

The trend for the inventory, however, is not flat. It's tilted upward, because the inventory keeps growing and growing. This makes sense; the number of patients in the waiting room also grows throughout the day. So how can the office staff use this new information to improve patient care and reduce waiting times?

The first thing they need to do is stabilize the system—and the tool we have for that is setting a WIP limit. They'll use the Kanban practice of evolving collaboratively and improving experimentally by deciding on a WIP limit together, and using that as a starting point. After looking at the data, everyone decides to add a WIP limit of six to the waiting room. But there's a tough decision that needs to be made: the doctors have to agree that if there are already six patients in the waiting room, then the office staff must start calling low-priority patients scheduled for the next hour and ask to reschedule their appointments (but they will find a way to handle more serious cases without compromising patient care). They'll also ask patients in the waiting room if anyone would be willing to volunteer to reschedule their appointment—and they promise to give that patient priority for the rescheduled appointment. This is a *new policy* that they need to make explicit. They'll do that by adding a WIP limit to the kanban board, and also posting a big notice to patients on a piece of paper at the front desk letting them know that this is the policy going forward.

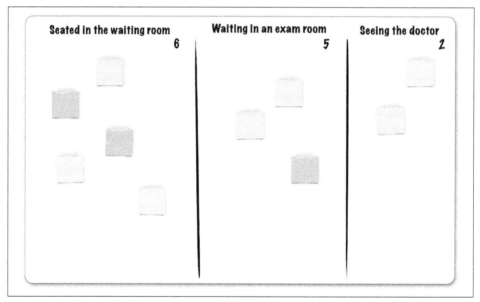

Figure 9-13. The staff sets the policy that there's a WIP limit of six patients in the waiting room. They enforce this policy by calling up patients and rescheduling them as soon as the waiting room hits its WIP limit. They use pink stickies to indicate patients with more serious problems who can't be rescheduled.

It takes a little practice, but after a few days the office staff gets used to the new policy. They discover that they need to take the patient's complaint into account. They decide to do this by defining the **class of service**: they'll use a pink sticky to indicate patients who have a more severe condition and cannot be rescheduled, and keep the yellow stickies to indicate patients who have more minor problems. This allows them to provide more prompt service for patients who need it the most.

And it works! The office staff discovers that once they impose the WIP limit, they no longer have to stop scheduling appointments at 4 p.m. in order to be done by 6 p.m. —they can schedule patients as late as 5:40 p.m. as long as they never schedule patients with more severe problems later than 4:40 p.m. (and they write down this policy as well). Obviously, if someone has a very severe problem and walks into the office, the doctor will see that patient (or send them to the emergency room)—but that's a rare exception, and because the office staff are smart and responsible, they can handle situations like that on a case-by-case basis. The patients seem much happier because they're not waiting as long to see the doctor.

Little's Law Lets You Control the Flow Through a System

The office staff took the Kanban practice of improving experimentally very seriously. And through their experiments, they discovered something interesting: once they found a good WIP limit, they *could control how long patients had to wait.*   If they scheduled more appointments every hour, there would be four or five patients in the waiting room, and patients would have to wait longer. If they scheduled fewer appointments every hour, there would only be two or three patients waiting to see the doctor, and they would wait less time. This gave them a feeling that for the first time, they were really in control of a system that had caused them so many headaches in the past.

So what's going on here?

What the office staff discovered is that in a stable system, there's a relationship between inventory, lead time, and arrival rate. For example, if the office staff schedules 11 patients to arrive every hour (so the arrival rate λ is 11/hour), and the office has average inventory of seven patients over the course of the day (so the inventory L is 7), then Little's Law tells us the average time patients have to wait:

$$W = L \div \lambda = 7 \text{ patients} \div (11 \text{ per hour}) = .63 \text{ hours} = 37 \text{ minutes}$$

But what if after some experimentation, they discover that scheduling 10 patients to arrive every hour causes the average inventory to drop to 4 patients? There are going to be peak times during the day when all of the exam rooms are filled, but most of the time there's one patient in the waiting room, one patient in an exam room waiting to see a doctor, and two patients in exam rooms talking to the doctors:

$$W = 4 \text{ patients} \div (10 \text{ patients per hour}) = .4 \text{ hours} = 24 \text{ minutes}$$

By using a kanban board and a CFD and experimenting with WIP limits, the office staff discovered that they could reduce the patient waiting time by almost 15 minutes just by scheduling one fewer patient per hour.

This works because Little's Law tells us that lead time in a stable system is affected by exactly two things, inventory and arrival rate—and WIP limits let you control one of those things. When you add WIP limits to your kanban board, you can reduce unevenness, which keeps inventory from piling up. That gives you a straightforward way to reduce lead time: by reducing the arrival rate (for example, by keeping work in a backlog until the team has time to deal with it, just like Scrum teams do—or by reducing the number of patients scheduled per hour).

This is why the office staff can use Little's Law to calculate the average lead time. But even if they never calculate it, *they're still affected by it*. The reason is that Little's Law *always* applies to every stable system, whether or not the team is aware of it. This affects your projects because it isn't just theory. It's a proven mathematical law that applies to any system with a stable long-term inventory.

So now that we've seen a simple example, let's have a look at an example that's closer to real life. Let's say that every three weeks, your entire team gets mired with supporting production releases.

Unfortunately, things aren't going so well for this team. At first everything was working just fine. But over time, problems started to crop up. Even though all of the support work eventually gets done, the team doesn't feel like there's enough time to do it. Instead, everyone feels like this month is always more stressful than last month—and everyone knows that if they don't get the support work done as quickly as possible, next month will be even worse.

This is a familiar feeling for a lot of teams. It feels like the project is slowly sinking in quicksand, and if it keeps up, eventually it will get so bad that the people on the team don't feel like they have enough time to think about their work. We learned in Chapter 7 what kind of damage an environment like that can do to the code: developers will end up building poorly designed software, and will create a codebase that has a lot of technical debt and is difficult to work with.

What can we do about this problem? It won't necessarily be obvious just from looking at the kanban board every day, because most of the time the board looks more or less healthy. There are some extra stickies on the board while the team is doing work to support the release, but that's expected. Eventually those stickies flow off the board, and it seems to return to normal. But it doesn't feel normal to the team (or, worse, it does feel normal—but it doesn't feel good!).

Can the tools that we've learned about help us find and fix the team's problem? Let's have a look.

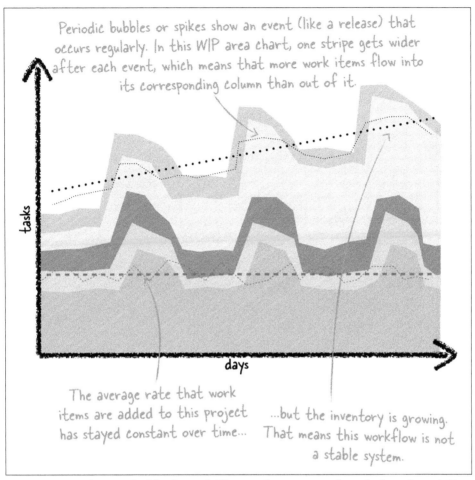

Periodic bubbles or spikes show an event (like a release) that occurs regularly. In this WIP area chart, one stripe gets wider after each event, which means that more work items flow into its corresponding column than out of it.

tasks

days

The average rate that work items are added to this project has stayed constant over time...

...but the inventory is growing. That means this workflow is not a stable system.

Figure 9-14. We've switched back to a WIP area chart to get a closer look at the stability of the system. This diagram shows that the arrival rate is constant but that the average inventory increases over time, which means the system isn't stable.

The additional work for each production release causes a visible spike in the CFD. Remember, each stripe corresponds to one of the columns on the board, and the vertical thickness of the stripe represents the number of stickies in its column for that day. In this CFD, one of the stripes gets thicker and thicker after each release, and that causes the total height of the diagram to slowly go up over time.

The WIP area chart makes the cause of the problem clearer: work is *accumulating* in that column because more work is flowing into it than out over time. If the team doesn't make a change, each new release will push them further behind and that stripe will keep getting thicker after every release. And we can see that the long-term inventory is going up, which means our system isn't stable—work isn't flowing. No wonder the team feels like they're sinking.

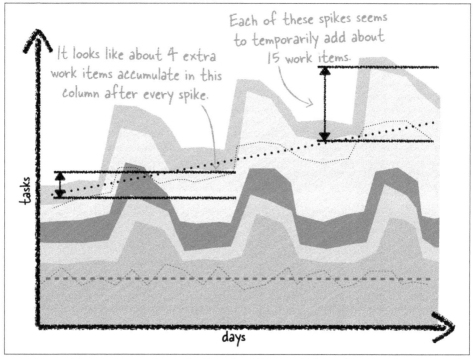

Figure 9-15. This WIP area chart also has clues that can help us figure out how to stabilize the system. The average inventory increases after periodic spikes in the work. If we can figure out how much extra inventory accumulates, it will help us choose a good starting point for experimenting with a WIP limit.

The team may not realize that work is getting "stuck" in one column on the kanban board. The WIP area chart makes this a lot easier to spot, because the corresponding stripe for that column gets thicker over time. Luckily, we already have a tool to smooth out this unevenness: adding WIP limits. And measuring the number of work items that seem to be getting "stuck" in the column can help us find a good starting point.

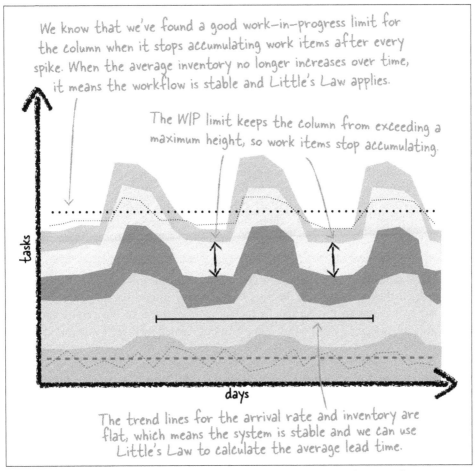

We know that we've found a good work-in-progress limit for the column when it stops accumulating work items after every spike. When the average inventory no longer increases over time, it means the workflow is stable and Little's Law applies.

The WIP limit keeps the column from exceeding a maximum height, so work items stop accumulating.

tasks

days

The trend lines for the arrival rate and inventory are flat, which means the system is stable and we can use Little's Law to calculate the average lead time.

Figure 9-16. When you find a good value for the WIP limit, the column no longer retains work, and the stripes on the WIP area chart don't accumulate work over time. How would this look on a CFD instead? Do you think a CFD would do a better job of visualizing this particular problem than a WIP area chart?

The spikes are still there, but there's *no longer an increase in the total number of tasks*. By adding a queue, we stopped extra work from flowing into the system, which increases the overall flow for the whole project. The work is more evenly distributed across all of the columns. When the overburdened column hits its WIP limit, the team shifts their focus to work items in earlier columns. You can see this on the WIP area chart: the bumps on the lower stripes are smaller than they were before the WIP limit.

Kanban teams don't just set a WIP limit and stop, however. They implement a feedback loop: as the project continues, they keep adjusting the WIP limit based on new information. If there's still accumulation, the team can experiment with different WIP limits until we find a value that gives us the most flow. Kanban teams take that experimentation seriously: they don't just randomly set these WIP limits; they run experiments by forming a hypothesis about how WIP limits will affect the system, and carefully prove them out by taking measurements. This is how the team can improve collaboratively and evolve experimentally.

As the team collaborates to evolve their system, they'll feel that increased flow in their day-to-day work. The support tasks won't cause them to feel like they're putting off important development work because they're treating the support work as features that need to be developed. By including work items for the support work on the board, the team has effectively promoted support tasks to first-class citizens of the project, and can focus on them and do a better job with them (instead of trying to cram them in and rush through them—and, in the process, create more work for themselves).

There's an added long-term benefit as well. Many of the support issues may be caused by technical debt that the team was forced to add in order to keep up with the backlog; now that they have time to do the job right, they might discover that they have fewer support issues in the future. In the meantime, the team can enjoy increased focus and a more energized work environment, which will let them build better software.

If the team still has to do all of that production support work, then what happened to the other work they were doing? Won't it accumulate somewhere else?

No. The reason that extra work isn't accumulating anymore is because *it isn't being added to the project in the first place*. This team was feeling stress because they were expected to put all of their effort into building software—but at the same time, they were also expected to stop every few weeks and concentrate on support without affecting development work. This was a choice made by their boss. Or, more accurately, it was a choice that the boss refused to make. His magical thinking let him pretend that the team could handle a full workload of development work while still taking on extra support work every few weeks. The queue will force the boss to choose which work the team will do.

But wait a minute—what if the support work takes up all of the slots in the queue? How will any development work get done?

If the support work seems to be "clogging" up the queue, that means the boss made a choice to prioritize support work over development work. It's the team's top priority, whether or not the boss explicitly acknowledges it; putting work items for support on the kanban board is a way for the team to give support the attention that top-priority items deserve. It's no longer the team's fault anymore if they don't do any new development. Of course, many developers prefer to do development than support; they might not like being turned into a full-time support team. But this is better than being responsible for all support work, while still being held responsible for all of the development work too.

And now the boss has much more accurate information about the progress that the team is making. This is one of the principles of agile software development from Chapter 3: *working software is the primary measure of progress.* Before, the overloaded team was seemingly able to produce software and do support; it wasn't immediately obvious that the extra load was causing them to build worse software that was more difficult to maintain, and potentially causing some of those support issues. Now that the team is delivering less software, the boss has a more accurate measure of progress. That makes it much more difficult for him to use magical thinking to pretend that the team can do much more work than is humanly possible. If he wants more software built, he either needs to prioritize it over support work, or hire additional people. But it's a lot less easy for him to simply blame the team.

Managing Flow with WIP Limits Naturally Creates Slack

Developers need slack, or "wiggle room," in the schedule. They need it to make sure that they have time to do a good job. We saw in the XP chapters that when a developer feels like he doesn't have enough time to think about the work, he cuts corners and adds technical debt. He has a mindset where he wants to get his current task done as quickly as possible, because there's always more work to do, and the project is always behind.

This kind of "always behind, always rushed" atmosphere leaves little or no room for creativity, and stifles innovation at every turn. It also kills quality practices, because teams that feel like they're running behind will often cut out any activity that doesn't directly produce code. This is why XP teams include Slack in their primary practices.

Teams using Kanban also value slack, and understand the impact that slack has on each team member's ability to do their best work. This is one of the main reasons that they limit work in progress. And when teams use Kanban to improve the process, instead of following a strict timebox they will adopt a **delivery cadence**. To do this, they commit to delivering software on a regular schedule (for example, a team might commit to releasing software every six weeks)—but they don't commit to a specific set of work items that will be included with the release. Instead, they trust their system to deliver work items. If they've removed overburdening and unevenness, then they will naturally get a set of completed work items to include in each delivery.

So what, specifically, causes a programmer or other team member to feel like there isn't enough time? That feeling is caused by a vivid awareness of the amount of work left to do, and that his or her current work is blocking the rest of the project. When someone feels like the current work is just an impediment preventing more work from getting done, he'll naturally try to get through it as quickly as possible.

This is why many people have a surprising reaction when the team gets their managers to agree to a WIP limit: *a feeling of relief.*

Before the WIP limit, extra work always seemed to sneak into the sprint, and the team had to rely on slack to cover that extra work. They'd always go into the sprint assuming that they'd only have, say, 70% of the work figured out, because impatient bosses and users would find a way to cram in the other 30% (or, worse, 40% or more!) with last-minute changes and emergency requests.

After the WIP limit—and, just as importantly, the agreement to stick to the WIP limit—these extra requests will still come in, but now the team doesn't have to try to absorb the impact of the unplanned work. Instead, the new work goes into a queue that's been created by adding a WIP limit somewhere in the workflow. There's less pressure, because they know that there won't be an unlimited amount of work that piles up. They've managed their flow (possibly using a CFD), so they know that the queue's WIP limit is set to a level that will give them enough time.

This is why many Kanban teams end up setting WIP limits on every column on the kanban board.

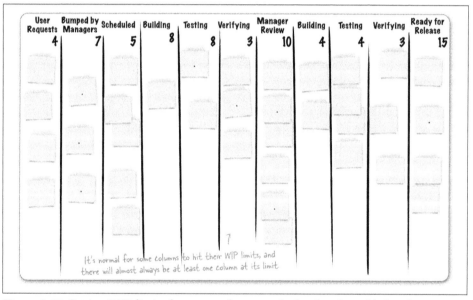

Figure 9-17. Setting WIP limits for every column on the kanban board helps the team maximize flow throughout the entire project.

This helps the team control the flow through each step in development. There's even a WIP limit on the "Ready for Release" column. If there is too much *"done"* done work that's piled up and is ready for release, they can find other work to do to prepare for the next release—and now they have better information to adjust their delivery cadence in the future by reducing the time between releases.

The team can't always get everyone to agree to WIP limits everywhere in the first step; this is why Kanban teams follow their cycle of improving collaboratively and evolving experimentally. After seeing that WIP limits help the team build software more quickly and reduce lead time after the first round of improvement, managers are more likely to agree to additional WIP limits in later rounds.

Controlling the flow across the entire project helps everyone on the team relax and focus on the work that they're doing now, without having to worry that tasks are piling up behind them. They can trust the WIP limits to keep the chaos out. And they know that if chaos starts to leak in, it will show up when they measure the workflow, and they can adjust the WIP limits and cadence to keep work focused and flowing.

Make Process Policies Explicit So Everyone Is on the Same Page

What would happen if you asked everyone on an effective Scrum team to write a detailed description of how they build software? There's a good chance that almost all of their descriptions will match up pretty well. That's because everyone on the team is familiar with the rules of Scrum, and they've all been working consistently with those rules. Every single person on an effective Scrum team has a common understanding of how the whole team builds software, and the rules for a Scrum project are simple enough that everyone on the team can understand them.

On the other hand, what would happen if you asked the same thing of a typical, ineffective waterfall team? There's a good chance that they have a fractured perspective (just like we learned about in Chapter 2). Everyone would probably write down how they do their own work on a day-to-day basis: developers would write about coding, testers about testing, business analysts about requirements gathering, etc. The project manager *may* have a larger perspective, because she needs to understand what everyone does in order to build a project plan, so she *might* actually write a description that includes the work done by everyone on the team. But she might also just describe the steps that she follows to plan and track the project.

Sometimes a complex process is important and useful; other times, it's wasteful bureaucracy. Say a team is in the habit of sending around many emails any time a specification is updated, and the team can't (or won't) make any changes until enough people seem to be on board. That's a process, and even if it's not written down it's part of the team's "tribal" knowledge. How do you know which of those categories this particular spec updating process falls into? The answer is in the Kanban practice **make process policies explicit**—in other words, write down a description of how the team works, and show it to everyone who's affected by it. It may be that a complex process is required. The project manager, for example, might point out that this spec change control process is required for regulatory compliance. But more often, simply making an unwritten policy explicit can cause people to shake their heads and agree that it's stupid.

Kanban teams don't need to write long documents or create huge Wikis to establish explicit policies. Policies can be as simple as WIP limits at the tops of the columns. Teams can also write down their policies by adding "definitions of done" or "exit criteria" bullets to the bottom of each column on a kanban board, so that the team members know exactly when to advance the work items through the workflow. This is especially effective when these policies were established collaboratively and evolved experimentally by the whole team, because it means that everyone understands why they're there.

Complex processes and unwritten rules tend to emerge over time, and they seem to be especially common on teams that have a fractured perspective. A complex change control process might come about because a business analyst has trouble keeping up with many last-minute changes, and is blamed loudly in front of the entire team any time the software doesn't meet a specific user's needs. He might impose a complex process to keep control of the scope, and to make sure that there's a paper trail so that he can CYA if someone decides later on to change his or her mind. It's hard to blame this business analyst for defensively creating bureaucracy; it may be the only way he can exert control over a spec that he's held accountable for.

Setting WIP limits is a policy choice, and that policy only works because everyone honors the agreement not to push more work on to a queue if it's full and has already reached its limit. Writing down the agreement—especially if it's in a visible place, like a kanban board—helps to make sure that everyone still agrees to it after it's written down. The team can point to that written policy any time an overeager manager or user tries to push additional work onto the queue. This gives the team solid ground when they need to pull another item off of the queue to make room for an urgent request. That discussion is much easier for the team if the manager or user has already agreed to a policy that was made explicit.

Emergent Behavior with Kanban

> The more you tighten your grip, Tarkin, the more star systems will slip through your fingers.
>
> —Princess Leia

Think back to the doctor's office example from earlier in this chapter. If you had asked a team of command-and-control project managers to help the office staff improve their process, what would have happened? The first step in command-and-control project management is often estimation, so they might make the doctors come up with an estimate for how long they would spend with each patient. That would require a lot of up-front analysis by the doctors, nurses, and office staff, but it would allow the project managers to take control of the system and create a complete schedule for all of the resources—the exam rooms, doctors, and nurses—and micro-manage every aspect of the practice.

This would be a stifling way to work; more importantly, it would be pretty ineffective. Doctors are trained in medicine, not estimation. It's possible that the project managers might come up with an ideal schedule; it's more likely that they'll create an unrealistic or ineffective one because the doctors will give them poor estimates. This is why Kanban looks at the entire system *in aggregate*. Instead of trying to micromanage every little activity, a team using Kanban uses systems thinking to understand, measure, and incrementally improve the system as a whole. They accept the fact that individual work items will vary, but the system as a whole acts predictably when unevenness, overburdening, and futility—muda, mura, and muri—are reduced.

When a team uses Kanban to gradually improve their process for building software, a funny thing often happens: the rest of the company starts to change. Consider the example of our team trying to reduce lead time. Before the team tried Kanban, the managers and users blamed the team for not responding to user requests quickly enough; the team reacted by creating project plans that "proved" that nothing was wrong. This led to conflict and bad feelings.

Kanban helped fix the underlying problem. The team used the Five Whys technique to find the root cause of the lead time problem, and introduced WIP limits to help fix it.

But how, exactly, did that fix the problem? Let's get back to the first two Kanban practices that we talked about in this chapter—**improve collaboratively**, **evolve experimentally**, and **implement feedback loops**—to understand what's going on. The first thing that it did was to *literally* change the way that everyone—including the managers—looked at the process. Visualizing the workflow with a kanban board helped to un-fracture their perspectives. Managers could see that work was piling up, and that helped convince them to agree to WIP limits, and to hold their reviews more often. This is an example of how setting a WIP limit causes behavior to change.

Consider, for example, a team that constantly gets requests from several different managers, and has to balance the requests between them. Each manager considers his or her request to be the most important one; if the team works on a request from one manager, another will feel snubbed. Everyone feels a lot of pressure because they're faced with an impossible choice.

If this team uses Kanban to visualize the workflow, all of the managers' requests for features will end up as work items in the first column. If there are more requests than the team can handle, then stickies will pile up in that column, and everyone can see it. Now the team knows what to do: get all of the managers to agree to a WIP limit on that column.

Let's say, just for this example, that they're able to get this agreement and establish that WIP limit. The managers will keep adding new feature requests as usual, and until that WIP limit is hit nothing changes. But as soon as that first manager hits the WIP limit, something interesting happens: she can't just add the new sticky to the board. Instead, she has to choose another one to remove. And if she doesn't want to remove one of her own, then she has to talk to the other managers.

That's worth repeating: when the manager ran into the WIP limit, she didn't blame the team. She *recognized it as a limitation of the system*, and worked with the other managers to find a solution. This is an important part of systems thinking. When everyone who works with the system recognizes it, they work within that system to solve their problems. And because everyone understands this system, the unevenness and overburdening are no longer just the team's problem. They're everyone's problem, including the managers.

This is how *new behavior emerges outside of the team*. Instead of just blaming the team for overburdening that isn't necessarily their own fault, everyone becomes very concerned with stickies queued up in that first column, because those are the ones that will be worked on by the team. They may have prioritization meetings, or do "horse trading" among themselves, or find some other way to decide on what tasks go into the queue. But there's one thing that does not happen anymore: the team no longer has to take the blame, because they're no longer expected to do more work than they are physically capable of.

In other words, before Kanban, the team had to deal with managers who had magical thinking, and expected to be able to push an unlimited amount of work on to the team. They were always disappointed with the results, and felt that they were promised things that were never delivered. With the WIP limit and an explicit policy, that magical thinking was eliminated. The managers changed their behavior, not because they were asked to change, but because they were working within a system that naturally encouraged them to behave differently. As a result, the team had the slack they needed to relax and do the work right. All of the effort that they'd been using to negotiate with managers individually about their requests could now be focused entirely on their work. That's a much more effective—and pleasant—way to run a team.

Key Points

- One goal of a Kanban team is to maximize the **flow**, or the rate at which work items move through the system.
- The Kanban practice **measure and manage flow** means taking measurements of the flow and making adjustments to the process to reach maximum flow.

- A **cumulative flow diagram** (or CFD) is a WIP area chart that also shows the number of work items added to the workflow every day (**arrival rate**), the total number of work items in the workflow (**inventory**), and the average amount of time each work item stays in the system (**lead time**).

- When the arrival rate and inventory do not change over time, the system is **stable**; Kanban teams set WIP limits to stabilize the system.

- When a system is stable, **Little's Law** applies, which means that the average lead time is always equal to the long-term arrival rate divided by long-term inventory.

- If your team can stabilize the workflow with WIP limits, you can reduce the lead time for your users by getting your stakeholders to agree not to add new work items, which reduces the arrival rate.

- Kanban teams often **make process policies explicit** by adding definitions of done or exit criteria to the bottom of each column on the kanban board.

- When Kanban teams gradually improve the system by adding WIP limits, managing flow, and making process policies explicit, improved behavior often emerges in the rest of the company.

 Frequently Asked Questions

You talk about WIP limits and explicit policies like they can completely change how a team operates. This sounds far-fetched. Is that really true?

Amazingly, yes. To understand why, it helps to go back to the origins of Lean and Kanban.

WIP limits are a simple but very effective tool for smoothing out flow, and this effect has been known for a long time. Kanban is based on a system for signaling work that originated at Toyota in the 1950s (like many of the ideas and tools of Lean). The name "Kanban" comes from the Japanese word that means "signal card" (literally "signboard" or "billboard"). In the manufacturing plant, a station on an assembly line would be given a certain number of kanbans—physical cards with a part number or name printed on it—for each type of part used at that station. When they ran low and needed more of that part, they would leave the kanban in an empty parts cart. The cart would get restocked with one new part for each kanban left in it, with the kanban attached to the part. As parts got used, the kanbans would go back into the cart. This is how the team at the assembly line station would pull only the parts they need, which allowed the entire company to reduce the total number of parts they had to keep in stock. Limiting the number of kanbans for each part allowed the team to set WIP limits.

For developers, it's sometimes hard to see how this pull system using kanban cards can be applied to software development. Programmers don't like being compared to assembly line workers—which is fair, because development is much more similar to what the automotive engineers and designers do than what the assembly line workers do. But Kanban isn't about treating people like assembly line workers, or like cogs in a machine. What Kanban has in common with assembly lines is how it uses kanbans —like cards in a parts bin or stickies on a board—to signal that more work is ready.

It's sometimes easier to understand this parallel by using an example that has nothing to do with either assembly lines or software. Every summer on a large fairground in St. Paul, the Minnesota State Fair is held, and well over a million Minnesotans attend. There are many food vendors scattered all around the fairgrounds. One of the most popular vendors is a large grilled-corn stand. Some other popular vendors have very long lines—for example, it's not unusual to have to wait behind two dozen people to buy deep fried olives on a stick.[4] But the grilled-corn stand is able to serve many people, usually with a very short wait and almost no lines. How do they do it?

Unlike the deep-fried olive vendor, which has two identical windows that often both have very long lines, the grilled-corn vendor has two separate stations set up. At the first station, you hand over your money and you're given a ticket. You then take the ticket over to the second station, where you hand it to a person and are given your grilled corn on a cob.

For first-time state fair attendees, this seems a bit superfluous: why did I just give my money to someone, take a ticket, and then immediately hand that ticket to someone else? But now you should recognize this extra step: the ticket is a kanban, and the grilled-corn vendor uses it to create a WIP limit and establish a pull system.

The people making the grilled corn at the second station know how many tickets are out at a time, and will only pass enough tickets to the first station so that there isn't a large line of ticket holders waiting for grilled corn. This lets them adjust the amount of corn that they keep on the grill so that during slower periods they don't keep corn on the grill so long that it turns into charcoal, and during peak periods they can keep a lot of corn on the grills to minimize lines. It also means that they can hire extra people to do the grilling, so that there are more people doing the time-consuming task of grilling without having to pause and take money. In the rare cases when the

---

4 The vendor selling deep-fried olives on a stick used a typical push system—a long line of people—as of 2014. They may have switched to a kanban system since this book was published.

number of people who want corn is greater than the amount that's ready to serve, the line only forms at the first station. The grillers are protected from the chaos of many people standing in line and trying to hand them money, which allows them to concentrate on grilling and causes the line to move faster and disappear more quickly. And because their work is flowing smoothly, the grillers can get into a rhythm, which causes them to feel more comfortable—and also do a good job.

Adjusting the WIP limit helps the grilled-corn vendor deal with variability. By increasing the number of tickets available and putting more corn on the grill during peak periods (like after a big show lets out at the nearby grandstand), they can ramp up production smoothly and quickly, and then reduce it just as smoothly after the peak disappears. And whether or not the corn vendors know it, they're taking advantage of Little's Law: by limiting the number of people arriving into the system, they can reduce the lead time for people who have handed over their money and are now waiting for their corn. (Can you imagine how this might look on a cumulative flow diagram?)

This example helps illustrate the difference between a push system and a pull system. The deep-fried olive stand uses a push system: a long line of people. The people are "pushing" because they're creating the demand as they line up. The vendors selling the olives don't have any control over that demand; they can only sell olives to the next person in line. At the corn vendor, the people at the grill station are "pulling" because they give tickets to the station that takes the money. They use those tickets to pull people to the grill station, and can limit the number of people they pull by limiting the number of tickets. This is how they set a WIP limit, which lets them match the number of tickets available to the amount of corn on the grill. Adjusting the WIP limit lets them adjust to variability on the fly.

I don't have a bunch of parts that need to be assembled in a car, or corn waiting to be grilled. I build software, so I'm constantly solving different problems all the time. How does this apply to me?

Kanban applies to you because it's just a system that lets you deal with project variability on the fly. Limiting WIP and controlling queue sizes reduces variability. Highlighting sources of delay and techniques like blocker clustering (or root-cause analysis and improvements designed to reduce the likelihood and impact of blockers) reduces variability. Attacking sources of variability that adversely affect the economic outcome and the risk management of the system is a core technique in Kanban.[5]

This is something that development teams need to do—a lot. In fact, you can argue that software teams actually need to deal with variability even more than car manufacturers or corn vendors. What makes software different than any other engineered product in the world is that it's *changeable*. Because it's not a physical object, software engineers have the ability to change software much more extensively and later in the

---

5 Thanks to David Anderson for helping us out with wording to explain how Kanban deals with variability.

project than other kinds of engineers. But each change carries risk, and if your project is tossed to and fro on the whims of variability, it introduces unevenness (mura) because the changes become very disruptive.

So what can you do to make sure that this unevenness doesn't disrupt the project?

In the traditional way of thinking used by most waterfall teams, this is done through a change control process. Changes are controlled, slowed down, and if possible, avoided. Changes to the plan must be proposed, considered by the team, analyzed for their impact on the project, and then agreed to by all parties before they can be implemented. This is an effective way to shield the project from variability, and it does reduce the risk on the project—but it also ensures that your team builds what was originally planned, whether or not it's actually valuable to the users.

The world of traditional project management isn't as bleak as this makes it sound. We saw in Chapter 6 and Chapter 7 that a team is more able to build software that can be changed easily if they're given a relaxed environment where they can work a reasonable number of hours, and mental and emotional space to think about the problems that they're solving. Good software project managers aren't idiots, and they recognize this. That's why they'll add slack to their schedules, just like XP teams do. But the change control process means that they don't have the XP option of adding low-priority tasks that the team can push to a later iteration, because that would require a change to the plan that has to be reviewed and approved. Instead, they'll add *buffers*, or extra tasks with no actual work planned that pad the schedule, often using formulas to determine how much padding to add at various points in the plan. Now they can follow the initial plan and give the team enough time to get their work done, while still removing that extra variability so that the project comes in on time.

In other words, when things get difficult for a team using traditional project management, the response usually involves padding the schedule—no matter what the source of the problem is.

Kanban teams don't put buffers in place or pad schedules, because those things hide the variability from anyone trying to make good decisions. Lean thinking values seeing the whole, and hiding information prevents that. Lean thinking also tells us that when there's waste caused by unevenness, we must find the root cause of the problem and fix it. Instead of hiding the unevenness with padding, Kanban teams expose it when they visualize the workflow and introduce WIP limits and other policies to fix it. They make the variability—and its root causes—explicit.

What if I can't get my manager to agree to limit work in progress?
Then you'll have trouble implementing Kanban. When you read about how Kanban works, it seems like creating queues and limiting flow can help you make substantial improvements for your team. But it all starts with setting WIP limits, which requires you to get your manager—or, often, several managers—to agree to stop adding more work when the team hits that WIP limit.

This can be the Achilles' heel of an improvement effort, especially when the boss uses magical thinking. Let's say that you've spent weeks or even months helping the team understand Kanban, working together to visualize the workflow, creating a kanban board, and taking careful measurements to identify a WIP limit. Now you've gathered your boss and the other managers together, and proudly present your proposal to them. Your boss looks through everything and considers it carefully. He responds, "I like the kanban board, I think these measurements are great, and I am completely on board with this. I just need you to make one tiny little change. Erase that number on top of the column in the kanban board."

To the boss, it seems like he's making the very smallest compromise that he can: just erase one little number. But the WIP limit is the "secret sauce" behind Kanban. Without setting WIP limits, the team has no way to limit flow, and Kanban does not work.

It isn't necessarily intuitive that slowing down the work in one step will make the entire project go faster. And even if you've visualized the workflow, taken measurements, and identified waste caused by unevenness, overburdening, and unreasonable or impossible work, that may not be convincing enough for the boss. When it isn't, he will focus on the WIP limit and look to compromise on it. It might feel to him like removing it will help the team to optimize their work, and prevent people from being underallocated. He probably feels like the WIP limit is going to prevent work from getting done, and he's helpfully pointing that out to the team. He may see that the WIP limit gives the team slack, and fears that they will abuse it by slowing down work to take time off. Or—to be charitable—he may not even really know why he doesn't like it; it just seems like a bad idea. Or he may be completely rational and not have magical thinking at all: he may recognize that a delivery cadence will occasionally cause the project to slip a feature from one release to the next, and when his users see that they'll go crazy and start getting people fired. But no matter what his thought process is, cutting out that WIP limit cuts the legs out from under the entire Kanban effort.

So what do you do if you can't get your managers to agree to limit work in progress?

This is a great opportunity to try Scrum instead, with its predictable timeboxes and scope that is decided up front and managed by a dedicated Product Owner.

One reason that Scrum is effective when managers face restrictions is that the backlog is *internal* to the project. Scrum teams rely on a Product Owner who has the authority to make decisions about what work items are added to the backlog and included in each sprint, and incorporates that Product Owner into the team. Now the team has control over the scope, and the managers and users can work with that Product Owner to absorb any changes and variability in the scope. This gives the team much more flexibility than a traditional change control process, but it still limits the variability that the company is exposed to. The team even uses a board to visualize the workflow—but it's a task board, not a kanban board, because it includes tasks and not just work items, and there are no WIP limits or other policies written on it.

Kanban, on the other hand, has queues and buffers that are *external* to the project. By agreeing to a WIP limit, the customers themselves (managers, users, Product Owners, etc.) decide what goes into the queue. They have to agree to the WIP limits and are not shielded from the variability, but in return they have much more control over what features get built, and in what order. In manufacturing terms, we call this *"just in time" delivery*, because the team decides what work is done next based on the work items waiting in various stages of the workflow (the stickies in the columns on the kanban board) and those decisions can be made very late in the project—even minutes before the team starts working on a work item.

Now, if what started as a Kanban effort ends up with your team adopting Scrum, that's a pretty good result. Once you've got the team working consistently within a stable system, you can help your team learn what it means to make process improvements. If you find that the team is getting better-than-not-doing-it results, it's a step in the right direction and you can continue to move forward. And using Kanban to improve how team builds software is a great way to move forward.

Kanban claims it's not a system for managing projects, but when you move work items around a kanban board, it sure looks like one. Are you sure it's not a project management system?

Yes, Kanban is definitely not a system for project management or a methodology for building software. Kanban is a method for process improvement.

Before you can improve a process, you need to understand it. The kanban board is a great tool for helping you to understand the system that you use to build software, because it is a very effective way of visualizing the workflow.

This is a very effective fix for a serious pitfall that a lot of process improvement efforts fall into: they don't really start off with a solid understanding of how their teams build software today. A typical process improvement effort starts out with a group of managers and project leaders getting together in a room and creating diagrams or descriptions of the current software process. They usually understand that process improvement needs a starting point, so they'll send out surveys, interview software teams, and find other ways to gather that information. Then they'll compile all of that information into some sort of documented process, and use that as the starting point for improvement.

The problem is that gathering information like this is very difficult, and rarely produces a realistic picture of how teams actually build software. Imagine that you're a team member asked by a committee of senior managers about how your project runs. Are you going to highlight your problems and failures? Or are you going to try to paint a rosy, optimistic picture? Even if you strive to give the best answers that you can, we all tend to recall our successes very well, while playing down our challenges and failures in our own memories.

This is where Kanban works better. At the start of the Kanban effort, the team visualizes the workflow by creating a kanban board. But they don't stop there—as the project progresses, they update that board with the work items. Everyone on the team understands that they're doing this not to manage the project, but because they're trying to create an accurate picture of the system that they use to build software. This picture is very accurate because they constantly keep it updated. And it's very useful —when they want to figure out what story or feature to work on next, they can see exactly what work is flowing through the system. But they don't use the kanban board to figure out what tasks they need to perform. The only information that's on the kanban board is at the work item level, not the task level. If their system involves a task board, or a Gantt chart, or some other way of managing projects, they'll still use that.

Because Kanban has such an effective way of visualizing the workflow (a kanban board) and measuring the flow through it (with a CFD), the team can find the most effective improvements. But that's not the only reason that teams using Kanban have a lot of success with process improvement. Kanban gets the best results when the team adopts a Lean mindset—and, just like we saw with Scrum and XP, an effective way to help your team adopt a Lean mindset is to start using the practices of Kanban. Once they start visualizing the workflow and measuring flow, they'll start to understand where the waste in the system is, use options thinking to create options for themselves, and learn to see the whole system that they work in.

 Things You Can Do Today

Here are a few things that you can try today on your own or with your team:

- If you were to build a kanban board today, what would the columns be? If you didn't already create value stream maps, this is a good time to do that—they'll help you figure out how your kanban board might look.
- Is one of the columns a good candidate for a WIP limit? Create sticky notes for work items for just that column. How many of them are actually being worked on right now? What would the WIP limit be?
- Figure out who you would need to talk to in order to create a WIP limit.
- Create a simple kanban board and track your project for a week. Create a CFD based on your data. Is your inventory stable? What about the arrival rate?

Where You Can Learn More

Here are resources to help you learn more about the ideas in this chapter:

- You can learn more about Kanban in *Kanban: Successful Evolutionary Change for Your Technology Business,* by David J. Anderson (Blue Hole Press, 2010).
- You can learn more about systems thinking in *Lean Software Development: An Agile Toolkit,* by Mary and Tom Poppendieck (Addison-Wesley 2003).

Coaching Tips

Tips for agile coaches helping their team to work with the ideas in this chapter:

- Kanban starts with a Lean mindset, so the first step in helping your team to use Kanban is to help them with lean thinking. The coaching tips in Chapter 8 will help.
- The single biggest barrier for teams who want to use Kanban to improve their process is to understand that it is not a system for project management. As a coach, your job is to help them learn what it means for something to be a system for project management, and how Kanban helps them understand their system, and not manage projects.
- Help your team start seeing when they're committing too early, and how that can cause waste in their project. Help them to identify options, and learn to make commitments at the last responsible moment. People—especially nervous managers or managers with magical thinking—will often demand that teams commit to a date. Help the team learn to make only the commitments that are needed for the project.
- Kanban also needs the team to adopt systems thinking. This is an important part of Lean, and it's one of the basic ideas that makes Kanban work. Helping the team to visualize the workflow with a kanban board is often a good first step toward mentally separating the "cogs" of the machine from the people who make it work.

CHAPTER 10

The Agile Coach

You've learned about Scrum, XP, Lean, and Kanban. You know what they have in common, and understand what they achieve. If you work with other people to build software, then you've spotted at least a few things—some practices, ideas, attitude changes—that will help your team.

OK! Now, go ahead and do it. Make your team go agile. Right now!

That doesn't seem quite realistic yet, does it? There's a big difference between reading about values, principles, mindsets, and practices in a book and actually changing the way that a team works.

Some teams are able to take a book on Scrum or XP, adopt the practices, and immediately see great results. After reading the first nine chapters of this book, you should recognize why: those teams already have a mindset that's compatible with the values and principles of the Agile manifesto and the methodology. To a compatible team like that, adopting agile feels easy because the individual people on the team don't have to change the way that they think about their work. So if you already have a mindset that's compatible with the agile methodology you're trying to adopt, you're much more likely to have a successful adoption.

But what if you don't already have a mindset that works for Scrum, XP, or another agile methodology? What if you're working in an environment where it's difficult to succeed with the agile values? What if individual contributions on your team are rewarded far more than team effort? What if mistakes are punished harshly? What if you're in an environment that stifles innovation, or where your team has no access to the customers, users, or other people who can help you understand what software you're building? These are all barriers to agile adoption.

This is where an **agile coach** comes in. An agile coach is someone who helps a team adopt agile. He or she will help each person on the team learn a new attitude and mindset, and get past the mental, emotional, and technical barriers that prevent the team from adopting an agile methodology. Agile coaches work with every person on the team to help him or her understand not just the "how" of the new practices that they're being asked to implement, but also the "why." A coach will help the team overcome the natural dislike—and even fear—of change that happens to anyone who is asked to try something new at work.

We've seen many examples throughout this book of people getting better-than-not-doing-it results: a team adopts the practices of an agile methodology, but the team members only get a marginal improvement because they don't really change the way that they think about the way they work, or their attitude toward working together to building software. In other words, *your team needs an agile mindset to get good results with an agile methodology.* Agile has the values and principles of the Agile Manifesto to help teams get into the right mindset, and each methodology comes with its own values and principles for the same reason. A team gets the best results from an agile adoption when each person gets into a mindset that's compatible with the values and principles of agile, and with the specific methodology that they're adopting.

The goal of the agile coach is to *help the team attain a better, more agile mindset.* A good coach helps the team choose a methodology that best fits their existing mindset, and introduces them to the values, principles, and practices of a methodology in a way that works for them. The coach will help the team adopt its practices, and then use those practices to help the team learn and internalize the values and principles, to slowly change their attitude, and to get into the right mindset so that they go beyond simply getting better-than-not-doing-it results.

In this chapter, you'll learn about agile coaching: how teams learn, how an agile coach can help a team change their mindset so that they can more easily adopt an agile methodology, and how that coach can help you and your team become more agile.

 ## Narrative: a team working on a mobile phone camera app at a company that was bought by a large Internet conglomerate

Catherine – a developer

Timothy – another developer

Dan – their boss

Act III: Just One More Thing (Again?!)...

"Hey, Cathy! Do you have a minute? I've got great news."

Catherine groaned silently as her boss, Dan, called her into his office. She thought to herself, *I'll never get used to that.* She steeled herself for the "great news" as she sat down.

"You've done a fantastic job with this whole agile thing. Really, just fantastic."

Catherine thought back over the last eight months that she and Timothy had spent using Kanban to improve their process. She'd identified several bottlenecks in their process, especially the big one where Dan and other managers would drop new features on them seemingly at random. An amazing thing happened when she added a queue: as they started fighting and jostling for position on the queue, they slowly stopped demanding that she and Tim do more work than they were physically capable of.

In fact, now that she thought about it, this was the first time in months that Dan had called her into his office with "great news"—which usually meant that he had a critical last-minute change that would completely derail her project.

"I'm glad to hear you're happy, Dan," said Catherine. She only meant it half-sarcastically.

Dan continued, "And people in our parent company have noticed. They've been reading about this agile stuff, and now that we've got some success under our belt, they want us to teach other teams how to do it."

Catherine said, "Wait a minute. So you're asking me to... what? Coach them?"

"Exactly," said Dan.

"I have no idea how to be a coach," replied Catherine.

Dan looked her straight in the eye. "This isn't optional, Cathy. Come on, just buck up and do it."

Coaches Understand Why People Don't Always Want to Change

> Most people in your organization are trying to do a good job. They want their peers and supervisors to see that they are good at performing the tasks assigned to them. When someone has developed a level of comfort and familiarity with his job, the last thing he wants is to have someone come along and make him adopt an entirely new way of doing things.
>
> —Andrew Stellman and Jennifer Greene, *Applied Software Project Management*

Agile coaches spend most of their time helping people on teams change the way that they work. This is challenging for both the coach and the team, because only the coach sees the big picture. To the people on the team, they're being asked to adopt new rules about how they work, but they don't necessarily know why they're doing that.

There are many ways that a well-intentioned team trying to adopt a practice can alter it so that it doesn't really work anymore. For example, we saw in Chapter 5 that teams will often turn the Daily Scrum into a daily status meeting. An important goal of the Daily Scrum is to replace command-and-control project management with self-organization; the three questions that each person asks during the meeting are aimed at giving the team control over their own project plan. But many teams that attempt to adopt Scrum end up just using it as a daily meeting for team members to report their individual statuses, in which the Scrum Master acts as a de facto project manager and assigns work to them.

Similarly, some teams add stories to business requirements documents, but otherwise treat those documents as specifications in the same way most waterfall teams do. They're still doing big requirements up front (BRUF) development, just with user stories added. Or instead of doing test-driven development, some teams attempting to adopt XP will just make sure that they have very high code coverage for the tests that they develop after they build the code—which means the tests don't have any impact on the design, because it's complete by the time the tests are written.

In all of these cases, the people on these teams are genuinely trying to adopt agile. But in each of these examples, the people on the team don't really understand how those practices fit into a larger ecosystem of a methodology. So instead of trying to change the way that they work, they *focus on the part of the practice that feels familiar*. And why should we expect any different? A team that has only known command-and-control project management has no experience with self-organization, and no context to help them understand the Daily Scrum beyond what they already know.

And let's give credit where credit is due. Most of the teams adopting agile already build software, and have some success. (Completely dysfunctional teams rarely have a manager who is open-minded enough to let them try agile in the first place.) They're naturally looking to make small, incremental changes, because they don't want to break what's currently working.

This leads to one of the biggest roadblocks for agile adoption: when a team member thinks, "I've seen agile, I've adopted the practices that are familiar to me, my team is working better than before, and that's enough for me." This is what we've been calling better-than-not-doing-it results, and it's what causes many people to dismiss agile by reducing it to specific, marginal improvements that are a letdown from the excitement and "hype."

Why do team members so often insist on adopting only the practices that seem familiar to them, and reject any practice that doesn't immediately translate to something that they're doing today?

Because every new practice is a change, and there's always a chance that any change won't work out. And when changes at the office don't work out, people get fired.

This is something that every agile coach needs to keep in the front of his or her mind. The job of coaching is to help teams to change, and change can cause an outsized— but *entirely rational*—emotional response from the people being asked to change. Why? Because *work is how you pay for your life and feed your family.*

When we're asked to learn and do new things at work, if we don't feel like we can master them quickly and easily, it causes us severe emotional discomfort. There's a basic hunter-gatherer part of our minds that thinks, "Yesterday I knew that I could do my job and bring home food for my family, but today I can't be sure of that anymore." This is an important reason why being expected to learn new things at work can cause anxiety and seemingly irrational reactions (which, in this context, don't really seem all that irrational).

Another reason why people push back against a change at work and gravitate toward what they already understand is that they don't feel like they have time to sit and think through all the reasons behind it. For example, it's very common for teams to adopt agile by simply trying it on a pilot project. This often starts when one person has read a book about agile, and is now leading the whole team through their adoption—while at the same time, dealing with deadlines, bugs, conflicts, changing requirements, and all of the other things that happen during a typical project. This is not an ideal proving ground for a completely new way of thinking about work. People will do the best they can, but if there's something they don't quite get, they'll keep the label "agile" and the names of the methodology and practices, but little else will change about how they work. Milestones in their old project plan are now labeled "Sprint," or maybe someone puts up a task board that never really impacts the work being done. In the end, the team will just do what they did before, because they know that it worked in the past, and there's a deadline.

When a team uses the names of agile practices but doesn't change the way they work, it's not hard to see why the team members quickly become disillusioned with the ideas behind agile. To them, it's a reasonable assumption to think that agile is just another name for whatever it is they're currently doing. They think that they've adopted agile, but they haven't changed the way they work, so they get the same results.

The people on the team will decide that agile doesn't work, without ever realizing that they never actually saw anything that resembles agile in real life. They have this reaction because they're being asked to change how they work without understanding why, and without someone to help them through the change without compromising the integrity of the new practices and ideas.

This is why teams need agile coaches. An important job of the agile coach is to recognize when people are being asked to do something new, and to help them feel comfortable with the change. The coach needs to give that person context for the change, so they understand *why* (and not just *what*). This helps the team actually change the way they work, rather than simply taking the name of something from an agile methodology and attaching it to a practice that they already do.

For example, a good coach will explain—in language that everyone understands—how the Daily Scrum helps the team self-organize, how test-driven development helps the team think functionally and move toward incremental design, or how user stories help everyone on the team understand the perspective of the people using the software. The coach helps everyone go beyond just adopting new rules, so they start to see where they're going and what these new things will eventually give them.

Coaches Listen for Warning Signs That the Team Is Having Trouble with a Change

If you spend time coaching many teams, you'll hear many of the same sentiments repeated from different people. Here are a few things that team members say that could indicate that they're uncomfortable with a change, and what you can do when you encounter them—which is useful for seeing things from the coaching perspective, even if you're not an agile coach:

"We already build software well. Why are you telling me to do something different?"
> It's hard to argue with success. If you're working with a team that has a history of getting software out the door, they have a right to know why they need to change at all—and it's not enough to tell them that the boss said so, because that will just undermine their morale. As a coach, you need to stay positive about the work that the team did in the past. But don't be shy about pointing out problems that they ran into. The practices in every agile methodology are aimed at fixing problems that teams have; if you can help your team understand why those problems are happening and give them solutions, they're much more likely to accept the change.

"This is far too risky."
> This is a very common response to agile, especially to someone who's used to a command-and-control style of project management. Where are all the buffers? Where's the risk register? Where's all the extra bureaucracy that slows down the project and gives me plenty of CYA? A project plan can be opaque, which can make teams comfortable: they don't need to share details beyond vague milestones, and can build in buffers to reduce and even eliminate variability. When

you use status reports as the primary measure of software progress, you can control the message that you give to the users and customers. To a team that's used to these things, agile can feel very risky. In Chapter 3, we learned about the agile principle that working software is the primary measure of project progress. If something goes wrong on an agile team, everyone knows. Your job as an agile coach is to help the managers, users, and customers to feel comfortable with this undiluted measure of progress—and give the team a safe environment where they're allowed to fail today, as long as they learn from it tomorrow. If this isn't realistic today, then your job is to help everyone, especially the boss, to set a goal to change the team's climate and attitude in the future.

"Pair programming (or test-driven development, or some other practice) just isn't going to work for me."

A developer used to working alone might feel in his gut that pair programming will slow him down. He may even have a legitimate point—if he works on a team (or for a boss) with a mindset in which mistakes are simply unacceptable, then it's reasonable for him to feel uncomfortable having another person watch him code. And anyone who's taught a teenager to drive can relate to the uncomfortable feeling that a senior team member might have thinking about letting a junior team member control the keyboard for their pair. There are a lot of reasons that people can rationally feel uncomfortable with these practices, especially when the team has a mindset that doesn't match the practice. A good agile coach will help the team first choose the practices that are compatible with their mindset. As the team members start working those practices, they'll see the benefits and understand how and why the practices work. With guidance from a good coach, everyone will naturally start to shift toward a more agile mindset.

"Agile doesn't work for a business like ours."

People often say this because they're used to building large and detailed plans or designs before work begins, and they can't imagine working any other way. Command-and-control project managers and bosses get a lot of comfort from having the scope, requirements, and project plan on paper before any work starts. And in the same way, architects and development leads are reassured when the entire design for the system is on paper before the first line of code is written. Now they're being asked to trust the team to make decisions at the last responsible moment—and that means giving up that control. So they'll say something like, "Our business is very complex. People in other companies may be able to jump right into projects, but because of how our particular business works, we need to do all of this planning and design ahead of time." The truth is, every business is complicated, and every project needs analysis and planning. A good agile coach will help the managers, businesspeople, and development leads to see that teams are much better at capturing that complexity when they're allowed to divide the project into smaller pieces, and have the freedom to make decisions at the last responsible moment.

"This is exactly like what we're already doing, just with a different name."
This is one of the most common reasons that people reject agile methodologies. They'll find ways to keep doing what they're doing today, and just choose new names for them that match agile practices they've read or heard about. This can make all of agile seem trivial—and even wrong, if they've decided to give the agile name to a practice that failed for them. In fact, if you do a web search for a term like "agile sucks" you'll find people who have done exactly this, denouncing agile as "hype" without substance because it's just another name for old waterfall practices. They'll even call agile an "obfuscation" of simple, commonsense software development. As a coach, you need to recognize that this isn't done with malice or ill intent; it's just a natural reaction from someone who's never actually seen agile (but thinks he has). Your job, as a coach, is to help your team understand that agile really is different from what they're doing, and that it doesn't suck.

Coaches Understand How People Learn

One good model for mastering anything (if that's possible) comes from martial arts. A martial arts student progresses through three stages of proficiency called Shu Ha Ri. Shu: Follow the rule. Ha: Break the rule. Ri: Be the rule.

—Lyssa Adkins, *Coaching Agile Teams: A Companion for ScrumMasters*

Kent Beck, author of *Extreme Programming Explained*, described the use of Extreme Programming (XP) using similar levels. Asked about XP and the five levels of the Software Engineering Institute's "Capability Maturity Model," he replied with XP's three levels of maturity:

1. Do everything as written.

2. After having done that, experiment with variations in the rules.

3. Eventually, don't care if you are doing XP or not.

—Alistair Cockburn, *Agile Software Development: The Cooperative Game,* 2nd Edition

Back in Chapter 2, you learned about how different people see agile differently. Like each of the blind men who encountered the elephant, different people will initially come to their own answers to the question, "What is agile?"

A programmer might see XP's programming practices like test-driven development and incremental design and decide that agile is about software programming, design, and architecture. A project manager, on the other hand, might decide that agile is about improving project management practices after reading about Scrum's sprints, planning, backlog, and retrospectives.

It's taken us hundreds of pages to explore Scrum, XP, Lean, and Kanban. We've talked about mindsets, values, principles, and practices. We've shown you how to put them all together to help your team deliver more value to your users and customers. We've helped you find things that you can do today to help your team, and given you tools (like playing "Are you OK with?") to help your team with their mindset. We've given you many tools for learning agile, and understanding Scrum, XP, Lean, and Kanban.

This is *not* how most people adopt agile.

As much as we'd love it if every developer in the world buys and reads our book, the truth is that most people on most teams don't learn agile by reading. They learn it by doing. And it's easier to do something if it's broken into small, straightforward chunks.

In other words, when most people first try to learn agile, what they really want is a simple list of rules that they can follow that will get them to build better software more quickly.

If you're new to agile coaching, this can be frustrating. Imagine that you're trying to teach a team how to effectively adopt Scrum. You know from Chapter 5 that if someone doesn't understand self-organization and collective commitment, they don't "get" Scrum. So you spend time explaining the Scrum values of openness, courage, focus, commitment, and respect, and you talk about how self-organization works. But the team gets frustrated—these seem like very abstract concepts. They just want to talk about task boards and stories. You want them to "get" Scrum; they seem determined to get better-than-not-doing-it results, and you don't seem to be able to do anything about it. What's going on here?

There's an old saying about teaching: *meet them where they are, not where you want them to be*. A good agile coach understands how people learn, and presents them with information, guidance, and examples to help them reach their next stage in learning. Coaches understand that people don't change overnight.

In *Agile Software Development: The Cooperative Game*, Alistair Cockburn talks about a basic idea of learning called **shuhari**, and it's a very valuable tool for a coach trying to figure out where the team is. Shuhari is adopted from martial arts, but it's a good way to think about how people learn about almost anything.

In Shuhari, learning comes in three stages. The first stage, *shu* (守, "obey" or "observe"), describes the mindset of someone who first encounters a new idea or methodology. He wants simple rules that he can follow. This is one reason that people latch onto practices: the team can make a rule about adopting sprints, pair programming, using a task board, etc., and everyone can tell whether or not it's being followed.

Rules are especially important for adults learning new things at work, because unlike kids in school, adults aren't in the habit of learning new things all the time. When you give someone who is learning a new system—like an agile methodology—simple rules to follow, it gives her a place to start. The straightforward practices that are part of agile methodologies like Scrum, XP, and Kanban work very well for someone in the *shu* stage, because they are simple enough that people can focus on getting good at them. By setting a rule for the team today (like "we have a Daily Scrum meeting at 10:30 every morning where each person answers three questions"), you can help get them on the right track to learn a principle ("we use self-organization to constantly review and adjust our plan").

Your goal as coach, however, is *not to establish an agile orthodoxy*. An agile zealot is someone who has decided that there is exactly one way of doing agile that will work for every team, and who loudly and forcefully pushes that way of doing things on everyone. Agile zealots tend to focus only on the rules that they've learned, and stop at the *shu* level. They believe every problem that they encounter can be solved with a rule that they already know and preach. Agile zealots do not make good coaches because they don't take the time to understand where the people that they're coaching are in their learning.

An agile coach needs to understand more than simple rules, which brings us to the next stage in Shuhari, *ha* (破, "detach" or "break"). This is the stage where people have gotten practice with the rules, and can start to understand and internalize the principles that drive them. Throughout this book you've learned how an effective way to change the mindset of your team is to adopt the practices of a methodology, and through its practices (and lots of team discussion) come to understand its values and principles. When people on a team reach the *ha* stage together, they start to progress from getting better-than-not-doing-it results to getting the real gains in productivity that come when a team truly adopts an agile mindset.

We haven't talked much about the last stage, *ri* (離, "separate"). When you reach the *ri* stage of learning, you are fluent in the ideas, values, and principles. You care less about the methodologies, because you've gone beyond them. When you have a problem that can be fixed with a specific practice, you and your team just do that practice. You don't really care if it's Scrum, XP, Kanban, waterfall—it doesn't matter, and your process doesn't need a name. But it's not like the chaos that you see on a team where nobody has tried agile. A team where everyone has reached *ri* is a smooth, well-functioning team, where everyone just does what's right.

Cockburn points out just how "distressingly Zen" this can sound. In *Agile Software Development: The Cooperative Game*, he talks about how people at the *ri* stage of learning say things that are difficult for a *shu*-level learner to understand:

"Do whatever works."

"When you are really doing it, you are unaware that you are doing it."

> "Use a technique so long as it is doing some good."
>
> To someone at the fluent level of behavior, this is all true. To someone still detaching, it is confusing. To someone looking for a procedure to follow, it is useless.

The first job of a good agile coach is to talk to everyone on the team and figure out each person's current stage of learning. To the coach, a team with people at the *ri* stage of learning is a team that's very easy to work with, because every team member knows how to learn, and is willing to adapt to new practices.

On the other hand, a person at the *shu* stage wants unambiguous rules. For example, do you use stickies or index cards on your task board? You may know as a coach that it doesn't really matter. But someone who has never used a task board has no way of knowing whether this is a trivial or critical decision, so your job is to give him a rule. Later you can help him understand why you chose, say, stickies, and that index cards will do just as good a job. They're a little different—for example, you can write on both sides of an index card, but only one side of a sticky—and you can use the similarities and differences to help the team members learn how they both fulfill the same principles.

Use Shuhari to Help a Team Learn the Values of a Methodology

Put yourself back into the shoes of the frustrated coach trying to teach the team to "get" Scrum. Shuhari can help you understand why the team is frustrated when learning about values, and why they only want to talk about the most tangible practices like task boards and stories. A task board or story is not hard to present as a *shu*-level concept: a straightforward rule that you can apply to a project today. Scrum is full of *shu*-level rules ("meet every day and answer these three questions"); this is one reason that teams find a lot of success in adopting its practices.

Values like openness and commitment, on the other hand, are *ha*-level ides: abstract concepts that govern how you employ rules in a system. Self-organization and collective commitment happen only when everyone on the team has really understood and internalized those values. Shuhari helps us understand why the team needs to first go through the motions of the practices before they can "detach" and start to understand what openness and commitment really mean.

This is why adopting the practices of Scrum is a very effective first step in helping the team to learn its values. A good coach is patient, and waits for opportunities during each sprint to teach the team about the values. Often, these opportunities happen when two people with different perspectives see different aspects of the Scrum "elephant."

For example, let's say that a developer discovers halfway through a sprint that a feature won't be finished, and at the next Daily Scrum he asks the Product Owner to push it to the next sprint. The Product Owner gets angry. She's afraid that a customer or manager will get mad about this, and wants the developer to "do whatever it takes" to get it in—even if it means cutting corners and not finishing all of the code. There's a *shu*-level answer to this problem: the rules of Scrum dictate that the team can only demo the feature at the sprint review if it's "*done* done," and incomplete work *must* be pushed into the next sprint. An agile coach understands the rules of Scrum, and can use them to resolve the conflict.

But a good agile coach also sees that there's a *ha*-level teaching opportunity here. By recognizing a fractured perspective (like we learned about in Chapter 2) that can be "un-fractured," the coach can help the Product Owner see things from the developer's perspective—that doing poor work will add technical debt, and this will make the entire codebase more difficult to maintain. That technical debt, in turn, will cause future sprints to take longer. So while the Product Owner might end up getting the feature to a customer sooner by ignoring the Scrum rule, in the end she will be worse off because future development will go more slowly. This an important lesson that will help the Product Owner learn more about the Scrum value of *focus*, and how a team that focuses on completing work delivers a higher quality product more quickly.

The coach can also help the developer understand how important the feature is, and how it delivers value to the customers—and how in the future, a better understanding of value can help the developer work more closely with the Product Owner to find a way to break features into smaller ones and deliver more value to the customers sooner. This is an important lesson that will help the developer learn more about the Scrum value of *commitment*, and that a team can be more effective when they really understand what's valuable to the customers and users.

This is an example of how the coach with a deep understanding of a methodology fills an important and valuable role on the team. The coach helps the team understand and adopt the practices and rules of the methodology. And through those rules, the coach can help everyone on the team understand the values of agile, and use those values to help every single person on the team grow into a more agile mindset.

Coaches Understand What Makes a Methodology Work

Conflicts and problems happen on projects every day. A good Scrum Master, for example, spends most of his time resolving issues and problems. Many of these problems won't necessarily present great opportunities to teach the team about Scrum.

So in the example that we just showed you, how did the coach know that there was an opportunity in this particular conflict to teach the team about the Scrum values of *focus* and *commitment*? What was it about this particular problem that the coach recognized?

The coach recognized the opportunity because he understands not just *how* Scrum teams use iteration, but *why* they use it. He knows that a timeboxed iteration can be rendered completely ineffective if the team is allowed to include work that isn't "*done done*." Without that rule, iterations turn into simple project milestones: the scope of each iteration becomes more and more variable, and the team no longer has to deliver working software at the end of each iteration.

This breaks several important values and principles that make agile work. For example, the coach knows that working software is the primary measure of progress, and delivering incomplete software at the end of a sprint gives the customers and users a false measure of that progress. The coach also knows that agile teams value customer collaboration—but he also understands that customer collaboration doesn't mean that the customer is always right. It means that if the team recognizes that there is a real problem with the plan, they can collaborate with the customer to come up with a solution that delivers the most value. He recognizes that if the customer and Product Owner can pressure developers to include software that isn't complete in a sprint review, the team will become more guarded about the true progress of the work, and eventually customer collaboration will give way to contract negotiation between the team and the customer.

The coach knows all of this because he understands the values and principles of agile and Scrum, and knows how those values and principles drive the practices. He recognizes what makes the methodologies "tick." A Scrum coach understands collective commitment and self-organization. An XP coach understands embracing change and incremental design. A Kanban coach understands how improving the team's process requires setting WIP limits and using them to control the flow of work—and that when someone tries to prevent those WIP limits from getting set, the entire methodology unravels.

In *Coaching Agile Teams*, Lyssa Adkins has a suggestion for how coaches can approach problems with the team—we talked about this earlier in the book, but it's worth repeating:

> **Let the team fail:** Certainly, don't stand idly by while the team goes careening off a cliff. But do use the dozens of opportunities that arise each sprint to let them fail. Teams that fail together and recover together are much stronger and faster than ones that are protected. And the team may surprise you. The thing you thought was going to harm them may actually work for them. Watch and wait.

This is excellent advice for any agile coach, especially one who is prone to what Adkins refers to as "command-and-control-ism," or a need to control every aspect of the team's learning and progress. A good coach understands that there are times when the team can and should fail, because that's the most effective and efficient path to a successful project and team.

This is where retrospectives are extremely valuable. We learned about how Scrum and XP teams use retrospectives to look back at the project and find ways to improve. To an agile coach, this is a great opportunity to help the team learn from the failure—

and learning is the whole goal of letting them fail. If the team failed because they didn't implement a practice well enough, the coach can help them learn the skills they need to get better at it. But sometimes failure happens because the teams need to improve their mindset—and because an agile coach knows why methodologies and practices work, he or she can use the failure to help the team learn more about the specific value or principle that would have helped them to make better decisions and avoid failure. This is how teams grow.

But a good coach also understands when a team can't be allowed to fail. Just like there are supporting beams and walls in a house that can't be moved during a renovation, every methodology has its "supporting beams" that cannot be changed without compromising the integrity of the project. A coach needs a *ha*-level understanding of the methodology: he has a deep knowledge of it as a system, and knows why it works. In Chapter 8, we learned about the boss who inadvertently cuts the legs out from under an entire Kanban effort by asking the team to remove the WIP limit. Someone with a *shu*-level understanding might let that WIP limit get changed, feeling like it's better to get at least some of Kanban in place. A good Kanban coach understands that while some things (like the specific columns on a kanban board) can be changed, the WIP limit must be left intact, because it's the lynchpin that holds the entire Kanban methodology together.

One of the more difficult parts of an agile coach's job is to figure out just how much of this to explain to the team, the boss, and the customers. A simple *shu*-level explanation of the rules of a methodology is enough to get the job done, but not enough to help the team get into the right mindset to get better-than-not-doing-it results. Sometimes the team is satisfied with a simple set of rules to follow; other times, they may feel like they've just traded an arbitrary set of waterfall rules for an arbitrary set of agile rules. A *ha*-level understanding will help them see why following these rules will produce better software; but it also may sound "distressingly Zen," as Cockburn put it. The agile coach is there to help the team move toward their *ha*-level of understanding at a pace that they can handle, and without overly abstract explanations that don't help them.

The Principles of Coaching

If there's one thing that we've reinforced throughout this book, it's that agile requires the right mindset, and that teams get to that mindset through values and principles. That's why every agile methodology comes with a set of values, and team members only approach the full potential of an agile methodology when they understand and internalize those values.

So it shouldn't come as a surprise that coaching has its own set of values. John Wooden, coach of the UCLA men's basketball team in the 1960s and 1970s, is widely considered one of the greatest coaches in the history of sports. In his book, *Practical*

Modern Basketball, he lays out five basic principles of coaching: **industriousness**, **enthusiasm**, **condition**, **fundamentals**, and **development of team spirit**. They make just as much sense for an agile coach as they do in basketball:

Industriousness

Changing the way a team builds software means working hard at things that they've never done before. Developers have to think about planning and testing, not just coding. Product owners need to understand what the team does, not just throw features over the wall at them. Scrum masters need to learn how to give the team control, while still staying involved with the project. These are all new skills, and all new skills require work.

Enthusiasm

When your heart is in your work, and you're excited about a new way of doing things, it rubs off on everyone around you. And there's a lot to be enthusiastic about: you're solving problems that have given you headaches in the past. When everyone goes into agile with a real enthusiasm toward it, you get more than just better software; you get a team where everyone is more innovative, happier, and excited about working together every day.

Condition

Agile works when every team member is good at what he or she does. There's a real, implicit assumption that everyone has pride of workmanship: they try to build the best software that they can, and work to get better at building it—and that they're genuinely motivated by pride in their work. This is why every member of an agile team continues to work hard at improving their skills, so that they bring their best condition to the project.

Fundamentals

Wooden writes, "the finest system cannot overcome poor execution of the fundamentals. The coach must be certain that he never permits himself to get 'carried away' by a complicated system"—and this is especially relevant for an agile coach. Agile works because its values are simple and straightforward, and its methodologies consist of uncomplicated practices. These are the fundamentals of agile, and a good coach works to keep the team focused on them, and helps the team to keep things simple.

Development of team spirit

We've talked about self-organization, whole team, energized work, and empowering the team: ways that agile teams build each other up and create a collaborative, innovative work environment. On the flipside, an agile coach needs to be on the lookout for team members who are primarily focused on their own personal performance, career goals, résumé, or getting promoted out of the team, and help them change their attitude. Wooden is clear about the effect that sort of person has on team spirit, and what to do about it: "The coach must use every bit of psychology at his command and use every available method to develop a fine team spirit on his squad. Teamwork and unselfishness must be encouraged at every opportunity, and each [team member] must be eager, not just willing, to sacrifice personal glory for the welfare of the team. Selfishness, envy, egotism, and criticism of each other can crush team spirit and ruin the potential of any team. The coach must be aware of this and constantly alert to prevent such traits by catching them at the source before trouble develops."

These five principles are a solid foundation for the mindset of an agile coach. An important step in becoming a great agile coach is to understand, internalize, and use them, in exactly the same way as you would use the values of the Agile Manifesto and any agile methodology.

Key Points

- An **agile coach** is someone who helps a team adopt agile, and helps each individual person on the team learn a new mindset.
- Effective agile coaches help teams get past their discomfort with new practices by focusing on the part of the practice that feels familiar.
- Coaches recognize the warning signs that teams are uncomfortable with change.
- People learn new systems or mindsets in three stages called **shuhari**.
- Someone who encounters an idea for the first time is in the first stage, **shu**, where she's still learning the rules—she often responds best to specific instructions.
- The **ha** stage is where someone starts to recognize the larger system, and has adapted his mindset to match it.
- In the **ri** stage, people are fluent with the ideas of the system—for example, they know when rules don't have to be followed.
- An effective agile coach knows why a system works, and understands why the rules are there.

Where You Can Learn More

Here are resources to help you learn more about the ideas in this chapter:

- You can learn more about agile coaching in *Coaching Agile Teams,* by Lyssa Adkins (Addison-Wesley, 2010).
- You can learn more about shuhari and how people learn and adapt to new systems in *Agile Software Development: The Cooperative Game,* 2nd Edition, by Alistair Cockburn (Addison-Wesley, 2006).
- You can learn more about the fundamentals of coaching in *Practical Modern Basketball,* 3rd Edition, by John Wooden (Benjamin Cummings, 1998).
- You can learn more about why teams resist change and how to help them move beyond that resistance in *Applied Software Project Management,* by Andrew Stellman and Jennifer Greene (O'Reilly, 2005).

Index

goals for, 8
inclusion of businesspeople on, 68
key points, 81
reflection and adaptation in, 80, 158
reward systems for, 70
self-organizing, 79
sense of community in, 68
simplifying development, 78
unifying mindset of, 82
vs. rugged individualism, 281
amplify learning (Lean value), 270
Anderson, David, 315
antipatterns, 223
automated build scripts, 24
autonomy, 250

B

baby steps (XP principle), 202, 205
backlog, 62, 69, 144
"Beautiful Teams" (Stellman and Greene), 126, 161
Beck, Kent, 197, 214, 222, 230, 265
blind men and the elephant metaphor, 39
Booch, Grady, 161
bottlenecks, controlling, 303
Brand, Stewart, 182
Brooks, Fred, 19, 190
BRUF (big requirements up front) approach, 17, 54, 111, 169
build integrity in (Lean value), 270, 288
build server, 24, 180, 187, 199, 254
build tokens, 180
burndown charts, 24, 149

C

Capability Maturity Model, 376
"caves and commons" office layout, 182
change
    embracing, 175, 219
    understanding resistance to, 372
    warning signs of trouble with, 374
    welcoming, 57
CHAOS report, 141
check outs, 180
Chrysler Comprehensive Compensation (C3) project, 222
class of service, 348
"Coaching Agile Teams" (Adkins), 160
Cockburn, Alistair, 42, 51, 377

code
    continuous integration practices, 241
    creating overly complex, 222, 247
    decoupling, 245
    last responsible moment decisions, 237
    monolithic design, 243
    recognizing overly clever, 230
    recognizing poorly behaved, 229
    recognizing poorly structured, 223
    refactoring
        benefits of, 240
        definition of, 237
        example of, 238
        reducing complexity with, 239
        vs. one-time coding, 240
    reusable, 232, 240, 255
    separation of concerns, 233
    technical debt problem, 239
    tightly coupled, 245
code antipatterns, 225
code smells
    decoupling code with, 245
    definition of, 225
    duplicated code, 227
    half-baked code, 226
    increased complexity due to, 236
    key points of, 236
    lasagna code, 228
    leaks, 228
    shotgun surgery, 226
    source of, 226
    spaghetti code, 228
    very large classes, 227
Cohn, Mike, 121, 157, 170
collective commitment, 89, 141
collective ownership, 214
command-and-control approach
    response of teams to, 100
    response to change, 59
    role of project manager in, 94
    status reports in, 74
    vs. options thinking, 274
commitment (Scrum value), 105, 163, 273
communication (XP value), 196, 198, 211
communication principle, 208
conceptual integrity, 289
conditions of satisfaction, 144
continuous delivery, 56, 127
continuous integration, 180, 199, 241, 248

contracts, 257
cost of delay, 304
coupling, 245
courage (Scrum value), 104, 107, 165
courage (XP value), 196, 211, 254
cumulative flow diagram (CFD)
    building, 341
    components of, 340
    managing flow with, 345
    vs. WIP (work in progress) area chart, 340
Cunningham, Ward, 225
customer collaboration over contract negotia-
    tion, 35, 56, 70, 79, 141
CYA (cover your ass) attitude, 71, 167, 192

D

Daily Scrum
    decisions at last responsible moment, 114
    functions of, 110
    holding effective
        adapting the plan, 117
        choosing new tasks, 115
        full participation, 117
        handling dependencies, 131
        inspect every task, 117
        non-status meeting approach, 117
        schedule follow-up meetings, 116
        stay engaged, 116, 172
        take turns going first, 116
    key points on, 118
    overview of, 90
    questions during, 87
    self-assignment of tasks in, 113
    standing vs. sitting during, 158
    user-stakeholder participation in, 141
    visibility-inspection-adaptation cycle, 111
daily standup, 3, 25, 34, 158
decide as late as possible (Lean value), 270
decision-making authority
    at last responsible moment, 132
    commitment level and, 105
    of Product Owners, 96
    on Scrum teams, 84
decoupling, 245
defect injection, 190
deliver as fast as possible (Lean value), 270, 295
dependencies, 78, 130
diversity (XP principle), 202, 205
documentation

approach to change, 190
    drawbacks of comprehensive, 66, 71
    optimum amount of, 47, 65, 72
    silver bullet methodology for, 64
    traditional approach to, 65
Done, concrete definition of, 145, 181
Downey, Scott, 172
duplicated code, 227

E

early delivery, 56, 127
Ebook Reader Project
    improved communication for, 72
    improved project delivery for, 61
    improved working environment for, 77
    varied concepts of value in, 53
economics (XP principle), 201, 208
edge cases, 229, 247
elevating goals, 126
eliminate waste (Lean value), 270, 283
embracing change (XP), 185
emergent design, 258, 358
empower the team (Lean value), 270
energized work practice, 249
execution (see project execution)
expertise, 273
external integrity, 289
"Extreme Programming Explained" (Beck), 214

F

face-to-face communication, 67
fail-fast systems, 242
failure (XP principle), 202, 208
fault tolerance, 242
feedback (XP value), 196, 198, 208, 211, 254
feedback loops, 112, 208, 213, 292, 320, 337,
    339, 359
Five Whys technique, 294
flow (XP principle), 202, 250, 263, 295
flow measurement/management
    creating Slack, 355
    cumulative flow diagrams, 340
    explicit policies in, 357
    Little's Law and, 349
    overview of, 339
focus (Scrum value), 105, 164
40-hour work week, 250
fractured perspective
    danger of, 40

Y

About the Authors

Andrew Stellman is a developer, architect, speaker, agile coach, project manager, and expert in building better software. He has over two decades of professional experience building software, and has architected large-scale real-time back end systems, managed large international software teams, been a Vice President at a major investment bank, and consulted for companies, schools, and corporations, including Microsoft, the National Bureau of Economic Research, Bank of America, Notre Dame, and MIT. He's had the privilege of working with some pretty amazing programmers during that time, and likes to think that he's learned a few things from them.

Jennifer Greene is an agile coach, development manager, business analyst, project manager, tester, speaker, and authority on software engineering practices and principles. She's been building software for over twenty years in many different domains including media, finance, and IT consulting. She's worked with teams of excellent developers and testers to tackle tough technical problems and focused her career on finding and fixing the habitual process issues that crop up along the way.

Colophon

The animal on the cover of *Learning Agile* is a Goeldi's marmoset or Goeldi's monkey (*Callimico goeldii*). It is the lone member of the *Callimico* genus, and is also sometimes called a callimico. It is sometimes classified separately from marmosets, because of characteristics such as having a third set of molars, bearing one child at a time, and having claws on most digits. It is named after the Swiss naturalist Emil August Goeldi, who discovered the species in the early 20th century.

These monkeys dwell in the upper Amazon Basin, in Brazil, Colombia, Peru, Bolivia and Ecuador. They tend to spend time in a forest's "understory," or scrubby low level near primary forest, stream, and bamboo habitats. Some of their favorite foods are insects, fungi (in the dry season), and fruit (in the wet season). They live in small packs of about six and don't like to get separated, so they keep in touch through a system of high-pitched calls. They move through the trees by vertically leaping, but spend most of their days sleeping in a tangle of leaves.

Their bodies are only about eight or nine inches long, a bit bigger than those of squirrels, but their tails can be up to a foot long. They have dark skin on their faces and their fur is either black or dark brown, often with lighter highlights. Females reach sexual maturity at 8.5 months; males, on the other hand, take 16.5 months. Females also outnumber males two to one and can give birth twice a year. The fathers become the primary caregivers to their children after the first three weeks or so.

Goeldi's monkeys can live to be over 20, at least in captivity. The conservation status of Goeldi's marmoset is classified as "vulnerable," however, and they are much scarcer than the common marmoset. Proposed development and other habitat changes threaten their population and ongoing survival. They prove elusive and difficult to observe in the wild.

Many of the animals on O'Reilly covers are endangered; all of them are important to the world. To learn more about how you can help, go to *animals.oreilly.com*.

The cover image is from Lydekker's *Royal Natural History*. The cover fonts are URW Typewriter and Guardian Sans. The text font is Adobe Minion Pro; the heading font is Adobe Myriad Condensed; and the code font is Dalton Maag's Ubuntu Mono.

Have it your way.

Get even more for your money.

Join the O'Reilly Community, and register the O'Reilly books you own. It's free, and you'll get:

- $4.99 ebook upgrade offer
- 40% upgrade offer on O'Reilly print books
- Membership discounts on books and events
- Free lifetime updates to ebooks and videos
- Multiple ebook formats, DRM FREE
- Participation in the O'Reilly community
- Newsletters
- Account management
- 100% Satisfaction Guarantee

Signing up is easy:

1. Go to: oreilly.com/go/register
2. Create an O'Reilly login.
3. Provide your address.
4. Register your books.

Note: English-language books only

To order books online:
oreilly.com/store

For questions about products or an order:
orders@oreilly.com

To sign up to get topic-specific email announcements and/or news about upcoming books, conferences, special offers, and new technologies:
elists@oreilly.com

For technical questions about book content:
booktech@oreilly.com

To submit new book proposals to our editors:
proposals@oreilly.com

O'Reilly books are available in multiple DRM-free ebook formats. For more information:
oreilly.com/ebooks

Ingram Content Group UK Ltd.
Milton Keynes UK
UKHW032350050723
424640UK00002B/4

9 781449 331924